DATE DUE			
APR 1 1 1996			
MAY 0 8 1996			
MAR 0 9 1997			
JUL 1 1 1997			
AUG 14 1997			
FEB 0 5 1998			
JUL 1 1 2001			

JUL 16 1986

John Berry born Sept. 17th 1843

Mary Berry do Jany 23rd 1845

Alexander Berry do Feb 21st 1846
Died Augt 3rd 1866

Frederick Berry do Aug 1st 1847

Annette Berry do Decr 29th 1848

Henrietta Berry do Oct 15th 1851

Georgianna Berry do May 29th 1853

Peter Berry do Sept 3rd 1854

Emily Berry do Sept 14th 1856
died March 6/57

Herbert Berry born Decr 13 1857

Nelson Berry born Decr 13th 1859

Kate Amelia Maude Decr 9th 1863.
Died March 7th 1895

John Berry & Amelia Mary Barnes

Married Decer 28th 1863

Annette Berry & Archibald George Butterfield

Married Decer 31st 1874

Henrietta Berry & Wm Farbon Married
Sept 25th 1877

The Dictionary of
GENEALOGY

Terrick V. H. FitzHugh

Barnes & Noble Books
Totowa, New Jersey

First published in Britain by
ALPHABOOKS
Sherborne, Dorset DT9 3LN

First published in the United States by
BARNES & NOBLE
81 Adams Drive, Totowa, NJ 07512

Library of Congress Cataloging in Publication Data

ISBN - 906670 38 1

FitzHugh, Terrick.

 Dictionary of genealogy.

 1. Genealogy--Dictionaries.   2. Great Britain.

Genealogy--Handbooks, manuals, etc.   I. Title.

CS6.F58 1985 929′.1′072041   85-1220

ISBN 0-389-20565-6

Designed and produced by Alphabet & Image Ltd,
Sherborne, Dorset, England

*The illustration on page 1 is the flyleaf of Katherine Berry's
bible, a wedding present to her in August 1842. It typically
records useful genealogical details about a Victorian family.
Photo: John Mennell*

*The illustration on the title page shows an indenture
document. British Library MSS Dept. (See* INDENTURES*)*

Phototypesetting by Margaret Spooner Typesetting,
    Dorchester, Dorset
Printed and bound by Butler & Tanner Ltd, Frome,
    Somerset, Great Britain

Contents

Acknowledgements

During my practice as a professional genealogist I compiled, as I went along, a collection of notes on genealogical sources and related matter, which I kept, in alphabetical order, at my elbow, where it served me as a rapid-reference aide-mémoire. The compilation, growing through fifteen years, was amplified from time to time with information from published material. In adding these latter jottings I kept no record of their sources, as I had no thought then of publication. I am therefore unable to acknowledge their authors' help as I should like. I cannot, however, forget being indebted at various times, both in my researches and note-taking, to A.J. Camp's *Wills and Their Whereabouts*, D.E. Gardner and F. Smith's *Genealogical Research in England and Wales*, G. Hamilton-Edwards's *In Search of Ancestry*, P. Litton's article on 'Foundlings' in the *North Cheshire Family Historian*, I. Mordy's article on 'Jewish Genealogy' in the *A.G.R.A. Newsletter*, L.M. Munby's *Short Guides to Records*, and D.J. Steel's *National Index of Parish Registers*, and also articles and news items too numerous to trace in *The Amateur* (and *Local*) *Historian*, archives, *Family History News and Digest* and *The Genealogists' Magazine*.

To Jeremy Gibson, who read the finished work in typescript, I am grateful for a number of suggestions. Finally, I should especially like to express my thanks to Faith and Nick Russel for inducing me to expand my private genealogical encyclopedia into its present, more readable form for the benefit, I hope, of other genealogists.

T.V.H.F.

Foreword

Everyone has wondered at one time or another, 'Where did my family come from? What sort of people were they? Rich or poor? Merchants or labourers? Royalists or Roundheads? Do the skeletons of gibbeted sheep-stealers or smugglers rattle in our family cupboard? Do we really have any link with the great man, or family, whose surname we share?'

For people of English descent, the tracing of bygone generations is now so much easier than it was for our fathers, because the essential sources of information have been brought together, catalogued and made freely available to the public. Before the Second World War there were only six county record offices in England, but during the late 1940s and '50s record offices were established in every county, not only for official county archives but also for the safe-keeping of a great variety of historical documents, many of which had previously been in private hands. Most of these county offices also became diocesan registries, thus bringing together under one roof thousands of parish registers and other church records alongside the civil archives of the area. This easy availability of the genealogically useful documents, in almost all cases free of charge, provided the initial impetus for the tremendous growth in the popularity of family history research.

Soon this growth of interest itself produced an important new development making genealogy even more popular. Until the mid 1960s there was only one family history society in England — The Society of Genealogists, in London. All over the country family researchers were treading solitary trails, but as their numbers grew the situation became transformed. First in Birmingham, then gradually all over the country, enthusiasts came together to form county or neighbourhood family history societies, and what had formerly been a lonely hobby became a sociable one. At regular monthly meetings, members are now able to hear talks by knowledgeable genealogists, to discuss problems they have encountered, and to share experiences.

From the development of the county societies came yet another stage in the genealogical 'revolution' — the mass indexing of Britain's basic genealogical source material. Where, twenty years ago, there were only two partial indexes to marriages recorded in parish registers, now nearly every society has an index in progress for its own county. This invaluable research aid has been matched by the Genealogical Society of Salt Lake City, Utah, with its INTERNATIONAL GENEALOGICAL INDEX containing millions of British baptismal entries and many thousands of marriages. Copies, on microfiche, are available at many of the county record offices, public libraries and family history societies.

All these developments are both cause and effect of the now widespread enthusiasm for researching our family past. But the interest has also deepened. All over England, university extra-mural departments and local Adult Education Institutes offer evening and day courses in genealogy that enable people to advance quickly from the hesitant gropings of the beginner to the real knowledge of how to go about their researches systematically and effectively.

The exceptional wealth of Britain's historical documentary material, now so readily accessible, can lead a genealogist on to discoveries he never dreamed possible. The compilation of a family tree is fascinating, and success a matter for pride; but the names that hang on its branches can provide, for the persistent researcher, a starting point for a quest, even more exciting, into the lives lived by those people, each in their generation and historical period. It may well be possible to discover the kinds of work by which they earned their living, the exact sites of their homes, the events that moulded their careers, and so place them in their historical, geographical and social context. It is astonishing how much can be found about ordinary private people. This final stage in the unfolding of our past can be the most rewarding, and should be crowned by the writing of a narrative history to pass the results of our researches on to future generations — incidentally immortalising the author as 'the family historian'.

Part One of this book, *The Guide to Ancestry Research*, outlines the various choices open to the researcher and describes, step by step, the main sources of information and the techniques to be used in tracing the family back through time. By concentrating on the basic principles and the logic behind them, and by reserving the indispensable, but initially overwhelming, detail for the dictionary section, the Guide spares the beginner the common difficulty of not being able to see the wood for the trees. Links between the Guide and the Dictionary are provided by cross-references indicated by SMALL CAPITALS.

Part Two, the Dictionary section, contains more than 1000 entries, setting out the essential information on virtually everything the researcher will need to know about genealogically useful records — where to find them and what they can reveal. Armed with this knowledge, the researcher will understand what to expect from each document and will know how to extract the maximum advantage from it. Sometimes a seemingly unimportant word can provide a pointer to a new source of information, and such clues are the very essence of family history research.

Some old documents present difficulties because they contain words and phrases that have disappeared from common use; so those most often met with are explained in the Dictionary, to enable the searcher to assess correctly what the record tells him.

The major part of the Dictionary was originally compiled by the author as an aide-mémoire for his own use during years of professional genealogical work. As such it proved its worth, and so now, greatly extended, provides a tested research tool for beginner and experienced researcher alike.

Part One

The Guide
to Ancestry Research

Several choices are available to the beginner in ancestry research. Many people set out to find all their ancestors on both their father's and mother's, grandfathers' and grandmothers' sides (their Total Descent). Some like to trace just their own family with its surname (their Family Tree), perhaps later spreading their interest to take in all branches of it, often including distant cousins in America, Australia and elsewhere (their Extended Family Tree). People with a fairly uncommon surname may decide to look for traces of all people of the same name, just in case they may be distantly related (Namesakes). And finally, for those who have compiled a family tree there is the fascinating quest to find out what kind of lives their forebears lived, and to write a narrative account of them (a Family History). Let us take a closer look at these aims.

Total Descent

For anyone ambitious to trace his descent as far back as possible this is the choice to make, because with every newly discovered generation the number of ancestors doubles (at least, it does in theory; in practice, the same ancestors crop up in different lines), so that when the scent on one trail dries up or is temporarily difficult to follow, there are plenty of others to turn to. As there has been a good deal of intermarriage between the social classes in England it is not uncommon to be able to trace one's ancestry back to William the Conqueror himself. An example of a Total Descent chart is given under the entry of that title in the Dictionary.

Family Tree

This shows descent in the male line through one's father, his father, and so on, and includes not only ancestors and ancestresses but also the ancestors' brothers and sisters. As the husband-cum-father was always the breadwinner, male-line research traces not only a biological line but also the social continuity of the family. There is an example of a Family Tree under the entry of that title in the Dictionary.

Extended Family Tree

Having traced a family tree, it is interesting to find other members of one's family, distant cousins descended from ancestors' brothers, and thus of the same name and blood as oneself. The short family tree on page 107 could be extended by tracing the descendants of John's brother Nicholas.

Namesakes

This type of interest, in all people of the same surname, has resulted in the formation of a number of One-name societies made up of namesake members, related or unrelated, engaged in joint research into every bygone person of their surname. This often leads to the discovery that some of the researchers are indeed distant cousins.

Family History

A development from the Family Tree. Knowing the names and dates of ancestors whets the curiosity to find out more about them, the things they did, the incidents that happened to them and the local backgrounds of their homes and places of work. This calls for searches into a wider range of records than those used to prove a descent. Nowadays the term 'family history' is applied to this type of research into biographical detail to distinguish it from the tracing of descents, for which the term 'genealogy' is reserved.

There are thus five avenues facing the newcomer to ancestry research. The following pages provide an outline guide to the basic principles and sources of information applicable to all of these.

Making a Start

First, it is best to check that no one has already researched your ancestors. The majority of existing family trees and histories are known only to their compilers and their close relations, but many have been printed and catalogued. Also, a large number in print, typescript and manuscript can be found in the library of the Society of Genealogists (*see* FAMILY TREES AND HISTORIES *and* NATIONAL PEDIGREE INDEX in the Dictionary section). If that does not lead you to the discovery, possibly disappointing, that all the work (or much of it) has been done already, you can start to blaze your own trail from the very beginning.

A tree of five generations can normally be made up right away from the living members of a family — grandparents, parents and children — and from the memories of the elderly. All relevant genealogical information should be entered on the chart, using the standard signs and abbreviations illustrated on page 107 and described in the FAMILY TREE entry in the Dictionary section. Dates and places of birth, marriage and death are needed to identify each person, and in constructing the chart ample space should be left at the top for the later addition of earlier generations.

Domestic Clues Stage two is to take a very careful look around the house, paying particular attention to old desks and chests, and of course attic and box-room storage areas, for articles that may throw light on the family's past. Other members of the family should also be asked to do the same in their own homes.

DOMESTIC CLUES include such items as the FAMILY BIBLE, so popular in the Victorian period; old letters and diaries giving personal and social details, and clues to the writers' whereabouts; newspaper cuttings; book prizes; cap badges, buttons, medals and other military service mementoes; professional qualification certificates, old photographs, and so on. Not only do these items carry information in their own right, they are often marvellous aides-mémoires when shown to elderly relatives.

Memories The final stage before embarking on documentary research is the questioning of all elderly members of the family about their own parents and grandparents, uncles and aunts, and others among whom they grew up. This stage, described under ORAL FAMILY HISTORY can be enormously rewarding. Each person interviewed will add something to the record, no matter how good or bad the memory, or how willing or reticent he or she may be — and reticence itself is a clue not to be overlooked.

Compiling the Record

All the information from these interviews, as well as that to be obtained later from records, must be meticulously transcribed for eventual use in compiling a descent chart or writing a history, and also as evidence for their accuracy. The proper method of doing this is described under TRANSCRIPT.

If the aim is eventually to write a narrative history, all family mentions found in records should be transcribed in generous extracts. For instance, an old local directory that supplies the address of an ancestor will also provide the names of his neighbours, and these should be noted because they may well crop up again in other connections, such as witnessing a wedding or a will. The odd names occurring around those of our ancestors are all part of the family background.

When the searching of historical records gets under way, the researcher will soon find a quantity of transcripts building up, so that orderly RECORD KEEPING becomes important. Three main categories of information will be kept, corresponding broadly with three of the principal lines of ancestral research. The main file and record book will contain information relevant to the male-line descent investigation — the Family Tree. A second series of files will contain records relating to the Extended Family Tree. A third set of records will contain every mention of the surname under investigation. This Namesake file acts as a 'holding' file, the names in it becoming either identified as family (in which case they are transferred to the main research files), or later as definitely not related (in which case they will be of no further use unless, at some future date, a One-name investigation is undertaken).

Beginning the Documentary Research

For the last four hundred years, nearly everyone living in England has left behind some trace of his or her existence. By law, certain records have been written down and preserved; for example, the entries of people's birth, baptism, marriage, death and burial, their tax assessments, the leases and title deeds of their houses, the census forms they filled out, and so on.

These records are the raw material of genealogical research, and the art and science lie in knowing what records to look for, where to find them, and — once found — how to understand them. This essential knowledge falls under four main headings, the four 'know-hows' of genealogy: Linkage Records, Location Records, The Records' Whereabouts, and Understanding the Records.

Linkage Records

To compile a family tree we need to know our ancestors' names and certain dates and places connected with them, and there is one more essential piece of information — clear proof of their relationship within the family. Just finding a person of the right name, in the right place, at the right time, is not enough. Their relationship to an already known member of the family has to be proved. What is needed, therefore, is a document bearing the names of two or more members of the family, at least one of which is already known, and which states the link between them. An example of such a Linkage Record might be a grandfather's birth certificate. It shows the names of three people: our grandfather (who is already known to us), plus two more, shown by the document to be his father and mother.

Linkage Records are the material for establishing genealogical descent. There are ten main records to which the researcher may turn with a reasonable expectation of success in making a proven addition to a family tree, and, for quick reference, these are shown in the table below, along with their locations. Each record is described in detail under the appropriate heading in the Dictionary.

Linkage records and their whereabouts

Birth, Marriage & Death Certificates	*General Register Office*
Census Returns	*Public Record Office* *County record offices*
Parish Registers	*County record offices* *Parish churches*
Bishops' Transcripts	*County record offices*
Non-parochial Registers	*Public Record Office (mostly)*
Memorial Inscriptions	*Burial grounds and churches* *Copies at family history societies*
Marriage Licence Records	*County record offices*
Wills and other probate records	*County record offices* *Public Record Office*
Apprentice Bindings	*Public Record Office* *Guildhall Library, London* *Some London gilds* *County and borough record offices* *Society of Genealogists*
Manor Court Rolls	*County record offices* *Public Record Office* *Lawyers' offices*

Location Records

When tracing a descent back as far as the year 1837, we are fortunate in having one GENERAL REGISTER OF BIRTHS, DEATHS AND MARRIAGES for the whole of England and Wales, so in whatever town or village the family was living their essential records will be found at the GENERAL REGISTER OFFICE. However, once 1 July, 1837, is passed on our backward journey through time, there is no longer one single source of information. Before that date the only comparable records were the local parish registers of baptism, marriage and burial, maintained by parish clergy and now to be found mostly in county record offices.

It follows, therefore, that before the right records can be consulted, the parish in which the family was then living must be identified. To do this without the wearying work of searching through one parish register after another, advantage can be taken of certain records that offer short cuts. These are the Location Records. They provide a thin coverage of a region — a county, an archdeaconry or a diocese — containing a large number of parishes, and thus enable a quick search to be made of the areas in which the ancestors are thought likely to have lived.

The seventeen types of Location Record are summarised in the list below, and, as with the Linkage Records, each is described in detail in the relevant Dictionary entry.

The importance of these Location Records must not be underestimated. Many beginners waste valuable time, and experience frustration, by searching through endless Linkage Records when they could be taking advantage of these valuable 'short cut' facilities.

Location records and their whereabouts

Census Returns	*Public Record Office*
	County record offices
Local Directories	*County record offices*
	Guildhall Library, London
	Society of Genealogists
Electoral Registers	*County record offices*
	Public Record Office
County Marriage Indexes	*Family history societies*
	Society of Genealogists
	Institute of Heraldic & Genealogical Studies
International Genealogical Index	*Family history societies*
	County record offices
	Society of Genealogists
	Guildhall Library, London
	Some libraries
Poll Books	*County record offices*
	Guildhall Library, London
	Society of Genealogists

Jurors' (Freeholders') Lists	*County record offices*
Marriage Licence Indexes	*County record offices*
Probate Indexes	*County record offices*
	Public Record Office
	Society of Genealogists
Land Tax Returns	*County record offices*
	Public Record Office
Lay Subsidies (Inc. Hearth Tax)	*Public Record Office*
Protestation Oath Returns	*House of Lords Record Office*
Collection for Distressed Protestants in Ireland	*Public Record Office*
Muster Rolls	*County record offices*
	Public Record Office
Society of Genealogists' Great Index	*Society of Genealogists*
Published Records with Indexes	*Society of Genealogists*
	County record offices
	Public libraries
Apprentice Bindings Index	*Society of Genealogists*

The Records' Whereabouts

Most Linkage and Location Records are housed in record repositories, of which there are four main kinds: national, regional, local and private.

The General Register of Births, Deaths and Marriages falls into the first category: it is a national repository, as is the Public Record Office, which houses government archives and law court records, and the Principal Registry of the Family Division with its accumulation of all wills proved in England and Wales since 1858. These are all to be found in London, where the researcher may also refer to the extensive collection of genealogical record copies housed in the library of the Society of Genealogists.

The main regional repositories are the county record offices, situated usually in the county towns and often also housing the archives of the local diocesan registries.

The principal local repositories are the record offices of cities and boroughs, and some of the public libraries. Until recently the vestries of Anglican parish churches formed a large class of record repository, but now the records once housed there have largely found their way to the appropriate county record office.

The only private archives of any size are those of the great land-owning families. The researcher who finds an ancestor living or working on one of these ancient estates may well find, in the account books, rent books, surveys and maps, a useful amount of biographical material. Long-established solicitors' firms also hold a variety of old family records, and from time to time these get deposited in the local county record office. The whereabouts of the Linkage and Location records are shown in the lists on pages 12-14.

Understanding the Records

Historical documents often say a great deal more — and occasionally a great deal less — than at first meets the eye, so some knowledge of what lies behind the wording is essential. The Dictionary aims to supply that information where necessary, but one example will illustrate the point: in the 'Age' column of the Census Returns of 1841, the figures appearing for people older than 14 are not intended to show their actual age, but only their five-year age group. For instance, the figure 15 stands for 15-19; 20 means 20-24; and so on. This does not apply in the later censuses.

Progress into the Past

All genealogical research must proceed backwards in time, working from the known to the unknown. In each period of history the law, for various purposes (but not for genealogy), has required certain official records to be kept; and today the genealogist consults these for the family evidence they contain. Given reasonable luck, he is carried along by them in his search from one generation to another. Assuming we have extracted all the oral evidence still available, let us now trace our steps further back, from period to period and from record to record.

The Victorian Era

The first year of Victoria's reign, 1837, saw the beginning of the General Register of Births, Deaths and Marriages, containing (at least in theory) a record of every one of these events in England and Wales since 1 July of that year. This Mecca for all genealogical researchers, formerly in Somerset House in central London, is now housed in the Office of Population Censuses and Surveys at St Catherine's House in nearby Aldwych (for births and marriages), and at Alexandra House in Kingsway (for deaths).

Here the researcher studies the huge index volumes, and, having found the wanted name, applies for a copy certificate for the event: no information is issued by the office except by certificate. When the copy document is received, usually a few days later, it will be found to show not only the date and place of the event, but also information hitherto unknown: such as, the father and mother of a newly born child; the fathers of both a bride and bridegroom, and their occupations; the maiden name of a wife and mother.

The exact wording of the document should be carefully transcribed into the family records, and the document itself filed away separately. For original documents such as this, and for photocopies, it is best to keep a separate storage file for each category — the file being clearly labelled with the class of document.

The Early Nineteenth Century

Census Returns 1841-81

To find where a family was living before 1837, use must be made of the first of the Location Records listed on page 13, the CENSUS RETURNS of 1851, 1861, 1871 and 1881. (The Return for 1841 is less informative.)

If the family was living in a village in or near a census year, the search will usually be easy: the Returns for the whole place can be searched in a matter of minutes. But if the family was resident in a large town or city, the first requirement will be an exact address. This may be obtained from a birth certificate or death certificate, registered in a year close to census year. A certificate for a birth registered in 1862, for example, would provide a guide to a search of the 1861 Census Return. Alternatively, the family may be looked up in another Location Record — either a LOCAL DIRECTORY published in or near a census year, or an ELECTORAL REGISTER.

Once the census entry has been found, it will provide, among other useful information, an ancestor's age and place of birth: this will direct the search to the PARISH REGISTER in which his baptismal entry will be recorded, and from that entry the names of his parents will be discovered. Thus the Census Return will have done its job as a Location Record; and it will also have served as a Linkage Record because the Return shows all members of the family who were at home on census night, and some of these may not have been previously known.

International Genealogical Index

Another very valuable Location Record, and one which will be of particular use over the next three hundred years of the search, is the INTERNATIONAL GENEALOGICAL INDEX of English baptismal registers, compiled at Salt Lake City, Utah, by the Church of Latter-Day Saints (Mormons). This is an index of parish baptismal entries, plus a smaller number of marriages taken from many English parish registers and arranged in alphabetical order of surname, by county. Though its coverage of the country is far from complete, the index contains many millions of names. Copies are housed at many of the county record offices, at the Society of Genealogists, and also with many of the family history societies.

Marriage Indexes

The computerised index of baptismal entries has its counterparts in a number of very useful marriage indexes. BOYD'S MARRIAGE INDEX, at the Society of Genealogists, gives partial coverage of sixteen counties with records going back to 1538; and PALLOT'S INDEX OF MARRIAGES AND BIRTHS, for the period 1780-1837, covers mainly London and

Middlesex. But the individual county family history societies are now engaged in compiling indexes of their own counties, and are only too pleased, for a fee, to provide enquirers with appropriate extracts. Their addresses may be found through the FEDERATION OF FAMILY HISTORY SOCIETIES.

Having discovered from an index the place and date of a baptism or marriage, the next step is to obtain a copy of the full original register entry, as this may contain valuable information not mentioned in the index. It will also act as a check on the accuracy of the index.

Parish Registers 1538 onward

The parish register containing a wanted entry for a baptism, marriage or burial may be found in a county record office, though a few are still housed in the local church vestry, in which case a search fee may be required. Alternatively there may be a modern copy in the library of the Society of Genealogists. In addition, there are a number of other copies elsewhere and the Society has a catalogue giving their location. (Non-members are allowed to use the library facilities of the Society on payment of a search fee.)

BISHOPS' TRANSCRIPTS provide yet another avenue. It was once the obligation of a parson to make a copy of his register at the end of each year and send it to his bishop. These valuable transcripts are now housed at the county record offices.

Where a sought-after record is housed in some distant part of the country, it may prove economical to write to the county archivist and request a list of local professional record searchers. The fee charged, particularly for a simple search, is likely to be less than the cost of travelling to the source of the record.

Once an ancestor has been located in a baptismal register the search should immediately be extended, initially for about ten years either side of the ancestor's entry, in order to discover any brothers or sisters registered in the same parish, and then earlier still to see whether earlier generations are present. A family may have lived in the same parish for many generations. Any moves that were made were usually of twenty miles or less. The eldest son usually inherited his father's land, no matter how small the holding, while his younger brothers moved away in search of employment. The search of the baptismal register having been completed, the ancestors so far found should also be looked up in the marriage register and burial register of that same parish, so providing further material for the Family Tree, the Total Descent record, and the Family History.

Memorial Inscriptions

Memorial inscriptions on the church walls and gravestones of an ancestral parish church should always be carefully inspected, as these often provide more information than the simple entry in the burial register. Several members of a family may be buried in the same churchyard, sometimes even in the same grave, and the inscription on the stone should be carefully examined: it may contain names not previously known. Memorial plaques may also reveal useful information about a man's former station in life, by referring, for example, to his regiment or to government service in some overseas territory.

Many family history societies are engaged in transcribing these inscriptions before the agencies of weathering and decay take their toll, and copies of these transcripts are usually presented to the Society of Genealogists.

Records of the Poor . . .

Even the poorest of our ancestors may not have gone unrecorded, thanks to the provisions of the Poor Laws of 1601 onward. Men and women who fell on hard times were entitled to parish relief: but from which parish?

A system of SETTLEMENT was laid down by law, and from 1697 parochial churchwardens were empowered to issue a parishioner with a Settlement Certificate acknowledging his right to their aid. Armed with this, a poor man could travel and take up residence elsewhere, and the wardens of his new parish would accept him because they had documentary evidence on which to return him, if necessary, to the parish that acknowledged responsibility for him.

More worrying for churchwardens were those who had neither Settlement in their parish, nor a certificate from any other. Such people were subjected to a verbal examination and details were recorded of their stated birth-place, apprenticeship, employment and so on, in an attempt to establish where they may last have gained Settlement — usually in order that they might be returned thither. The answers given in these Settlement Examinations were written down and many have survived, ironically providing life-stories that are often the envy of researchers whose forebears were more successful in making ends meet.

. . . and of the Prosperous

One more Location Record, and an associated Linkage Record, concerns mainly, though not entirely, the more prosperous section of the community. The former are the indexes to probate records, and the latter the records themselves. Only a minority of people made wills, but a very much larger number of people are mentioned in them, and in most cases their relationship to the testator is clearly stated.

Wills were required to be proved in ecclesiastical courts, which would also grant LETTERS OF ADMINISTRATION in cases of intestacy where the estate was considerable. Such matters were not taken out of church hands until 1858. Probate records before that date are now generally in the county record office, together with indexes. These indexes are useful Location Records, as they can be searched quickly and usually mention the testator's parish. The wills themselves are among the most useful of all Linkage Records, because they commonly mention most of the closer living adult relatives of the deceased, and sometimes also their children. Letters of Administration are less useful, because they specify only the relative appointed to administer the estate.

Non-parochial Registers and the Dissenters

The Church of England parish registers are not the only records of baptisms and burials. From the late seventeenth century onward, an increasing number of people belonged to churches of dissenting denominations, including the BAPTISTS, CONGREGATIONALISTS, METHODISTS, PRESBYTERIANS, QUAKERS, UNITARIANS and many smaller sects. Though their earliest records date from the 1600s, few survive from much earlier than 1780, but, fortunately for the modern researcher, from 1754 onward all marriages with the exception of those of Quakers and JEWS had to be performed in Church of England churches or chapels. It was not until 1937 that marriages by Roman Catholic and Protestant dissenting rites were made legal, providing they were registered in the civil register.

Most non-parochial registers prior to 1837 are now held at the Public Record Office: records of Catholic marriages, baptisms and burials are less centralised, and reference should be made to the extensive Dictionary entry for details of their location (*see* ROMAN CATHOLICS).

The Hanoverian Period 1711-1837

For the greater part of this period the Linkage Records continue as for the later nineteenth century, except, of course, for the General Register and the Census Returns. Non-parochial registers, however, become few and far between. Location Records differ somewhat; electoral registers and census returns are left behind and few local directories show private residents.

Location Records

There are, however, others to take their place in indicating a family's movements from place to place. The Jurors' Lists (*see* FREEHOLDERS' LISTS) of each parish show every person owning a freehold of 40 shillings per year or more, and these will be found in the county record offices. There are also the POLL BOOKS, printed lists showing how people voted in county parliamentary elections before the introduction of the secret ballot, and the LAND TAX records, mainly from 1780 onward, housed in the county record offices. And we have, too, for this period the thousands of names in the Great (card) Index of the Society of Genealogists, compiled from many different kinds of records.

Records of Apprentices

From the year 1710, whenever a boy was apprenticed to a trade a stamp duty had to be paid, and these records of the binding of APPRENTICES survive to provide the name of the apprentice, that of his father or widowed mother, and his master, as well as his parents' abode. Apprentice Records serve, therefore, as both Linkage and Location Records, and are held at the Public Record Office, where they form a part of the Inland Revenue archives; at the Society of Genealogists; and, for the London LIVERY COMPANIES, at the Guildhall, London.

In addition to the trade apprentices there were also Poor Apprentices, whose destiny, in the main, was governed by the *Poor Law Act*. Churchwardens and Overseers of the Poor were empowered to apprentice to husbandry any child under the age of 16 whose parents they judged unable to maintain him. If a master could be found in a neighbouring parish, this form of apprenticeship was often a convenient way of getting rid of a pauper child, because the apprenticeship conferred Settlement after a period of forty days. 'Husbandry' for a boy, or 'housewifery' for a girl, simply meant being a servant on the land or in the house: later, in the Industrial Revolution, it might mean life in the mill, or even down a mine.

1752: a Date to Remember

In the middle of the eighteenth century, two changes were made in the English calendar. The first, and the only one of importance to genealogists, moved the official start of the year from 25 March (Lady Day) to 1 January, so changing January, February and March from being the last three months of the old year to the first three months of the new. The second, by 'losing' eleven days from September, was from the Julian calendar to the Gregorian, bringing England into line with the rest of Europe where the Gregorian system had been in use since 1582.

As the new system was adopted by some people *before* its official introduction, great care must be taken in transcribing extracts containing dates in January, February and March before 1752. The correct procedure is to transcribe the dates in both Old Style and New: 5 Feb. 1626 O.S., should therefore be shown as 5 Feb. 1626/7.

The Use of Latin

In the period before 1733, many legal documents were written in what is known as Medieval Latin, and this can naturally cause some difficulties for researchers. Nor is the knowledge of classical Latin a complete answer. The language is full of later, but now archaic, words and expressions, many of them abbreviated, but fortunately the vocabulary needed to deal with the more genealogically useful documents is not extensive, and, as the same words and phrases recur time and time again, any researcher armed with one of the useful aids described in the Dictionary (*see* LATIN, MEDIEVAL) will, with a little practice, become able to cope with most Latin records. Should an unfamiliar or unusually difficult document need to be deciphered or translated, the staff of the record office are usually ready to help.

The Stuart and Late Tudor Period 1600-1700

A more common difficulty in this period is the handwriting used in sixteenth- and seventeenth-century documents. It is known as SECRETARY HAND and differs considerably from that we use today. The Dictionary entry under HANDWRITING contains a specimen alphabet, and with a little practice most difficulties in transcribing such documents can be overcome.

Most of the Linkage Records remain the same as in the Hanoverian period, but one important set that runs through both periods comprises the estate records described in some detail in the Dictionary entry under MANOR. In addition to rent books, surveys and maps, these court rolls note the passing of copyhold properties from father to son on the thousands of manors that were once the unit of English local government. Until the Commonwealth in the mid seventeenth century these records were written in Latin, to which language most manors returned after the Restoration of the monarchy, and the researcher about to tackle any manorial records would be well advised first to acquire and study some of the aids and word-lists referred to above.

Among the Location Records, Jurors' Lists and Poll Books are no longer (on our backward journey) available, but in their place we have the taxation records known as the LAY SUBSIDY ROLLS for every parish in the country. These include the HEARTH TAX Returns of 1662 and 1689. Similarly useful are the PROTESTATION OATH RETURNS of 1641/2. By order of Parliament the Returns listed all who signed, and all who refused to sign, an oath to live and die for the true Protestant religion, the liberties and rights of subjects, and the privilege of Parliaments. Many of the lists are housed in the House of Lords Record Office, but some survive only among local parish records. Other useful Location Records of the same year are the parochial lists of those who subscribed to a Collection for DISTRESSED PROTESTANTS IN IRELAND, mentioning many more women than the Lay Subsidy lists. Lastly, there are the MUSTER CERTIFICATES that list, in each parish, men between the ages of 16 and 60 available for service in the militia.

For Apprentice Records in the period before 1710, it is necessary to turn to the archives of the London LIVERY COMPANIES and those of the Craft Gilds (*see* GILD, CRAFT) of provincial boroughs. The former are often very detailed and of great value to the genealogist: the latter, although of undoubted historical interest, are less detailed.

Tudor, Plantagenet and Beyond

The parish registers which, until now, have provided by far the most valuable source of Linkage information, come to an end (or, more properly, their beginning) during this period. Most of those now surviving do not go back beyond 1558: the oldest of all date from 1538.

In these oldest parish registers the entries tend to be very brief, and information sparse. Parents are usually omitted from baptismal records, and sometimes even the wife's name does not appear in a marriage entry. Only a very fortunate few will find it possible to trace their descent beyond this period. There are mentions of many people (most, but not all, of the upper classes) in the early sixteenth-century records that have been summarised and printed under the title *Letters and Papers of the Reign of Henry VIII*. Also, descents can sometimes be traced well back into the Middle Ages for those families whose ancestors were tenants-in-chief of the king in feudal times, or were the lords or tenants of manors of which the medieval court rolls have survived.

Of the handful of families for which records go right back to the Norman Conquest, the male-line descents have already been well researched.

The Oldest Documentary Records

The study of very old documents naturally presents a great many difficulties. Latin and Court Hand scripts are two; the physical ageing of the materials causes others. Inks fade, the parchment becomes brittle and discoloured. Special facilities may be required for handling and reading them.

Fortunately for the researcher, however, many of the most useful of the medieval records have been calendared (i.e their gist has been briefly rendered into English, with all names of people and places mentioned), and they are usually indexed. These published

Calendars can be found on the open shelves of the British Library at the British Museum, and at the Public Record Office. They include the CLOSE ROLLS and PATENT ROLLS (the two forms in which records were kept of the King's Letters issued by the Court of Chancery; the INQUISITIONS POST MORTEM and their associated documents, introduced by Henry III to control the handing-on of lands held by tenants-in-chief; the FEET OF FINES (final agreements establishing titles to land); and a number of others.

This Guide has outlined the trails along which the researcher may travel in tracing the history of his family: detailed guidance will be found in the Dictionary that follows. But there are still a couple of useful hints to be given.

When visiting any repository of manuscript records, take a pencil, because you will not be allowed to use ink or a ball-point pen. Go with a clear idea, gleaned from this Dictionary, about what records you wish to consult, and ask for them to be brought to you. You will find the archivists very helpful, and you will feel an urge to tell them your family history, but this is a temptation to be resisted. Two-thirds of all their visitors are on a similar quest. In the case of county or borough record offices, it is as well to check in advance on the opening days and times, that they have the records you wish to see, and that they have room for you. Some of the smaller offices can only accommodate visitors by prior appointment.

Genealogy is a fascinating kind of detective work. We find clues, often in little bits of seemingly irrelevant information; we make guesses from them and follow them up. Every piece of evidence we find we must interpret critically, never letting the wish be father to the thought. Each new generation we discover gives us a greater sense of achievement.

Luck will play its part, both good and bad. Some records on which we could expect to depend will turn out to be damaged or lost, or never written at all. But there are often ways around these checks, and every now and then strokes of luck occur that take the search forward in leaps. Somehow, the more experienced we become the better luck we get! As the great bio-chemist, Pasteur, once said: 'Chance favours the prepared mind.' An Englishman put it another way: 'The winds and waves are on the side of the ablest navigators.' The purpose of this Dictionary is to prepare your minds, and so bring you luck.

Major record repositories are located within a small area of central London. The above map by Peter Haillay shows where they are.

Abbreviations The following are abbreviations commonly found in English records (although some are Latin) or used by genealogists.

Admon. Letters of Administration
Ag. Lab. Agricultural Labourer
AGRA Association of Genealogists and Record Agents
B Burial Register
b. buried
BL British Library
bp or *bpt.* baptized
bur. buried
C Christening Register
c. or *ca.* *circa*
Cal. Calendar
Chan. Proc. Chancery Proceedings
Cit. Citizen
CLRO Corporation of London Record Office
CMB All 3 types of parish register
Co. County
CRO County Record Office
d. died, also *denarius* (penny)
dau. daughter
d.b.n. *de bonis non administratis*
DNB Dictionary of National Biography
d.s.p. *decessit sine prole* (died without issue)
d.s.p.leg. died without legitimate issue
d.v.p. *decessit vita patris* (died within his father's lifetime)
Exch. Exchequer, Court of
FHG Fellow of the Institute of Heraldic and Genealogical Studies
FHS Family History Society
fo. folio
F. of F. Feet of Fines
f.p. foreign parts
F.R. Hist. S. Fellow of the Royal Historical Society

F.S. Female servant
F.S.A. Fellow of the Society of Antiquaries
F.S.G. Fellow of the Society of Genealogists
FWK Framework knitter
gent. gentleman
GLCRO Greater London Council Record Office
GRO General Register Office
HEIC Honourable East India Company
Hist MSS Comm Royal Commission on Historical Manuscripts
IGI International Genealogical Index
Ind. of independent means
IOLR India Office Library and Records
I.P.M. Inquisition Post Mortem
k killed
M Marriage Register
m married
mem. membrane
M.I. Monumental Inscriptions
M.L. Marriage Licence records
M.S. Male servant
MS Manuscript
N.R.A. National Register of Archives
ob. *obiit* (died)
o.t.p. of this parish
p. page
PCC Prerogative Court of Canterbury
PCY Prerogative Court of York
Pec. Peculiar Court
pr. proved
PRO Public Record Office
R.D. Registration District
R.O. Record Office
s. & h. son and heir
S.P. State Papers
TS Typescript
unm. unmarried
VCH Victoria History of the Counties of England

Part Two

The Dictionary

Abbey In the Catholic England of the Middle Ages, the term 'abbey' described a community of monks and also the building in which they lived and prayed. The community might also have several subordinate monasteries, called priories. The abbot, who was the head of the community, was usually elected by his brethren but subject to confirmation by the bishop of the diocese within which the abbey lay; but some abbeys were exempt from episcopal jurisdiction, in which case the new abbot would go to Rome for confirmation.

In the course of time many abbeys came to own extensive lands, granted by benefactors, and their abbots became men of secular and political influence, at the same time tending to lose much of their religious character. At the Dissolution of the Monasteries by Henry VIII, abbots against whom no offences were alleged were pensioned off. Many manorial families held their lands of abbeys and priories.

Records of monastic estates are to be found at the Public Record Office and in the British Library MS Department.

Abeyance A peerage falls into abeyance when more than one heir is equally entitled to inherit. This occurs in baronies (*see* BARON) created by writ of summons when, for want of a male heir, the right of succession is divided equally between sisters who are all co-heiresses — the law of primogeniture not applying in such cases. The peerage can be brought out of abeyance only after all but one of the sisters' lines of descent have become extinct.

Abjuring the Realm *see* **Sanctuary**

Abroad, Britons The following London repositories contain records of many births, baptisms, marriages and burials of Britons on the continent of Europe and in other overseas territories.

The General Register Office holds indexes to the following:

Marine Births and Deaths, 1837 onward
Air Births and Deaths, 1949 onward
Army Chaplains' Returns of Service Men, 1796-1880
Army Returns of Births (1896 onward), *Marriages* (1796 onward) and *Deaths* (1881 onward)
Army Regimental Registers, 1761-1924
Royal Air Force Returns, 1920 onward
Consular Returns, 1849 onward
Natal and South Africa Field Forces Deaths, 1899-1902
Deaths of Men in the three Services and the Indian Service in the two World Wars, 1914-21 and 1939-48
Service Department Deaths, 1851 onward
Births, Marriages and Deaths in the Ionian Isles, 1818-64
Miscellaneous Foreign Births, 1946-50, plus some in more recent years

The Guildhall Library, in Aldermanbury, London EC2, holds registers of a number of congregations abroad, and those performed by the chaplains licensed by the Bishop of London (1816-1924), in addition to copies of memorial inscriptions.

The Public Record Office has, among its Foreign Office records:

Foreign Registers and Returns, 1627 onward (RG.33)
Miscellaneous Foreign Returns, 1831 onward (RG.32)
Miscellaneous Foreign Marriages, 1826 onward (RG.34)
Miscellaneous Foreign Deaths, 1830 onward (RG.35)
Registers and Returns of Births, Marriages and Deaths in the Protectorates of Africa and Asia (RG.36)

The India Office Library and Records (Orbit House, Blackfriars Road, London SE1) have *Ecclesiastical Returns* of baptisms, marriages and burials from India, Burma and St Helena from the early part of the eighteenth century. The Society of Genealogists also has printed volumes of memorial inscriptions from India.

The volumes of *Miscellanea Genealogica*, and *Notes and Queries*, also contain memorial inscriptions of Britons buried abroad.

For memorial inscriptions of Britons who died in the East, the British Association of Cemeteries of South Asia (Mr T. Wilkinson, 76 Chartfield Avenue, London SW15 6HQ) should be contacted. Also, Miss S.M. Farringdon, 68 Tachbrook Street, London SW1, has transcripts of British memorials in Pakistani cemeteries.

For the working careers of Britons overseas, *see* CHARTERED COMPANIES.

See also EMIGRANTS; LICENCE TO PASS BEYOND THE SEAS; PASSPORTS.

Abstract When there is no need, or no time, to transcribe a document in full, an abstract can be made, containing all the necessary genealogical and family history information. An abstract should include, in addition to the document's title, reference number and location and a note of what it is about (e.g. a conveyance, obligation, or whatever), all names of persons and places, all dates, names of any offices or courts involved, all occupations and sums of money. 'All' includes details of persons outside the family who may seem unimportant or irrelevant. You never know whether further searches may reveal them to be relations by marriage or persons who influenced the family in some way. If you are planning an eventual narrative history of the family, then mentions of household possessions, statements quoted and other human details should be noted, also the wording of sentences or phrases that convey atmosphere or character. *See also* RECORD KEEPING; TRANSCRIPT.

Account, Action of An action at law to oblige a bailiff to submit an account of moneys administered by him. In more recent times it has been used of a similar action against a partner.

Achievement A complete representation of a family's heraldic insignia, including the coat of arms, crest, helmet, mantling, torse and motto; plus, in the case of peers, chapeau, coronet, supporters and compartment.

Acre The word sometimes meant nothing more than a piece of arable land without reference to size. It is never safe to assume that it corresponded to our present statute acre. In Lancashire there were three different acres in use well into the nineteenth century.

Act Book A register in which the minutes of a court were written. Some entries are very cramped and difficult to read, because the same page space was allowed under each heading.

Actors Information about the careers of actors can best be found in the advertisement and review columns of national and local newspapers, and in the journals devoted to the profession, namely *The Era* (from 1838), *Theatrical Journal* (1839-73), *Theatre* (1877-97), *The Stage* (from 1879). All these can be found at the British Newspaper Library at Colindale, and the specialist journals can also be consulted at the Westminster Central Library, St Martin's Street, Leicester Square, London WC2. Two useful reference books are *Who's Who in the Theatre* and *Spotlight*.

The Enthoven Theatre Collection at the Victoria and Albert Museum has photographs, press-cuttings, programmes and playbills. Most theatrical companies deposit copies of their programmes there and the collection is card-indexed. The British Library also has a collection of programmes and playbills.

The British Theatre Association's library is at 9 Fitzroy Square, London W1. The Society for Theatre Research, 13 Woronzow Road, London NW8, has a library in the University of London Library, at Senate House, Malet Street, London WC1.

For further reading on records, see *London Theatres and Music Halls, 1850-1950*, by D. Howard (Library Assoc., 1970).

Acts of Parliament All Acts of Parliament since 1500 are contained in the Statute Rolls housed in the Victoria Tower at the House of

Lords. Public Acts are those intended to alter the general law. Private Acts, of which there are 34 categories, alter the law relating to a particular locality or confer rights on, or relieve from liability, a particular person or body of persons. From 1797 Local, Personal and Private Acts are also to be found among the Parliament Rolls at the Public Record Office.

Public Acts from 1485 to 1702 have been printed under the title *Statutes of the Realm* together with the titles, but not the texts, of Private Acts for the same period. From 1702, Public Acts are printed as *Statutes at Large*. Private, Personal and Local Acts not printed can be inspected at the House of Lords Record Office in the Victoria Tower on payment of a search fee for each Act. Application should be made to The Clerk of the Records, Parliament Office, House of Lords, London SW1. Most of the House of Commons Records were destroyed by fire in 1834.

For the period before 1800 there is no complete index of Personal or Local Acts, but there is a privately produced index, called *Analytical Table of the Private Statutes from 1727 to 1812*. It does not contain Local Acts, because at that time they were classified as semi-public Acts. In the eighteenth century, annual lists of Private and Personal Acts were published and these can sometimes be found at the front of the Statute volume for the year.

There are printed sets, perhaps not complete, of Local and Personal Acts at the British Library. Some printed eighteenth-century Acts are really Bills.

See also PARLIAMENTARY PAPERS.

Administration, Letters of When a person died intestate, i.e. leaving no will, the next-of-kin or a close friend or creditor was supposed to apply to a probate court for Letters of Administration of the estate. Unfortunately, in the majority of cases where the estate was small and there was no doubt as to who should inherit, no application was made and so no record remains. Where letters were sought, the applicant had to swear that there was no will, that he would pay all funeral expenses and debts, administer truly, and submit a true inventory and account of his stewardship. The court granted the Letters and entered the Administration Act, in Latin until 1733, into a register, sometimes in the same book as its Probate Acts. The court might require the administrator to enter into a bond to administer the estate faithfully, in which case a copy of the Act was endorsed on the bond document before it was filed.

The court's annual index of Administration Acts (popularly called Admons.) may be combined with that of its wills, or it may be listed separately. Sometimes the index shows an 'Admon. with Will Annexed'. This usually means that a will had been made but that the executors named in it were unavailable, through death or otherwise, so Admon. was granted to someone else, usually the next of kin. Admon. records are kept with those of wills. For their location, *see* the section on wills under the relevant county heading.

A typical Latin Administration Act can be translated word by word, as follows:

Vicesimo sexto die mensis Martii
On the twenty-sixth day of the month of March

1596 Venerabilis Vir Magister Egidius
1596 the Worshipful [man] Master Giles

Richardson legum doctor surrogatus etc.
Richardson of laws doctor surrogate etc.

commisit administrationem bonorum etc.
committed the administration of the goods etc.

Johannis Mercer nuper de Farnham defuncti
of John Mercer formerly of Farnham deceased

Jacobo Mercer filio naturale et legitimo ejus
to James Mercer son natural and lawful of him

de bene et fideliter administrando, etc, jurato
to well and truly administer, etc, being sworn

etc, salve, etc, Maria
etc, saving (the rights of others), Mary

relicta dicti defuncti renunciante.
the relict of the said deceased renouncing.

Adopted Children The first mechanism for regulating adoption was set up in 1926. Before that year, adoption was often covered by a deed drawn up between parents and adopter, or simply by unrecorded verbal agreement. However, from the year 1927 onward a register of adoption exists at the General Register of

Births, Deaths and Marriages. Birth certificates can be applied for from the Adopted Children's Register there. These show the dates of birth and adoption and the names of the adopting parents. The child's original surname and the names of its natural parents are not shown. Even its Christian name may be changed. Adopting parents are not informed of the identity of the natural parents, and vice versa.

By the *Children Act*, which came into force on 12 November 1975, an adopted person over the age of 18 may apply for his original birth certificate at the General Register Office (on Form CA8), or by writing to the General Register Office (CA side), P.O. Box 7, Titchfield, Fareham, Hampshire PO15 5RU. If the Adoption Order was made before the date of the *Children Act*, the applicant will be interviewed by an experienced social worker before the certificate is issued; if adopted after that date he or she can decide whether or not to be interviewed, and can also choose whether to be interviewed at the General Register Office in St Catherine's House (London WC2), at the office of his or her own local authority, at the office of the authority of the area where the adoption was made, or at the office of the approved adoption society.

Affeerer The officer of a manorial court whose responsibility it was to assess the amount of the monetary penalties which offenders were sentenced to pay. To affeer means to assess.
See also MANOR.

Affidavit A written statement, made on oath or by affirmation. It was, among many other occasions, required in the case of burial in woollens. For that purpose some clergy kept Affidavit Books of record.
See also PARISH REGISTERS (Burials).

Affinity (i) A relationship other than one of blood, e.g. a spouse, in-law, step relative. Such a relative is an 'affine'. A Table of Affinities, to be found in the *Book of Common Prayer*, lists degrees of relationship within which marriage is forbidden. At one time 'Deceased Wife's Sister' and 'Deceased Husband's Brother' were on this list, but they have now been removed. Earlier still a 'spiritual affinity', such as the relationship between godparent and godchild or between

baptizer and baptized, constituted an impediment to marriage. This could be removed by papal or episcopal dispensation.

(ii) The followers of a magnate in the system of MAINTENANCE were known as his 'affinity'.

Agnate A relative descended in the male line from a common male ancestor, related on the father's side. An agnatic line of descent is one entirely through males.
See also COGNATE.

Agricultural Labourers Before the Industrial Revolution, workers on the land constituted the largest single class of the community, but also one that left few records in virtue of their occupation. However, that does not necessarily mean that their lives cannot be successfully researched. As members of the population they appear in the General Register of Births, Deaths and Marriages, and (as Ag.Labs.) in the census returns. As members of religious denominations their baptisms, marriages and burials can be found in either parish or nonconformist registers. As occupants of cottages they are to be found named in land tax and manorial records and in the estate accounts of landowning families, which may also mention the type of work they did. When moving from one place to another, they were liable to give rise to settlement documents. In times of misfortune they will have received parochial assistance and so be mentioned in the accounts of Overseers of the Poor and churchwardens. They may well at some time have been involved, perhaps only as witnesses, in parochial troubles brought to the attention of ecclesiastical courts or ecclesiastical visitations. In lawsuits tried in the courts of Chancery, Exchequer, Star Chamber, and Requests they may have been called upon to make depositions. The indexes of Quarter Sessions records, where they exist, are also worth consulting. As children they are likely to have been either trade or parochial apprentices. If the poet Thomas Gray could return to life today, he would be surprised to find how modern genealogy had outdated much of his *Elegy in a Country Churchyard*.

Aid A feudal due payable by a tenant to his lord, either to ransom him after capture or on the occasions of the lord's eldest son being knighted and his eldest daughter being married. Feudal Aids were abolished in 1660.

Ale (i) A country festival at which ale was the usual drink; often one held to raise funds for a particular purpose, e.g. a Church Ale for the maintenance of the building. Ale Plays were sometimes performed at such events.

(ii) An Assize of Ale was the inspecting of ale, by tasting and other means, by assessors appointed by the Quarter Sessions. These officials called from time to time to ensure that ale and beer were being sold by the correct measures, and at the price and quality laid down. The manorial or parochial official responsible to the assessors was the Aleconner, also called Aletaster and Alefounder.

Alias Latin for 'otherwise'. When a person changed his surname, or was known by more than one name, he might sometimes be described in records as 'Smith alias Jones'. The term had no disreputable connotation. In a few cases both names joined by 'alias' were retained for several generations and so became the equivalent of our hyphen in a modern 'double-barrelled' name. Once hereditary surnames became established, a change of name might be caused by the inheritance of a property from a maternal relative, by a young person's being adopted, by becoming known by a stepfather's surname, or by a number of other causes. In legal papers a married woman often had her maiden name added as an alias to show her connection with the matter in hand.

Alienation The transfer of a property, holding or lease, from one person to another by sale, inheritance or any other means whatsoever.

Aliens, Return of From 1792 a foreigner arriving in England had to register with a Justice of the Peace. Householders accommodating aliens were obliged to inform the parish constable, who passed the information to the Clerk of the Peace of his county.
See also DENIZATION; IMMIGRANTS.

Allegation A solemn statement, usually made on oath, most commonly met with by genealogists when made to obtain a marriage licence. The word has much the same meaning as affidavit.

Amateur Historian, The *see* **Local Historian, The**

Amen The words 'In the Name of God Amen' appear at the commencement of almost all wills and of some other documents. They are a short prayer that the provisions about to be described may be carried out, the word 'Amen' in that context meaning 'So be it'. In other contexts it can mean 'Verily'.

Amerce To levy a money penalty for an offence at a manorial court, the culprit being said to be 'in mercy'. The penalty itself was called an amercement.

Anabaptist Properly used, this term denotes a member of a German Protestant sect that repudiated the interference of any secular authority in religious affairs. However, as found in the records of the English church, it is usually a loose derogatory term for a Baptist or a Quaker.

Ancestor A person from whom others are descended, but sometimes used loosely by a descendant to mean an ancestor's brother, for want of any other genealogical term. In English, the only way of identifying an ancestor three or more generations removed is by prefacing the word 'grandfather' with the word 'great' one or more times. The Latin usage is more economical:

Grandfather = Avus
Great-grandfather = Proavus
Great-great-grandfather = Abavus
Great-great-great-grandfather = Attavus

Ancient Demesne Land that had belonged to the Crown in 1066. By the thirteenth century the law afforded special privileges to the tenants of such manors, even in cases where they were no longer held 'in chief'.
See also DEMESNE.

Angel A gold coin introduced in the reign of Edward IV. It bore the image of St Michael and varied in value from six shillings and eightpence to ten shillings.

In the sixteenth century it was the coin given to those touched for the King's Evil (scrofula). It was withdrawn as legal tender under Charles I, but small copies were struck for the later Stuarts to present at the traditional touching ceremonies.

Anglo-Norman language *see* **Norman-French language**

Anglo-Scottish Family History Society This society promotes research into families who have crossed the border in either direction. At present it operates under the umbrella of the Manchester and Lancashire Family History Society.

Angwite A fine paid to compound, i.e. to settle out of court, for bloodshed. Also called Blodwite.

Anilepman A smallholding tenant of a manor.

Annuities The first state life annuity was launched in the 1690s and was not followed by others until 1745, but between that date and 1789, ten were available. The records at the Public Record Office in Kew (NDA.1-3), show the participants' names, addresses, ages at entry, and the dates of the last payments made, also some marriages, deaths and wills. There were over 15,000 of these nominees. A full account is given in F.L. Leeson's *A Guide to the Records of British State Tontines and Life Annuities of the 17th and 18th Centuries*.
See also TONTINE.

Antiquaries of London, Society of The oldest historical and archaeological society in the country. Originally founded in 1572, it was banned in 1604 by James I on political grounds. Meetings were resumed in 1707, and the Society was formally re-established in 1717. Its papers were printed in 1720, but regular publication started in 1747 with *Vetusta Monumenta*. In 1751 the Society obtained a Charter from George II, and its *Archaeologia* began publication in 1770.

The Society has a fine library, open to members only, at Burlington House, Piccadilly, London W1.

Apothecaries In the sixteenth century apothecaries dispensed drugs and generally acted as family doctors. In London they were incorporated in 1606 in conjunction with the Grocers' Company, but became a separate body in 1617. Their right to prescribe medicines was hotly resisted by the Physicians (incorporated in 1518) as an encroachment on their proper sphere. In 1722 the Company gained the right to inspect all druggists' shops in London and destroy any drugs found unfit for use. In 1815 the Apothecaries' Company was empowered to license apothecaries throughout England and Wales, and all candidates for licences were obliged to have served a five-year apprenticeship.

The early records of the Worshipful Society of Apothecaries (from 1670) are at the Guildhall Library, London. The apprenticeship details usually include the date of the lad's baptism, the name and abode of his father, the date of his binding, and the name of his master.
See also APPRENTICES; LIVERY COMPANIES.

Apparitor The official messenger of an ecclesiastical court, responsible for summoning people to appear. Also called a Summoner.

Apprentices Apprentices were of two kinds: Trade Apprentices, bound by their parents voluntarily to a master to learn a town trade, and Poor Apprentices — pauper children put out by the parish churchwardens and Overseers of the Poor to service with householders or their wives.

Trade Apprentices

By the *Statute of Labourers and Apprentices* of 1563 it was enacted that no person should exercise any of the crafts or mysteries at that time exercised in England, unless he had served an apprenticeship of at least seven years. Previously, a similar arrangement had been laid down in some towns in corporation by-laws, but even when it became law, the Statute applied only to market towns. It required that the boy must be over 10 and under 18 years of age, and that his apprenticeship must last until he was at least 21. He must be the son of a freeman, not 'occupying husbandry', and not a labourer. The master must be a householder, at least 24 years of age, and exercising an 'art, mystery or manual occupation'.

In corporate towns, special conditions applied to merchants, mercers, drapers, goldsmiths, ironmongers, embroiderers and clothiers. They could only be masters of either their own sons or the sons of a parent (father or widowed mother) who had an estate of inheritance or freehold of forty shillings per year or more. This qualification had to be certified by three Justices of the Peace living where the property lay, and then presented to the mayor, who had to enroll it in the corporation records. This property qualification was probably intended to ensure that the boy would have the means to set up for himself when he became free. In small towns the apprentice might come from another town within the county, and in such cases his parent had to have an estate of sixty shillings a year. Many other trades, including the following, were under no conditions: bricklayers, brickmakers, burners of ores and wood ashes, carpenters, coopers, earthen potters, fullers, limeburners, linenweavers, millers, millwrights, plasters, ploughwrights, rough masons, sawyers, shinglers, slaters, smiths, tilemakers, wheelwrights, and woollen weavers of household cloth.

By a statute of 2 & 3 Anne (her REGNAL YEARS), a boy of 7 or more could be apprenticed to a shipowner, a fisherman, a ship's gunner or a shipwright, for ten years or less. In 1710 a stamp duty was levied on bindings, and this caused the establishment of a central register which is now among the Inland Revenue records at the Public Record Office, Kew (IR.1, and Index IR.17). The register gives the name of the apprentice and his father (or mother, if she was widowed), the name and trade of the master, and the abodes of them all. After 1760 the information is not so full and often omits the father's name. If the indenture fee was less than one shilling, no stamp duty was charged, and so no record exists. Such cases were usually of boys bound to relatives. In many trades there were regulations as to how many apprentices one master might have, and as to his apprentice/journeyman ratio. In 1766-7 the maximum age for an apprentice

was reduced from 24 to 21. Compulsory binding to the specified trades was abolished in 1814.

Records The indentures were held by the master and the father, and so are usually lost; but register books are available, kept by the Corporation (from 1681) and livery companies of the City of London (from the sixteenth century) and by some corporate boroughs. An index of the Inland Revenue records, 1710-74, is available at the Society of Genealogists and the Guildhall Library, London. The Society also has a collection of original indentures with an index, but there is as yet no index to the Inland Revenue Apprentice records after 1774. The Society also holds a microfilm of the Bernau Index, which covers apprenticeships subject to Inland Revenue taxation.

If the search is for a London apprentice and his company is not known, one can write to the Clerk of the Chamberlain's Court, The Guildhall, London EC2, who has a register of all London freemen from 1681. He will allow a search or have a search made through five years of the register for a small fee, and if the name is found will give more details for a further small fee. The Corporation of London Record Office has a card index of freedom entries in the Repertories (Court of Aldermen proceedings) between 1495 and 1649.

Poor Apprentices

Parish officials also put out apprentices under the Statute of 1563, but most of their activities were governed by the *Poor Law Act* of 1601. Churchwardens and Overseers of the Poor, with the consent of two justices, were empowered to apprentice to a trade or husbandry any child under 16 whose parents they judged not able to maintain him, until the age of 24 in the case of a boy, and 21 or marriage in the case of a girl. Masters failing to provide for the apprentice or carry out the conditions of the indenture could be fined by Justices of the Peace, with appeal to Quarter Sessions. The master of every ship of 30-50 tons was obliged to take an apprentice over 10 years of age, one more for the next 50 tons and one more for every additional 100 tons.

Poor Apprenticeships were exempt from stamp duty. Until 1757 apprenticeship was by indenture; after that by any properly stamped deed. Both before and after that date it was often done merely by agreement and entered in the vestry minute book.

In the eighteenth century, apprenticeship to someone in another parish was often no more than a convenient way of getting rid of a pauper child, because apprenticeship conferred settlement after 40 days. Instead of a trade, a boy learned 'husbandry', and a girl 'housewifery'. In other words, they were just servants. Anyone taking an apprentice in husbandry had to be a householder and have, and use, half a ploughland in tillage. In the Overseers' and child's own parish the master chosen was compelled to receive the child. He was often picked in rotation, or 'house row', and could be fined for refusal. In some parishes he could pay to be excused. Sometimes the children were drawn for in a lottery. If the pauper's parent disagreed with the Overseers' decision, he might find his relief docked. In the Industrial Revolution, pauper children were often apprenticed by the waggon-load to a mill-owner in another town.

Records Documentary evidence of Poor Apprenticeships is to be found in the records and accounts of the Overseers of the Poor, and in the vestry minutes of the parishes concerned. A free leaflet, *Apprenticeship Records as Sources for Genealogy in the Public Record Office*, is available at the Public Record Office.

Approvement An early form of enclosure of common land, especially unredeemed waste, by a lord of the manor under the statutes of *Merton* (1235) and *Westminster II* (1285).

Approver A hired false witness.

Appurtenances The rights and duties attached to the holding of manorial land. The most important were submission to the manor court, grazing rights and the payment of various fines to the lord of the manor. A pew, or part of a pew, in church was often an 'appurtenance' of a specific house in the parish.

Archbishop The bishop in charge of an ecclesiastical province. He also exercises episcopal authority in his own diocese. In England there are two Church of England provinces; Canterbury and York. The Archbishop

Among other APPURTENANCES of a manorial tenancy were the grazing rights for the tenant's animals. The extent of these depended upon the number of acres of arable land in the common fields that went with his holding. These seventeenth-century manorial 'Orders' put on record the grazing rights of the tenants of Uphoe Manor, Buckinghamshire. Part of the document is transcribed as follows:

Orders

Wee order that every acker of Greene sward Grown may keeape upon the Common three sheeape, and every tow ackers of areable Land one sheepe and no more, upon payne for every defalt to forfitt to the Lord of the maner [£]0-1-0

Wee order that every six acres of Land may keepe upon the Common one Cow & no more, upon payne [etc.]

Wee order that every 12 acres of Land may keepe upon the Common one horse & no more, [etc.]

Wee order that the sheepe shall not come upon the lean stuble untill St Luke [18 October], upon pain [etc.]

Wee order that the Cowes shall not come upon the barly stuble untill three dayes after all the barly be att home, [etc.]

Wee order that every inhabitant shall keepe for every two cowes Common one hogg & no more, [etc.]

Courtesy Buckinghamshire Record Archaeological Society

Orders

Wee ȳ that every acker of Groend Sward ground
may keepe upon the Common three sheepe and every tow
ackers of ould[able] Land one sheepe and nomore upon payne
for every default to forfitt to the Lord of the manor — 0 — 1 — 0

Wee order yt every 50 acres of Land may keepe upon ye Common
one Cow & no more upon payne for every default to forfeit
to ye Ld of ye manor — 0 — 1 — 0

Wee order yt for every 12 acres of Land may keepe upon ye Common
one gerse & no more upon payne for every default to forfeit to ye Ld
of ye manor — 0 — 1 — 0

Wee order yt ye sheepe shall not runn upon ye leaze stuble
untill yt Luke upon payne for every default to forfeit to ye Ld of
ye manor — 0 — 1 — 0

Wee order yt ye Cowes shall not come upon ye barly stuble untill three
dayes after all ye barly be att hand upon payne to forfeit to ye
Ld for the first offence — 0 — 1 — 0 & for every offence after — 0 — 5 — 0

Wee order yt every inhabitant shall keepe for every two townes Common
one hogg & no more upon payne to forfeit for every Hogg — 0 — 1 — 0

Wee order yt no horse, mare, Colt, or Cow shall be kept or grased in ye
follow field upon payne to forfeit to ye Lord of ye manor — 0 — 1 — 0

Wee order yt no mare and Colt shall be grased in ye barly fields after ye
Colt be a month old upon payne for every offence to forfeit to ye Ld — 0 — 1 — 0

Wee order yt ye sheepe shall not runn upon ye barly stuble untill six
dayes after al ye barly be at home upon payne to forfeit to ye Lord — 0 — 1 — 0

Wee order yt no leanes shall be gleaned but upon every ones ould
land upon payne to forfeit to ye Ld ye manor — 0 — 3 — 4

Wee order yt no man shall lett any towne to any Inhabitant in
any new erected Cottage upon payne to forfeit to ye Ld of ye manor — 0 — 1 — 0

Wee order yt no man shall cutt any bushes or willowes yt are not
in his owne ground upon payne to forfeit to ye Ld of ye manor — 0 — 1 — 0

Wee order yt no horse mare or Colt shall lye a loose in
ye meadow in ye night till harvist be home upon payne to
forfeit to ye Ld of ye manor — 0 — 1 — 0

Wee order yt no person shall fish in ye Lds waters without his
licence upon payne to forfeit to ye Ld of ye manor — 0 — 1 — 0

Wee order yt no Hogs shall goe unrringed from St Michaelmas
untill yt George upon payne to forfeit to ye Ld of ye Manor — 0 — 0 — 6

Wee order yt no Colltes shall goe loose in

of York is Primate of England; the Archbishop of Canterbury is Primate of All England and has precedence. Wales formerly fell within the Province of Canterbury, but has lately become a separate archbishopric.

Archdeacon The ecclesiastical dignitary next under a bishop of the Church of England, having jurisdiction over either the whole or part of a diocese. It is his duty to visit the parishes of the archdeaconry from time to time to see that the churches are in good repair, that parish affairs are being carried out according to Canon Law, and to hear reports from churchwardens on any public scandal. All the larger dioceses have more than one archdeaconry.

The most important archdeaconry records for genealogists are those of the probates granted in their courts, but the judicial records of the archdeaconry courts (*see* ECCLESIASTICAL COURTS) and the records of the archdeacons' visitations (*see* ECCLESIASTICAL VISITATIONS) can also supply valuable information.

Arches, Court of The Provincial Court of Appeal of the Archbishop of Canterbury. In the late Middle Ages it was held in Bow Church, the church of 'Blessed Mary of the Arches', which was exempt from the jurisdiction of the Bishop of London. The judge, appointed by the archbishop, was known as the Dean of the Arches. Appeals from the decisions of the court had to be made to the king in chancery. The court records are in the Lambeth Palace Library.

The Court dates from the thirteenth century, but few medieval or sixteenth-century records survive. The series now extant starts in 1660, but many documents are in a bad state, having at one time been stored in a well in St Paul's Churchyard. Until 1733 some are in Latin. There are over 10,000 cases, of which more than half deal with disputes over Prerogative Court of Canterbury wills and Letters of Administration, and with matrimonial troubles including applications for nullity and separation, which continue till the *Court of Probate* and *Matrimonial Causes* Acts of 1857. Other cases concern defamation, the morals and church duties of clergy and laity, liability for tithes, and the structure of churches.

Cases in the Court of Arches, 1660-1913,

published by the British Record Society, is an index and calendar to all the cases.

Arches, Deanery of the *see* **London**

Architects Details of the careers of early architects are to be found in two works: *English Mediaeval Architects, a Biographical Dictionary down to 1550,* by John Harvey, and *A Biographical Dictionary of English Architects, 1660-1840,* by H.M. Colvin.

For the sixteenth to eighteenth centuries, the archives of the Masons', Carpenters' and Bricklayers' Companies (*see* LIVERY COMPANIES) are useful for ancestors in the building trades. Researchers should also consult the publications of the Wren Society.

In 1985, *Edwardian Architecture* — a biographical dictionary by A. Stuart Gray — was published, giving details of the career and often the ancestry of architects and sculptors who flourished in the first decade of the twentieth century.

For architects of more recent times, reference should be made to the Royal Institute of British Architects, 66 Portland Place, London W1.

Archive Class *see* **Class, Archive**

Archives Documents that were originally drawn up, with no thought of posterity in mind, in the course of administrative or executive transactions. Having passed out of current use, they were preserved by the transactors and their legitimate successors. For instance, the archives in a county record office are the multifarious official records of the County Council and its predecessor, the Court of Quarter Sessions. Other records deposited there, e.g. parish registers, are more properly designated 'Collections' of various kinds.

Ark A chest, often found mentioned in the inventories of the possessions of deceased persons.

Arms, Coat of To find out whether your ancestors bore a coat of arms the best first step is to inspect their original wills, most of which until the mid nineteenth century were not only signed but also sealed with a signet. Inspecting

Crest

Torse

Helm

Mantling

CANDIDE COMME LA FLEUR

Shield with
Arms

Motto

The armorial achievement of the Fenton
family. The blazon of the arms in heraldic
terminology is: 'azure, on a chevron
between three secretary birds' heads
erased argent as many fleur de lis of the
field'; which means that the background
(field) is blue, the chevron and birds'
heads silver (in practice, white), and the
fleur de lis the same as the background.
'Erased' means that the head looks as
though it had been forcibly pulled off.
Drawing by Peter Haillay

them is not always possible. Some probate
courts (*see* WILL), after copying a will brought to
them by an executor, handed the original back to
him, in which case it is almost certainly now lost;
but other courts made two copies, one in their
Register Book and another for the executor, and
they kept the original. The probate court in
which the wills of England's most prosperous
testators — who were also the most likely to be
armigerous — had their wills proved in the
Prerogative Court of Canterbury. This court
retained original wills, many of which survive at
the Public Record Office (PRO) repository at
Hayes, Middlesex. They have to be ordered at
the PRO, Chancery Lane, London, under call
number PROB.10. Delivery to the Wills Room
there takes about a week.

Not all wills, even those of armorial persons,
were sealed with heraldic signets. Some show
non-heraldic devices from signets probably
handed to the testator for the purpose, by the
lawyer who drew up the will or the scrivener

who wrote it out. When the device is heraldic it
may be that of a crest or a coat of arms, or both,
and sometimes shows the ancestor's arms
impaling those of his wife's family, a useful
additional piece of information. The tinctures of
course are not shown; for these, see Papworth's
Ordinary of British Armorials or Burke's *General
Armory*, both mentioned later in this article.

The fact that an ancestor used an heraldic
signet is no guarantee that he was genuinely
entitled to arms, but the discovery that he made
an armorial seal makes it more worthwhile to
engage in the process of checking with the
College of Arms, the only authoritative source of
such information.

To be entitled to arms by inheritance, a family
of today needs to prove a direct legitimate male
line descent from an ancestor who is on the
official record of the College as being entitled to
the same arms. Modern firms which advertise
shields of arms 'associated with your surname'
are using a vague phrase to sell armorial insignia

to people not entitled to them, and, in doing so, cause future confusion to genealogy.

Armorial bearings were originally marks of identification for knights in armour, whether in war or at tournaments. The earliest known are those of Geoffrey of Anjou, father of Henry II, described in a chronicle of 1127. Heraldic devices probably came into England in the reign of Stephen (1135-54).

The personal identifying device of those days, the equivalent of our signature, was the engraved seal. On this a knight or lord was usually depicted fully armed and on horseback; so, once armorial bearings came into widespread use they were soon visible on the seal's shield and/or lance flag. Because they were more readily identifiable than the mounted figure they soon came to form the whole of a seal's device, at least on one side. The earliest known English seal showing arms is of 1136-8. Later in the century part of a knight's bearings also came to be displayed on his helmet, and this gave rise to the crest, of which the earliest known example is of 1198.

In the thirteenth century the application of armorial bearings spread to horse-trappings and surcoats, from which came the name 'coat of arms'. The supporters that later became the privilege of peers were at first merely decorative additions on the larger seals used by magnates.

Like surnames at this time, arms were becoming hereditary and therefore no longer confined to actual knights but spread among their male-line descendants, thus becoming a symbol of social status. By the year 1300, about 1500 families were armigerous and so some regulation of armorial bearings was required to prevent duplication. This responsibility was laid upon the heralds — the officers whose work, at tournaments and in the armies, already entailed a professional knowledge of such matters (hence the name 'Heraldry' for the science and art of armorial display). The earliest extant English grant of arms is of 1389. It was also about this time that the hereditary nature of arms led to the quartering of an 'heiress's' coat by her descendants when her father's blood and name became extinct in the male line.

In the fifteenth century, the senior heralds, called Kings of Arms, were given the right to grant arms; and in March 1483, or 1484, the College of Arms was incorporated by Richard III. Coats of arms were to be granted to 'men of virtue and repute, worthy to be received among noble gentlemen', and also to guilds and other corporate bodies. Crests were not automatically included in such grants. The heralds began to compile registers both of the arms they granted and of those already in approved use.

The sixteenth century saw the establishment of minimum property requirements (land worth £100 per annum or movables worth £360) before grants of arms would be approved; and at the same time a drive was made to tighten controls on the use of arms and ensure the proper registration of those already justifiably borne. The Kings of Arms made tours of the country from 1530 onward to examine gentlemen's claims. They took consideration of personal knowledge, family muniments, family traditions and the records of previous visitations, and finally either confirmed or disallowed the claim. This gave rise to a large number of written family trees of varying reliability.

The heralds' visitations continued until 1686. During the seventeenth century, crests first became an automatic feature in grants of arms. The Harleian Society has printed copies of visitation pedigrees, but some of these contain unauthorised additions to the originals at the College.

Arms and quarterings should, ideally, assist the genealogist in one of his problems, that of distinguishing armigerous families of the same surname from one another. Unfortunately many people in the past used arms to which they had no real right. This practice was even condoned by some heralds, though sometimes the latter salved their consciences by adding marks of difference. If a researcher can establish a descent from a person who rightly bore arms, he may be able to obtain considerable information about previous generations from the College of Arms.

Women's use of arms An unmarried woman bears her father's arms upon a diamond-shaped 'lozenge' instead of a shield. A widow bears her late husband's arms on a lozenge 'impaled' with her father's, or with the latter on an escutcheon of pretence if she is an heiress. (For an explanation of this, *see* HATCHMENT.) It is inferred from hatchments that a married woman may, during the life of her husband, use a shield of his arms, but suspended from a ribbon and without a helmet, mantling, crest or motto. The latter four items are never used by women, except in the case of Royal arms. (*See also* ACHIEVEMENT).

To obtain a grant of arms a 'petition' or 'memorial' must be addressed to the Earl Marshal, which will be drawn up for the petitioner by one of the heralds. He will be asked for personal details to ensure that he has the standing of a Gentleman. If he has served in the regular armed forces, he will be expected to have been an officer. If the College is satisfied with the replies, the petitioner will then be asked if he has formed any opinion as to the bearings he would like to have on his shield. If he has not, he will be asked what his, or his family's, interests or occupations have been, so that appropriate charges may be chosen. He will also be asked to choose a motto. An artist employed by the College will prepare a coloured sketch of the proposed arms, which is submitted to the petitioner for his approval and initialling. In due course, Letters Patent granting the arms will be issued to him. The arms are granted to a person and his male-line descendants; so the petitioner needs to register details of his family at the College. If he applies in his own name, he need only give particulars of himself, his wife, children and grandchildren, and he need not offer documentary evidence. If he applies in the name of his father (who must be living), he must also give details of his father, mother, siblings, sisters- and brothers-in-law, nephews and nieces. This latter type of petition enables the arms to be borne by his brothers and sisters and his brothers' descendants.

The Harleian Society has also printed lists of numerous persons who received grants of arms between 1687 and 1898. The descents of many armigerous families appear in the issues of Burke's *Peerage, Baronetage and Knightage* and *Landed Gentry*. The British Library MSS department, at the British Museum, has a collection of MS pedigrees compiled at the times of the Visitations and sometimes added to later.

A classified list of arms arranged under blazons is contained in the *Ordinary of British Armorials* by J.W. Papworth and A.W. Morant (1961 reprint of 1874 edition). It refers to arms listed in Burke's *General Armory*, which gives an alphabetical list of families, with blazons of the arms they use, with or without authority, and is very inaccurate. Crests are listed in Fairbairn's *Book of Crests* (1905), and mottoes in Elvin's *Handbook of Mottoes* (1860). Their accuracy cannot be relied upon. For further reading, see *A Complete Guide to Heraldry* by A.C. Fox-Davies, revised by J.C. Brook-Little (1969). The Society of Genealogists has published a leaflet on *The Right to Arms*.

See also ARMS, COLLEGE OF; HERALDRY.

Arms, College of This is the corporation of heralds responsible for controlling, granting and confirming arms in England under the general supervision of the Duke of Norfolk in his capacity of Earl Marshal. It was incorporated by Richard III in March 1483, or 1484. Its activities and those of the heralds are described under ARMS, COAT OF. The Officers of Arms are:

Kings of Arms

Garter (the Senior)

Clarenceux   Norroy and Ulster

Heralds

Somerset   York   Lancaster

Chester   Windsor   Richmond

Pursuivants

Bluemantle   Rouge Croix

Rouge Dragon   Portcullis

The College, in Queen Victoria Street, London EC4, is open daily from 10 am to 4 pm, with an Officer of Arms always in attendance to deal with enquiries.

The Official Registers of the College include the armorial bearings granted or confirmed to English and Welsh families from the fifteenth century until today, and family trees of thousands of families of English and Welsh origin.

Army The records to be consulted will depend upon whether the man to be researched was an officer or a member of the other ranks.

Officers The first source to consult is that of the

printed *Army Lists* issued annually since 1754 and twice annually since some time in the nineteenth century. They are indexed by the end of the eighteenth century. There is also a printed issue for 1740, but for the period 1702-54 there are the *MS Army Lists* at the Public Record Office (PRO) Kew, under reference WO.64.

From 1727 back to the beginning of the regular army in 1661, there are two printed compilations by Charles Dalton called *English Army Lists and Commission Registers, 1661-1714*, and *George I's Army* which covers 1714-27. These printed sources can be found on the shelves at the PRO, at the National Army Museum in London and at the Society of Genealogists. They supply details of an officer's progress and promotion, his regimental unit, whereabouts and retirement or death, but contain nothing about his origins or family.

For pre-1660 officers, *The Army Lists of Roundheads and Cavaliers* by E. Peacock (1865) lists the officers of both armies under their regiments, with an index. For the Parliamentary side, there is much information in *The Regimental History of Cromwell's Army* by Firth and Davies (1940). Other printed sources held at the PRO for this period are *Calendars of State Papers* and, in manuscript, *Commonwealth Exchequer Papers* (SP.28). Before the Civil Wars of 1642-9 there was no regular standing army.

Services of Officers Retired on Full and Half-Pay (WO.25) was compiled for the year 1828. This class of record gives the officer's age on being commissioned, the date of commission, his regiment, promotions (with dates), and whether placed on half-pay by reduction in the services or by the purchase of a half-pay commission and desirous of further service. It also mentions the family items of marriage (with date), births of children, and place of residence during the preceding five years. Finally, the record contains the officer's signature. There is an index of the half-pay returns.

Services of Officers on the Active List, 1829-1919 (WO.25 and 76) periodically give the same details plus the officer's date and place of birth, whether the first commission was by purchase or otherwise, details of any campaigns in which he took part and of service abroad, date and place of marriage and name of wife, indication of whether she is still alive, names of children with date of birth and place of baptism. They are slip-indexed in the Search Room at the PRO, Kew.

Reports of Officers' Marriages (WO.25) In the early nineteenth century officers were ordered to report their marriages. These reports gave the officer's age at marriage, name and age of bride, place and date of the ceremony, names of the witnesses and officiating clergyman. These are now card-indexed from 1810.

Commander-in-Chief's Memoranda, 1793- (WO.31) This class contains the letters of application for commissions and their recommendation by influential persons. The letter will usually bear the address of the applicant and mention the regiment in which he desires a commission, giving his reasons. These may include the fact that he has had relatives serving in it.

Paymaster General's Records of Full and Half-Pay (PMG.3 and 4) contain the date of the officer's death.

Note Disappearance of a name from the *Army List* can mean that the officer sold his commission.

Other Ranks (other than Royal Artillery and Royal Engineers) The records at the PRO are arranged by regiment, so the man's regiment must first be known. Old cap badges may be a help, but for an article on further clues, see 'World War I Army Ancestors' by Norman Holding in *Bedfordshire FHS Journal*, Vol.4, No.1. If the man is known to have been serving at a certain place at a certain time, the regiment or regiments stationed there can be found at the PRO from the *Monthly Station Returns* (WO.17, and WO.73 after 1859). Having discovered the man's regiment, the next step is to refer to:

Discharge Certificates in *Regular Soldiers' Documents* (WO.97) These date from 1756 and, until 1883, are in two series: men discharged to pension and men discharged for other reasons, e.g. limited engagements and discharge by purchase. From 1883 all army discharges are in one alphabetical series. Soldiers who died or were killed during their service will not, of course, have had any discharge records. Discharge certificates, except for a few of the earliest, record a man's birthplace and age on enlistment. After 1883 his next-of-kin, wife and children are sometimes given. The records at the PRO extend to 1913.

Pay Lists and Muster Rolls, 1760- (WO.12 and 16) These are yearly regimental volumes enabling one to follow a man from enlistment till discharge or death. In many volumes, a form showing *Men becoming Non-effective*, i.e. discharged or dead, will be found at the end of each quarter. This will show the man's birthplace, previous trade and date of enlistment. From about 1868, marriage details and the names of children are also included.

The following classes of record at the PRO may provide additional information, as indicated.

Description Books, 1795- (WO.25/266-688) Age, trade and birthplace, and sometimes height, colour of hair, eyes and complexion.

Casualty Returns (WO.25/1359-2410, 3251-3472. India, 7880-8223) Name, rank, birthplace, previous trade, type of casualty and next-of-kin.

Depot Musters - 1872 (WP.12/12122-13184 or in Muster Rolls at home).

Pension records include:
Widows' Pensions 1735-1912 Proof of marriage and often date and place of birth.

Chelsea Hospital Pension Registers 1715- (WO.116/1-151; WO.117/1-70; WO.121/136).

Royal Hospital, Kilmainham, Dublin, Pension Registers (WO.118/1-43; WO.119/1-70).

Regular Soldiers' Documents c.1760-1900 Before 1883 these refer to pensioners only.

There are, additionally, the following registers for all ranks, at the Office of the Registrar General, St Catherine's House, London WC2 (*see* GENERAL REGISTER OFFICE).

Garrison Registers Christenings, marriages and burials (CMB) of soldiers' families.

Chaplains' Returns 1796-1880 Births, baptisms, marriages and deaths while on service abroad, with one consolidated index.

Regimental Registers Original registers both at home and abroad, with an index of births and baptisms, and others showing soldiers' marriages and the births and baptisms of their children.

Chelsea Hospital Registers CMB records: christenings 1691-1812; marriages 1765 onward; burials 1856 onward.

Army records are normally open to inspection by the public at the PRO when they are 30 years old.

Background Information Histories have been written of most British regiments. These give details of the movements about the world of each battalion and of the campaigns and minor engagements in which they have been involved. The names of even junior officers may be mentioned, and occasionally those of other ranks. A large collection of regimental histories may be consulted at the National Army Museum, Royal Hospital Road, Chelsea, London SW3.

Infantry regiments were initially known by the name of their colonel, but during the period 1820-80 they were designated by numbers in their order of precedence. In 1880, regiments consisting of only one battalion were merged with other one-battalion regiments. Most regiments have their own museum, some with archive material. Addresses can be obtained from the National Army Museum.

The Commonwealth War Graves Commission will supply information on twentieth-century grave locations, photographs of graves and memorials and copies of cemetery register entries. Enquiries should be addressed to: The Information Officer, Commonwealth War Graves Commission, 2 Marlow Road, Maidenhead, Berkshire SL6 7DX.

For the Indian Army, *see* EAST INDIA COMPANY.

For further reading, see *In· Search of Army Ancestry* by G. Hamilton-Edwards (Phillimore, 1977); the leaflets *Operational Records of the British Army, 1660-1914*, and *British Military Records as Sources for Biography and Genealogy*, available free at the PRO; also *Tracing Your Ancestors in the PRO* by J. Cox and T. Padfield, and *Records of Officers and Soldiers who have served in the British Army* (PRO).

Array, Commission of Commissions of Array were instituted by Edward I to raise armed forces in each shire whenever necessary. The commissioners appointed were usually barons, knights of the shire, or officers of the royal household. They were commanded to call up a certain number of men from each township, working from muster rolls prepared in each hundred. The *Statute of Winchester* laid down what equipment each man between the ages of 15 and 60 had to bring with him, according to the value of the land or goods he owned.

Land	Goods	Equipment
	Under 20 marks	Sword and dagger
20 marks p.a.		Halberd and dagger
£2 p.a.		Sword, bow and arrows and dagger
£5 p.a.		Doublet, helmet, sword and dagger
£10 p.a.	20 marks	Coat of mail, helmet, sword and dagger
£15 pa. and over	40 marks	Coat of mail, helmet, sword, dagger & horse

Twice a year a view of arms, or muster, was held in each hundred and liberty. Any man required to serve abroad was paid wages. This system enabled forces to be raised and maintained for the duration of any emergency in a way that was impossible under the obligations of feudal tenure. In Tudor times the Commission was replaced by the appointment of Lieutenants in each shire (*see* LORD LIEUTENANT). The Commissions are entered on the backs of Patent Rolls, reference C.66 at the Public Record Office, Chancery Lane, London.

Arrentation The commutation of manorial services for rent.

Artillery A term that covered all types of military missile weapons; and an Artillery Ground was an area set aside for practising marksmanship with both bows and arrows and hand firearms. The general term for cannon was Ordnance.
See also ROYAL ARTILLERY.

Ascent A term, unfortunately little used, to describe an ancestral line when thought of as running back into the past; the reverse concept to a descent, which applies to the same line when considered as leading down from the past to the present. In researching a family tree one is, in practice, tracing an ascent, i.e working backwards from later generations to those earlier.

Assart A piece of land recently brought under cultivation after woodland clearance. The field name and family name Newlands usually derive from such a development.

Assize From the thirteenth century onward an Assize was the periodic regulation and examination of the quality, weights, measures and prices of certain products offered for sale, notably ale, bread and cloth.

The term originally applied to the jury appointed to deliver verdicts, hence the derivation of the name of the later Courts of Assize (*see* ASSIZE, COURTS OF).

Assize, Courts of Since Plantagenet times, a county court presided over by the king's judges on circuit, administering the Common Law. The judges held commissions of OYER AND TERMINER, GAOL DELIVERY and NISI PRIUS.

Freeholders could buy royal writs that obliged persons with whom they were in dispute to come to court. The name of the writ in question was often added to that of the court that tried the case, e.g. an Assize of Darrein Presentment. In Tudor and Stuart times the most important function of the Courts of Assize, which worked in seven circuits with two judges at each, was the control of local justice, as the judges were more susceptible to royal authority than the county Justices of the Peace sitting in Quarter Sessions. The judges also reported back on political feeling in the provinces. No hard and fast rule distinguished the types of case heard by the Assize courts, but after about 1590 the prestige of the judges led to the more serious felonies being sent to the Assizes in addition to those involving any finer points of law. As they represented the king, the judges were able to arbitrate between local magnates and decide on inter-jurisdictional disputes. The trials, however, were often hurried through, and the penalties were severe, so much so that juries often returned verdicts of 'not guilty' in order to save the neck of those charged with minor offences. However, they could be fined if they refused to return a verdict as the judges directed. The records are at the Public Record Office, Chancery Lane, London, under groups JUST and ASSI.1-76, except those for London (which are at the Corporation of London Record

Office), the printed Old Bailey Sessions Papers (at the Guildhall Library), and those of Middlesex (which are at the Greater London Council Record Office). The most useful are the Minute Books and Indictments. Those of some counties have been calendared and printed. The official records are laconic, but those of the nineteenth century can often be supplemented by reports in local newspapers. The Gaol Calendars attached to the Indictments give the names, ages, occupations and abodes of prisoners awaiting trial, accompanied sometimes by lists of gentry eligible for grand and petty juries.

See also PRISONERS.

Association Oath Rolls The *Act of Association*, 1695/6, in consequence of a Jacobite plot against the life of King William III, required all office holders to take a Solemn Oath of Association vowing to combine with others for the better preservation of His Majesty's royal person and government. Actually, most men of any standing took the oath. The rolls containing the names of the oath-takers, mainly under parish headings, are now at the Public Record Office, Chancery Lane, London, under reference C.213. A list of the surviving ones is given in *The Genealogists' Magazine* of December, 1983. There are separate lists for the livery companies of the City of London, but under the same call number.

Association of Genealogists and Record Agents In 1968 a few of the leading professional genealogists in England came together to form the Association (known as AGRA), with the objects of upholding the standards of professional genealogy and record research and of protecting the interests of those requiring such services. A distinction is made between genealogists and record agents. The former class of members are recognised as qualified to direct genealogical research on behalf of clients, and the latter to carry out searches in records specified by clients in any field of enquiry. The membership of the Association is now around one hundred. Management is by an elected Council. A list of members' names and addresses is obtainable from the Secretary, Mrs Jean Tooke, 1 Woodside Close, Caterham, Surrey CR3 6AU.

Attach To place under constraint pending attendance at a court, by virtue of a writ or precept. It differs from an arrest in that the latter lies only against the body of a person, whereas an attachment may alternatively lie against a person's goods.

Attainder A declaration of Attainder, by Act of Parliament, was made after judgement of death or judgement of outlawry on a capital charge. The consequences were forfeiture and 'corruption of blood' (see below). From 1539, Attainder Acts were used in lieu of trials.

In a case of treason, lands and any rights in them were forfeited to the Crown for life, or for a term of years. For murder, the forfeiture to the Crown was of the profits of any freehold land, or, if the lands were held in fee simple (*see* FEE), of the lands themselves, for a year and a day. In both cases goods and chattels were also forfeited. In the case of lands, the forfeiture was backdated to the date of the crime in order to obviate sales in the meantime, but in the case of goods and chattels it dated only from the conviction.

'Corruption of blood' meant that the attainted person could neither inherit nor transmit lands; they would escheat (revert) to the superior lord, subject to the Crown's rights of forfeiture. Attainder was ended by the *Forfeiture Act* of 1870.

The verb 'to attaint' could mean no more than just to convict.

See also ACTS OF PARLIAMENT.

Augmentation, Court of A branch of the Exchequer formed in 1535 to carry out the dissolution of the monasteries and to administer their lands, properties and revenues about to accrue to the Crown. Its records contain a number of cases between owners and/or claimants of such lands. In 1547 it was combined with the Court of General Surveyors. The Proceedings are at the Public Record Office, Chancery Lane, London, under references E.315 and 321. Some of them have been calendared by the List and Index Society. The Court was abolished in 1554 as a separate section of the Exchequer.

Aulnager An official responsible for inspecting

and measuring woollen cloth and seeing that it was sold in correct widths and lengths. Approved cloth bore his stamp.

Avon A county formed in 1974 out of parts of Gloucestershire and Somerset. For the Bristol and Avon Family History Society, *see* GLOUCESTERSHIRE.

Avowry A protector or guardian, such as the lord of a manor in relation to the manor's tenants. Also such a guardianship. A stranger outside any tithing could purchase a lord's avowry by paying a fine. The word has other legal meanings.

B

Badge (i) A heraldic device, not part of an ACHIEVEMENT, used to mark property or allegiance. In modern times, it is recommended by the College of Arms as a convenient property mark for anciently armorial families having no crest.

(ii) A military cap badge is a useful clue for discovering the regiment in which a soldier served.

Badge-Man By an Act of 1697 the poor in receipt of parish relief were obliged to wear badges bearing the letter 'P', and were forbidden to beg. However, at certain hours they could beg broken victuals from their neighbours, who were pledged to give none to unbadged applicants.

Badger In Tudor times a licensed beggar: later also meaning an itinerant pedlar, chapman or other type of dealer.

Bailiff A manorial lord's local manager, appointed from outside the tenantry. He watched his lord's interests, superintended his demesne land and conducted relations with the tenants of the manor through their representative, the reeve. He was responsible to the lord or his steward for the efficient carrying out of his duties.

42

Bait To break a journey for food or refreshment, for either travellers or horses. In farming, a baiting-place was where the cattle were gathered for feeding.

Balk An unploughed length of turf between the FURLONGS in the open fields, not those between the strips. Those running parallel to the SELIONS were 'sidebalks'; those at right-angles to them, 'waybalks' or 'headlands'.

Bankrupts Bankruptcy is a legal declaration of a debtor's insolvency. The courts that had jurisdiction in such matters consisted, until 1831, of commissioners appointed by the Lord Chancellor. Later, two judges of the Chancery division dealt with them in the London area, and county court judges in the rest of the country. Notice of every adjudication was, and is, published in the Government's official paper, the *London Gazette*, and advertised in a local paper. The winding-up proceedings before 1710 are among the records of the Court of the King's Bench at the Public Record Office (PRO), Chancery Lane, London. After 1710 they are among the records of the Court of Bankruptcy, also held at the PRO, under group B and indexed. They are available for search after 75 years. Insolvents of the period 1820-43 are listed in *The Bankrupt Directory, 1820-43* by George Elwick (1843).

Banneret, Knight Once a military rank. The banneret was a small square banner distinguishing the knight banneret from the knight bachelor. On promotion to this rank, the man-at-arms might have his 'banner' created by cutting the points off the forked pennant of his former rank. Such promotion might be conferred on the field of battle. The knight banneret had command of a group of men-at-arms and was superior to a knight bachelor.

Banns of Marriage A proclamation of

RIGHT This Banns Book of 1824 shows the marital status of contracting parties, their parish(es) of residence, the dates of the three Sundays on which their banns were called, and the names of the clergymen who read them. In cases where only the groom's parish is known and there is no record of his having been married there, a banns book can lead the searcher to the bride's parish and the approximate date of the marriage there — provided, of course, there was no last-minute hitch. *Chertsey Parish Church*

BANNS published in the Parish Church of *Chertsey* in the County of *Southampton* in the Year 18 24

NAMES.	Residence.	Publication.	When	By whom.
William Skeet Bachelor & Sarah Paice Spinster	both of the Parish of Chertsey	1 2 3	Sep 26th Oct 3d Oct 10th	Thos Chas May V C Pembroke cur C Pembroke cur
James Dolby Bachelor and Mary Pullen Spinster	both of the Parish of Chertsey	1 2 3	Sep 26th Oct 3d Oct 10th	Thos Chas May V C Pembroke cur C Pembroke cur
William Stephen bachelor and Harriett Ellis Spinster	both of the Parish of Chertsey	1 2 3	Oct 10th Oct 17th Oct 24th	C Pembroke cur C Pembroke cur C Pembroke cur
Benjamin Moram Bachelor and Ann Snelling Spinster	both of the Parish of Chertsey	1 2 3	Oct 17th Oct 24th Oct 31th	C Pembroke cur C Pembroke cur C Pembroke cur
Richard Hearley Bachelor and Ann Warner Spinster	both of the Parish of Chertsey	1 2 3	Oct 17th Oct 24th Oct 31th	C Pembroke cur C Pembroke cur C Pembroke cur
John Watt, Bachelor Martha Stent Widow	both of the Parish of Chertsey	1 2 3	Oct 24th Oct 31th Nov 7	C Pembroke cur C Pembroke cur James R Le

intended marriage, repeated three times at weekly intervals in the parish churches of the bride and bridegroom, was ordered by the Lateran Council in 1215. To dispense with banns required the obtaining of a marriage licence.

In 1653, under Cromwell's Protectorate, marriage was made a civil contract performed by a Justice of the Peace, and banns had to be published either on three consecutive Sundays after 'the Morning Exercise' or on three market days in three consecutive weeks in the market place. The Banns were then recorded, sometimes in a separate book and sometimes in the marriage register, either as a full entry or by adding the letter M (for Market) after the marriage entry. At the Restoration of the monarchy, marriage once more became a sacrament of the Church.

On 25 March 1754, Lord Hardwicke's *Marriage Act* brought Banns Registers into regular keeping, sometimes in separate books and sometimes in the parish marriage registers. Separate Banns Books tended to be discarded after they were filled, so only a comparatively small number survive today. The requirement to register banns continued until 1812.

A typical wording is: 'Banns published between John Smith, bachelor of this parish, and Jane Brown, of the parish of Aldford, spinster. 7th June 1806, 14th June, 21st June.'

Banns Registers may still be found in a few church vestries, but where marriage registers have been deposited at the county record office any surviving Banns Books have usually gone with them. They offer a substitute for a missing marriage register and provide a cross-reference from the parish of one party to that of the other. Where the corresponding marriage entry still exists, the banns entry may supply additional information. However, a banns record by itself is no guarantee that a marriage actually took place. See also PARISH REGISTERS.

Baptismal Register *see* Parish Registers

Baptists In 1611 the English Baptist movement was founded in Amsterdam by John Smith, an English Puritan in exile. In 1612 one of his followers, Thomas Helwys, came to London and formed the first Baptist church in England in Newgate Street (one authority says, in Spitalfields). This was the origin of the General Baptist denomination. They repudiated infant baptism and Calvinistic predestination, and affirmed the Arminian view of individual responsibility for the salvation of one's soul.

1633 A church of Independents broke away and founded the first Calvinistic or Particular Baptist Church in Southwark. They, too, rejected infant baptism.

1640 The first local Baptist Association was founded at Bristol.

1644 A Confession of Faith was published by the Particular Baptists. This was a theological agreement, but not an organisational conjunction, between the General and Particular churches. They adopted baptism by immersion, and most Baptist churches admitted only those who had been so baptized. The Bedfordshire and Hertfordshire churches, influenced by John Bunyan, were the chief exceptions to this rule.

1660 At the Restoration, persecution of the Baptist and other nonconformist churches began. In the following year, the *Corporations Act* restricted membership of corporations to those who took the sacrament according to the rites of the Church of England.

1673 The *Test Act* intensified the restrictions on opportunities for nonconformists, by requiring holders of civil or military office to produce SACRAMENT CERTIFICATES and take an oath recognising the king as supreme head of the church.

1689 Under William III the *Act of Toleration* ended the persecution. Dissent increased, especially in manufacturing districts. The Particular Baptists became more numerous than their General Baptist brethren. Applications for the registration of new chapels came in to both the diocesan and archidiaconal registrars and also to the county Clerk of the Peace. These are now to be found at county record offices.

In the eighteenth century a Baptist theological academy was founded in Bristol. Many General Baptist churches became Unitarian in theology. Before 1754, marriages were sometimes performed in meeting-houses, the fact of public contract making it lawful.

1754-1837 Baptists could only marry lawfully in a licensed Church of England church or chapel, so the records of the ceremonies must be sought in parish registers.

1770 The General Baptists founded the General Baptist New Connection, and since then the Old Connection has gradually merged with the Unitarians. In 1800, the New Connection had 40 churches and 3,400 members.

1828 The *Corporation* and *Test Acts* were repealed.

1837-40 Nearly all Baptist registers were deposited with the Registrar General, and are now at the Public Record Office, Chancery Lane, London, under references RG.4, 5 and 8. New registers were started from 1837, after the old ones had been sent in for inspection.

1891 The General and Particular Baptists united in the Baptist Union of Great Britain and Ireland.

Minutes of congregations, committees and associations are at the Baptist Union Library, 4 Southampton Row, London WC1, which incorporates the Baptist Historical Society Library. Other archives are at Baptist Church House, Southampton Row, and at Dr Williams's Library, Gordon Square, London WC1 (formerly the accepted place for registers of non-conformist marriages), and with the church secretaries and trustees' secretary. The Secretary of the Baptist Historical Society is the Reverend P.J. Wortley, 96 Palmerston Rad, Buckhurst Hill, Essex. The Society publishes the *Baptist Quarterly*, formerly entitled its *Transactions* (*see also* WILLIAMS'S LIBRARY, DR).

The Baptist College, Rusholme, Manchester 14, has records of the college only. Bristol Baptist College, Woodland Road, Bristol 8, has archives of the college, of the Western Baptist Association and of Dr John Rylands (1753-1835). It also has the MSS of William Prynne, Puritan pamphleteer (1600-99).

For further reading, see *Sources for Nonconformist Genealogy and Family History*, by D.H. Steel (1973).

Barbers The Company of Barbers was first incorporated in 1461, but under Henry VIII it was united with the Company of Surgeons. Apart from shaving and the cutting of hair and beards, the barbers were only allowed to undertake such minor 'surgery' as blood-letting and tooth-drawing, while the surgeons were barred from 'barbery and shaving'. In 1745 the companies were again separated as the surgeons strove for higher professional status. The barbers' sign was a spirally striped pole with a basin hung from the end. The white stripe signified the filet or bandage used in blood-letting, and the basin was the receptacle for the blood. Barbers' shops were popular places of resort for news and chat. Stringed musical instruments were often kept for the use of waiting customers. The records of the Barbers' Company are held at the Guildhall Library, London.

Bargain Formerly meant any contract, not necessarily advantageous.

Bargain and Sale A procedure for the private and secret conveyance of property, devised to take advantage of a loophole in the *Statute of Uses* of 1535-6. When property was transferred, the Statute made possession pass at once to the person who was to have the use of the land, instead of to any trustee who was the nominal purchaser. By Bargain and Sale procedure, the vendor bargained and sold a property to a purchaser and so found himself holding it to the purchaser's use, but, according to the Statute, ownership had passed at once to the user, so there was no need to enrol any conveyance documents and so make the sale public. However, the *Statute of Enrolments* was quickly passed, enforcing enrolment of such transfers either at one of the central courts or before a Justice of the Peace. This regulation made the procedure less popular and it was gradually replaced in favour by that of LEASE AND RELEASE.
See also ENFEOFFMENT TO USE.

Barnardo's Homes, Dr The archives of these homes for orphans and foundlings now belong to the University of Liverpool. The records are closed for one hundred years after they are made, but there is provision for bona fide academic researchers to apply to consult within the closed period. Records more than one hundred years old are available for research; enquiries should be addressed to the University Archivist, P.O. Box 147, Liverpool L69 38X.

Baron The lowest and second oldest of the five ranks of the peerage. Originally a 'baro' was the king's, or a great magnate's, 'man' who held the land of him, having done homage for it, as distinct from the 'homo' of lesser magnates. The barons became differentiated into greater and lesser barons. The former were summoned by writ directly to the king's council, the latter through the county sheriffs. Barons as peers of the realm are the successors of the greater barons. The earliest writs now considered to have created hereditary peerages are those of Edward I. The limits of the inheritance of a hereditary baronage are defined by the Letters Patent creating the barony. Today a baron is styled 'Lord' both in conversation and also, unlike other ranks of the peerage, in formal written address. His wife is styled 'Lady', his children 'The Honourable' in formal written address, and 'Mr', 'Mrs' or 'Miss' in conversation.

Baron and Feme (i) A man and his wife legally considered as one person.

(ii) In heraldry, the situation in which the arms of a man and his wife (not being an heiress) are borne side by side on a shield.

See also ARMS, COAT OF; HATCHMENT.

Baronet The lowest hereditary dignity and not of peerage rank, it takes precedence above that of knight and below that of baron, and carries the title of 'Sir'. The rank, the latest to be created, was instituted by James I in 1611 to raise money for the maintenance of troops in Ulster, the fee payable by the new baronet being £1,095. It was at first limited to those who held land worth £1,000 per year and whose paternal grandfather had borne heraldic arms. Separate baronetcies of Ireland and Nova Scotia were created. Those of Nova Scotia were descendable to heirs collateral of the original grantee, as well as to his descendants.

1616   As an inducement to potential applicants, the eldest sons of baronets became entitled to claim knighthood on coming of age.

1634   Englishmen and Welshmen became eligible for Nova Scotia baronetcies, originally instituted in 1625 for Scotsmen, to provide for settlement in that transatlantic colony.

1783   During the eighteenth century a number of baronetcies were illegally assumed, owing mainly to the large numbers of collateral descents from Nova Scotia baronets; so new grantees became obliged to register their arms and descents at the College of Arms.

1827   The right of the eldest sons to claim knighthood was rescinded.

1898   The Honourable Society of the Baronetage was formed to maintain the privilege of the rank. Its name was later changed to the Study Council of the Baronetage.

1910   To prevent the continued illegal assumption of baronetcies, an official roll of the rank was established by royal warrant.

In conversation and correspondence, baronets are styled 'Sir' followed by their forename alone. Their formal title — on an envelope, for instance — is 'Sir' followed by both forename and surname and 'Bart.', to distinguish them from knights. Their wives are styled 'Lady' (formerly 'Dame'), and their children 'Mr', 'Mrs' or 'Miss'. The arms of baronets are distinguished by the Red Hand of Ulster either on a canton or on an inescutcheon, except for those of Nova Scotia titles, which display a saltire badge. The conferring of baronetcies has been discontinued.

For families in which there is, or was, a baronetcy, *see* Burke's *Peerage and Baronetage*, and Burke's *Extinct and Dormant Baronetage* (1844).

Barons of the Exchequer Four judges, usually not peers, appointed to deal with causes between the king and his subjects on matters of revenue.

Barton (i) The home farm of the lord of a manor. (ii) A monastic farm. (iii) A barley farm.

A 'bartoner' was the supervisor of a monastic barton or grange.

Bastardy The state of being begotten and born out of lawful wedlock. In the Middle Ages, the term 'bastard' referred only to the baseborn child of a father of gentle or noble birth, but later applied to any illegitimate child. The Common Law descent of land was to legitimate heirs only, but land could be passed to a bastard by enfeoffment to trustees, combined with a last will.

Bastardy is a circumstance which presents

problems for a genealogist tracing a male line of ascent. The baptismal entry in a parish register for an illegitimate child will normally mention the fact of bastardy and omit the name of the father, which was also usually omitted from birth certificates issued by registrars from 1837 onward. However, arriving back at an ancestor who was illegitimate is not necessarily the end of the road. Bastardy was a condition liable to give rise to a number of documents. Sometimes the father and mother of the child would marry later, and this is a possibility that should be explored first, though it may not always be possible to be sure that the husband was the same man as the father. The Christian name given to the child is sometimes an indication.

If no marriage took place and the mother seemed likely to 'fall on the parish', she would be questioned on oath by the Overseer of the Poor and the churchwarden, as to the father's identity. The answer would be recorded among the records of either the vestry or the Overseer. The putative father would then be required to enter into a bond to pay for the woman's lying-in and to support the child. Such a bond is known as a Bastardy Bond or Indemnity Bond, and may survive among the parochial records. Alternatively, a parent of either the father or mother could give an Indemnity Bond to the same effect.

If no bond was forthcoming, the churchwardens would apply to the Quarter Sessions for a court order obliging the father to do his duty. This document was a *Maintenance Order* or *Filiation Order*, and a copy will be in the Quarter Sessions records. If the father ignored it, he would be brought before the court by the issue of a summons. Sometimes the desired result could be reached without fuss by the father agreeing verbally to pay the Overseer his paternal dues, and this may be discovered from entries of moneys received and disbursed in the Overseers' Accounts. The regulations with regard to the illegitimate children of the poor varied from time to time.

Bastardy appears to have increased considerably from the sixteenth to the nineteenth century, although all children born more than a month after marriage were considered legitimate. The following parliamentary Acts were passed on the subject:

1575-6   Justices were empowered to charge either the mother or the putative father with the cost of the child's upkeep, either directly or by reimbursing the parish. The father often discharged himself by payment of a lump sum, until, in the eighteenth century, this was made illegal. The *Application Order* made by the justices gives the mother's name and sometimes the names of both parents. It remained the basis of the law until 1834.

1609-10   Any mother of a bastard who became chargeable to the parish might be sent to the county House of Correction for one year. On a second offence, she had to be. The murder of bastards therefore increased. At this period the whipping of both mother and father was a common sentence at Quarter Sessions.

1662   If the mother and father of a bastard ran away, the overseers might, on the order of two justices, seize their goods.

1732-3   A woman pregnant of a bastard was required to declare herself and name the father.

1733   Any man convicted of being the father of a bastard was to be gaoled until he gave security to indemnify the parish from its expense.

1743-4   A bastard was to have the settlement of his or her mother, wherever he/she was born. The mother was to be publicly whipped. Previously a bastard had had settlement where he/she was born.

After 1750, illegitimacy rose sharply. If the father married the mother during pregnancy, the child had its paternal settlement. This might lead to the deportation of the family to the father's parish. Applications for this can be found in the Quarter Sessions records. The vast majority of bastard births have no record except in the baptismal registers.

The above documents and other mentions may be found among the parish registers, in vestry minutes, and in churchwardens', constables' and overseers' accounts, which may have been deposited at the County Record Office, and also in Quarter Sessions records at the CRO. If paternity was not contested, Justices of the Peace normally issued maintenance orders in Petty Sessions, and of these virtually no records remain.

Settlement Examinations may also contain evidence of illegitimate children (*see* SETTLEMENT).

Other sources of information about bastards

are the records of the ECCLESIASTICAL COURTS, in which the churchwardens of the parish are likely to have presented the mother and, in many cases, named the father. The mother will then have been sentenced to do penance in the church. *See also* FOUNDLINGS.

Beadle (i) A minor official with disciplinary duties. In some parishes another term for constable. (ii) A law court messenger.

Bear in hand To delude someone.

Beast Gate The right to pasture one animal on the manorial common.

Beasts, Great These, in connection with tithes, were equine animals (horses, mules, donkeys) and bovine animals (oxen, bullocks, cows). The latter were also known as rother beasts.

Bederepe A special reaping service carried out for the lord of the manor by his tenants, originally as boonwork, but later compulsory.

Bederoll The list of a church's benefactors, for whose souls the faithful were asked to pray. It was read out from the pulpit each Sunday, and at Christmas and Michaelmas.

Bedesman (i) A person paid, endowed or voluntarily vowed to pray for others.

(ii) Any person obliged to pray for the benefactors of an institution of which he is a member.

(iii) A polite self-description — 'your bedesman' — acknowledging obligation; used, for example, in a letter applying for a favour.

Bedfordshire The Bedfordshire Family History Society holds meetings in Bedford and publishes a regular quarterly journal. Enquiries should be sent c/o the Federation of Family History Societies, 31 Seven Star Road, Solihull, West Midlands B91 2BZ, marked 'Please forward' and enclosing a stamped self-addressed envelope.

Record Repositories The County Record Office (CRO), Shire Hall, Bedford (tel: 0234.63222);

The Town Hall, Bedford (for borough records).

Parish Registers and Indexes (*see* comment under COUNTY) Virtually all the registers of the 127 ancient parishes have been deposited at the CRO, though records for Whipsnade are at the Hertfordshire Record Office. More than three-quarters of them have been copied. The INTERNATIONAL GENEALOGICAL INDEX (IGI) covers, at least in part, nearly every parish to 1812. The family history society (FHS) and the CRO have an index of all marriages not included in the IGI. The FHS has a marriage index in progress. Pallot's Marriage Index covers 45 of the parishes for the years 1790-1812, and the CRO has the Bishops' Transcripts and marriage licence records.

Wills before 1858, proved in the following courts, are at the CRO and are card-indexed:

Archdeaconry Court of Bedford.
Peculiar (Pec.) Court of Biggleswade.
Pec. Court of Leighton Buzzard.

For Bedfordshire wills proved in the Commissary Court of London and the Archdeaconry Court of Huntingdon, *see* HUNTINGDONSHIRE. As the county lay in the Diocese of Lincoln and Province of Canterbury, wills could also be proved in the Consistory Court of Lincoln and the Prerogative Court of Canterbury.

The Society of Genealogists has the following probate calendars: Bedford Archdeaconry Wills, 1498-1526; the same, 1496-1857 on microfilm; and 1480-1590 in Vol.45 of the Bedfordshire Historical Record Society publications.

Non-parochial Registers The registers of 28 chapels are deposited at the Public Record Office (PRO), Chancery Lane, London, and the IGI includes nearly as many again.

Memorial Inscriptions of some 130 Church of England churchyards have been transcribed by the FHS.

Census Returns These are at the PRO, Portugal Street, London, and at the CRO. Indexing by the FHS is in progress.

Heralds' Visitation Pedigrees have been printed for 1566, 1582 and 1634.

The Bedfordshire Historical Record Society has published many volumes of the county's records, including the Hearth Tax Returns.

Settlement Certificates The CRO has 5000 of these that were issued in the eighteenth century.

Genealogia Bedfordiensis is a well known printed source of transcripts, but experience has shown that it has a 28 per cent discrepancy from the originals, so all information from it should be checked.

Benefice Properly, the established income from an ecclesiastical office, derived from land appertaining to it, but popularly used for the office itself, which could be held for life. A Donative Benefice was one to which a parson could be appointed without any presentation to a bishop.

Benefit of Clergy A product of the conflict between the claims of Common and Canon Law. As a compromise, the Common Law courts abandoned the death penalty for some less serious capital crimes when the person convicted was a clericus (clerk), and a secondary punishment was inflicted. As a result, offences came to be classed as 'clergyable' and 'unclergyable'. The term 'clerk' had always included a large number of people in minor orders, but in 1305 it was extended to apply to secular clerks able to read and understand Latin. The test text was the first verse of the Fiftieth Psalm in the *Vulgate* (the Latin version of the Bible), popularly known as the 'Neck Verse'. In English it reads, 'Have mercy upon me, O God, according to thy loving kindness; according unto the multitude of thy tender mercies, blot out my transgressions.' This requirement degenerated into the ability to read the same verse — which in the Authorised Version became the first verse of the Fifty-first Psalm — in English. If a convicted prisoner on a capital charge read this successfully, he was merely branded on his thumb. The device had become a legal fiction to modify the severity of the English criminal law for first offenders. Even the test was abandoned in 1705, but it was not until 1827 that Benefit of Clergy itself was abolished.

Berkshire In 1974 the northern part of the county was transferred to Oxfordshire. The Berkshire Family History Society and the Windsor, Slough and District Family History Society hold regular meetings and issue journals. Enquiries should be sent c/o the Federation of Family History Societies, 31 Seven Star Road, Solihull, West Midlands B91 2BZ, marked 'Please forward' and enclosing a stamped self-addressed envelope.

Record Repositories Berkshire Record Office, Shire Hall, Shinfield Park, Reading (tel: 0734.55981); The Aerary, St George's Chapel, Dean's Cloister, Windsor Castle; Reading Corporation Archives Department, Central Public Library, Reading.

Parish Registers and Indexes (*see* comment under COUNTY) Virtually all the registers of the ancient parishes have been deposited at the county record office (CRO), but Hinksey South is at the Bodleian Library, Oxford, and Combe is at the Hampshire Record Office, Winchester. Many registers have been transcribed and published, and the Society of Genealogists lists forty in its catalogue. The INTERNATIONAL GENEALOGICAL INDEX (IGI) includes, at least in part, about two-thirds of the county's baptismal registers. A marriage index, males only, is complete for 1700-1837 and is in the custody of Mr J.W. Brooks, 'Murchison', Grubwood Lane, Cookham Dean, SL6 9UD. Pallot's Marriage Index covers thirteen parishes, mostly 1800-37. The Bishops' Transcripts until 1836 are at the Wiltshire Record Office. Later ones are at the Bodleian Library.

Marriage Licence Records Those of the Bishop's office are at the Wiltshire Record Office. Those of the Archdeacon were destroyed by enemy action in the war, but had been indexed.

Wills before 1858 proved in the following courts are located as shown.
At the county record office:
    Archdeaconry Court of Berkshire
    Peculiar (Pec.) Court of (Great) Farringdon.
At the Bodleian Library, Oxford:
    Pec. Court of the Dean and Canons of Windsor in Wantage, 1582-1668.
At the Wiltshire Record Office:
    Pec. Court of the Dean of Salisbury
    Pec. Court of the Dean and Canons of Windsor in Wantage, 1669 onward.
The county lay in the Diocese of Salisbury and Province of Canterbury, so wills could also be proved in the Consistory Court of Salisbury and the Prerogative Court of Canterbury (PCC).

The Society of Genealogists has the following indexes:

Archdeaconry of Berkshire, 1508-1857, on microfilm.

Archdeaconry of Berkshire Registered Wills, 1653-1710.

Snell's Berkshire Wills proved in the PCC, 1731-7.

Non-parochial Registers These are at the Public Record Office (PRO), Chancery Lane, London. The IGI covers about thirty.

Census Returns These are at the PRO, Portugal Street, London, with a copy at Reading Central Library.

Memorial Inscriptions Windsor family history society has transcription in progress.

Heralds' Visitation Pedigrees have been published for 1532, 1566, 1623 and 1665/6.

Protestation Oath Returns The Berkshire family history society (FHS) has an index of these.

Poor Law Records Many of these at the CRO are being indexed by the Berkshire FHS.

A Guide to the Berkshire Parish Registers and Transcripts has been published by the Berkshire FHS and CRO jointly.

Betrothal From the twelfth century, a betrothal followed by a pregnancy, or even simply by consummation, was considered a valid marriage, though a formal declaration of matrimony before witnesses was expected. An entry in a sixteenth or early seventeenth century parish register of a baptism shortly after, or even before, the marriage of the parents may be due to an official betrothal. Espousal Books, recording such contracts, survive for a handful of parishes. Betrothals gradually declined to the freely breakable status of engagements.

Bibliographies (of Genealogy) The following are recommended:

Gatfield, George *Guide to Printed Books & MSS Relating to English and Foreign Heraldry and Genealogy* (1892)

Harrison, H.G. *Select Bibliography of English Genealogy* (1937)

Humphery-Smith, Cecil R. *A Genealogist's Bibliography* (Phillimore, 1976)

Kaminkow, M.J. *A New Bibliography of British Genealogy* (Magna Charta, 1965)

Steel, D.J. *National Index of Parish Registers* Vol.1. (Society of Genealogists, 1968)

Swinnerton, Ian S. and P.A. Saul *Books for the Family Historian* (Federation of Family History Societies, 1980).

Bid Ale A social function organised by the churchwardens of a parish to raise money for those in need or temporary distress.

Bigamy (i) In ecclesiastical law, a second marriage or a marriage with a widow or widower.

(ii) Having two wives or husbands at once.

Bill (i) A document acknowledging an obligation to pay money.

(ii) In law, a declaration in writing, e.g. a Bill of Complaint, expressing a wrong alleged to have been suffered, thus initiating a law suit.

(iii) An infantry weapon consisting of a long shaft mounted with a metal pike at its end, a short pike at right-angles to the first and a hook-shaped blade for pulling an enemy off his horse. This was the weapon required of most men at musters of the militia.

Bill of Exchange A written request or order from one person (the drawer) to another (the drawee) to pay a stated sum of money to a third person (the payee) at a certain date. If the drawee accepts the bill — normally by an arrangement made in advance — he thereby becomes the acceptor. Such bills were sometimes discounted at an earlier date by a money-lender. Eventually the drawer has to repay the drawee. Bills of exchange were much in use before bank cheques became the normal method of payment.

Birmingham and Midland Society for Genealogy and Heraldry *see* **Warwickshire**

Birth Brief *see* **Total Descent**

Birth Certificate *see* **General Register of Births, Deaths and Marriages**

Births at Sea *see* **Sea, Births and Deaths at**

Bishop A priest consecrated for the spiritual direction of a diocese. A Coadjutor Bishop or Suffragan Bishop is an assistant to a Diocesan Bishop. Bishoprics were abolished in 1645 but restored on the Restoration of the monarchy. Bishops have the right to confer holy orders, administer confirmation, and consecrate churches. Since the Reformation the appointment of bishops has been vested in the Crown, but the form of election by the cathedral chapter is retained. Their consecration is carried out by an archbishop. A bishop can dispense with the proclamation of banns by issuing a marriage licence. As spiritual peers all bishops once had seats in the House of Lords, but these are now limited to 25, of which five are always occupied by the two English archbishops and the bishops of London, Winchester and Durham.

Bishops' and Archbishops' Registers
The Registers, extant from the early thirteenth century, record matters dealt with in an official capacity by the archbishop, his suffragan and his vicar-general, and by the bishop and his chancellor, including always the institution of parochial incumbents. The patrons of benefices are mentioned and also any special conditions attached to the institution. The building or repair of a church gives rise to entries, as do legal disputes, tithes, the endowment of chantries and the relations between vicar and rector and any neighbouring religious houses.

For further reading, see *Guide to Bishops' Registers of England and Wales*, ed. D.M. Smith (Royal Hist. Soc., 1981).

Bishops' Transcript A copy of one year's entries in a parish register, sent by the incumbent to his bishop, usually at Easter. This practice was made general in 1598 in accordance with an archiepiscopal order of the previous year, but in some dioceses it had been the custom from about the beginning of Queen Elizabeth I's reign.

In almost any series of Transcripts there are annual gaps and also errors and omissions owing to insufficient care in copying. However, they sometimes contain entries and valuable details omitted from the original registers. This stems from the practice by some incumbents of making notes of all baptisms, etc., on loose sheets or in rough notebooks and copying them into the register book at the end of the year, at the same time as making another copy for the bishop. During the Commonwealth, very few Transcripts were made. From 1813 all Transcripts had to be sent to the Diocesan Registrar. Incumbents of peculiars sent their Transcripts to their ecclesiastical superior instead of to their bishop, but from 1813 they were obliged to conform to the general practice. Bishops' Transcripts should not be treated as a source alternative to registers, but as a check on them and as a substitute when the registers are missing or contain gaps or omissions. The spelling of personal names often differs from that in the parish register, which may be a help in identification.

The Federation of Family History Societies has published a useful guide to the location and indexes of the Transcripts, entitled *Bishops' Transcripts and Marriage Licences*, by J.S.W. Gibson.

Bishops' Visitations *see* **Ecclesiastical Visitations**

Black Death *see* **Plague**

Blodwite A fine paid as compensation for bloodshed. Also called Angwite.

Blood Descent *see* **Total Descent**

Board of Guardians *see* **Guardians of the Poor**

Bona Notabilia These words (Considerable Goods) appear as a note in probate records to indicate that the estate was of the value of £5 or over. Sometimes they also implied that it came under more than one probate jurisdiction, and so might need to be dealt with in an episcopal court. The phrase 'having etca' in an Act Book entry refers to *bona notabilia*.

Bond A binding engagement with a penalty for non-performance. A bond deed is in two parts, the *Obligation* and the *Condition*. Before 1733 the *Obligation*, which records the penalty, was written in Latin. The *Condition* describes what the bonded person has undertaken to do, or otherwise committed himself to (e.g. the truth of a statement), and was always in English.

Bookland Land held by rights granted by a written 'book' or title deed. It was transferable by the holder.

Bookplate *see* Domestic Clues

Boonmaster One of the many local names for the parochial official usually known as the Surveyor of the Highways.

Boonwork Major seasonal labour services on a medieval manor, such as ploughing, haymaking or reaping. Originally done as a favour to the lord, but later compulsory. The tasks had to be performed at certain times during the year, for example at the spring and autumn ploughing and at harvest. These were, of course, particularly inconvenient to the tenant.

Bordar A small-holder, usually on the outskirts of the village. It has been suggested that the word derives from the French *borde*, meaning 'a hut'. Bordar is a term occurring frequently in the *Domesday Book*. *See also* COTTAR.

Border Marriages The practice by English couples of contracting marriage at villages just over the Scottish border became common as a result of Lord Hardwicke's *Marriage Act*, which came into force in 1754. As that Act made marriages in England legal only if performed in a building licensed for that purpose, it became necessary for runaway couples to cross into Scotland, where marriage by mere consent, given before witnesses and followed by cohabitation, was legally valid. As even the presence of a priest was unnecessary, a number of men set themselves up in business in Scottish border villages solely to perform such marriages. Gretna Green has become the best known of these places, but the 'ceremony' was also available at Springfield, Halidon Hill, Coldstream, Sark Toll Bar, Lambton Toll Bar and Alison's Toll Bar. In 1825 one of the 'priests' turned Old Gretna Hall into a marriage centre and hotel, thus offering facilities for both ceremony and consummation.

The various 'priests' kept their registers in their own custody, for which reason many of them no longer exist. However, the following are still extant at the places shown.

Place of Marriage	Period	No. of Entries	Location
Alison's Toll Bar	1843-65	Upwards of 6000	Messrs Wright, Brown & Strong, Solicitors, 7 & 9 Bank St, Carlisle
Gretna Hall	1825-55	1134	Ewart Library, Catherine St, Dumfries.
Spring-field (by D.S. & W. Long)	1783-1895		Messrs Robert Mickle, Son & Hall, 12 New Bridge St, Newcastle on Tyne.
Spring-field (by R. Elliot)	1811-38	?	Mrs Pearson, 51 St Nicholas Street, Carlisle.
Spring-field (by J. Linton)	1825-40	600	J.L. Armstrong, Dumfries.
Spring-field (by J. Douglas)	1843-62	910	Gretna Council Registry Office, Glasgow Road, Gretna.
Lamber-ton Toll (by H. Collins)	1834-48	?	New Register House, Edinburgh EH1 3YT.
Cold-stream	1793-97	?	Revd M.D. Ryan, The Vicarage, Cornhill-on-Tweed, Northumberland.
Sark Toll Bar	1832-45	342	Ewart Library, Catherine St, Dumfries.

In 1856, Lord Brougham's *Marriage Act* made it illegal to be married, except by licence, where neither of the partners had been resident during the preceding twenty-one days. From 1878, marriages in Scotland had to be performed in buildings licensed for that purpose, and from 1 July, 1940, marriage by consent was abolished.

For further reading, see 'Irregular Border Marriages', by G.S. Chrichton, in *The Genealogist's Magazine*, Vol.20, No.8.

Borough English A custom of inheritance in certain ancient boroughs and manors in southern England, where the youngest son, and not the eldest, was considered the heir to his father's burgage of copyhold tenement. The custom died out with the ending of copyhold tenure.

Borough Records In the Middle Ages a large number of towns and villages were granted royal charters giving them powers of local government. Their records, therefore, are those of bodies carrying out the same administrative and judicial functions as those of the counties, plus a number dealing with specifically urban problems. Not all ancient borough archives have been carefully preserved, but some extend back into the Middle Ages. For the genealogist, the most important are the Minute Books and the Orders and Decrees of the Common Council, which may be supplemented by Depositions and Books of Examination covering preliminary enquiries. Also useful are the account books of the chamberlain, steward and treasurer, and the records of municipal properties and their tenants. For judicial purposes, several courts would be operating within a borough, such as a manorial Court Leet, the Mayor's Court, Court of Orphans, of Conscience and Requests, and of Pie-powder (*see* PIEPOUDRÉ, COURT OF), as well as those of Gaol Delivery and Sessions of the Peace. There are also separate records of the borough's manifold responsibilities, such as Watch and Ward, Street-lighting, Paving, Turnpike Trusts and Schools. Those of the merchant and craft gilds may also be there. The names of the burgesses were enrolled on their being appointed, as also are those of apprentices. Political information may be gleaned from any correspondence between the Common Council and their elected Members of Parliament. By the *Municipal Corporation Act*, 1835, the minutes and proceedings of borough councils had to be printed and available to the public on request.

A borough's archives may be found at the town hall, often without any full-time archivist in charge of them, but in many cases they have now been deposited at the county record offices or county library.

For further reading, see *Municipal Records*, by

F.J.C. Hearnshaw, and *The Mediaeval English Borough*, by J. Tait (1936).

Borsholder A local name, especially in Kent, for the parish constable.

Borthwick Institute of Historical Research Based at St Anthony's Hall, York, this department of the University of York has as its main purpose the furtherance of research into ecclesiastical history, particularly that of the Province of York. However, in addition to the diocesan archives, it houses parish registers, bishops' transcripts and other parochial records; also Poor Law records, the probate records of the Prerogative, Consistory, Chancery and Exchequer courts and a number of Peculiars, marriage licence allegations and bonds, manor court rolls and tithe awards. Searchers wishing to visit the Institute should make an appointment. A charge is made for searches by genealogists in 'parish register transcripts'. The Institute has published a very useful *Guide to Genealogical Sources in the Borthwick Institute of Historical Research*.

Bote The right, common to all tenants of a manor, to take timber from the waste for the repairing of hedges, fences or houses, or for firewood, tools, and so on. Often more specifically called haybote (for hedges), housebote, firebote, ploughbote.

Bottom A low-lying meadow, as distinct from an upland or dry one.

Bovate One eighth of a ploughland. Also called an Oxgang.

Bow The six-foot longbow came into its own during the Hundred Years' War, especially after its success at Crécy. As its use called for a high degree of skill, an Act of Edward IV compelled every Englishman between the ages of 16 and 60 to own a bow of his own height, and every township to set up its own butts on Artillery Grounds, where shooting practice was compulsory on Sundays and feast days. Games that might draw men away from archery, such as football, were designated 'unlawful sports'.

Though firearms came into use in the fifteenth century, the bow was still valued for its mobility, its speed of fire, which was six times that of the musket, and also for its cheapness. Every local militia was expected to include bowmen. The longbow played its last important role in battle in the reign of Elizabeth I, but archery was still officially encouraged for Londoners under Charles I. In early Victorian times it experienced a popular revival as a sport among the upper classes.

The cross-bow was used mainly by the French, who placed their faith in men-at-arms, the cavalry arm. Henry VIII forbade the use of the cross-bow in England, regarding it as an inferior weapon.

Bower Hold Land held in customary tenure.

Boyd's Marriage Index This index of marriages covers, in varying degrees of completeness, the marriage registers of sixteen counties from their beginnings until the year 1837. It was compiled by Percival Boyd mainly from printed register copies, and is available to searchers at the Society of Genealogists and the Guildhall Library, London. Each of the counties listed below is indexed in a separate series of volumes. Others are grouped together in two miscellaneous series, containing additional parishes of the named counties. Each volume, except the first and last, covers 25 years. The Society has published *A Key to Boyd's Marriage Index*.

The counties included, and the number of parishes covered, or partly covered, in each, excluding the miscellaneous series, are:

Cambridgeshire	169	Lancashire	101
Cornwall	202	London & Middlesex	160
Cumberland	34	Norfolk	146
Derbyshire	80	Northumberland	84
Devon	169	Shropshire	125
County Durham	72	Somerset	120
Essex	374	Suffolk	489
Gloucestershire	121	Yorkshire	174

See also MARRIAGE INDEX.

Breach The removal of dead hedges after the corn or hay harvest.

Bread, Assize of In 1266 the principle was established that the price of a loaf of bread should remain fixed, but that its weight might vary according to the price of wheat. The Assize was the inspection and weighing of loaves, one of the functions of an official of the manorial Court Leet.

Break *or* **Breck** A temporary enclosure, especially from forest land. It often became permanent. A type of ASSART.

Bride Ale A function organised in the parish by the churchwardens, to raise money to help a young married couple to set up house.

Bridewell At first a workplace for vagabonds and beggars, but, by the 1750s, used as a county gaol or House of Correction.

Bridgewardens' Accounts During Tudor and Stuart times the transportation of goods by road was increasing, and could not be allowed to be held up by broken bridges for which no one would assume responsibility. In 1531 the *Statute of Bridges* authorised Justices of the Peace 'to enquire, hear, determine in the King's General Sessions of the Peace all manner of annoyances of bridges broken in the highways'. The responsibility was placed upon the city, borough or parish in which the bridge was situated. Sometimes a gild undertook the upkeep of a bridge as a pious duty. Many people also left legacies for this purpose.

Boroughs appointed bridgewardens to collect rents from lands donated for the upkeep of the bridge. The earliest bridgewardens' accounts date from 1526. Such accounts usually mention by name men paid to work on the bridge, and people from whom materials were brought. The records will now usually be at the county, city or borough record office.

The Bridge House records of Old London Bridge are at the Corporation of London Record Office at the Guildhall. In addition to the usual details of maintenance, they contain the names of the leaseholders of the houses and shops on the bridge, which in most cases were not those of the actual inhabitants.

Brief A royal mandate for a collection towards some deserving object. It was addressed to the parish incumbent and churchwardens, and was read from the pulpit. At the end of the service the clerk took the collection at the church door. The funds were handed to an authorised travelling collector, and the brief was returned with an endorsement of the amount raised. The sum was also entered in the parish records, often in the parish registers. The mandate was sometimes called a Church Brief, or King's Brief.

Bristol and Avon Family History Society *see* **Gloucestershire** *and* **Somerset**

British Library The Reference Division's Department of Printed Books is situated in the British Museum in Great Russell Street, London WC1, and was formerly known as the British Museum Library. A reader's ticket is required for access to the Reading Room, and this has to be applied for personally at the Library.

Under the *Copyright Acts*, the British Library is given a copy of every book printed in the country, so almost any book required by the genealogist will be found here, and some of those most commonly consulted are immediately available on the open shelves — including the *Annual Register, Calendars of State Papers, Gentleman's Magazine, Historical MSS Commission Reports, Notes and Queries*, the *Rolls* series, *The Times* index, and the *Victoria County Histories*.

London newspapers before 1801 are also here, but later ones are at the British Library's Newspaper Library, for which *see* NEWSPAPERS. A guide to the use of the catalogues is available.

The Reading Room is open from 9 a.m. and closes at 9 p.m. on Tuesday, Wednesday and Thursday, and at 5 p.m. on Monday, Friday and Saturday. There is also a Map Library in the King Edward Building on the north side of the British Museum, open from 9.30 a.m. to 4.30 p.m., Monday to Saturday. Also in the British Museum, the British Library has a Department of Manuscripts containing deposited collections from numerous sources. These are all well catalogued. Printed indexes to the Library's manuscripts can be found in some of the larger public libraries.

British Newspaper Library *see* **News-papers**

British Record Society Formerly the Index Society (founded 1888) it publishes the Index Library, consisting of indexes of important groups of historical records, nearly all of assistance to genealogists. The records include wills, marriage licences, Chancery proceedings and Inquisitions Post Mortem. There is particular emphasis on indexes to probate records pre-1750, though many continue until later.

British Records Association Founded in 1932, the Association's main purpose is to advise and to give assistance on all matters which relate to the preservation of records. To the Association's influence has been largely due the establishment of the National Register of Archives, the setting up of county record offices and the professional status of archivists.

Brother A term often used to mean a brother-in-law. Sometimes, to make clear which is meant, a real brother is referred to as 'my own brother'.

Brownists An alternative name for the Separatists, the earliest sect of Puritan dissenters. They were led by Robert Browne (*c.*1550-*c.*1633), a schoolmaster. His following, suppressed in England, fled to Middelburg and Amsterdam and in time gave rise to the Independent (Congregationalist) and Baptist denominations.

Buckinghamshire The Buckinghamshire Family History Society holds meetings at Aylesbury and publishes a quarterly journal, *Origins*. Enquiries should be sent c/o the Federation of Family History Societies, 31 Seven Star Road, Solihull, West Midlands B91 2BZ, marked 'Please forward' and enclosing a stamped self-addressed envelope.

Record Repositories Buckinghamshire Record Office, County Hall, Aylesbury HP20 1UA (tel: 0296.5000); Buckinghamshire Archaeological Society, The Museum, Church Street, Aylesbury; County Reference Library, Aylesbury.

Parish Registers and Indexes (see comment under COUNTY) More than three-quarters of the 206 ancient parishes have deposited their registers at the county record office (CRO). Twenty volumes of registers have been published by the Buckinghamshire Parish Register Society. The Society of Genealogists lists 104 in its catalogue. The INTERNATIONAL GENEALOGICAL INDEX (IGI) covers, at least in part, about a quarter of the parishes. The family history society (FHS) has the IGI for the county, and the CRO has those for the county and for Oxford. Pallot's Marriage Index covers 72 parishes for the years 1790-1812, and the FHS has a marriage index in process of compilation. Bishops' Transcripts are held at the CRO, as are marriage licence records. An index of marriage licence bonds for 1617-1726 is held by the Society of Genealogists.

Wills before 1858 proved in the following courts are located as follows.

At the county record office:
Archdeaconry of Buckingham.
Peculiar (Pec.) Court of the Dean and Chapter of Lincoln.
Pec. Court of the Archbishop of Canterbury.
Pec. Court of the Prebend of Aylesbury.
Pec. Court of the Prebend of Buckingham.
Pec. Court of Monks Risborough.
Pec. Court of Thame.

At 'Penzance', Eton College, Berkshire:
Pec. Court of the Provost of Eton.

At Hertfordshire CRO, Hertford:
Archdeaconry Court of St Albans.

At the Bodleian Library, Oxford:
Pec. Court of Bierton.

As the county lay in the Diocese of Lincoln and in the Province of Canterbury, wills could be proved in the Consistory Court of Lincoln and in the Prerogative Court of Canterbury. The Society of Genealogists has an index and calendar of the Archdeaconry Court of Buckingham, 1483-1858, on microfilm.

Non-parochial Registers The registers of 33 chapels are at the Public Record Office (PRO), Chancery Lane, London. The IGI covers a very few.

Census Returns 1851-71, are at the County Reference Library. High Wycombe Library holds the 1841 Returns for Desborough Hundred.

Memorial Inscriptions A few transcripts are in the library of the Society of Genealogists. The family history society (FHS) has transcription in hand.

Heralds' Visitation Pedigrees have been printed for 1566 and 1634.

Protestation Oath Rolls 1641-2, are being transcribed by the FHS.

Buckinghamshire Record Society has been publishing historical records of the county since 1937, including the muster rolls for 1522 and *Buckinghamshire Wills, 1483-1519*.

Burebrige A breach of surety.

Burgage A small-holding in a town, rented by a free burgess under burgess tenure.

Burgess A person holding some of the privileges conferred by a municipal corporation. Also a person elected to Parliament to represent a borough.

Burgess Tenure A form of tenure peculiar to boroughs. The tenant had the free disposal of his land or property in accordance with the custom of the borough, and paid only a nominal rent (called a land-gable) which made him quit of all other services to his feudal superior. If the lord was the king, the tenant held in chief.

Burial Register *see* **Parish Register**

Buried, Partly An expression meaning that the heart of the deceased was buried separately from the rest of the body, usually in conformance with a will or dying wish.

Burleyman Another name for the manorial beadle or constable, probably a corruption of 'bylawman'.

Butchers Men of this trade had to be licensed annually by the Quarter Sessions. The licence records are therefore at county record offices.

Butt (i) A land (or selion) in a common field abutting more or less at right angles upon another selion.
(ii) A land which, because of the irregular shape of the field, falls short of the full length.
(iii) A mark to be shot at.

Buttery A room or area where beer was brewed.

Button, Military *see* **Domestic Clues**

By-and-by Immediately.

Byblow An illegitimate child.

C

Calendar (i) A catalogue of documents that gives the essential data contained in them, and the names of all persons and places mentioned.

(ii) The system fixing the civil year's beginning, length and sub-divisions. In the Middle Ages, dates were usually indicated (for years) by the REGNAL YEAR of the reigning monarch, and (for days) by the number of days before or after the nearest church festival or fast. When *Anno Domini* years were shown, there was no regularity as to the day on which the year was considered to have begun. To the writer of the document, New Year's Day might have been 1 January, 25 March or 25 December. At the Reformation it was laid down in the *Book of Common Prayer* that 'the Supputation [reckoning] of the year of our Lord in the Church of England beginneth the Five and twentieth day of March, the same day supposed to be the first day upon which the world was created and the day when Christ was conceived in the womb of the Virgin Mary'. In the 1662 version, that date for New Year's Day was retained but the reason for it was omitted.

In 1752 two changes were made in the English calendar. The first was from the Julian to the more accurate Gregorian system that had been introduced in Catholic countries by Pope Gregory XIII in March 1582. A difference of eleven days had accumulated between the systems, so the change necessitated England's 'losing' that number of days. To bring that about, the day following 2 September 1752 was renumbered 14.

The second change, of far greater importance to genealogists, was that the commencement of that year was brought forward from 25 March to the preceding 1 January. This changed January, February and most of March from being the last months of the Old Year to the first of the New. As the new system had already been put into use by some people in advance of its official introduction, care has to be taken when transcribing documents of the pre-1752 period dated between 1 January and 24 March. The correct transcription procedure is to use both Old and New Reckonings; for example, by copying '5th February 1626' as '5th February 1626/7'.

The months of September, October, November and December, which used to be the seventh to tenth months of the year, are sometimes found abbreviated to the '7ber, 8ber, 9ber and 10ber' respectively, and must not be mistaken for the present seventh to tenth months, July to October.

The festivals and fasts often used to date events are too numerous to list here *in toto*, but the following are the fixed ones most often found, plus some of the dates observed as 'solemn days'. In most parishes the day of the saint to whom the local church is dedicated may also be found used for dating purposes.

January	1 Circumcision
	6 Epiphany. Twelfth Day
	13 St Hilary the Bishop
	30 Death of Charles, King and Martyr (solemn day)
February	2 Purification of the Blessed Virgin Mary (Candlemas)
	24 St Matthias*
March	25 Annunciation of the Blessed Virgin Mary* (Lady Day, a quarter day)
April	23 St George
May	1 St Philip and St James the Less (May Day)
	29 Restoration of Charles II (solemn day)
June	24 Nativity of St John the Baptist* (Midsummer Day, a quarter day)
	29 St Peter the Apostle*
July	25 St James the Apostle*
August	24 St Bartholomew the Apostle*
September	21 St Matthew the Apostle*
	29 St Michael and All Angels (Michaelmas, a quarter day)

Year			Year			Year			Year			Year			Year			Year		
1500	A	19	1556	A	5	1612	A	12	1668	M	22	1724	A	5	1778	A	19	1834	M	30
1	A	11	7	A	18	3	A	4	9	A	11	5	M	28	9	A	4	5	A	19
2	M	27	8	A	10	4	A	24	1670	A	3	6	A	10	1780	M	26	6	A	3
3	A	16	9	M	26	5	A	9	1	A	23	7	A	2	1	A	15	7	M	26
4	A	7	1560	A	14	6	M	31	2	A	7	8	A	21	2	M	31	8	A	15
5	M	23	1	A	6	7	A	20	3	M	30	9	A	6	3	A	20	9	M	31
6	A	12	2	M	29	8	A	5	4	A	19	1730	M	29	4	A	11	1840	A	19
7	A	4	3	A	11	9	M	28	5	A	4	1	A	18	5	M	27	1	A	11
8	A	23	4	A	2	1620	A	16	6	M	26	2	A	9	6	A	16	2	M	27
9	A	8	5	A	22	1	A	1	7	A	15	3	M	25	7	A	8	3	A	16
1510	M	31	6	A	14	2	A	21	8	M	31	4	A	14	8	M	23	4	A	7
1	A	20	7	M	30	3	A	13	9	A	20	5	A	6	9	A	12	5	M	23
2	A	11	8	A	18	4	M	28	1680	A	11	6	A	25	1790	A	4	6	A	12
3	M	27	9	A	10	5	A	17	1	A	3	7	A	10	1	A	24	7	A	4
4	A	16	1570	M	26	6	A	9	2	A	16	8	A	2	2	A	8	8	A	23
5	A	8	1	A	15	7	M	25	3	A	8	9	A	22	3	M	31	9	A	8
6	M	23	2	A	6	8	A	13	4	M	30	1740	A	6	4	A	20	1850	M	31
7	A	12	3	M	22	9	A	5	5	A	19	1	M	29	5	A	5	1	A	20
8	A	4	4	A	11	1630	M	28	6	A	4	2	A	18	6	M	27	2	A	11
9	A	24	5	A	3	1	A	10	7	M	27	3	A	3	7	A	16	3	M	27
1520	A	8	6	A	22	2	A	1	8	A	15	4	M	25	8	A	8	4	A	16
1	M	31	7	A	7	3	A	21	9	M	31	5	A	14	9	M	24	5	A	8
2	A	20	8	M	30	4	A	6	1690	A	20	6	M	30	1800	A	13	6	M	23
3	A	5	9	A	19	5	M	29	1	A	12	7	A	19	1	A	5	7	A	12
4	M	27	1580	A	3	6	A	17	2	M	27	8	A	10	2	A	18	8	A	4
5	A	16	1	M	26	7	A	9	3	A	16	9	M	26	3	A	10	9	A	24
6	A	1	2	A	15	8	M	25	4	A	8	1750	A	15	4	A	1	1860	A	8
7	A	21	3	M	31	9	A	14	5	M	24	1	A	2	5	A	14	1	M	31
8	A	12	4	A	19	1640	A	5	6	A	12				6	A	6	2	A	20
9	M	28	5	A	11	1	A	25	7	A	4	New style			7	M	29	3	A	5
1530	A	17	6	A	3	2	A	10	8	A	24				8	A	17	4	M	27
1	A	9	7	A	16	3	A	2	9	A	9	2	A	2	9	A	2	5	A	16
2	M	31	8	A	7	4	A	21	1700	M	31	3	A	22	1810	A	22	6	A	1
3	A	13	9	M	30	5	A	6	1	A	20	4	A	14	1	A	14	7	A	21
4	A	5	1590	A	19	6	M	29	2	A	5	5	M	30	2	M	29	8	A	12
5	M	28	1	A	4	7	A	18	3	M	28	6	A	18	3	A	18	9	M	28
6	A	16	2	M	26	8	A	2	4	A	16	7	A	10	4	A	10	1870	A	17
7	A	1	3	A	15	9	M	25	5	A	8	8	M	26	5	M	26	1	A	9
8	A	21	4	M	31	1650	A	14	6	M	24	9	A	15	6	A	14	2	M	31
9	A	6	5	A	20	1	M	30	7	A	13	1760	A	6	7	A	6	3	A	13
1540	M	28	6	A	11	2	A	18	8	A	4	1	M	22	8	M	22	4	A	5
1	A	17	7	M	27	3	A	10	9	A	24	2	A	11	9	A	11	5	M	28
2	A	9	8	A	16	4	M	26	1710	A	9	3	A	3	1820	A	2	6	A	16
3	M	25	9	A	8	5	A	15	1	A	1	4	A	22	1	A	22	7	A	1
4	A	13	1600	M	23	6	A	6	2	A	20	5	A	7	2	A	7	8	A	21
5	A	5	1	A	12	7	M	29	3	A	5	6	M	30	3	M	30	9	A	13
6	A	25	2	A	4	8	A	11	4	M	28	7	A	19	4	A	18	1880	M	28
7	A	10	3	A	24	9	A	3	5	A	17	8	A	3	5	A	3	1	A	17
8	A	1	4	A	8	1660	A	22	6	A	1	9	M	26	6	M	26	2	A	9
9	A	21	5	M	31	1	A	14	7	A	21	1770	A	15	7	A	15	3	M	25
1550	A	6	6	A	20	2	M	30	8	A	13	1	M	31	8	A	6	4	A	13
1	M	29	7	A	5	3	A	19	9	M	29	2	A	19	9	A	19	5	A	5
2	A	17	8	M	27	4	A	10	1720	A	17	3	A	11	1830	A	11	6	A	25
3	A	2	9	A	16	5	M	26	1	A	9	4	A	3	1	A	3	7	A	10
4	M	25	1610	A	8	6	A	15	2	M	25	5	A	16	2	A	22	8	A	1
5	A	14	1	M	24	7	A	7	3	A	14	6	A	7	3	A	7	9	A	21

58

October	25 St Crispin, anniversary of Agincourt
	28 St Simon and St Jude the Apostles*
November	1 All Saints (Allhallows)*
	2 All Souls
	5 Gunpowder Plot (solemn day)
	30 St Andrew the Apostle*
December	6 St Nicholas
	21 St Thomas the Apostle*
	25 Christmas Day* (a quarter day)
	26 St Stephen
	28 Holy Innocents

* The eve of the festivals marked thus was kept as a fast, but when the festival fell on a Monday, the fast was kept on the previous Saturday.

The most important movable feast is Easter, for which see the table opposite. The dates of the other movable feasts are governed by that of Easter, as follows:

Septuagesima ⎫
Sexagesima ⎪ Sunday is — nine weeks ⎫
Quinquagesima ⎬ eight before
Quadragesima ⎭ seven Easter
 six Day

Ash Wednesday is six and a half weeks before Easter Day.

Rogation Sunday ⎫
Ascension Day ⎪ is — five weeks after
Whitsunday ⎬ forty days Easter
Trinity Sunday ⎭ seven weeks Day
 eight weeks

Advent Sunday is the nearest to the feast of St Andrew the Apostle, whether before or after.

For further reading, see *A Handbook of British Chronology* by Sir Maurice Powicke and D. & E.B. Fryde, and *A Handbook of Dates* by C.R. Chaney. *See also* PERPETUAL CALENDAR.

Cambridgeshire Since the boundary changes of 1974, Cambridgeshire has included the Isle of Ely, the ancient county of Huntingdon and the Soke of Peterborough. For information about the latter two, *see* HUNTINGDONSHIRE. The Cambridgeshire Family History Society and the Peterborough and District Family History Society hold regular meetings and issue journals. Enquiries should be sent c/o the Federation of Family History Societies, 31 Seven

Star Road, Solihull, West Midlands B91 2BZ, marked 'Please forward' and enclosing a stamped self-addressed envelope.

Record Repositories (*see also* HUNTINGDONSHIRE) Cambridgeshire and Isle of Ely County Record Office, Shire Hall, Castle Hill, Cambridge (tel: 0223.58811); University of Cambridge Archives, The Old Schools, Cambridge; The Diocesan Registry, Ely.

Parish Registers and Indexes (*see* comment under COUNTY) Most registers are at the county record office (CRO) The Society of Genealogists has copies of almost all of them. Boyd's Marriage Index covers nearly all, and the CRO also has a marriage index. The family history society (FHS) and the Cambridge Reference Library each has a copy of the INTERNATIONAL GENEALOGICAL INDEX (IGI). Pallot's Marriage Index covers 44 parishes, 1790-1837. The Bishops' Transcripts are at the Cambridge University Library.

Marriage Licence Records Those for the Diocese of Ely are at the Cambridge University Library. Those for the Archdeaconry of Sudbury are at the Suffolk Record Office, Bury St Edmunds. Those for the Archdeaconry of Norwich are at the Norfolk Record Office.

Wills before 1858 proved in the following courts are located as follows.

At the University of Cambridge Archives:
 Archdeaconry of Ely.
 Court of the Chancellor of the University, for members of the University.
 Peculiar (Pec.) Court of Thorney.
 Pec. Court of King's College.

At the Suffolk Record Office, Bury St Edmunds:
 Archdeaconry of Sudbury.
 Pec. Court of the Bishop of Rochester, for Isleham.

The Archdeaconry was in the Diocese of Ely, Diocese of Norwich, so wills could also be proved in the Consistory Court of Ely, the Commissary Court of Norwich and the Prerogative Court of Canterbury.

Non-parochial Registers The registers of 35 chapels are at the Public Record Office (PRO), Chancery Lane, London. The IGI covers a large number of chapels.

Census Returns for Cambridgeshire and the Isle of Ely are at the PRO, Portugal Street, London, with copies at the Cambridgeshire Record Office, Wisbech Library and Bedfordshire Record Office.

Memorial Inscriptions Transcripts of over 150 churches and burial grounds are in the Society of Genealogists' library. The FHS and the Women's Institutes of the county have widened the coverage.

Heralds' Visitation Pedigrees have been published for 1575 and 1619.

The Cambridge Camden Society publishes its Transactions.

Camden Society *see* **Royal Historical Society**

Campipars Rent of land in the form of a proportion of the crop.

Candlemas The 2nd of February; the Feast of the Purification of the Blessed Virgin Mary. The stock of candles required for use in the church during the ensuing year was consecrated on this day.

Canon (i) A law of the Church. All clerics were subject to Canon Law.

(ii) A cleric in a group observing a definite rule of life, for example an Augustinian Canon.

(iii) A cleric possessing a prebend for his support in a cathedral or collegiate church.

Cantref The name given to some fiefs on the Wales-Cheshire border. Though they came under the jurisdiction of the justices of Chester, they were also partly subject to Welsh customary law.

Cap Money To promote the wool trade, a statute of 1571, repealed in 1597-8, laid down that all persons of common degree should wear a cap of English wool on Sundays and holy days. Cap money was the fine paid for non-observance — three shillings and four pence.

Capias A warrant for an arrest.

Capite, Tenant in One holding his land by feudal tenure direct from the king. This Latin term is often used in English documents instead of Tenant-in-Chief.

Caption, Letters of A letter from an ecclesiastical dignitary invoking the aid of the secular government against an obdurate excommunicate.

Cards, Genealogical Record Printed cards, 6 x 4 inches, with spaces allotted for card number, name of person, dates and places of birth, baptism, marriage, death, burial and probate of will; also names of father, mother, spouses and children. A useful aid for rapid reference and the reconstitution of families. Available from the Society of Genealogists.

Cartulary A register of the estates and liberties granted to owners (e.g. monasteries and manorial estates) by charter, together with the charters themselves. The term is also used to include additional classes of record such as rentals. Surviving cartularies are listed in *Medieval Cartularies of Great Britain*, by G.R.C. Davies. Those held at the Public Record Office, Chancery Lane, London, can be found under references E.36, 132, 135, 164 and 315, LR.2 and DL.42.

Carucate In the Danelaw, an area of ploughland assessed for taxation. As much land as an eight-ox plough team could maintain in cultivation, which varied between 160 and 180 acres, according to the soil and lie of the land. About the same area as a Hide. By 1086 it had come to mean a unit of taxation.
See also PLOUGH TEAM.

Cathedral The chief church of a diocese, where the bishop's throne (*cathedra*) was located. Often referred to as the 'mother church'.

Catholic Apostolic Church *see* **Irvingites**

Catholic Record Society *see* **Roman Catholics**

Cemeteries Burial grounds not appertaining to any church or chapel were first made available as private ventures, but in 1852 for London and in 1853 for the rest of the country, an Act of Parliament enabled local authorities to purchase and use land for that purpose, and many cemeteries came into existence shortly afterwards. The superintendent normally has a small office near the entrance to the ground, where burial registers are housed and grave-lots listed as a guide for visitors looking for a particular grave. The registers of cemeteries in existence before 1837 are now at the Public Record Office, Chancery Lane, London. One of the earliest non-parochial cemeteries was that of Bunhill Fields, London. It was open to the deceased of all denominations, but in fact was mostly used for nonconformist burials.

For further reading, see *Greater London Cemeteries and Crematoria and their Registers.*

Census Returns A census of the population of England and Wales, the Isle of Man and the Channel Isles, was first taken in 1801. This was followed by others every ten years, except for 1941 when the country was at war. The original purpose of the census was to provide population statistics, so the existing records (with a handful of exceptions) do not show the names of individual people until the Returns of 1841. From then onward the records show the names of each person at the address at which he or she spent the night of the census date.

The Returns become available for public inspection as soon as they are one hundred years old. They are an invaluable aid to the genealogist in enabling him to discover where his ancestors were born in the early nineteenth and late eighteenth centuries, and in revealing the existence of unsuspected members of the family.

The Census of 1841 was taken on Sunday, 6/7 June, 1841, not only of every person in each house that night, but also of night workers who would return to the house in the morning. The Returns were compiled in parishes, and the families are shown in the order in which their houses were visited by the enumerators. The Registration Districts were the same as for the General Register. Each was sub-divided into Enumeration Districts of not less than 25, and not more than 200, inhabited houses. The forms were distributed to householders and collected and checked by the enumerators. At hotels, hospitals, ships and other institutions, the forms were filled in by the official in charge. The

enumerators were volunteer schoolmasters, clergymen, businessmen and other persons of some education. The Returns were then copied, in pencil, into printed books of blank forms. These are the Enumeration Schedules, microfilms of which are now available for searching. Each one is prefaced with a description of the boundaries of the enumerator's district.

The forms show the street in which each house stood, and sometimes the number of the house or its name. Each household also has an enumeration number which should not be mistaken for its street number. The questions asked on the forms are: names of persons in the house, their ages, occupations, whether born in the same county, and whether born in Scotland, Ireland or Foreign Parts.

Names Only the surname and first Christian name are given.

Ages Exact ages in years are given for children up to the age of 14 inclusive. For persons of 15 and older, ages are given in five-year groups indicated by the youngest year of the group; that is, ages from 15 to 19 inclusive are shown as 15, from 20 to 24 as 20, and so on. People, however, did not always state their ages correctly.

Occupations Often abbreviated: for example, Ag.Lab. for agricultural labourer; F.S. for female servant; F.W.K., framework knitter; Ind., of independent means; J, journeyman; M.S., male servant; N.K., not known.

Born (County) This question is only answered by 'Yes' or 'No', abbreviated to 'Y' or 'N', depending on whether or not the person was born in the county in which he was residing on census night.

Born (Country) This is answered by 'S', 'I' or 'F', for Scotland, Ireland or Foreign Parts.

No relationships between members of the household are given, but the head of the house usually heads the list. Children may be nephews and nieces. A single stroke in the margin marks the end of a family; a double stroke, the end of a household.

The Returns are at the Public Record Office (PRO) under the Class HO.107. These are at present housed at the Land Registry building in Portugal Street, just south of Lincoln's Inn Fields in the City of London. Place indexes are available. Large towns have separate index

PLACE	Uninhabited or Building	Inhabited	NAMES of each Person who abode therein the preceding Night	Males	Females	PROFESSION, TRADE, EMPLOYMENT, or of INDEPENDENT MEANS	Whether Born in same County	Whether Born in Scotland, Ireland, or Foreign Parts
Mill Gate	16	1	John Hammond	50		Ind	yes	
			Isabella Varley		65	F.S	y	
do		1	John Grime	40		Bankers Cl	y	
			Mary Ellwood		50	F.S	y	
do		1	Matthew Spence	45		Shoemaker	y	
			Mary do		50		y	
			John do	15			y	
			William do	13			y	
			Alice do		7		y	
			William Lye	20		Shoem Ap	y	
			William Graham	15		Shoe m Ap	y	
			James Lumbley	15		Shoem Ap	y	
			William Lumbley	25		Shoem Jour	y	
			John Bolton	25		do	y	
			Jane Milner		15	F.S	y	
			John Hepple	55		Ag Lab	y	
do		1	James Metcalfe	40		Plumber and Glazier	y	
			Caroline do		40		y	
			Mary do		17		y	
			Maria do		13		y	
			George do	8			y	
			Henry do	6			y	
			Margaret do		2		y	
do		1	Peter Dobson	33		Plumber & Glazier	y	
			Thomas Sanderson	25			y	

A page from the Census Record of 1841. *Crown copyright: H0.107/1254 S*

RIGHT A page from the 1851 Census Return for Chertsey, Surrey. Most of the information in the 'Where Born' column shows the genealogist what parish register to search next, but the first, third and fourth entries are annoyingly vague in this respect. *Crown copyright: HO.107*

Place	Name and Surname of each Person who abode in the house, on the Night of the 30th March, 1851	Relation to Head of Family	Condition	Age of Males	Age of Females	Rank, Profession, or Occupation	Where Born	Whether Blind, or Deaf-and-Dumb
	William Childs	Head	Mar.	62		Labourer Burnet	Berkshire	
	Robert Do	Wife	Mar.		10		Surrey Chertsey	
	Eliza Do	Dau.					London	
	William Middleton	Lodger	Mar.	33		E.I. Company Invalid Service Yorkshire		
	Harriet Do	Wife	Mar.		24	Backeeper	do Chertsey	
	Emma Ann Do	Dau.			4	do	do Chertsey	
	Eliza Maria Do	Dau.			18	do	Berkshire	
	Arthur Taylor	Lodger		18			Bridge Piccadilly	
	Walter Do				11		Essex Barnet	
	Eliza Elizabeth Do	Dau.			3		Surrey Chertsey	
	John Burt	Lodger	Wid.	27		Labourer	do	
	Thomas Shore	Son		64		Gen Servant Berks. Wallingford		
	James Do	Son		13		Scholar	Surrey Chertsey	
	George Do	Son		5		Scholar	do	
	James Do	Grandson					do	
	Mary Do	Dau.					do	
	George Field	Wife	Mar.	25		Gardener	Yorks Cottage	
	Rebecca Do	Wife	Mar.		49		Berks Twickenham	
	Emily Do	Dau.				Scholar	Middlesex Westminster	

Total of Persons... 9 11

volumes showing each street separately. The number shown after the bundle number is that of the book in the bundle.

The Census of 1851 was taken on 31 March for the night of 30/31 March, using methods similar to those of 1841. However, the questions asked make this census considerably more useful than the earlier one.

Names Christian and surname. Sometimes a second Christian name or an initial is given.

Relation to head of family Essential genealogical information, but beware of assuming that a person's relationship to the head of family is the same as the relationship to his wife. The man may have married twice, in which case his wife may be stepmother to some or all of his children.

Condition Married, Unmarried, Widower or Widow.

Age Shown in two columns, one for males, the other for females. Verbal Returns were sometimes misheard. Again, ages were not always correctly stated.

Occupation As for 1841. Children being educated were shown as 'scholars'.

Where born Parish and county if in England or Wales, but the country only if in Scotland or Ireland. 'Foreign Parts' if abroad. Verbal Returns by illiterates were sometimes misheard.

Whether blind, deaf-and-dumb, imbecile or lunatic.

Deposited, as for the 1841 census, at the PRO. *Enumeration Schedules* are mostly written in ink on blue paper. They are in bundles, books and divisions, with the parishes arranged in the same sub-districts and districts as the General Register. Each house has an enumeration number and is shown in the order in which it was visited by the enumerator. The reference is HO.107. The page numbers of the books are apt to be confusing, there being three for each, one in pencil, one in print and one mechanically stamped. To find the right microfilm, consult the *Alphabetical List of Parishes and Places*, which is available in the Search Room.

This census also included Returns from all existing places of worship, with dates at which dissenting congregations were founded and their size.

The Census of 1861 was taken on 8 April for the night of 7/8 April. The information given on the Returns is the same as at the census of 1851. The call number is RG.9. The papers were badly kept by the Registrar General before being made available for study at the Public Record Office in 1962, and many are missing.

The Censuses of 1871 and 1881 were taken for the night of 2/3 April and 3/4 April respectively. The call numbers are RG.10 and 11. The information is as for 1851 and 1861.

In order to find the entry for a family living in a town it is necessary to find out in advance their exact address. This can be done either from a local directory or an electoral register, or by obtaining a birth or death certificate of a member of the household who was born or who died at a date as close as possible to a census night.

Censuses after 1881 are still in the custody of the Registrar General. Returns are not open to the public sooner, because people still alive may be included in them, and the original information was obtained under a pledge of secrecy. However, an extract covering members of a family in one household may be obtained on application to the Registrar General, by, or with the written authorisation of, a descendant of the family concerned. The application must mention the exact address in the census, because no searches can be undertaken. An undertaking must be given that the information will not be used for the purposes of litigation. A fee is charged. Apply to The Registrar General, General Register Office, St Catherine's House, Kingsway, London WC2.

The copies of the Returns, shown under county headings in this Dictionary as being held elsewhere than at the Public Record Office, may not be for every available census.

The Federation of Family History Societies has published two useful booklets, *Census Indexes and Indexing* and *Marriage, Census and other Indexes for Family Historians*.

Cess A parochial rate, tax or assessment.

Champion Open-field land as distinguished from land held in SEVERALTY.

Chanceling An illegitimate child.

Chancery, Court of The court and the office of Chancellor date from the reign of Edward the Confessor. The Chancellor was then a sort of Secretary of State for all departments. The records of his Chancery date from 1199, when important letters from the king began to be enrolled in Charter Rolls, Patent Rolls and Close Rolls. The very earliest are in Norman-French, but later ones in English. Charter Rolls contain grants and confirmations more formal than those in Letters Patent. Fine Rolls record moneys received by the king for grants and privileges accorded, and the Parliament Rolls record transactions in Parliament down to 1886.

Chancery as a court of law dates from about 1348. It was a court of equity based on Roman Law to deal with cases for which the Common Law made no provision, and later with cases remediable under Common Law but in which the plaintiff would have found himself under a legal disadvantage. Any propertied family is almost sure to have been concerned at some time in a chancery suit. It is the court with more surviving records than any other. The Bills and Answers down to the year 1875 amount to 19,000 bundles, each containing on average 70 cases, making more than a million in all. Evidence was received in writing, and the Depositions make up a further 4000 bundles. These records, exceptionally rich in information for the family historian, are housed at the Public Record Office, Chancery Lane, London, and are of two main kinds:

(a) *Proceedings*

(1) Bill of Complaint by the plaintiff (or of Information by the Crown) addressed to the Lord Chancellor or the Lord Keeper of the Great Seal.

(2) Writ of Subpoena, ordering the defendant to appear. Few of these survive.

(3) Answer by the defendant, or a Plea to reject the Bill on legal grounds.

(4) Replication, or Exception, by the plaintiff.

(5) Rejoinder by the defendant.

(6) Rebuttal by the plaintiff (sometimes).

(7) Surebuttal by the defendant (sometimes).

(8) Interrogatories — lists of questions drawn up by counsels for both parties — to be put to witnesses.

(9) Depositions by witnesses, whose names, abodes, ages and occupations are shown.

(10) A Bill of Revival became necessary if one of the parties died before the case was heard.

(b) *Registers*

(1) Orders and Decrees — injunctions (for example, to appear in court or to produce papers or witnesses) and decisions of the court.

(2) Awards and Agreements, which were decisions by arbitration.

Decrees

In addition to the Register note of the court's decision, a document was issued recording it in full. Samples of those decrees that have survived at the PRO have been indexed.

The following are the indexes and calendars to the above-mentioned records:

PRO 'Lists & Indexes'	Title	Period	Call No.
Vol. 12	Early Chan. Proc. Vol. 1	Rich.II-1466	C/1
16	2	1467-85 & undated	C/1
20	3	1485-1500	C/1
29	4	1500-15	C/1
38	5	1515-29	C/1
48	6	1529-38	C/1
50	7	1533-38	C/1
51	8	1538-44	C/1
54	9	1544-53	C/1
55	10	1553-58	C/1
7	Chan.Proc. (Series 2) 1	1558-79	C/3
24	2	1579-1621	C/3
30	3	1621-60	C/3
39	Chan.Proc. (Bridges Div.) A-C	1613-1714	C/5
42	D-H		C/5
44	I-Q		C/5
45	R-Z		C/5
47	Chan.Proc. (Series 1) A-K	James I	C/2
MS Calendar	L-Z		C/2
Brit. Rec. Soc. Index Library Vols 2,5,6, & 14		Charles I	C/2

PRO 'Lists & Indexes'	Title	Period	Call No.
MS Calendar	*Chan.Proc. Before 1714*	1649-1713	
	Bridges Div.		C/5
	Collins Div.		C/6
	Hamilton Div.		C/7
	Mitford Div.		C/8
Brit. Rec. Soc. Index Library	Reynardson Div.		C/9
MS Calendar	Whittingdon Div.		C/10
	All Divs	1714-58	C/11
	All Divs	1758-1900	C/12
	All Divs	1800-42	C/13

Chancery Depositions

MS Calendar	Country Depositions	Eliz-Chas I	C/21
	Country Deps	Chas I-1713	C/22
	Deps Never used (no trial)		C/23
	Town (London) Deps	Henry VIII-1853	C/24
	Country Deps	1714-	In Cha. Pro.

Chancery Answers   No list   C/4

Chancery Decrees & Orders

Contemporary Annual Lists under Plaintiffs	38 Henry VIII-1875	C/33
	1876-today	J/15

Chancery Decree Rolls

Typescript Index   C/78

Chancery Interrogatories
Town   C/25

Pedigrees in Masters Records

Mostly 19th century	Earliest person d.1699	J/46, 63, 64, 66, 67

Of the above, only the *Lists & Indexes* edition of the Bridges Division 1613-1713, and the *Decree Rolls*, provide a full index of litigants. The rest,

including the *Depositions*, merely list the cases under the initial letters of the first plaintiff. Some do not show more than his single name. Where defendants are shown and there are more than one, only one may be given and that not always the same in every listing of the case. The Bernau Index, which the Society of Genealogists has on microfilm, lists all litigants, but for the 1613-1713 period covers only the Bridges Division. The Society's *Great Slip Index* covers all the divisions in that period but fails to give the divisions' names, so the bundle and piece numbers still have to be searched for at the PRO before the right call number can be found. Also, when making out the slips for defendants, the compiler reversed the order of the names of the disputants, thus converting the defendant into the plaintiff and vice versa. This needs to be kept in mind when searching the PRO lists for the call number.

Until the time of the Commonwealth, suits brought in the Court of Chancery can only be dated, and that approximately, from the name of the Lord High Chancellor or Lord Keeper of the Great Seal to whom the Bill of Complaint is addressed. The following is a chronological list of these officers of state for the Tudor and early Stuart periods.

1485	Thomas Barrow, Keeper, 1 August
1485	Thomas Rotheram, *alias* Scott, Archbishop of York
1486	John Alcock, Bishop of Ely, 1 March
1486	John Morton, Archbishop of Canterbury, 8 August
1501	Henry Deane, Bishop of Salisbury, Keeper, 13 October
1502	William Warham, Bishop-elect of London, then Archbishop of Canterbury, Keeper, 1 August
1516	Thomas Wolsey, Cardinal, Archbishop of York, 7 December
1530	Sir Thomas More, 25 October
1533	Sir Thomas Audley, Keeper, 20 May; Chancellor the following 6 Jan
1534	Thomas Goodrick, Bishop of Ely
1545	Thomas, Lord Wriothesley, 3 May
1547	Sir William Paulet, Lord St John of Basing, 29 June
1547	Richard, Lord Rich, 30 November
1551	Thomas Goodrick, Bishop of Ely, 19 January

1551 Sir Nicholas Hare, Lord Keeper
1553 Stephen Gardiner, Bishop of Winchester, 21 September
1555 Nicholas Heath, Archbishop of York, 1 January
1559 Sir Nicholas Bacon, Lord Keeper, 20 December
1579 Sir Thomas Bromley, 25 April
1587 Sir Christopher Hatton, 29 April
1592 Sir Thomas Egerton, 6 May
1603 ditto, as Lord High Chancellor
1616 Sir Francis Bacon, knt, Lord Keeper, 7 March
1617 ditto, as Lord High Chancellor
1621 Henry, Viscount Mandeville, Keeper, 3 May
1621 John Williams, Dean of Westminster, Lord Keeper, 10 July
1625 Sir Thomas Coventry, knt, Lord Keeper, 1 November
1639 Sir John Finch, knt, 23 January
1640 Sir Edward Littleton, knt, Lord Keeper
1641 ditto, as Lord Littleton
1645 Sir Richard Lane, knt, 27 August
1646 Edward, Earl of Manchester, Keeper

The Court of Chancery's *Guardianship Orders*, creating Wards in Chancery, do not survive unless there was litigation on the subject. For 'Money in Chancery', *see* DORMANT FUNDS.

The various courts of equity competed against one another; so, at different times, a case may have occurred in different courts. *See* EXCHEQUER, COURT OF; REQUESTS, COURT OF; STAR CHAMBER, COURT OF.

A useful booklet, *Chancery and other Legal Proceedings* by R.E.F. Garrett, has been published by Pinhorns.

Change of Name *see* Surnames

Chantry In its most modest form, a chantry was the provision of church services of intercession for the dead, usually parents, ancestors or benefactors, performed in a parish church by a cleric who was usually paid from the proceeds of land granted for that purpose. More elaborately it might be, for the same purpose, an altar or chapel in a church or even a separate building, to which the name became attached.

Chapel (i) A small Church of England church without parochial status or rights of sepulture (burial), etc., usually dependent on a parish church. Widespread parishes consisting of several hamlets, very common in the north of England, often contained chapelries served by chapels, some of which kept independent registers and were, after 1754, licensed for the performance of marriages.

(ii) An enclosure for a side altar in a large church.

(iii) The religious meeting-house of a nonconformist sect.

Chaplain (i) An unbeneficed priest, living on a stipend from an employer.

(ii) The priest in charge of a chapel.

Chapman A buyer or seller, often both and sometimes itinerant.

Chapter (i) The governing body of a cathedral or secular collegiate church, consisting of a dean, archdeacon, precentor, chancellor, treasurer and canons.

(ii) The periodic assembly of a religious community, originally so called from the custom of reading a chapter from the Rule of the Order (e.g. of St Benedict) in such assembly.

Charter Properly a document granting lands or privileges, but also loosely used to cover related documents. The Charter Rolls record royal grants of land or rights to boroughs, churches and families, in copies of the originals, from 1199 to 1537.

Chartered Companies Companies of merchants incorporated by Royal or Parliamentary charters, and engaged in foreign trade to areas of the world for which they were granted monopolies. Among the most famous and successful were the Merchant Adventurers (to the Netherlands and Hamburg), the East India Company (to southern Asia), the Levant Company (to the Turkish Empire), the Royal African Company (to West Africa), the Hudson's Bay Company (to what is now Canada), the Virginia Company (to the new American colonies of the sixteenth century), the Russia Company (to Muscovy), the Eastland

Company (to the Baltic), and the South Sea Company (to South America).

The records of some of these great companies survive and provide historians with a wealth of biographical material.

Chase A hunting area presented to a subject by the king, as distinct from a forest which was exclusively for the king's use. Offences committed in a Chase were not usually dealt with under forest law.

Chattel Any kind of property except a freehold and things appertaining to it. A more extensive term than 'goods' or 'effects'. In old wills it is sometimes written 'cattel', causing some doubt as to its true meaning. Both 'cattel' (beasts) and 'chattel' come from the Old English and Old French words meaning 'property', and the Latin *catallum* served both meanings.

Cheat Second-quality wheaten bread.
See also MANCHET.

Chelsea, Royal Hospital A Middlesex retreat for army pensioners, founded by Charles II and housed in a building designed by Christopher Wren and completed in 1692. Its registers of baptisms (1691-1812), marriages (1691-1765) and burials (1692-1856) are now at the General Register Office.

Cheminage A toll charged on roads in royal forests during the month when hinds were dropping their calves.

Cheshire The county now includes the southern border of Lancashire. The Family History Society of Cheshire and the North Cheshire Family History Society hold regular meetings and issue journals. Enquiries should be sent c/o the Federation of Family History Societies, 31 Seven Star Road, Solihull, West Midlands B91 2BZ, marked 'Please forward' and enclosing a stamped self-addressed envelope.

Record Repositories Cheshire Record Office, The Castle, Chester (tel: 0244.602574); Chester City Record Office, The Town Hall, Chester.

Parish Registers and Indexes (*see* comment under COUNTY) Nearly all the registers have been deposited at the Cheshire Record Office. The Society of Genealogists has copies of a number of them, and some are indexed in the INTERNATIONAL GENEALOGICAL INDEX (IGI). Manchester Public Library and the Family History Society of Cheshire each have a copy of the IGI. Marriage index entries are available from B. Merrell, 29128, 2520 W. Granger, Salt Lake City, Utah 84119, U.S.A. Mr R.B. Trunkfield of 7 North Downs Road, Cheadle Hulme, Cheshire, has an index of Cheshire people who married outside the county. Pallot's Marriage Index covers nine parishes, mostly 1790-1812. The Bishops' Transcripts are at the county record office (CRO).

Marriage Licence Records These, too, are at the CRO.

Wills before 1858 can be found at the CRO, but until 1541 the county lay in the Diocese of Lichfield and Province of Canterbury, so wills before that date could also be proved in the Consistory Court of Lichfield and the Prerogative Court of Canterbury (PCC). Since 1541 the county has been in the Diocese of Chester and Province of York, so wills could be proved in the Prerogative Court of York and the PCC. Indexes of wills, 1545-1837, have been printed by the Lancashire and Cheshire Record Society.

Non-parochial Registers These are at the Public Record Office (PRO), Chancery Lane, London. The IGI covers more than a hundred of them.

Memorial Inscriptions The North Cheshire Family History Society has transcription in hand.

Heralds' Visitation Pedigrees have been published for 1533, 1566, 1580 and 1613.

Census Returns are at the PRO, Portugal Street, London, and at the CRO.

Record Publishing Societies Chetham Society; Lancashire and Cheshire Record Society.

Chevage (i) A payment made by a villein to his lord for permission to live away from the manor.

(ii) A payment to the lord by an outsider for permission to live within the manor.

Chirograph A document written more than once on the same sheet of parchment, for example in an indenture.

Chirurgeon A SURGEON.

Cholera This disease was widespread in England in 1831-2 and 1849, causing great anxiety and a large number of deaths. Places with high mortality rates can be identified from parish registers and local newspapers.

Chrism A mixture of oil and balsam, consecrated by the bishop on Maundy Thursday and used throughout the succeeding year in baptism, confirmation and extreme unction, being kept in a chrismatory. When brought out it was covered with a silk cloth called a chrism cloth, which is not to be confused with a CHRISOM cloth.

Chrisom A Chrisom cloth was the white shawl, provided by a baby's parents and put upon the child by the minister during the baptismal ceremony. The child continued to wear it until its mother was 'churched', at which time the cloth was presented to the church for use in ablutions. If the child died before its mother's churching, the cloth became its shroud. Such a child would be entered in the burial registers as a Chrisom Child, Chrisomer, or Innocent. In some parts of the country this term was applied to children dying before they could be baptized.
See also CHURCHING OF WOMEN.

Christian Names Within two or three generations after the Norman Conquest, Anglo-Saxon names had disappeared from among the upper classes, though they lingered on among the peasantry until the end of the thirteenth century. The few pre-Conquest names that survived were those of saints and kings, notably Alfred, Edmund, Edward, Hilda and Mildred. The most popular Norman men's names were William, Robert, Richard, Ralph, Eudes, Hugh, Walter and Alan. In a few cases Anglo-Saxon names became changed to more Norman-French forms, such as Ethelward becoming Aylward, and Regenwald, Reynold.

In the Plantagenet period, under church influence, saint's names grew in popularity, particularly Matthew, Mark, Luke, John, Philip, Simon and Michael, and, from the Mystery plays, Adam, Daniel, Isaac, Joseph and Noah. Biblical women's names were even more popular, especially Mary, Anne and Elizabeth, and also those of post-biblical saints such as Agnes, Catherine and Margaret and the Mystery play characters, Eve, Sarah and Anna. However, during this period the range of Christian names in use progressively lessened until, in the fourteenth century, the five men's names of William, Richard, Harry, Robert and John comprised nearly two-thirds of all those recorded. For long after that time the restricted choice of Christian names poses problems for genealogists in distinguishing one person of the same surname from another. In documents, Christian names were latinised, and the Latin versions often gained favour; the English name Harry became less popular than Henry (from Harry's Latin version *Henricus*), and Piers less popular than Peter (from *Petrus*). The popularity of a Christian name under the Plantagenets can be estimated from the extent to which it gave rise to patronymic surnames; compare Harrison with Henryson, and Pearson with Peterson.

Women were often given men's names, such as Philip, Alexander, Nicholas and James, but the confusing effect is minimised by the Latin versions, which were always of feminine gender; for example, Philippa and Alexandra, which have become the modern forms. Nicholas, however, was retained as a girl's name as late as the eighteenth century.

Before the Reformation it was a grave offence under Canon Law to change a name that had been given at baptism, and anyone guilty of such a change was obliged to perform a penance. Surnames, on the other hand, could be changed at will. However, pet names and nicknames were countenanced, such as Will, Sim, Wat, Dick and Hodge (Roger), and Bess, Betty and Molly; and this was necessary when parents gave more than one of their living children the same name. One reason suggested for this is that it was to preserve intact a 'lease for three lives' in which the leaseholders-to-be had to be named.

After the Reformation, post-biblical saints' names fell into disrepute as being papistical. Biblical names, on the other hand, increased in popularity because of the Puritan emphasis on the Bible as the sole authority for truth. In the seventeenth century the religious influence on Christian names reached heights now considered absurd, with children being named Praise-God, Much Mercy, Repentance, Sin-deny and Livewell. Twins might be called Moses and Aaron, Esau and Jacob, Joseph and Mary. The influence of an extreme Puritan parish minister was often behind such excesses, and foundlings were, of course, particularly vulnerable. Names such as Flee-Fornication and Misericordia-Adulterina tell their own story.

The genealogist may encounter difficulties from the fact that some women's names were interchangeable. The most common are Elizabeth and Isobel, Anne and Agnes, Gillian and Julian, Anne and Hannah, Hester and Esther, Phyllis and Felice, Marion and Mary Ann, Joan and Jane.

The Renaissance period saw the beginning of the use of surnames as Christian names. One of the first to be so christened was Lord Guildford Dudley, the husband of Lady Jane Grey, whose mother's maiden name was Guildford. Often the surname was that of a godparent. Sometimes a godfather conferred his surname on his goddaughter. A married woman who has what appear to be two Christian names, of which the second is a surname, may turn out to be a Scot, conforming to the custom north of the border of retaining her surname in addition to that of her husband.

Before the Stuart period it was very rare for a man to have two Christian names, but the practice became more noticeable in the seventeenth century, though still not common. King James I had two names, Charles James; and so had his eldest son, Henry Frederick, who died before his father. But for men, two names only became really common from the end of the eighteenth century. After the Revolution of 1688 appeared the female pair-names Mary Anne, Mary Jane, Sarah Jane and Anne Maria, which were treated as one and went out of fashion only after they had dropped in social status in the mid nineteenth century.

The early part of the Georgian period was classical in mood, and a fashion developed for the classical forms of women's names, such as Anna, Maria, Sophia, Olivia, Evelina, Amelia, Cecilia and Juliana, and also for Latin names that had no English equivalent, such as Lavinia.

At the end of the Georgian period, England, indeed Europe, was dominated by the Romantic movement stressing the beauty of strangeness. This made people look back to early times,

because they were little known. So Anglo-Saxon names came in again. Edward had never gone out entirely, but new favourites were Edgar, Edwin, Alfred, Emma, Ethel, Matilda, Arthur and Wilfred.

In the Victorian period, the Tractarian Movement, reinforcing the Romantic trend, revived the names of long-neglected saints such as Aidan, Augustine, Theodore, Benedict and Bernard. The pre-Raphaelites and Tennyson increased the taste for medievalism and revived such names as Lancelot, Hugh, Walter, Ayhmer, Roger, Ralph, Ella, Alice, Mabel, Edith and Gillian. The influence of royalty made Albert a popular name.

The following are the Latin versions of a number of common Christian names. They will sometimes be found under variant spellings; for example, ae for e, and au for al. Men's names that are virtually identical with the English, except for the suffix -us, -ius or -dus, have been omitted, as have women's names ending in -a and -ia.

Agneta	Agnes
Aluredus	Edward
Alienora	Eleanor
Aloysius	Lewis
Amabilia	Mabel
Amia	Amy
Amicius	Amyas
Andreas	Andrew
Caius	Kay
Carolus	Charles
Coleta	Nicholas (f)
Constantia	Constance
Dionisia	Denise
Dionisius	Dennis
Egidius	Giles
Emelina	Emily
Francisca	Frances
Galfridus	Geoffrey
Godefridus	Godfrey
Gratia	Grace
Gualterus	Walter
Guido	Guy
Gulielmus	William
Hamo	Hamon
Helena	Ellen, Helen, Eleanor
Henricus	Henry, Harry

Horatius	Horace
Hugo	Hugh
Isabella	Isabel, Elizabeth
Jacobus	James, Jacob
Jocosa	Joyce
Johanna	Joan, Jane
Johannes	John
Joscia	Joyce
Juetta	Jowet, Ivote
Lucas	Luke
Marcus	Mark
Marta	Martha
Milo	Miles
Paganus	Payn
Petronilla	Parnell
Petrus	Piers, Peter
Radulfus	Ralph
Ro(h)esia	Rose
Tedbaldus	Theobald
Villefridus	Wilfred
Willelmus	William

Latin names are often abbreviated to the first syllable, followed by the declension ending, e.g. Willus (William), Rici (of Richard). A special case is Xpoferus (Christopher), in which the first two letters are not really X and p but the Greek letters X (Ch) and p (r). Xp was the customary abbreviation for Christ. In 'Xmas' the second letter has been dropped.

Chronicle A record in which events are set down one after the other without any attempt to analyse or explain them. Famous examples are the Anglo-Saxon Chronicles, entered up annually by monastic chroniclers. The term is used in a derogatory sense of a historical work that fails to probe beneath the surface of events, or investigate cause and effect. For want of sufficient data, it may be difficult for a family history to be more than a chronicle.

Church Ale Periodic festival gathering for the purpose of raising money for the parish church. The ale for the occasion was brewed in the church house from malt either bought or begged by the churchwardens. In 1603 it was forbidden to hold such functions within churches, chapels or churchyards, but the ban was not always effective.

Church Hay Another term for a churchyard.

Churching of Women A purification ceremony performed for a mother shortly after the birth of each child. *See also* CHRISOM.

Church of England Hierarchy *See below.*

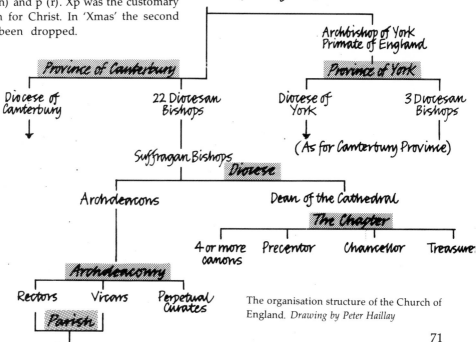

The organisation structure of the Church of England. *Drawing by Peter Haillay*

Churchwardens Men acting as the chief lay officers of a parish. The office has been in existence at least since 1127. There were commonly two wardens, the Rector's (or Vicar's) Warden and the People's Warden, but in the north-west and in populous towns it was common to have more. The method of selection varied with the custom of the parish. A 'tied' churchwarden was one who served by rota by virtue of his occupation of a certain house or certain land. During the fifteenth and early sixteenth centuries, as the parish took the place of the manor as the effective unit of local government, many civil duties were placed upon the wardens. They were *ex officio* the senior members of the parish vestry. Levying church and other rates was among their responsibilities, and their books of accounts are an important source of parish, and often of family, history. In some places they were known as churchmen or church reeves.

Clandestine Marriages Before 1754 it was the rule that the clergy could perform marriage ceremonies only for people who either had banns called, or had obtained a marriage licence, but the breaking of this rule did not invalidate the marriage. The bride and bridegroom were liable merely to be censured, and even the penalties inflicted on the parson did not involve his permanently losing his benefice or going to prison. This laxity led to a large number of clandestine marriages, and certain churches became known for providing the facility.

In addition to some of the churches, prison chapels were especially liable to be used for clandestine marriages. The most notorious of these was the Fleet Chapel in London, but the prison chaplains soon began to perform marriages outside the prison, in rooms in taverns fitted up as pseudo-chapels. On the day before Lord Hardwicke's *Marriage Act* came into force (25 March 1754), 217 Fleet marriages were performed. About 300 registers recording clandestine marriages are now at the Public Record Office, Chancery Lane, London, under reference RG.7.

Class, Archive The technical term indicating the coverage of a single type of record, intermediary between a group and a piece. For example, the Public Record Office reference for the microfilm of the 1871 Census Return of Cleator in Cumberland is RG.10/5261. RG are the Group letters, showing that it came from the Registrar General's Office; 10 is the Class number of the 1871 Census; and 5261 is the Piece number of the microfilm covering the parish of Cleator.

Class, Social Nowadays the differences between social classes are very much smaller than they used to be, yet not so long ago they were immediately apparent — in speech, dress, manner and education. People recognised who were their 'betters' and who their 'inferiors', and accepted their own state of life as being that (in the words of the Catechism) to which it had pleased God to call them. The main classes were the aristocracy, the gentry, the middle class, lower middle class and working class, though those are modern terms for them. The following brief generalisations, on constantly changing conditions, have most relevance to the early nineteenth century.

The *aristocracy* consisted of titled families and their relatives. Their wealth came mainly from large landed estates. From one generation to another, the head of the family lived in the same stately home; at his death his personal papers tended not to be destroyed, but to be removed to capacious attics or cellars, and so great family archives accumulated. The pedigrees of the aristocracy have been published in the recurrent volumes of Burke's *Peerage*.

The *gentry* had much in common with the aristocracy, but on a smaller scale. They were armigerous, had private incomes and were educated at public schools and universities. The heads of county families inherited manor houses, and younger sons became officers in the navy and army, or barristers, clergy and bankers. The pedigrees of many gentry families have been published from time to time in Burke's *Landed Gentry*.

The *middle class* made their living as master tradesmen and businessmen, as physicians, surgeons, solicitors and yeomen farmers, and their sons attended grammar schools.

The *lower middle class* consisted of small master craftsmen, keepers of small shops and alehouses, and husbandmen cultivating their

April y 7th 1760
Officers Chosen for this Ensuing year are
as follows
Mr Farindon ⎱ Church
William Laker ⎰ wardens

Francis Killick ⎫
Robert Head ⎬ Overseers
Richard Agate ⎪
Charles Komber ⎭

The Account of the Legacy given by the last will
and testament of William Saxby Gent: to the Parish
of Lingfield for Ever and was Disposed of by
Ellis Bostock Esq: and Anthony Farindon Esq
Church Wardens for the year 1759

John Long a Coat and ———————	00 = 01 = 00
Thos: Everest a Coat and ———	00 = 01 = 00
Willm White a Coat and ———	00 = 01 = 00
Willm Bongs a Coat and ———	00 = 01 = 00
John Brown a Coat and ———	00 = 01 = 00
Robt Webb, wife a Gown and —	00 = 01 = 00
Thos: Jupp, wife a Gown and —	00 = 01 = 00
Peter Everist wife a Gown and —	00 = 01 = 00
Robt Dinnis wife a Gown and —	00 = 01 = 00
Widow Robt Lock a Gown and —	00 = 01 = 00

Churchwardens' Accounts of Lingfield, Surrey, 1760,
showing the names of the men and women in the
parish who received coats and gowns from a charitable
bequest. *Courtesy the Vicar and Parochial Church Council,
Lingfield*

own small plots of land. Many were unable to read or write, but in the early nineteenth century their children were the first to attend the new schools being opened by church bodies.

The *working class* was made up of journeymen, agricultural labourers and servants, working for wages and liable, in times of misfortune, to become 'paupers' dependent on parish relief. Some were able to attend charity or church schools, but only a minority was literate. Of the whole population, agricultural labourers formed the largest occupational group for men, and domestic servants for women.

In England, the dividing lines between classes have never been impassable. Men of ability have risen in the world, while the less able, the younger sons of large families, and the wastrels, have correspondingly sunk. Neighbouring classes have intermarried, and this, too, has led to class mobility. The industrial revolution gave all social classes a big shake-up, as agriculture ceased to be the largest sector of the economy. The professions moved up in the world because of the intellectual attainments that became increasingly necessary in their practitioners.

See also peerage titles, and BARONET; KNIGHT; ESQUIRE; FRANKLIN; GENTLEMAN; GOODMAN; HUSBANDMAN; MR; VILLEIN; YEOMAN.

Clergy, Church of England The records of the clergy of the Established Church are contained in the bishops' registers of the various dioceses. Those concerning ordination may, according to their parish, include a testimonial of character, a certificate of baptism, a nomination by the incumbent whose curate the ordinand was to be, a certificate that his intention to enter the church had been published in his own parish church, and covering letters. Later career information in the register is revealed by his institution to benefices. From 1556 such information can be found at the Public Record Office (PRO) in the Institution Books. Appointments during the period 1800-40 have been published in J. Foster's *Index Ecclesiasticus*. Thereafter *Clergy Lists* began publication, and Crockford's *Clerical Directory* has appeared regularly since 1858. It covers Anglican clergy anywhere in the world. Until quite recently it gave no information about date of birth, but the normal minimum age for

ordination was 23½. Incumbents are mentioned in ecclesiastical visitations, at which they were obliged to exhibit their written credentials and those of their curates and lecturers. Many clergy were university graduates, so details of their parentage can be found in the university registers; but from the mid nineteenth century, theological colleges were founded, and these accepted non-graduates. Such students often commenced their careers as curates in the colonies. An Ecclesiastical Census was taken in 1851 and is available at the PRO, Kew (HO.129).

The official term for a clergyman is 'clerk in holy orders', and until the mid nineteenth century that is what is meant by the simple term 'clerk'; a commercial clerk was called a 'writer'. Until the eighteenth century a graduate clergyman will be found in Latin records entitled *Magister* (Master); and a non-graduate, *Dominus* (Sir). Many churches display a tablet showing a chronological list of their incumbents from the Middle Ages until today (*see* INCUMBENT).

In the mid seventeenth century many clergy were ejected from their livings for failing to adapt to the changes introduced by a Presbyterian parliament and, later, to the Anglican restoration of 1662. Details of these, including in many cases the parentage of the parson, can be found in two volumes by A.G. Matthews, *Walker Revised* and *Calamy Revised*.

Nonconformist ministers The records of the clergy of many nonconformist churches for the seventeenth to nineteenth centuries were less systematically kept. The best course is to apply to the archivist of the denomination concerned. In more recent times the names of the clergy can be found in the annual directories published by the churches.

See also articles on the various denominations, and WILLIAMS'S LIBRARY, DR.

Clerical Subsidy Whenever lay subsidies were levied by Parliament, religious bodies also paid taxes, which were assessed and voted upon in the councils of the two archiepiscopal provinces. At the Public Record Office, Chancery Lane, London, the records are under the same class as Lay Subsidies, E.179.

Clerk (i) A man or boy who had been

ceremonially tonsured by the bishop, whether he subsequently took holy orders or not.

(ii) A clergyman, in which case the term is an abbreviation for 'clerk in holy orders'.

(iii) A man skilled in writing work; but a clerk in the modern sense of one engaged in office work was called a Writer.

(iv) The Clerk of the Peace was the principal legal officer of the Quarter Sessions. He was a trained attorney who guided the court proceedings and superintended all county business in the intervals between sessions.

(v) The Parish Clerk was often responsible for entering up the registers of baptisms, marriages and burials, and might keep a draft register from which the official register book was posted up at intervals. Today, if a clergyman is asked to make a search in his parish register for genealogical purposes, he is liable to pass the job on to his parish clerk, a fact worth bearing in mind.

Cleveland A county formed in 1974 out of parts of Durham and Yorkshire. For the Cleveland Family History Society, *see* YORKSHIRE.

Close A piece of land enclosed within hedges, fences or walls.

Close Rolls These contain the registered copies of Letters Close issued by, and private deeds enrolled in, the royal Court of Chancery. Many of the private deeds are conveyances. The copies were written on parchment sheets, or membranes, which were then stitched together and rolled into one or more rolls for each year of the king's reign. They are housed at the Public Record Office, Chancery Lane, London, under C.54 with annual calendars. The original Letters derive their name from the fact that they were folded before being sealed, and so could only be read after first breaking the seal. They issued orders to royal officers and writs of summons to Parliament.

Cognate A term meaning related on the mother's side.
See also AGNATE.

Collectioner A pauper in receipt of parish relief.

Collector of the Poor An early name for the Overseer of the Poor, because of his duty to collect the Poor Rate.

College A body of people, living together in the same endowed foundation, such as the members of a collegiate church, school or university. Also the buildings for such a body.

Colonial Records Index *see* Currer-Briggs Colonial Record Index

Commissary One to whom is committed some charge, duty or office by a superior power; a commissioner. In the Church of England, he was an officer of the diocesan bishop, empowered to exercise ecclesiastical jurisdiction on his behalf over an area at some distance from the bishop's residence — by presiding over a Commissary Court (*see* WILL). A Commissary General was a general assistant to a bishop, empowered to perform a number of functions on his behalf.

Common Law The law of the king's courts, as distinct from that of the local courts, because it was common over the whole country. It was also distinct from Statute Law and equity. The records start with the Curia Regis (King's Court) Rolls down to 56 Henry III (*see* REGNAL YEARS), containing pleas heard in the courts both of King's Bench and Common Pleas, but from the reign of Edward I these were separated.

Common Pleas, Court of Henry II appointed five justices to sit permanently in his Curia Regis (King's Court) to cope with the increasing number of pleas being brought by his subjects, one against another. The court was usually held at Westminster, but did sometimes follow the king from place to place as a section of his Curia (Court). This mobility was raised by the barons as one of their grievances against King John, and *Magna Carta* laid down that the Court of Common Pleas should stay in one place which, eventually, became a certain spot in the vast Westminster Hall.

From 1272 the court was granted its own Chief Justice, and so its separation from the Curia Regis became complete. In 1873 its jurisdiction was transferred to the King's Bench Division of the High Court of Justice. The early rolls of the Court of Common Pleas are called De

Banco Rolls, after the bench of judges, and the later ones Common Rolls. At the Public Record Office, Chancery Lane, London, the records are located in Group CP.

Common, Rights of These were the rights enjoyed by householders living within the manorial system in virtue of the MESSUAGE they held.

The rights were of many kinds, agricultural, beast-owning and miscellaneous. Common of Stock was the right to graze a certain number of cattle and sheep (according to the tenement held) upon the ploughland left fallow that year, and the land from which the crop had been reaped. Common of Turbary was the right to cut turf and other fuel within the manor. Common in Gross was a right detached from house or land, unlike the more usual Common Appendant (or Appurtenant) — rights that went with a holding.

See also APPURTENANCES; WASTE.

Commonable Land Manorial land held in SEVERALTY, but subject to common rights for part of the year; specifically, after the hay crop·from the meadow and the harvesting of the arable.

See also LAMMAS.

Commoners, History of the Four volumes of this work by John Burke appeared between 1836 and 1838. They contain narrative pedigrees of county families of that period. The series was continued under the title of the *Landed Gentry.*

Comperta Literally 'Things discovered', and written up for a bishop or archdeacon after his visitation of a parish. Together with detecta — things of which people had been accused (or, in the language of the courts, for which they had been 'presented') — they formed the basis of the bishop's or archdeacon's injunctions.

See also PRESENTMENT.

Compotus Rolls These are estate accounts by royal and seignorial officials, of which there are about 1200 bundles at the Public Record Office, Chancery Lane, London, under the title *Special Collection No. 6, Ministers' Accounts.* Many of them are the records of the royal escheators.

Compters The common gaols of London and elsewhere, used for debtors. Also written 'Counters'.

Compurgator One who swore to the truth of a statement made in court by another.

Computers The electronic indexing, sorting and editing of information is already having its effect on genealogy and is likely to have considerably more in the future. Most ancestry researchers will be familiar with the International Genealogical Index which became available from Salt Lake City in 1978. Since then, the development of the computer, with its handy size and low cost, has stimulated family history societies and other bodies to press on with the indexing of census returns, marriage registers, memorial inscriptions and other source material, because with computers the process is so much quicker and less liable to error than by two-stage manual copying. However, the indexing of historical records is only one aspect of computer use in genealogy. Many genealogists now possess microcomputers and use them not only to store record information and to process it in order to discover connections not otherwise apparent, but also to draw up family trees and birth brief pedigrees which are amendable without having to be rewritten. In fact, at present (1984) it is in the home that the computer is exerting its greatest impact on genealogy.

The Society of Genealogists has a Computer Committee and has formed a Computer Interest Group which holds frequent meetings — open also to non-members of the Society — at Charterhouse Buildings, London EC1, and elsewhere, with sub-groups for beginners and users of particular types of equipment. Since September 1982, the Society has published a quarterly magazine, *Computers in Genealogy*, in which methods of using the various types of hardware for ancestry research are discussed, and the inevitable problems aired.

The greatest single problem in computer use by genealogists is the diversity caused by the variety of hardware and software available. There is a need for some standardisation if information is to become readily exchangeable between users, but the time to take decisions on standardisation has not yet come, because the rapid advances being made in computer technology will soon render today's problems out of date and give rise to others.

There are indications that genealogists will soon be able to make use of commercially written programs for storing their data, and, indeed, some are already on the market. This tendency will be reinforced by the trend for computers to be sold as a system, with peripherals and a suite of programs written to work together.

As more source material becomes computer-indexed, traditional publishing in print will become relatively expensive, both in money and shelf space, and microfiches produced from computer files may become the preferred medium of publication.

Any genealogist thinking of buying a computer for his hobby without previous experience of using one is recommended to subscribe to *Computers in Genealogy*, and to consult a fellow genealogist already using a computer. Information on computer users can be sought through one's area family history society.

(Acknowledgements
to Mrs Evelyn Kenward)

Congregationalists This nonconformist denomination began as a movement within the Church of England, founded by Robert Browne. Its followers were at first called Separatists or Brownists, but were later known as Independents, and still later as Congregationalists. They were firmly suppressed, and in 1608 Browne's followers emigrated for a time to Amsterdam to escape persecution. But some returned, and in 1620 the church provided the London contingent of the passengers of the *Mayflower* when she sailed for America.

During the Commonwealth, Cromwell and several of his closest associates were Independents, though the official doctrine of the established church was then Presbyterian. When the monarchy was restored, the 1662 *Act of Uniformity* placed legal disabilities upon the sect, as it did upon other nonconformists. Although the persecution was ended under William and Mary, by the 1689 *Act of Toleration*, meeting-places were still subject to the granting of licences by either the county justices, the bishop or the archdeacon.

In 1742/3 a register of births for the Three Denominations (Congregationalists, Presbyterians and Baptists) was started at Dr Williams's Library (*see* WILLIAMS'S LIBRARY, DR).

1832 saw the Union of Congregationalist Churches inaugurated, and five years later, on the commencement of civil registration, marriages were allowed to be performed by Congregationalist ministers before a registrar.

In 1837, nearly all known registers were sent to the Registrar General for authentication, and in 1840 the records were deposited with that office on a permanent basis. Registers discovered later were added in 1858. The Births Register of the Three Denominations was also deposited. All are now held at the Public Record Office, Chancery Lane, London, under references RG.4, 5 and 8. Some of the undeposited registers have since been published. The earliest registers of baptisms and burials began in 1644, but comparatively few are extant earlier than the late eighteenth century. They often give more information than parish registers. The churches also kept Minute Books and Rolls of Church Members, but most of them have been lost.

Miscellaneous records and histories of individual churches are kept at the Congregational Library, Memorial Hall, Farringdon Street, London EC4. Others are kept at the New College Library, Hampstead, North London.

County record offices have Quarter Sessions records that contain presentments of persons for not attending parish churches as required by the *Act of Uniformity*, and for holding conventicles contrary to the Clarendon Code.

The Congregational Historical Society, founded 1899, publishes its *Transactions*, which are indexed, and the Society has also published C.E. Surman's *Bibliography of Local Congregational History* (1947).

For further reading, see *Sources for Nonconformist Genealogy and Family History*, by D.J. Steel (1973).

See also NON-PAROCHIAL REGISTERS.

Coniger A rabbit warren.

Consistory A solemn assembly or council. In the Church of England, a Consistory Court was normally the spiritual court of a diocesan bishop held before his Official or Chancellor in his cathedral church or other convenient place. The term consistory is occasionally used by other courts, such as that of a dean.

See also COMMISSARY.

Constable (i) The High Constable was the official of the hundred to whom petty (i.e. parish) constables were responsible for some of their duties. He was an assistant to the Lieutenant of his county in carrying out his military functions. When a muster was ordered by the Crown, the Lieutenant passed the word to his High Constables, giving each one the quota of men required of him. Each High Constable then passed the order and individual quotas on to the constables of the parishes in his hundred. The office was abolished in 32 & 33 Victoria (her thirty-second and thirty-third regnal years).

(ii) The Petty Constable was one of the most ancient of the offices of the manor and later of the parish. In the Middle Ages he was chosen by the manor, but served for the township.

He had to report, and take action on, a great many matters, among them: felonies committed, escaped prisoners, riots and unlawful assemblies, non-attendance at church, oppression by other officers, commercial irregularities, licensing of ale houses, compiling Jurors' Lists, drunkenness, his assistants, unauthorised building of additional cottages and dovecotes, vagabonds, intruders, militia Muster Rolls, taking lewd women before the Justice of the Peace, and detaining refractory fathers of bastards.

The appointment of the constable was taken over from the manor court by the parish vestry in the early seventeenth century. The position was an honorary one and required no property qualification until 1842, when anyone taking the appointment had to occupy lands or tenements assessed to poor rate or county rate at £4 or more per year. Constables' account books often throw interesting light on family history. Many of them have now been deposited by parish incumbents at county record offices.

Consul It was not until 1825 that consuls abroad became members of the Civil Service. Before that, the title was conferred on a prominent member of an English business community abroad, chosen by them to represent and lead them in negotiations affecting their status and safety with the authorities of the country in which they were residing. Even today, in smaller towns abroad, the British 'Consul' is often not a career official, or even British, but a trusted resident and citizen of the country of residence.

Consular Returns *see* **General Register Office**

Contumacy (i) A refusal, after a threefold citation, to appear before an ecclesiastical court.

(ii) Refusal by an excommunicate to submit to ecclesiastical authority.

Convent A community of monks, friars or nuns living in a single house. The popular restriction of its meaning to nunneries is late, as also is its application to the community's building.

Conventicle An assembly for the exercise of religion, otherwise than as sanctioned by law. The term was commonly used in the seventeenth century for meetings of non-conformists.

Conveyance *see* **Title Deed**

Copyhold A form of tenure for land held of a lord of a manor in return, originally, for agricultural services but, since Tudor times, for money payments. On the admission of a new tenant, a payment (fine) to the lord was required, and on the death of the tenant a HERIOT. Tenure of such land could be transferred only by its surrender to the lord, and by admission by him of the new tenant, who might be the heir of the old one. Each admission was recorded in the Court Rolls and a copy of the entry given to the new tenant, for whom it fulfilled the function of a title deed; hence the name Copyhold.

This form of tenure was made commutable to freehold by an Act of 1841, but it was an Act of 1853-4 that brought about a general commutation, although copyhold tenure was not finally abolished until 1 January, 1926. Copyhold is also known as customary tenure, since its conditions were governed by the custom of the manor.

Cordwainer Pronounced 'cordner'. A worker

or trader in leather goods. The name derives from Cordovan, a resident of the Spanish town famous for its fine leather. In general its use means a shoemaker or cobbler.

Corndealers Men of this trade had to be licensed annually by the Quarter Sessions. The licence records are at the county record offices.

Cornet The lowest commissioned rank in a cavalry regiment, equivalent to the present 2nd Lieutenant. The equivalent rank in the infantry was that of ensign. Like the latter, he carried the regiment's colours.

Cornwall Cornwall Family History Society holds regular meetings and issues a journal. Enquiries should be sent c/o the Federation of Family History Societies, 31 Seven Star Road, Solihull, West Midlands B91 2BZ, marked 'Please forward' and enclosing a stamped, self-addressed envelope.

Record Repositories Cornwall County Record Office, County Hall, Truro (by appointment. tel: 0872.3698); Royal Institution of Cornwall, River Street, Truro.

Parish Registers and Indexes (*see* comment under COUNTY) Many of the registers have been deposited at the county record office (CRO). The Society of Genealogists has copies of over 200 in its library. Boyd's Marriage Index covers 202 parishes, mostly down to 1812. The INTERNATIONAL GENEALOGICAL INDEX (IGI) has a good coverage of baptisms, and the family history society has a copy. Pallot's Marriage Index covers 153 parishes, 1790-1812. The Bishops' Transcripts for 1670-1736 and 1741-72 are at the CRO. Those for 1737-1812 are at the Devon Record Office (RO), Exeter.

Marriage Licence Records These are at the Devon RO, Exeter.

Wills before 1858, proved in the following courts, are located as follows.

At the CRO:
    Archdeaconry of Cornwall.
    Royal Peculiar (Pec.) Court of the Deanery of St Bunyan.
Destroyed by bombing in 1942 (but see below):
    Pec. Court of the Bishop of Exeter.
    Pec. Court of the Dean and Chapter of Exeter.

    Archdeaconry of Totnes.
As the county lay in the Diocese of Exeter until 1876, and in the Province of Canterbury, wills could be proved in the Consistory Court of Exeter, the Episcopal Principal Registry of Exeter and the Prerogative Court of Canterbury (PCC). These wills, too, were destroyed by enemy action. However, some probate records did survive and for details of these, see *Wills and Their Whereabouts*, by A.J. Camp.

Non-parochial Registers These are at the Public Record Office (PRO), Chancery Lane, London. The IGI covers many of them.

Census Returns These are at the PRO, Portugal Street, London, with a copy at the CRO.

Memorial Inscriptions Transcriptions of a few burial grounds are in the library of the Society of Genealogists.

Heralds' Visitation Pedigrees These have been printed for 1530, 1573 and 1620.

Protestation Oath Returns have been printed for 1641-2.

Devon and Cornwall Record Society has made a number of historical records available in print.

Coroner The office originated in 1194 as Keeper of the Pleas of the Crown, when four keepers were appointed for each county, three of whom were knights and the remaining one a clerk. By the early thirteenth century they had been reduced to two, both knights, each assisted by a clerk. They were elected by the knights and freeholders of the county, and the office was unpaid. From 1200 some boroughs had coroners of their own.

The duties of the office included holding inquests on the dead, hearing Abjurations of the Realm appeals and confessions (*see* SANCTUARY), and carrying out the confiscations that arose from declarations of outlawry. The coroners had to keep records and present them at the Eyre court, after which they were usually destroyed. However, from 1337 the records handed in to Superior Eyres were preserved, and these are at the Public Record Office (PRO) under *Justices Itinerant* (JUST).

The office was radically revised, first by the *Coroners Act*, 1887, and then by the *Coroners Amendment Act*, 1926. A coroner is now either a barrister, a solicitor, or a qualified medical practitioner, and may have deputies and assistant deputies. Their records are not available for public perusal. In the period immediately prior to the Acts, coroners regarded their records as their private property. Accounts of the proceedings of their courts are best discovered through reports in the local press (*see* NEWSPAPERS).

Corporal Oath An oath taken with one hand on a sacred object, usually a volume of the Gospels.
See also PROBATE (translation of Latin probate act).

Correction, House of A type of county gaol, especially one founded in accordance with Acts of 1575-6 and 1603-4, for rogues, vagrants, unmarried mothers and parents who had left their children chargeable to the parish.

From 1697, paupers who refused to be badged (*see* BADGE-MAN) could be sent to a House of Correction for whipping and three weeks' hard labour. The records are at the county record office.

Corrody Originally the right of free accommodation to be provided by a vassal to his lord when on his circuit; later the term came to apply to the boarding provisions made by monasteries to their living benefactors.

Corruption of Blood *see* **Attainder**

Cote (i) An enclosure for sheep or cattle.
(ii) A cottage.

Cottar The tenant of a cottage, with or without a small piece of land. After villeins, the largest class of people in the Domesday record (*see* DOMESDAY BOOK). A cottar's land was probably insufficient to support him, so he would also work on the land of others.
See also BORDAR.

Counters *see* **Compters**

Country A word often used, until the nineteenth century, in the modern sense of 'county', or, even more loosely, as 'neighbourhood'.

County The counties of England are of Anglo-Saxon origin. At the Conquest, the leaders of the county organisation were the ealdorman (an Anglo-Saxon term soon changed to the Danish earl) and the sheriff. As earldoms under the Normans became very large, it was left to the sheriff to carry out the county's administrative duties, and in time an earldom ceased to be an office and became merely a title.

In the sixteenth century the sheriff's military functions were handed over to a lieutenant, later known as the Lord Lieutenant, who in time also took over a number of the sheriff's other duties.

The county was administered through the holding of Quarter Sessions until, by the *Local Government Act* of 1888, elective county councils were established. At the same time, the Isle of Ely, parts of Lincolnshire, London, the Soke of Peterborough, East and West Suffolk, East and West Sussex, the Isle of Wight and the Ridings of Yorkshire, all became separate administrative counties. In earlier centuries certain cities and boroughs had been made corporate counties, and many of them became county boroughs under the 1888 Act.

As from 1 April 1974, the boundaries of a number of counties were adjusted. Some counties disappeared; for example, Cumberland and Westmorland were combined, along with an area of northern Lancashire, to become Cumbria, while Yorkshire was divided into North, West and South Yorkshire and the new counties mentioned below. Huntingdonshire was absorbed into Cambridgeshire, Rutland into Leicestershire. Several new counties and metropolitan counties were formed; i.e. Tyne and Wear (from SE Northumberland and NE Durham), Cleveland (from SE Durham and NE Yorkshire), Humberside (from SE Yorkshire and N Lincolnshire), Greater Manchester (from the area around that city), Merseyside (from SW Lancashire and the north Wirral), West Midlands (from the areas around Birmingham), Avon (from S Gloucestershire and N Somerset), and Herefordshire and Worcestershire were combined under their joint name. About one third of the area of Berkshire was transferred to Oxfordshire. At the present time (1985), the above metropolitan counties and Greater London are under threat of abolition, and it is not known what will replace them.

Under the headings of the historical counties, the sources and some of the facilities (indexes, transcriptions, etc.) relevant to each are listed, but the facilities are in such a constant and rapid state of development that it is impossible to give a full picture of them. To keep in touch with these developments, membership of the area's family history society is strongly recommended.

County Record Office (CRO) Before the Second World War only six counties had record offices, but today all English counties have one or more. They house the archives of the County Councils, Courts of Quarter Sessions, Boards of Guardians, Lords Lieutenant, Sheriffs, etc., and have attracted deposits of many other archives and collections of value to genealogists, such as parish registers, wills, marriage licence records, manor court rolls, as well as documents of private owners, solicitors, businesses and semi-public bodies. In most cases the CRO and the Diocesan Registry are now combined.

The record offices have the duty not only of housing records in conditions suitable for their preservation, but also of maintaining them by fumigation, repair and reprographic copying, and of making them available for research by listing, calendaring, indexing and rapid production. The present popularity of genealogy is due in large part to the facilities provided by CROs. For their location, *see* the relevant counties. The Federation of Family History Societies has published a useful booklet with town plans, entitled *Record Offices: How to find them*.

County Families, Walford's Volumes issued periodically from 1860 to 1920, giving details not of families but of individuals considered to be members of county families. *See also* LANDED GENTRY.

Court Baron A term distinguishing one aspect of the work of a manorial court. *See also* MANOR.

Court Leet A term distinguishing one aspect of the work of a manorial court. *See also* MANOR.

Court Deal Demesne lands arrented; also called Boardland. *See also* ARRENTATION.

Courtesy of England, Estate by the A widower's right to hold for life his deceased wife's dower land held in Fee Simple (*see* FEE) or Estate Tail (*see* ENTAIL). He had this right only if he had had, by her, a child, who was thus the wife's heir or would have been so had it lived.

Cousin A term formerly loosely used, and often meaning a nephew or niece. A cousin German is a first cousin, i.e. the child of an uncle or aunt. A cousin-once-removed expresses the relationship between a person and his cousin's child or parent, the 'once removed' referring to a difference of one generation: hence, 'twice removed' indicates a difference of two generations, and so on. People who are 'second cousins' to each other are the children of first cousins.

Creature A baptismal name bestowed, according to some opinions, when the sex of the child was not known at the hurried baptism of a weak new-born baby, but more likely, perhaps, when a name had not yet been chosen and the baby seemed unlikely to survive to need one. It is an anglicisation and abbreviation of the Latin *Creatura Christi*, which was sometimes the wording of the register entry.

Crenellation The technical term for the fortification of a house, for which a royal licence was required. Many of the records are to be found in the Patent Rolls from Henry III onwards. To surround a house by a moat also required a licence. Most of the licences issued were to religious houses or the palaces of bishops. (*See* the article 'Licences for Crenellation' by J.H. Parker in *Gentleman's Magazine* for 1856).

Crest A heraldic device depicted in an ACHIEVEMENT as mounted upon the helmet. It seems to have originated in decorative representations painted upon the body of the helmet itself, or upon a protective fan-shaped ridge or crest that surmounted it. The earliest known example of a crest in its present form is one of 1198. Thereafter the choice of device seems to have remained personal long after arms had become hereditary, and crests were more usually worn in tournaments than in battle. In the later years of Queen Elizabeth I's reign it became a common practice to issue grants of crests to men already bearing ancient arms; and during the seventeenth century most new grants of arms included crests. The practice was invariable by the eighteenth century, but today many older arms are still without crests. *See also* ARMS, COAT OF; ARMS, COLLEGE OF; HERALDRY.

Croft Land adjoining a house, often enclosed.

Cucking-stool Equipment for ducking a female scold.

Cumberland The ancient county is now absorbed in Cumbria. The Cumbria Family History Society holds regular meetings and issues a newsletter. Enquiries should be sent c/o the Federation of Family History Societies, 31 Seven Star Road, Solihull, West Midlands B91 2BZ, marked 'Please forward' and enclosing a stamped self-addressed envelope.

Record Repositories Cumbria Record Office, The Castle, Carlisle (tel: 0228.23456); Cumbria Record Office, 140 Duke Street, Barrow-in-Furness (tel: 0229.31269); Cathedral Library, The Fratery, Carlisle Cathedral.

Parish Registers and Indexes (*see* comment under COUNTY) A number of parishes have deposited their registers at the county record office (CRO). The Society of Genealogists has copies of some in its library. Boyd's Marriage Index covers 34 parishes, but only for the seventeenth century. Pallot's Marriage Index covers 17 parishes, mostly 1790-1812. The CRO has yet another index of marriages. The INTERNATIONAL GENEALOGICAL INDEX (IGI) has a good coverage of baptisms. The Bishops' Transcripts are at the CRO.

Marriage Licence Records A calendar of those for the Diocese of Carlisle is at the CRO; the originals no longer exist. Those for the Archdeaconry of Richmond are at the Lancashire Record Office.

Wills before 1858, proved in the following courts, are located as follows.

At the county record office:
   Consistory Court of Carlisle.
   Consistory Court of Durham (for Over Denton before 1703 and Alston).

At the Lancashire Record Office:
   Archdeaconry Court of Richmond.

As the Archdeaconry of Richmond lay in the Diocese of Chester, wills could be proved in the Consistory Court of Chester. As the county lay in the Province of York, wills could also be proved in the Prerogative Court of Yorkshire (*see* YORKSHIRE) and the Prerogative Court of Canterbury. The Society of Genealogists has a microfilm index of Carlisle Consistory Court wills.

Non-parochial Registers The registers of 24 chapels are at the Public Record Office (PRO), Chancery Lane, London. The IGI covers even more.

Census Returns Those for Cumberland are held by the PRO, Portugal Street, London, and the Workington Public Library.

Memorial Inscriptions A private collection of transcripts is available to members of the family history society. A few transcripts are in the library of the Society of Genealogists.

Heralds' Visitation Pedigrees have been printed for 1530 and 1615.

Cumbria A county formed in 1974 from Cumberland, Westmorland and part of Lancashire. *See also* under these county headings.

Curate Until the seventeenth century the term 'curate' was often synonymous with 'incumbent', but latterly it has applied almost exclusively to an assistant parish priest, paid a salary or stipend and removable by the incumbent or bishop. A Perpetual Curate is one in charge of a parish church where the tithes have been impropriated and there is no endowed vicarage. *See also* CHURCH OF ENGLAND HIERARCHY.

Curia Regis The King's Court. Originally the permanent royal judicial tribunal, but during the thirteenth century it gradually became divided into the separate courts of Common Pleas, King's Bench and Exchequer. At the Public Record Office, Chancery Lane, London, the records from the fifth year of Richard I to the fifty-sixth of Henry III are under reference KB.26. In order to establish their right as free subjects to plead, plaintiffs often submitted their pedigrees to the court.

Currer-Briggs Colonial Records Index
An index of emigrants to the southern colonies of America during the period 1560-1690. Compiled from unpublished sources in England and Virginia, it contains the names of almost 50,000 persons. Enquiries should be addressed to N. Currer-Briggs MA FSG, Les Chiseaux, Celles 24600, Riberac, Dordogne, France.

Curtilage A plot of land near a house, usually a vegetable garden.

Customary Tenure *see* **Copyhold**

Custumal One of the records of a manorial or monastic estate. Drawn up at fairly long intervals, it lists the customs guiding administrative procedures, and the rents payable.

Dame A form of address once customarily applied to the wives of baronets, knights and untitled gentlemen in positions of some authority, but sometimes to any elderly woman.

Danelaw That part of northern and central England once controlled by the Danes and, later, Norwegians, and in which Scandinavian laws, customs and to some extent language prevailed.

Dates *see* **Calendar** *and* **Regnal Years**

Daughter-in-law In old records this term is liable to mean what is now called a step-daughter. Also, a daughter-in-law is often referred to as 'daughter'.

Deacon A clerk in holy orders, but one below the status of priest. He was not qualified to perform marriages but could officiate as a private chaplain, as curate to a beneficed clergyman, or as lecturer to a parish church; and he could administer the wine to communicants.

Dean The senior dignitary of a cathedral or collegiate church, such as Westminster or Windsor. *See also* CHAPTER.

Death Certificate *see* **General Register of Births, Deaths and Marriages**

Decimation A 10 per cent tax on income from land, imposed on Royalists in 1655.

Decree The judgement of a court. A note in probate calendars 'by decree' or 'int. dec.' (interlocutory decree) indicates that contested proceedings came before the grant of probate. Alternatively referred to as Sentence.

Deed Poll A deed by one person, or by several having exactly the same interest, as distinct from one in which the interested persons are of the first and second (and more) parts. A deed poll would, for example, be used to change a surname.
The word 'poll' here means 'cut smooth', distinguishing this type of deed from that which needed to be indented.
See also INDENTURE.

Defaulter In a Manor Court Roll, an absentee from the court without excuse. Such a person would be fined.

Deforciant In a legal document, a defendant.

Delegates, Court of The ecclesiastical court of appeal from sentences pronounced by the Prerogative Courts of Canterbury and York. *See also* WILL.

Demesne Those parts of the land and rights of a manor that the lord retained for himself, as distinct from those used by his tenants. What might now be called the 'home-farm'. Ancient Demesne was a manor that had been in the king's hands at the death of Edward the Confessor.

Demise To convey by will or lease an estate either in Fee Simple (*see* FEE) or Fee Tail (*see* ENTAIL), or for a term of life or years. When applied to the crown of England it signifies its transmission to the next heir on the death of the sovereign. *See also* DEVISE.

Democracy Government by the common people. Until well into the nineteenth century, this word had the meaning of 'mob-rule'.

Demography, Historical The statistical study of population, population growth and movement, and the factors involved in them. The researches of historical demographers, especially the Cambridge Group for the History of Population and Social Structure, using parish registers and employing advanced techniques of analysis and interpretation, are beginning to throw fresh light on the ways of life of our forebears.

Denization The granting to an alien of some of the privileges of naturalization. The grant was made by Letters Patent instead of by a Private Act of Parliament, which was necessary for full citizenship.

A 'denizen' was allowed to buy and devise (grant by will) land, which was forbidden to aliens, but he could not inherit land and nor could any of his children born before denization; nor could he hold any office of trust or receive grants of land from the Crown. The records are at the Public Record Office, Chancery Lane, London (C.66, 67 and 54), and are open for inspection once they are one hundred years old. They usually show the immigrant's place of origin.

See also IMMIGRANTS.

Deodand A legal term for the instrument, animate or inanimate, that brought about a person's death.

Deponent One who makes a statement on oath in a court of law, or a written statement on oath (deposition), in connection with a legal case.

Derbyshire Derbyshire Family History Society holds regular meetings and issues branch news quarterly. Enquiries should be sent c/o The Federation of Family History Societies, 31 Seven Star Road, Solihull, West Midlands B91 2BZ, marked 'Please forward' and enclosing a stamped self-addressed envelope.

Record Repositories Derbyshire Record Office, County Offices, Matlock (tel: 0629.3411); Chesterfield Public Library, Corporation Street, Chesterfield.

Parish Registers and Indexes (*see* comment under COUNTY) Most of the ancient parishes have deposited their registers at the county record office (CRO). The Society of Genealogists has copies of many in its library. Boyd's Marriage Index covers nearly a third of the parishes. Pallot's Marriage Index covers 75, from 1790 to 1812 or 1837. Miss S. Brown, 25 Homecroft Drive, Packington Road, Ashby-de-la-Zouch, also has a marriage index. The INTERNATIONAL GENEALOGICAL INDEX (IGI) has a good coverage of baptisms; there is a copy at Lichfield Joint Record Office (*see* STAFFORDSHIRE), where the Bishops' Transcripts are also held.

Wills before 1858, proved in the following courts, are located as follows.

At Staffordshire and Lichfield Joint Record Office, Bird Street, Lichfield:
> Consistory Court of Lichfield
> Peculiar (Pec.) Court of the Dean and Chapter of Lichfield
> Pec. Court of Hartington
> Pec. Court of Peak Forest
> Pec. Court of Sawley

At Nottinghamshire Record Office:
> Manorial Court of Dale Abbey

As the county lay in the Province of Canterbury, wills could also be proved in the Prerogative Court of Canterbury.

Non-parochial Registers The registers of 63 chapels are at the Public Record Office (PRO), Chancery Lane, London. The IGI covers a similar number.

Census Returns These are at the PRO, Portugal Street, London, and at the County Library, Matlock, and the Central Library, Derby.

Memorial Inscriptions The family history society has transcripts from a number of churches, as also has the Society of Genealogists.

Heralds' Visitation Pedigrees have been printed for 1530 and 1615.

Derbyshire Record Society has made a number of historical records available in print.

Descend In connection with real property, this word meant 'to pass at death to the common law heir or heirs'.

Detecta Things of which people had been accused, or, in the language of the courts, for which they had been presented at an Ecclesiastical Visitation.

See also COMPERTA; PRESENTMENT.

Detinue, Writ of A writ issued for the recovery of a specific chattel, such as a plough or horse, wrongfully detained.

Devise To leave, by will, land as distinct from personal property. In the latter case, the term 'bequeath' is used. *See also* DEMISE.

Devon The Devon Family History Society holds monthly meetings and issues *The Devon Family Historian*. Enquiries should be sent c/o The Federation of Family History Societies, 31 Seven Star Road, Solihull, West Midlands B91 2BZ, marked 'Please forward' and enclosing a stamped self-addressed envelope.

Record Repositories Devon Record Office, Castle Street, Exeter, with West Country Studies Library adjacent (tel: 0392.79146); Devon County Library, Barley House, St Thomas, Exeter; Exeter City Library, Castle Street, Exeter; Exeter Cathedral Library, Bishop's Palace, Exeter; West Devon Area Record Office, Clare Place, Coxside, Plymouth.

Parish Registers and Indexes (*see* comment under COUNTY) Nearly all the ancient parishes have deposited their registers at either the county record office (CRO), Exeter City Library or West Devon Area Record Office. The Society of Genealogists has copies of over one hundred. Boyd's Marriage Index covers 169 parishes. Pallot's Marriage Index covers 26 parishes, from 1790 to 1812 or 1837. The INTERNATIONAL GENEALOGICAL INDEX (IGI) has a good coverage of baptisms, with copies at the Latter Day Saints Chapel, Plymouth, and at public libraries at Exeter, Plymouth, Torquay and Barnstaple. The Bishops' Transcripts are at the CRO, the West Devon Library in Plymouth, and the North Devon Library, Barnstaple.

Marriage Licence Records These are at the CRO. The Society of Genealogists has some indexes of Devon licences.

Wills before 1858, once deposited at the Probate Registry, Exeter, were destroyed by bombing in 1942, but some collections of abstracts have been copied and are available at the CRO, the

Devon County Library and Exeter City Library. Also, lists of wills had been previously published. Wills relating to tenements in the City of Exeter and proved in the Court of the Mayor of Exeter are at the Exeter City Library, and also an index of wills proved at Exeter.

Non-parochial Registers There are 112 of these at the Public Record Office (PRO), Chancery Lane, London. Most have been indexed in the IGI.

Census Returns These are at the PRO, Portugal Street, London, at the Plymouth Central Library and at the Exeter City Library.

Memorial Inscriptions The Society of Genealogists' library has transcripts of a few.

Heralds' Visitation Pedigrees have been printed for 1531, 1564 and 1620.

Hearth Tax Returns are on microfilm at the CRO.

Devon and Cornwall Record Society has made a number of historical records available in print.

Diary A number of diaries dating from the sixteenth century onward have been published, and are often to be found in the main public library of the county in which the diarist lived. They can reveal interesting local happenings and weather conditions useful to the family historian.

See also DOMESTIC CLUES.

Diem Clausit Extremum The Latin name for a writ ordering an inquiry into the lands held by a tenant-in-chief on the day he died.

Diocese The area of a bishop's jurisdiction. Before 1541-2 there were fourteen English dioceses, and thereafter, until the nineteenth century, eighteen, plus four for Wales. For administrative purposes a diocese might be divided into several archdeaconries (*see* ARCHDEACON), many of them having much the same boundaries as the counties within the diocese. Every diocese has a registry for its records. In many cases the registry and the county record office are now combined.

Diplomatic The science of documentary criticism involving, among other things, a knowledge of formally laid down procedure and forms of words.

Map showing dioceses (bounded by unbroken lines), and their relationship with the pre-1974 county boundaries (pecked lines). *Drawing by Peter Haillay*

Northumberland

Durham

Cumberland

Durham

Carlisle

Westmorland

Yorkshire

Isle of Man

Sodor and Man

West
land

Yorkshire

Chester

Lancashire

Anglesey

Caernarvon

Bangor
(Part)

Denbigh

Saint
Asaph

Merion.

Bang.

Chester

Cheshire

Derbyshire

York

York

Nottingham

Merioneth

Montgomery

Lichfield

Staffordshire

Leicestershire

Part of Lincoln

Norfolk

Shropshire

Rutland

Hereford

Northants

Peterborough

Hunts

Ely

Norwich

Cardigan

Radnor

Warwickshire

Worcester

Northants

Cambs

Suffolk

Pembroke

Herefordshire

Worcs

Beds

Saint Davids

Carmarthen

Brecknock

Bucks

Part of Lincoln

Herts

Glamorgan

Monmouth

Gloucester

Oxford

Herts

London

Essex

Llandaff

Glamorgan

Berks

Middx

Rochester

Salisbury

Kent

Winchester

Surrey

Kent

Canterbury

B

Wiltshire

Bath and Wells

Somerset

Hampshire

Chichester

Sussex

Part of Bristol
till 1836
Dorset

Devon

Exeter

Cornwall

Directories, Local The first local directories were published in the latter half of the seventeenth century, and were intended for business purposes. One that appeared in 1677 was called *A Collection of the Names of the Merchants living in and about the City of London: Very Usefull and Necessary*. During the eighteenth century the number of directories increased, but nearly all listed only commercial concerns. It was not until the early nineteenth century that private persons were regularly included. From that time onward they may provide the quickest means for finding out where a family lived, but not, unfortunately, in the case of all families.

Directories were compiled and issued at frequent intervals by private publishing concerns, sometimes by several in competition. The most famous are those by the firms of Pigot and Kelly, the latter being still in business today. The area covered by any particular volume varies greatly, from the whole of England and Wales to a single town. Most of them cover either a single county or a group of three or four contiguous counties. In these, each town and rural parish is dealt with in alphabetical order, with hamlets usually included under their parochial heading. There is normally a prefatory chapter on the history and geography of the area, and a list of people holding official positions. In a volume for a single city the inhabitants and businesses will then be listed in two sections — a Court Directory and a Commercial Directory — and sometimes also a Trades Directory and a Street Directory. The first gives names and private addresses of the gentry and more prosperous middle-class householders, the second gives the business addresses of professional and commercial people and firms. The Trades Directory groups these people under occupational headings, such as Bakers, Attorneys, etc., and the Street Directory includes private and business names under street headings. Thus the whole directory is liable to mention the same persons three or even four times. As the information supplied about any given person may not be the same in each section, it is worth searching them all.

Directories do not cover every household. Labourers were never included and only a small proportion of craftsmen — those usually in rural villages. Self-employed tradesmen appear in large numbers but are not necessarily all covered. In a town, the central shopping streets seem to be favoured at the expense of outlying areas, but the directory is not always to be relied on for the relative importance of the town's businesses. In villages, the squire, parson, farmers, graziers, innkeepers and blacksmiths are regularly included. It should be remembered that a directory is at least six months out of date on the day it is published.

The largest collections of old directories are those in London in the Guildhall Library, the Victoria and Albert Museum, and at the Society of Genealogists. A catalogue of the latter has been published. Another useful source of directory information is the firm of KELLY'S DIRECTORIES, which still publishes telephone directories and manufacturers' guides.

For further reading, see *A Guide to the National and Provincial Directories of England and Wales before 1856*, edited by Jane E. Norton (Royal Historical Society), and *A Bibliography of Trade Directories of the British Isles in the Victoria and Albert Museum*, by M.E. Keen (1979).

Disseisin Forcible eviction. Novel Disseisin was a claim in a court of law that the plaintiff had been recently dispossessed.

Dissolution of the Monasteries In March 1536 all monasteries with an annual income of less than £200 were dissolved by Act of Parliament, their inmates pensioned off, and their buildings and estates confiscated by the Crown. During the following four years the remaining, larger, monasteries and friaries were also dissolved. Many of their properties eventually passed into private hands.

Distressed Protestants in Ireland, Collection for Towards the end of 1641 the Catholic Irish rose against the Protestant English immigrants who had been forcibly intruded upon them. The English settlers fled in conditions of destitution. The winter was hard and probably destroyed more of the refugees than were killed by the Irish, but atrocity stories spread throughout England and in March 1641/2 King Charles approved an Act for raising, from every parish in the country, a total of £400,000 for their relief. The returns of the collections, arranged under parish headings, can be found at the Public Record Office (PRO), Chancery Lane, London, under references SP.28 and E.179. The contributors are all listed by name, with the sums they gave, and include many women, who are of course not named in the contemporaneous Protestation Oath Returns. As the latter do not survive for every parish, the records of the Collection supply a valuable supplementary location record for the period. A list of all surviving returns and their PRO class numbers has been published by the West Surrey Family History Society.

Distributor A name sometimes applied to the Overseer of the Poor or his assistant. It originated from his duty of giving out the proceeds of the Poor Rate for the support of the parish paupers.
See also COLLECTOR OF THE POOR.

Ditchsilver A payment by tenants towards the cost of clearing the ditches of the manor.

Divorce Separation of husband and wife *a mensa et toro* (from board and bed) could be granted by ecclesiastical courts, but from 1668 until 1857 full divorce *a vinculo matrimonii* (from the bands of matrimony) could only be effected by a Private Act of Parliament. It was therefore available only to those of ample means.

From 1669 onward the records of Divorce Bills are in the House of Lords Record Office, indexed in Part XIII of *The Index to Local and Personal Acts*, and accounts of the proceedings can be found in the published *Journals* of the House. The original records may also include those of any prior relevant proceedings in an ecclesiastical or civil court. Records of later divorces are kept at the Divorce Registry of the Family Division of the High Court, at Somerset House, Strand, London. Application may be made by post or in person at Room G.44. Details, if known, of the husband, wife, co-respondent and approximate date must be given on a form supplied, and a search fee paid. The search is made by the Registry staff during the next few days. If successful, the enquirer receives, for a further fee, a 'Certificate of Making Decree Nisi Absolute (Divorce)'. For postal applications, the address is: Divorce Registry, Somerset House, Strand, London WC2R 1LP.

Petitions for divorce, once they are one hundred years old, can be found at the Public Record Office, Chancery Lane, London, among the records of the Supreme Court of Judicature in class J.77.
See also ARCHES, COURT OF.

Doctors, Medical In the sixteenth century, licences to practice medicine were granted by diocesan bishops and can be traced in the records of their courts. Then and much later, no professional qualifications were required.

In 1518 the London College of Physicians, now the Royal College of Physicians of London, was founded by Thomas Linacre and granted the power to supervise the practice of 'physic' within seven miles of the capital. Its members were freed from social obligations that might interfere with their work, such as serving on juries, acting as constables, keeping watch (*see* WATCH AND WARD), and militia duties.

Later many medical men became graduates in medicine and can be found in the registers of the universities of Oxford and Cambridge. In 1845 the unofficial *Medical Directory* began to appear, and the official *Medical Register* has been published since 1858. Besides giving details of the living, it also provides obituaries of doctors recently deceased. Biographies of the Fellows of the Royal College since 1518 have been compiled by Dr William Munk in four volumes, the last posthumously, under the title *Munk's Roll of Physicians*. Some Vestry Minute Books give the names of doctors contracted to attend the parish poor.
See also APOTHECARIES; PHYSICIANS; SURGEONS.

Doe, John *see* **Roe, Richard**

Dole (i) A charitable donation.
(ii) A share in the common arable fields and/or meadow, distributed afresh periodically

RIGHT A document relating to the Collection for Distressed Protestants in Ireland, made in the spring of 1641/2. The parochial lists of this collection tend to reveal more than the Lay Subsidy and Protestation Oath Lists of the same period, because the names of many married women are shown on them. *Crown copyright: SP.24/194 (pt II)*

St: Margarets:

Monies contributed and collected out of the parish
of St Margarits in Norwich, towards the releife
of our afflicted bretherin in Ireland:

Mr Samuel Dobson:	ten shillings
Mres Newson	ten shillings
Mr Tho: Bigg	five shillings.
Mres Bigg.	three shillings.
Will Hardingam. sen:	seuen shillings
Will: Brooks	ten shillings
Joseph Brooke	sixe shillings
Daniel Winter	sixe shillings
Edward Boote	foure shillings
The wife of Edward Boote	One shillinge
Richard Howse	seuen shillings
Ambrose Norris	fiue shillings
Edward Beuis	fiue shillings.
Edmund Newman	fiue shillings.
William Lawes	foure shillings
Nic: Swetman	three shillings
Goodwife Swetman	One shillinge
John Goodings	three shillings.
Will: Hardingham. iun:	two shillings
Anne Dubery	two shillings ———— Six pence
William Shetringe	two shillings ———— Six pence
John Nobbs	One shillinge
Edm: Turner	One shillinge
Will: Linstead	One shillinge
Rich: Lathe	One shillinge ———— Six pence
Tobit Holfer	One shillinge
Will: Hargraue	One shillings
Mathew Guiton	One shillinge: ———— Sixe pence
John Danny	———— Sixe pence
Jane Danny	———— Sixe pence
John Eckleston	One shillingo.
Jeremiah Brooke	One shillinge.
Hen: Blanch	One shillinge.
John Webster	———— Seuen pence
Peregrine Ransome	———— Sixe pence
Robt: Browne	———— Six pence
Edward Caruer	———— Six pence
Rachel Burman	———— Six pence
Will: Curtesse	———— Six pence
Simond Coo	———— Six pence
John Lampkin	———— Six pence
William Horne	———— Six pence
Henry Palmer.	———— Six pence
wid Lane	

in some manors, either by lot or rotation. Also called Lot-meadow.

Domesday Book A two-volume report of a survey of land holdings made in 1086 at the order of William the Conqueror. One volume deals with Essex, Norfolk and Suffolk, and the other with the rest of England except for Northumberland, Durham, Cumberland, northern Westmorland, Winchester and London, which are omitted. The information was compiled by Royal Commission, and every hundred court appointed four Norman and four English members to co-operate by giving sworn answers to their inquiries. The result was later checked by a second commission.

The report is arranged county by county, and under the headings of the tenants-in-chief in each county. These tenants and their sub-tenants, both at the time of the survey and those at the Conquest, are the only persons named, the rest of the householders merely being numbered class by class, as villeins, cottars, slaves, freemen and sokemen; and in spite of an impression cherished by many families, the only buildings mentioned are churches and mills. The bulk of the report is taken up by the extents of arable, meadow, pasture and woodland, and the number of plough-teams estimated as necessary and actually in use. The first volume of the *Victoria County History* for each county deals with the Domesday returns, and separate Domesday volumes for each county are now being published.

Domestic Clues At the very beginning of research into the family past, much time and expense can sometimes be saved by making sure that no clues have been overlooked that may be lying about the house. The best known of these is the Family Bible, in which births, marriages and deaths in the family may have been recorded by a Victorian paterfamilias. Lucky is the family in which such a volume has been handed down.

Other family relics provide useful clues rather than ready-made additions to the family tree. Old letters will show, either from their headings or from their postmarks, where people lived, which will be a pointer for future research; and they probably contain interesting information

about the family, otherwise they would not have been kept. Old diaries can be a mine of information about the family's life-style, as can newspaper cuttings, although unfortunately in too many cases the name of the newspaper and its date will not have been preserved. Other indications of where members of the family lived can be found in visitors' books and address books. Certificates of qualification tend to be among the documents preserved after the death of a professional man.

Dates of birth and marriage are among the most important items of information to be discovered for every member of the family. Birthday Books, once a popular means of remembering people's anniversaries, usually show the day and month, but not the year of birth; but in a search of the indexes of the General Register of Births a birthday date can be useful in picking out the right person from a number of namesakes born in, or about, the same year.

Books received as prizes will have inscriptions showing the boy's or girl's school or college, the subject of study and the date. This can lead the researcher to school attendance records or printed registers, or, failing any of these, enable him to write to the present Head Teacher for further information about the former pupil, which may well include his parentage. Inscriptions in books given as Christmas or birthday presents may reveal unknown uncles and aunts, but it must be remembered that 'uncle' and 'auntie' are terms often loosely used. A Bookplate often shows only a name, but if it is heraldic the clue of the arms can be followed up (*see* ARMS, COAT OF).

Cap badges and metal buttons bearing insignia are clues to members of the family in the army or navy, or other uniformed services. Service medals, often for individual campaigns and bearing clasps for battles, are helpful for narrowing down the field within which a man's regiment and battalion may be identified (*see* MEDALS). Decorations for bravery or distinguished service are also useful for this purpose, and some provide an indication of whether or not the recipient held commissioned rank. An old uniform would, of course, show the exact rank its owner held, probably at the end of his service career.

Among the family records most likely to be treasured and passed down are photographic portraits. Too often these bear no name and so in a generation or two become difficult to identify, but comparing several photographs can be a help. Nineteenth-century photographs will usually have been taken by a professional whose name and address will appear either below the picture or on the back. Reference to old local directories to find the period during which the practitioner was in business at that address may enable the photograph to be dated approximately (*see* DIRECTORIES, LOCAL). The photographer's address may also give some indication of the district in which the sitter lived, but photographers at holiday resorts tended to draw their customers from a wide catchment area. The clothes of the sitter are another clue. The *Handbook of English Costume in the 19th Century* by C.W. and P. Cunnington, lavishly illustrated, shows how the fashions changed from year to year for both men and women. The apparent age of the sitter acts as another check on the dates deduced from other evidence.

Doncaster Society for Family History *see* **Yorkshire**

Doom A judgement delivered by a court.

Doomsman A member of the jury of a manorial court, who were also known collectively as the Homage.

Dormant Funds This term is applied to sums of money usually belonging either to people who died intestate and for whom no next-of-kin could be found, or to testators whose legatees could not be traced after advertisement in the national press had produced no claimants, and which have since lain undealt with for fifteen years. The funds are now in the custody of the Supreme Court of England and Wales.

Until 1938, lists of sums of £50 or more were published every five years as supplements to the *London Gazette*. Since 1954, lists have been published annually. All such lists can be perused, free of charge, in Room 60, Court Funds Office, Eastern Corridor, Ground Floor, at the Royal Courts of Justice in the Strand, London, and for the period since 1893, at the Public Record Office, Chancery Lane, London. Information about the sums shown may be supplied by the Accountant General in response to a written request from a person believed to be beneficially interested, after advance payment of the fee laid down. Such applications, enclosing evidence of the beneficial interest, but not original documents, should be addressed to The Principal, Court Funds Office, Royal Courts of Justice, The Strand, London WC2A 2LL. The majority of such sums is of less than £150, and so not worth the expense of claiming.

Dormant Peerage One for which, on the death of the holder, no heir can be traced, although it is likely that a potential claimant is living. Not to be confused with a peerage in ABEYANCE.

Dorse The reverse side of a sheet of paper or parchment. Anything written on it was called an Endorsement.

Dorset Since 1974 the Bournemouth area has been included in the county. The Somerset and Dorset Family History Society holds regular meetings and issues a journal, *The Greenwood Tree*. Enquiries should be sent c/o The Federation of Family History Societies, 31 Seven Star Road, Solihull, West Midlands B91 2BZ, marked 'Please forward' and enclosing a stamped self-addressed envelope.

Record Repositories Dorset Record Office, County Hall, Dorchester, Dorset (tel: 0305.63131); County Library, Colliton Park, Dorchester; Town Hall, Dorchester; Town Hall, Shaftesbury.

Parish Registers and Indexes (*see* comment under COUNTY) Registers of most parishes are at the county record office (CRO). The Society of Genealogists has a number of copies. Boyd's Marriage Index includes a number of parishes in its Miscellaneous Series. Pallot's Marriage Index covers 74 parishes, 1790-1812. The family history society (FHS) has another marriage index in progress. The INTERNATIONAL GENEALOGICAL INDEX (IGI), of which the FHS has a copy, covers many baptisms. The Bishops' Transcripts from 1731 are at the Wiltshire CRO.

Marriage Licence Records These are at the Wiltshire CRO.

Wills before 1858, proved in the following courts, are located as follows.

At the CRO:
>   Consistory Court of Bristol (Dorset Division)
>   Archdeaconry Court of Dorset
>   Peculiar (Pec.) Court of Corfe Castle
>   Pec. Court of Great Canford and Poole
>   Pec. Court of Milton Abbas
>   Pec. Court of Sturminster Marshall
>   Pec. Court of Wimborne Minster
>   Manor and Liberty Court of Frampton

At the Wiltshire CRO:
>   Prebendal Courts of Fordington and Writhlington; Lyme Regis and Halstock; Netherbury in Ecclesia; Preston and Sutton Poyntz; Yetminster and Grimston.
>   Royal Pec. Court of Gillingham
>   Pec. Court of the Dean of Sarum
>   Pec. Court of the Dean and Chapter of Sarum

The county lay in the Diocese of Salisbury (Sarum) until 1542, in the Diocese of Bristol from then until 1836, and then again in Sarum. The county was always in the Province of Canterbury, so wills could be proved in the Consistory Courts of those dioceses and in the Prerogative Court of Canterbury. The Society of Genealogists has some will indexes.

Non-parochial Registers There are 40 at the Public Record Office (PRO), Chancery Lane, London, and the IGI includes a larger number.

Census Returns These are at the PRO, Portugal Street, London, and at the County Library, Dorchester.

Memorial Inscriptions The Society of Genealogists has transcripts from a number of churches, and the FHS is transcribing at burial grounds in danger of clearance.

Heralds' Visitation Pedigrees have been printed for 1531 and 1623.

Dorset Record Society has made many historical records available in print.

Dower The portion to which a widow was entitled of the estate of her late husband for her sustenance and the education of their children. By Common Law it was fixed at one-third, but this could be over-ruled by the customary law of the manor (or other area) to one-quarter or one-half, or his whole estate. In connection with copyhold property, the last-mentioned right was called Freebench. Dower is also used of a daughter's portion of inheritance.

Dower (Latin *dotarium*) is not to be confused with DOWRY.

Dowry was the property in land or money that a wife brought to her husband at their marriage. This may have been given her by her father, or it may have been property already in her possession by inheritance.

Dowry (Latin *maritagium*) is not to be confused with DOWER.

Dozener (i) A borough official elected by the householders of a ward or street to make presentments at the Court Leet or Wardmote.

(ii) A juryman.

Drop-line Pedigree *see* **Family Tree**

Duke The first English dukedom was that of Cornwall, created in 1337 by Edward III for his son, the Black Prince. It took precedence over all earldoms, hitherto the highest rank of English nobility. Before that date, the kings of England alone had been dukes, but even then only of their possessions in France, i.e. of Normandy and Acquitane. The first non-royal duke was Sir William de la Pole, K.G., Marquess of Suffolk, created Duke of Suffolk in 1448.

The wife of a duke is a duchess. Their eldest son normally takes, by courtesy, his father's second title (usually either Marquess or Earl), and the younger sons and the daughters are styled, also by courtesy, Lord and Lady before their Christian names.

Durham The southeast corner of the county is now in the county of Cleveland, and the northwest in Tyne and Wear. The Northumberland and Durham Family History Society and the Cleveland Family History Society hold regular meetings and issue journals. Enquiries should be sent c/o The Federation of Family History Societies, 31 Seven Star Road, Solihull, West Midlands B91 2BZ, marked 'Please forward' and enclosing a stamped self-addressed envelope.

Record Repositories Durham County Record Office, County Hall, Durham (tel: 0385.64411); Priors Kitchen, The College, Durham (tel: 0385.64561); Department of Palaeography and Diplomatic, University of Durham, South Road, Durham; Durham Cathedral Library, The College, Durham; University Library, Palace Green, Durham; Gateshead Central Library, Prince Consort Road, Gateshead.

Parish Registers and Indexes (*see* comment under COUNTY) Registers of many parishes have been deposited, nearly all at the county record office (CRO). The Society of Genealogists has a number of copies. Volume 11 of the *National Index of Parish Registers* deals with County Durham. Boyd's Marriage Index covers 72 parishes. Pallot's Marriage Index covers 21, from 1790 to 1812. There are also the following marriage indexes: Northwest Durham, by G. Nicholson, 57 Manor Road, Concord, Washington, County Durham; Northeast Durham, by W.E. Raunce, 40 Salcombe Avenue, Jarrow, Tyne and Wear; South and Southwest Durham, by R. Joiner, Greystones, The Spittal, Yarm, Cleveland. The INTERNATIONAL GENEA-LOGICAL INDEX (IGI) has a fair coverage of baptisms. The Bishops' Transcripts are at the Department of Palaeography and Diplomatic, University of Durham.

Marriage Licence Records These are at the Department of Palaeography and Diplomatic, University of Durham.

Wills before 1858, proved in the following courts, are located as shown.

At the Department of Palaeography and Diplomatic:

    Palatine and Consistory Court of Durham
    Episcopal and Chancery Courts of York (for some clergy)

The county lay in the Province of York, so wills could also be proved in the Prerogative Courts of both York and Canterbury. The Society of Genealogists has an index of wills.

Non-parochial Registers There are 54 registers at the Public Record Office (PRO), Chancery Lane, London, and the IGI covers these.

Census Returns These are at the PRO, Portugal Street, London, and at the CRO.

Memorial Inscriptions There are a few transcripts in the Society of Genealogists' library.

Heralds' Visitation Pedigrees have been printed for 1575, 1615 and 1666.

Durham and Northumberland Parish Register Society has published a number of registers. The *Surtees Society* has published the Protestation Oath Returns and other records.

E

Earl Under the last pre-Conquest kings, earls were the highest rank of nobility and also the king's officials over wide provinces. They presided over the shire courts and commanded the FYRD. As the rank became hereditary and the work increased, the authority in each county passed to the sheriff, and an earldom became merely a title. After the Conquest, the titles first of Duke and later of Marquess were introduced as ranks taking precedence over that of Earl. The wife of an earl is a Countess, and, except for formal purposes, an earl and countess are referred to as Lord and Lady (So-and-so). Their eldest son takes, by courtesy, his father's second title (usually that of Viscount or Baron). The younger sons are styled Honourable (Mr, in conversation), and the daughters Lady before their Christian name.

East India Company The East India Company was incorporated by Queen Elizabeth I on 31 December, 1600. It became a joint stock company and established a number of factories (trading stations) on the mainland of India, in the Spice Islands and elsewhere in the East. The Company's earliest major factory was at Surat in northwest India, followed soon after by one at Madras, called Fort St George. When Charles II married a Portuguese princess in 1662, she brought him the Portuguese-occupied island of Bombay as part of her dowry, and he leased it to the Company. In the latter part of the seventeenth century, the stockholders and, indeed, the factors became so wealthy that their monopoly was resented by English merchants, and after an appeal to the House of Commons the formation of a second company was allowed. However, rivalry between the two sets of factors in the East did both organisations so much harm that they were glad to amalgamate, in 1708, as The United Company of Merchants of England Trading to the East Indies.

During the period of rivalry, the Old Company had acquired by treaty a site on the Hooghly River on which they built Fort William, close to the village of Calcutta. The United Company's territories became organised in three 'presidencies': Bengal (administered from Fort William), Madras (Fort St George), and Bombay, each headquarters having authority over a number of satellite factories. For a time, Bencoolen (Fort Marlborough) in Sumatra was the headquarters of a separate presidency.

In the mid eighteenth century, the Company established a permanent factory at Canton in China, in order to engage in the growing tea trade, and this station became one of the most lucrative. By this time, the French were the Company's chief rivals in India. Both enlisted the influence of Indian rulers and this led to open warfare between them, in which the British were finally successful.

The safeguarding of their interests led the Company to acquire more and more Indian territory, in spite of protests from their directors in London. This led, in 1773, to the intervention of the British Government. The Company's Bengal Governor was appointed Governor-General of all its Indian lands, with succession confined to Government-approved nominees. In 1784 William Pitt created a Board of Control to supervise the Company. In 1857 came the sepoy rising, known as the Indian Mutiny, and on its suppression the Company was taken over by the Crown. India was thenceforward ruled by a British Viceroy in conjunction with the newly created India Office in London.

Many middle-class families have had members in the East India Company, and probably more than one, because service with 'John Company' was considered the high-road to a fortune, and entry depended largely on inside influence. Many families served the Company for three or four generations.

The Company's records are a uniquely rich source of biographical material. They comprise those created by the London Head Office, those of the factories in Asia, those of the Company's armed forces, and the log-books and other records of the Company's merchant ships. The records include returns of baptisms, marriages and burials in India from the end of the seventeenth century; and there are also, from 1803, annual printed *India Lists* giving names of all Company servants. These records now constitute the India Office Library and Records, and are housed at Orbit House, Blackfriars Bridge Road, London SE1, where they are open to public inspection. The Office has issued a useful 53-page *Brief Guide to Biographical Sources*, by Ian A. Baxter.

Ecclesiastical Courts Under the Norman kings, separate courts were created for the hearing of judicial cases under Canon Law. They were on two levels — the Bishops' Courts and the Archdeacons' Courts — and their records survive from the fifteenth century. They dealt with such matters as heresy (bishops only), attendance at church, behaviour in church and in the churchyard, the conduct of the parson and church officials, the state of the church building and its furniture, payment of parish dues, betrothal, marriage, immorality, slander, wills, parish boundaries, usury and perjury. So many of the cases were about fornication and adultery that the court became known in some places as the 'Bawdy Court'. The cases arose very largely from presentments made at the Archdeacon's or Bishop's Visitations (*see* ECCLESIASTICAL VISITATIONS).

Archdeacons' Courts were held at about three-weekly intervals in some central or important town; more frequently if necessary. The court often occupied the west end of one of the aisles of the church. Either the Archdeacon himself or his Official Principal presided as judge. There was no jury.

An Apparitor served a citation on the accused to appear at the court. The case might be of two kinds, either an Office Cause or a Cause of Instance. The former was brought by the Office of the Judge against the defendant, but the Office might be prompted thereto by another party. The latter type was brought by one private person against another.

Many of the Office Causes could be dealt with simply. If the accused pleaded 'Guilty' the judge proceeded at once to sentence, if 'Not Guilty' the accused was examined under oath and witnesses made their depositions. The judge then ordered the accused to purge himself, which meant that he was given the chance to find a certain number of neighbours (usually about six) to be his compurgators and swear to his innocence. If he did this, the case was dismissed. If not, the judge sentenced the accused. The punishment of the guilty was normally by penance, which up to the sixteenth century might be accompanied by castigation and fines, although sometimes penance was commuted to a fine. Penances could be private (i.e. performed before only the parson and churchwardens), or public. Serious offences could be punished by excommunication, as could failure to appear in answer to a citation (this offence was 'Contumacy'). Excommunication was performed by sending a Letter of Excommunication to the accused's parish, to be read aloud in service at church.

Causes of Instance always involved a more formal procedure, beginning with the appointment of Proctors by both sides to represent them in court. The following documents record the successive stages of the cause, always carried on under oath: *Libel of Articles*, the case for the prosecution; *Responsions*, the reply made by the defence (the 'respondent'); *Attestations* (or Depositions), the witnesses for the prosecution; and *Interrogatories*, the questioning of the witnesses by the defence. In the next stage, the defence normally made its case and the same four stages were proceeded with by the opposite side. Sometimes, however, instead of making a case for itself, the defence attacked the credibility of the prosecution witnesses in *Articles of Exception*, which could give rise to another series of *Responsions*, and so on. In the end the judge gave his sentence, and also a Bill of Taxed Costs.

After the close of the court, often considerably later, the judge's registrar wrote a description of the case in his Act Book (or Court Book). Except for the names of the parties, these contain little of interest, sometimes not even the charge against the defendant. Of Office Causes, the record is often in a separate Corrections Book, but sometimes the two types of case are in the same volume. Non-judicial administrative business of the court is entered in separate volumes, such as those for faculties, marriage licences, probate records and inventories. Though in all the above-mentioned records the narrative is in Latin, any words spoken are given in English.

For genealogists the most valuable of these records are the *Attestations* (Depositions). Each begins with an account of the witness himself, his name, sex, condition, occupation, age, length of abode in the place about which he is giving evidence, where he now lives if different, and where he lived previously, right back to his birthplace. It has been reckoned that about 7 per cent of the population were deponents at one time or another.

The records are kept in the Diocesan Registries, which today may be incorporated in the county record office. Where the records are indexed, it is usually only under the names of the parties. Many Act Books are highly abbreviated notes in a technical scribble. The clerks would enter the headings of the cases first, allowing four entries to a page, and then fill in the business at a later date. For some entries the space is not enough, leading to cramped writing and sometimes even to the finishing of an entry in some blank space several folios away, accompanied by cross-reference marks. The reduced volume of business during the Civil War ended this practice.

For further reading, see *Shakespeare and the Bawdy Court of Stratford*, by E.R.C. Brinkworth.

Ecclesiastical Visitations Archdeacons were supposed to visit their archdeaconries once a year, and bishops their dioceses every three years. The Visitor would send out a Citation Mandate to all incumbents, who read it out in church, calling upon them and the church officials to appear before him at a date and place named. The latter would be a church either in a central position or in the most important town. At about the same time he would issue his Visitation Articles, listing the subjects into which he wished to enquire. These would include the church, the living, the clergy, hospitals, the parish, the parishioners and the ecclesiastical officers. All those people summoned would be required to obtain a copy of the Articles beforehand.

The Archdeacon arrived with his Registrar, bringing his Call Book and Fees Book to record attendances, absences and fees collected. The visited included the clergy, churchwardens, parish clerks, schoolmasters, surgeons and midwives, unless excused. The clergy brought their Letters of Orders proving their right to their cures (spiritual charges), with dispensations when they held more than one living. The parish clerks, schoolmasters, surgeons and midwives brought their licences. The clergy and churchwardens had certain fees to pay.

The clergy and churchwardens then handed in their presentments, reporting on the conduct of their parishioners since the last Visitation and answering the points in the Visitation Articles. Executors and administrators of people who had lately died were also required to come and prove the wills, or take administration, a function that at other times was performed at the relevant ecclesiastical court. The presentments were discussed and some verdicts given on the spot; the Visitation ended with the Archdeacon's Charge, an address delivered during a service in the church.

After the Visitation, the Archdeacon issued, through his Registrar's office, a number of Injunctions setting out in detail, in numbered paragraphs, his orders for the amendment of any faults revealed. Among these were penances imposed, together with a certificate to be signed by the incumbent and a church-warden that the penance had been performed. After the mid sixteenth century, the penance was normally just a Declaration Penance, which was a confession to be read publicly, usually in church, reciting the offence and expressing penitence. Sometimes the incumbent or churchwardens would give a certificate that the offender was of a sufficiently good general character — or perhaps social standing — to be allowed to perform his penance privately.

Other documents kept by the Registrar for permanent reference included the DETECTA and COMPERTA volumes, containing copies of all the presentments with a few brief additional notes; copies of Citation Mandates, summoning the more serious offenders to appear before the Archdeacon's Court; and the Act Book, recording the action taken against them there. This last overlaps the records of the court.

Exhibitions list the licences and other documents produced in court.

Though visitations began in the tenth century, the records are only numerous from the reign of Elizabeth I. Bishops' three-yearly visitations are similar to those of Archdeacons, but less numerous. The presentments are usually written in English and the originals sometimes survive on single sheets of paper. They are full of human interest, naming and reporting on the most important parish functionaries. People who neglected or refused to receive Holy Communion (Recusants) were presented; they might be Protestant nonconformists or Roman Catholics. The state of the church might also be given in some detail, mentioning any 'popish monuments of superstition' such as candlesticks, a crucifix, handbells or banner cloths. Rogation-tide perambulations of the parish are sometimes mentioned, with the boundaries described. Non-payment of tithe is always mentioned. The morals of the parishioners form the largest subject of the presentments. Not even the parson was exempt from presentment.

Eftsoons A second time.

Electioner A person qualified for election to a parochial office by virtue of his holding in the parish.

Electoral Register The *Reform Act* of 1832 greatly enlarged the county franchise. As a consequence, it required the parochial regis-tration of every person qualified to vote, and the publication of such registers. The entries show the name and abode of each elector, the property (owned or leased) that qualified him to vote, and its name and situation in the locality. Later volumes give the voters' addresses in fuller detail, including the house names or numbers. County Electoral Registers are to be found at county record offices.

Emigrants Emigration proper, the permanent settling of English men and women in communities overseas, began in the sixteenth century and has continued ever since. The causes have always been various: religion, politics, transportation for crime, service indenture, escape from poverty, and enterprise in search of prosperity. The chief destinations of large-scale emigration were, in roughly chronological order of their commencement, North America, the West Indies, Australia, South Africa, New Zealand and East and Central Africa. This excludes consideration of those who went abroad, for example to India, in pursuit of a career but with the intention of returning to the mother country on retirement.

Emigration to America and the West Indies

The following passenger lists and related records have been published:

Destination and date	Title	Editor
N. America 1538-1825	*A Bibliography of Ship Passenger Lists*	H. Lancour & Wolfe (1963
America 1600-1700	*The Original Lists of Persons Emigrating to America*	J.C. Hotten (1880, 1968)
America 1607-1657	*Founders of Early American Families*	Meredith B.
Plymouth 1620-3	*The English Ancestry of the Pilgrim Fathers*	Colket (1975) C.E. Banks, (1929, 1968)
Boston & Bay Colony 1620-40	*The Planters of the Commonwealth*	C.E. Banks, (1967)
New England 1620-50	*Topographical Dictionary of 3885 English Emigrants*	C.E. Banks, (1937, 1963)
New England 1623-50	*Ancestral Roots of 60 Colonists who came to New England, 1623-50*	Weis
New England 1630	*The Winthrop Fleet*	C.E. Banks, (1930, 1968)
Maryland 1633-80	*The Early Settlers*	G. Skordas, (1968)
America 1635-7	*Two Early Passenger Lists*	E. Putnam, (1964)
New England 1637-9	*Three Registers of Passengers from Gt Yarmouth to Holland to New England*	C.B. Jewson, (1964), Norfolk Record Society 25
America 1654-85	*Record of the First Settlers in N. America*	R. Hargreaves -Mawdsley (1929, 1931, 1967)
Pennsylvania prior to 1684	*Penn's Colony: Passengers and Ships*	W.L. Shepherd Jr. (1970)
America 1683-96	*Some Early Emigrants to America*	C.D.P. Nicholson (1965) *The Genealogists' Magazine*, Vol.12
America 1682-92	*List of Emigrants to America*	J. Wareing, M. Ghirelli (1968)
America 1683-4	*Some Early Emigrants to America*	J. Wareing *The Genealogists' Magazine*, Vol. 18, No.5
America 1690-1811	*List of Emigrant Ministers*	G.G. Fothergill (1904, 1965)
New England before May 1962	*Genealogical Dictionary of the First Settlers*	J. Savage (1860-62, 1969)
America 1697-1707	*List of Emigrants to America from Liverpool*	Elizabeth French (1913, 1969)
New England 1700-75	*Immigrants to New England*	Ethel S. Bolton (1967)
America 1718-59	*List of Emigrants*	J. & M. Kaminkow (1964)
America & W. Indies 17272-31	*Agreements to Serve in America and the West Indies*	D. Galenson *The Genealogists' Magazine*, Vol. 19, No.2
America before 1750	*Immigrant Ancestors*	F.A. Virkus (1963) *Compendium of American Genealogy*
Virginia in the Colonial Period	*Some Emigrants*	W.C. Stanard (1915, 1964)
America 1773-6	*Emigrants from England*	G. Fothergill (1913, 1964)

North Caro-lina 1774-5	Records of Emigrants from England & Scotland	A.R. Newsome (1963)
Connec-ticut	Catalogue of the First Puritan Settlers	R.R. Hinman (1846, 1968)
America	Early Emigrants from Liverpool	R. Sharpe France 1965, & Genealogist's Magazine 12 & 13
Georgia	List of the Early Settlers	E.M. & A.B. Saye 1949, 1967
Mass. Nantucket	Early Settlers	L.S. Hinchman (1934)
America	Bonded Passengers to America	Gen. Publ. Co. Inc., Baltimore (3 Vols.)
Mississippi, Natchez District	Early Inhabitants	N.E. Gillis (1963)
Missouri, Cape Girar-deau Country	A Belated Census	W.J. Gammon (1958) National Genealogical Society Quarterly (1967)
America 1819-20	Passenger Arrivals, Letter —, from Secretary of State	
Cali-fornia	San Francisco Ship Passenger Lists,	L.J. Rasmus-sen (1965)
USA & Canada 17-19th Centuries	Passenger Immigration Lists Index and Supplement	P.W. Filby & M.K. Meyer (1981, 1982)

Primary evidence can be obtained from the Colonial Office records at the Public Record Office (PRO), Kew. *Colonial Papers, General Series* (CO.1) relate to the period down to 1688. *Board of Trade Minutes* (CO.391) cover later years. Both are indexed in the 38 published volumes of *Calendar of State Papers; Colonial, America and West Indies*, covering 1574-1737. From then until 1782, there are the fourteen indexed volumes of the *Journals of the Commissions for Trade and Plantations*. Another Colonial Office source is *America and West Indies Original Correspondence* (CO.5), with separate classes (grouped under the names of the colonies) for *Original Correspondence, Entry Books, Acts, Sessional Papers, Miscellanea*, etc. These are described in PRO *Lists and Indexes*, Vol.36.

Privy Council records at the PRO contain petitions and letters of people going to America, which have been printed for the period 1613-1783, in *Acts of the Privy Council of England*, Vols.1-5. The Exchequer records have Licences to Pass Beyond the Seas, listing those licences issued to travellers to New England, Maryland, Virginia and Barbados in the period 1634-77. Treasury Records (T.47), Vols 9-11, give details of emigrants during the period 1773-6, for which there is a card index. The information includes name, age, occupation, reason for emigration, last abode, date of departure and destination. The Poor Law Union Papers (MH.12) at the PRO list parish-assisted emigrants from 1834 onward. The Guildhall Library, London, has memoranda of indentured servants sent to the West in the period 1718-60. Mr F. Leeson, FSG, of 108 Sea Lane, Ferring, Sussex BN12 5HB, has a name index to nearly one hundred published and unpublished sources for emigrants to America, Canada and the West Indies, 1600-1850. (*See also* CURRER-BRIGGS COLONIAL RECORDS INDEX).

Emigration to the Cape Colony Emigrants to South Africa, 1814-25, can be found in *Cape Colony Correspondence* (CO.48). There are also Entry Books (CO.49) from 1795, and Registers (CO.336 and 462). Descriptions of these records can be found in PRO *Lists and Indexes*, Vol.36.

Emigrants to Australia For settler emigrants to New South Wales, *Original Correspondence* (CO.201) has lists for 1801-21. Correspondence for 1823-33 has been indexed. CO.384 contains many letters from settlers or intending settlers, from 1817 onward, and Entry Books (CO.385) start in 1814. Also useful are Land and Emigration Commission Papers, 1833-94 (CO.386), Colonies General, Original Corres-pondence (CO.323) and Entry Books (CO.324 and 381). (*See also* TRANSPORTED CONVICTS). Dr M. Watts, of 77 Church Lane, Lowton,

Warrington, Lancashire, is compiling an index of emigrants to Australia and New Zealand.

Emigrants to Tasmania Free immigrants from Britain have been calendared in *Records Relating to Free Immigration* (Tasmanian Archives Office).

A free leaflet, *Emigrants, Documents in the Public Record Office*, is available at the PRO.

For further reading, see *Tracing Your Ancestors in the PRO*, by J. Cox and T. Padfield (HMSO, 1983).

The descendants of emigrants are usually interested in their British ancestry, so contact with them may well be possible through one or more of the following overseas family history societies:

Australia

Australian Institute of Genealogical Studies, P.O. Box 68, Oakleigh, Victoria 3166

Society of Australian Genealogists, Richmond Villa, 120 Kent Street, Observatory Hill, Sydney, NSW 2000

Heraldry and Genealogy Society of Canberra, G.P.O. Box 585, Canberra, ACT 2601

Genealogical Society of Northern Territory, P.O. Box 37212, Winnellie, Northern Territory 5789

Queensland Family History Society, P.O. Box 171, Indooroopilly, Brisbane 4068

Genealogical Society of Queensland, 2nd Floor, 329 Logan Road, Stones Corner, Queensland 4120

Genealogical Society of Victoria, Room 1, 1st Floor, Block Arcade, 98 Elizabeth Street, Melbourne, Victoria 3000

South Australian Genealogical and Heraldry Society, P.O. Box 13, Marden, South Australia 5070

Western Australia Genealogical Society, P.O. Box 7, West Perth, Western Australia 6005

Nepean Family History Society, 1 Napier Avenue, Emu Plains, NSW 2750

Genealogical Society of Tasmania, P.O. Box 6406, Hobart, Tasmania 7001

Canada

Alberta Genealogical Society, P.O. Box 12015, Edmonton, Alberta T5J 3L2

British Columbia Genealogical Society, P.O. Box 94371, Richmond, British Columbia V6Y 2A8

Manitoba Genealogical Society, P.O. Box 2066, Winnipeg, Manitoba R3C 3R4

Genealogical Association of Royal Nova Scotia Historical Society, P.O. Box 895, Armdale, Nova Scotia B3L 4K5

Ontario Genealogical Society, P.O. Box 66, Station Q, Toronto, Ontario M4T 2L7

Ontario Genealogical Society, Toronto Branch, P.O. Box 74, Station U, Toronto, Ontario M8Z 5M4

Prince Edward Island Genealogical Society, P.O. Box 2744, Charlottetown, Prince Edward Island C1A 8C4

Quebec Family History Society, P.O. Box 1026, Station Pointe Claire, Quebec H9S 4H9

Saskatchewan Genealogical Society, P.O. Box 1894, Regina, Saskatchewan S4P 3E1

New Zealand

New Zealand Family History Society, P.O. Box 13301, Armagh, Christchurch

New Zealand Society of Genealogists, P.O. Box 8795, Auckland 3

United States of America

National Genealogical Society, 1921 Sunderland Place, N.W., Washington D.C. 20036

Society for British Genealogy and Family History, P.O. Box 20425, Cleveland, Ohio 44120

Santa Barbara County Genealoogical Society, P.O. Box 1174, Goleta, California 93116

Florida Genealogical Society, P.O. Box 18624, Tampa, Florida 33679

Jefferson County Genealogical Society, P.O. Box 174, Oskaloosa, Kansas 66066

English Interest Group, Minnesota Genealogical Society, 9009 Northwood Circle, New Hope, Minnesota 55427

Houston Genealogical Forum, 7130 Evans, Houston, Texas 77061-2738

Seattle Genealogical Society, P.O. Box 549, Seattle, Washington 98111

Enclosures In the Middle Ages the typical method of agriculture was by what is now called the Open Field System. Householders in the manor held strips of land scattered among larger open fields, and they also held haymaking and grazing rights in the meadowland and pasture in proportion to the number of strips they held in the arable. The fields are called 'open' because there were no hedges or fences between the various strips.

In time it became apparent that it was more efficient for a man to hold one substantial block of land, rather than these scattered strips, so first the lord of the manor tended to withdraw his strips into one group and to take in land from the waste. These became part of his demesne. The same process was later followed by others, but affected mainly the pasture land because individuals were primarily concerned to increase their sheep-grazing capacity. However, arable land was also affected. The legal process is often spelt 'Inclosure', and the physical process of partition 'Enclosure'.

In 1517-18 the *Domesday of Inclosure* was drawn up, showing what land had been inclosed in six or seven counties. However, in 1533-4, as a result of numerous protests against inclosure, an Act was passed against the process, though it was widely ignored.

In the seventeenth century the process gathered speed, and tended to be brought about by people bringing suits in Chancery or other courts of equity, probably mostly collusive. The resulting decisions were recorded in the rolls of the court. Some enclosures were arranged within the locality, either by the Court Leet or the Vestry.

In the eighteenth century, agriculture became more scientific. This again hastened the process of inclosure — which now tended to be brought about by private Acts of Parliament, some of which merely confirmed what had already been agreed in the manor.

In 1836, a *General Inclosure Act* enabled enclosure to proceed without the cumbersome preliminary of a private Act of Parliament, provided it had the consent of a majority of the people concerned; and a further Act of 1845 set up a board of Inclosure Commissioners, in London, to supervise all inclosures. The bulk of all inclosures took place between 1750 and 1850.

The rolls of the Court of Chancery and other equity courts contain accounts of sixteenth, seventeenth and eighteenth centuries' enclosures, under reference C.54. Enclosures enrolled on the Common Pleas rolls are under reference CP.43. Under private inclosure Acts the original Award documents were given to the parish concerned, with a copy to the Clerk of the Peace of the Quarter Sessions. A list of these has been printed by the House of Commons. Under the *General Inclosure Act* of 1836, one copy of the Award document was the property of the enclosed parish and another was deposited with the Clerk of the Peace for the Quarter Sessions. Most of the latter are now at the county record offices, but some are at the Public Record Office (PRO), Chancery Lane, London, and a few among parish records. They consist of a list of owners, descriptions of the enclosed land portions and a map showing their situations. In places where tithes have been commuted mainly under inclosure Acts, the Enclosure Award maps give a wider survey than those of the Tithe Awards. Awards made under the Act of 1845 are at the PRO, Kew, in class MAF.1.

The Minute Books of Commissioners, where they exist, have been listed, and the list printed in the *Bulletin of the Institute of Historical Research*, Vol.XXI, 1946-8. The parish copy of an Agreement and Award can sometimes be found still in the custody of the incumbent.

For further reading, see *A Domesday of English Enclosure Acts*, by W.E. Tate (University of Reading, 1978), and *Summary of Proceedings at 2nd British Family History Conference* (West Surrey Family History Society, 1982).

Enfeoffment to Use In the Middle Ages a man who did not wish his land, or, at least, not all of it, to pass to his eldest son by primogeniture under the Common Law, could make it over during his lifetime to trustees by a written legal deed. The trustees then held it, but to the 'use' of the original owner. The latter then executed a 'last will' — not a testament — expressing his wish regarding who should be the user of the land after his death. This practice deprived the king and other lords of their escheats and fines, avoided forfeiture in cases of felony, and defeated the provisions of the Statutes of Mortmain, so a *Statute of Uses* was passed in 1535-6 to make it illegal. However, by the *Statute of Wills*, 1540, land was allowed to be legally devised on the death of its holder, and so Last Wills came to be customarily executed in the same document as Testaments.

See also JOINT ENFEOFFMENT; WILL.

Englishry From the Conquest to the mid fourteenth century, it was necessary to establish whether a murdered person was Norman or English by descent: the penalties for killing a Norman were much the more severe. All doubtful cases were considered to be Norman. Unless the accused person could successfully plead 'Englishry' (i.e. that the deceased was English and not Norman), he would face severe penalties and a fine would be imposed on the hundred in which the crime was committed.

Engrossing (i) The gathering into single ownership, or tenancy, of lands and houses formerly supporting two or more families.

(ii) The writing out in formal script of a legal deed, a procedure that required calligraphic skill.

Enrolled Deeds In order to ensure the survival of an authentic copy of a conveyance or title, it was open to any party concerned to have it registered in some official roll or record, i.e. to 'enroll' it. This was not obligatory, but the *Statute of Inrollment*, 1535, was intended to encourage the practice. Many deeds are to be found in the Close Rolls of the Court of Chancery, the Plea Rolls of the Courts of Common Law, the Memoranda Rolls of the Court of Exchequer, and among the records of various local courts. Deeds of Bargain and Sale could be enrolled with the Clerk of the Peace among his county archives. These archives will be found at county record offices, and those of the central courts at the Public Record Office, Chancery Lane, London. Some of the latter have been calendared and printed. From the early eighteenth century, statutory registers were in existence in Middlesex (1708) and the Ridings of Yorkshire, for the recording of deeds relating to those areas. These registers are indexed under vendors.

Ensign The lowest commissioned rank in an infantry regiment, named after his duty of carrying the flag. The term for the rank was changed to 2nd Lieutenant in 1871. Also written as 'Ancient'. *See also* CORNET.

Entail was originated by the *Statute De Donis Conditionalibus* of Edward I. An owner of lands in

Fee Simple (Absolute: *see* FEE) could, by a grant of land to a person 'and the heirs of his body', tie up that land in one family. Such land was called Estate Tail, and the mode of tenure 'Fee Tail'. Each successor would enjoy only a life interest in it, but it would pass to his heirs on the principle of primogeniture. If ever the direct issue of the original grantee died out, the land reverted to the grantor or his heirs.

Leases of entailed land became void on the death of a landlord who was a tenant in tail. Debts were not chargeable on such land. Heirs could not be disinherited. In cases of treason (until Henry VII) or other offences, such land could not be forfeited to the Crown for longer than the tenant's life, though it did escheat to the lord. In 1833 any tenant in tail was allowed to break the entail by a deed enrolled in the Court of Chancery.

See also RECOVERY.

Entertain To employ.

Equity In the Middle Ages, people who did not, or could not, obtain justice at law were entitled to appeal to the king. Edward I directed his Chancellor to deal with the more important petitions, and his justices with the lesser ones. When, under Edward III, the Chancellor ceased to follow the king on his peregrinations of the kingdom, his Chancery office became a court of jurisdiction. It dealt with civil cases and administered a system of law known as Equity. It did not rely on juries, but could summon witnesses or have depositions taken in the provinces by local commissioners. Both plaintiff and defendant were placed on oath and were not allowed to remain silent. Where the Common Law courts would fine, Chancery could imprison or impose forfeiture of property, but it could not inflict capital punishment, or mutilation such as hand-amputation. Petitions were addressed to the Lord Chancellor or, in periods of vacancy in that office, to the Lord Keeper of the Great Seal. At first precedents were not required, but when, in the seventeenth century, decisions began to be recorded, lawyers took to quoting them and equity settled into as much a set of principles as was the Common Law.

Escheat To revert to the superior lord. When a tenant of land died and there was no Common Law heir, or if the heir had forfeited his right on account of a felony, the land escheated to the immediate lord. Escheators were the royal officials who, with their deputies, usually held jurisdiction over one or more counties, and were responsible for effecting escheats of land held of the king. On the death of a tenant-in-chief, the escheator called an enquiry entitled Inquisition Post Mortem, with a local jury, to ascertain what lands the deceased had held and who was the heir. He was also responsible for wardship and the administration of Crown lands in his area.

Espousal Until the early seventeenth century an espousal, or betrothal, was considered to have almost the validity of marriage, and may sometimes, at that period, account for a first child being born less than nine months after the wedding. Only a few parishes have surviving Espousal Books, which are now probably all at county record offices.

Esquire In the Middle Ages a squire (escutifer) carried the shield and other armour of the lord or knight he served, but this duty passed later to pages. Squires in this sense were of gentle family. By the sixteenth century, Esquire was a title acquired by holding an office under the Crown, and so was not necessarily superior to 'gentleman', but in practice such office-holding carried distinction. Esquires proper held such Crown commissions as Justices of the Peace, army officers, Royal Navy commanders (but not junior naval officers), the common hangman, etc. The modern courtesy use of the style became common in the nineteenth century. The squire in a country parish was the colloquial designation for the lord of the manor, or chief landowner.

Essex The Essex Society for Family History holds regular meetings and issues *The Essex Family Historian*. Waltham Forest Family History Society also holds meetings and issues a Newsletter. Enquiries should be sent c/o The Federation of Family History Societies, 31 Seven Star Road, Solihull, West Midlands B91 2BZ,

marked 'Please forward' and enclosing a stamped self-addressed envelope.

Record Repository Essex Record Office, County Hall, Chelmsford (tel: 0245.67222).

Parish Registers and Indexes (*see* comment under COUNTY) Most of the 405 ancient parishes have deposited their registers at the county record office (CRO). The Society of Genealogists has copies of some of them. Boyd's Marriage Index covers 374 parishes. Pallot's Marriage Index covers 22 parishes, from 1790 to 1812 or 1837. The INTERNATIONAL GENEALOGICAL INDEX (IGI) includes many parishes, and there is a copy at Saffron Walden Library. A few Bishops' Transcripts of the seventeenth century are at the Guildhall Library, London.

Marriage Licence Records These are at the CRO and have been indexed. The Society of Genealogists also has some early indexes.

Wills before 1858 are located at the CRO, with a published index. As the county lay within the Diocese of London and the Province of Canterbury, wills could also be proved in the Consistory Court of London, the Commissary Court of London for Essex and Hertfordshire, and the Prerogative Court of Canterbury. The Society of Genealogists has indexes of wills proved in the several courts.

Non-parochial Registers There are 81 at the Public Record Office (PRO), Chancery Lane, London, and these are also covered by the IGI.

Census Returns These are at the PRO, Portugal Street, London, and also at Colchester Public Library.

Memorial Inscriptions The Society of Genealogists has copies from some Essex churches.

Heralds' Visitation Pedigrees have been printed for 1552, 1558, 1570, 1612 and 1668.

Essoin An excuse for absence from attendance at a manor court for a good and accepted reason, and with someone present at the court to answer for the absentee and pay his fine of 2 pence.

Estate Archives The account books, terriers, surveys, extents and rent books of a landowner's estate. These throw light on many more people than the landowning family themselves. In a country parish, the squire was normally the chief employer of labour. The account books of his estate name the people paid, the amount of their wages, and the type of service rendered. The surveys or extents of the estate describe the copyhold tenements and name their occupants. Maps of the village may be attached, showing each building and field with acreages, arable, meadow or pasture, and cultivators. Many of these records, originally with the owners or their solicitors, have now been deposited at county record offices.

Estate Duty *see* **Will**

Estate Tail *see* **Entail**

Estreat An extract from, or a copy of, a list of monetary penalties to be collected by the sheriff on behalf of the king, imposed by a court and delivered to the Exchequer. Filed among the Exchequer records at the Public Record Office, Chancery Lane, London.

Evidence The evidence upon which a family tree or history can be compiled is of two kinds — primary and secondary — with a grey area between them.

Primary evidence should always be sought, as being the most reliable. It is provided by documents or other artefacts, created at the time, or nearly so, of the events they record, and with no thought of historiography or genealogy in mind. Primary evidence requires effort not only to discover but also to interpret, since it calls for some understanding of the type of record itself. Nearly all such records have been caused in consequence of some law, the exceptions being private correspondence, accounts, etc.

Secondary evidence is that which has been brought into existence at a later period, such as histories and family trees. Every family tree and family history should be made referable to an accompanying list of the sources upon which it is based. Otherwise, generations hence, some conscientious genealogist of the family will treat it as secondary evidence which he will need to check by research all over again.

In the grey area are such contemporary records as newspaper reports, autobiographies and histories of the writers' own times, in which experience or research have been subjectively predigested.

Exchequer, Court of One of the three courts that evolved from the Curia Regis (King's Court), the others being those of Common Pleas and King's Bench. The name originated from the chequered cloth that covered its table for the purposes of calculation. It was an administrative body for collecting the royal revenue, and its judicial business arose out of that function. In time this side of its activities developed into an ordinary court of justice for suits between subject and subject. The Exchequer was a court of equity until early in Queen Victoria's reign. The best finding-aids are the Bill Books, which are arranged under counties. The evidence of witnesses was taken in writing and often contains interesting biographical material. The records are at the Public Record Office, Chancery Lane, London. Bills and Answers are in class E.112, Depositions in E.133 and 134, and Decrees and Orders in E.123-7. The Bernau Index, kept at the Society of Genealogists, lists county depositions taken on commission between 1559 and 1800.

The records of the Upper Exchequer, or Exchequer of Audit, are divided into those of the Treasurer's Remembrancer's Office and the King's Remembrancer's Office. The former includes the Pipe Rolls, Foreign Rolls, Originalia Rolls (extracts from Chancery Rolls) and Memoranda Rolls. Those of the King's Remembrancer's Office are of most use to family historians, since they include the Court's judicial cases. Among the Lower Exchequer records are suits involving Jews, and the archives of the Court of Augmentations. The Exchequer's most famous record, older than the department itself, is the *Domesday Book*.

Excommunication Exclusion from the communion of the Church; a penalty imposed by an ecclesiastical court in cases of heresy, simony, adultery, non-attendance at public worship, contumacious words, non-payment of fees or costs, etc. In pre-Reformation days, the greater excommunication deprived the condemned not only of the sacraments and the benefits of divine offices, but also of the society and conversation of the faithful, and even

Christian burial. In the cases of sovereigns excommunicated by the Pope, their subjects were absolved from their allegiance. Both King John and King Henry VIII suffered excommunication. The excommunication of a whole country was called an Interdict.
See also ECCLESIASTICAL COURTS.

Exigend A writ issued when a person indicted of a felony did not appear in court and could not be found. It rendered him liable to forfeiture of his goods and, in earlier days, to outlawry.

Ex Officio Suit *see* **Office Suit**

Extent A detailed survey and valuation of manorial or other estates. Useful to genealogists because the names of the tenants were mentioned.

Extinct Title An hereditary title became extinct when the holder died leaving no heir eligible to inherit it.
See also ABEYANCE; DORMANT PEERAGE.

Extra-parochial This term applied to land uninhabited in Anglo-Saxon times, and so outside the bounds of any parish, civil or ecclesiastical; this meant that it was exempt from church and poor rates and sometimes tithes, though such places were generally supposed to pay tithes to the Crown. People living in such areas would be baptized, etc., at the nearest convenient church. Extra-parochial places were made civil parishes in 1894.

Eyre The word derives from the Latin *Iter*, meaning a journey, and in law means the court of itinerant royal justices. Hence the expression, 'Justices in Eyre'. In the Middle Ages they were competent to hear all kinds of cases, and administered the Common Law as a check on the local courts. Representatives of each hundred and township, and all freeholders, were required to be present at court. To initiate a suit, the plaintiff had to purchase a writ from the king, and this soon became an important source of royal revenue.

The Eyre courts became progressively more unpopular and eventually, by a statute of 1284-5, were replaced by Assizes.

Factory Originally the work-place of a company's factors, i.e. a trading station. A term employed by chartered companies for their branches abroad. The modern sense of the word did not come into use until the mid nineteenth century. Before that, production work-places were called 'manufactories'.

Faculty Office The office of the Master of Faculties of the Archbishop of Canterbury. Applications for marriage licences had to be addressed to him if the contracting parties lived in different provinces of the Church of England. Records of the common and special licences issued by this office survive from 1660, the earlier ones having been destroyed in the Great Fire of London. They are now housed in Lambeth Palace Library, London, and can be inspected after prior notification to the librarian.

Fair The right of a market town to hold a fair was granted by Letters Patent from the Crown. Fairs were usually held annually or half-annually, and were extra-large markets accompanied by facilities for participating in shows and games. The date of such a function might be fixed to coincide with the festival of the patron saint of the parish church, starting on the eve of the feast and ending on its morrow. Traders and customers of all kinds were attracted from considerable distances. Many fairs were specific to a certain type of merchandise — horses, sheep, cheese, and so on.
See also HIRING FAIRS; PIEPOUDRÉ, COURT OF.

Falling sickness Epilepsy or convulsionary hysteria. Prior to the late nineteenth century, illnesses were commonly named after their symptoms, since their causes were unknown.

Fallow That part of the arable land of a manor that was left untilled every second or third year to allow the soil to recover, and to provide weeds and grass for grazing cattle, who would at the same time manure it.

Family Until the seventeenth century the term 'family' signified a household, including any servants and apprentices. In genealogical usage the term includes all people of the same name and blood descended from a common male-line ancestor, as distinct from its colloquial use to include close relatives on both father's and mother's sides, and grandchildren by both sons and daughters.

Family Bible A popular publication in the nineteenth century; usually a large edition of the Bible, in which several of the preliminary pages were either left blank or ruled with lines, to allow the owner to record the dates and places of such family events as births, baptisms, marriages, deaths and burials. Frequently these are found to be supplemented by earlier ones referring to events that occurred before the birth of the owner. For some of the later of these, the information may have come from parents or other elderly relatives then living, and can therefore be assumed to be reliable, but others may hark back to much earlier generations and so, unless documented elsewhere, must be open to doubt. Such entries, not made from personal knowledge, should be treated merely as a guide to the research needed to confirm them.
See also EVIDENCE.

Family History (i) Until recently this term was used as a synonym for genealogy, but now, in ancestor-tracing circles, it applies specifically to biographical research into one's forebears with the object of compiling a narrative history of the family; and the term 'genealogy' is reserved for the tracing of an ascent and the compilation of a Family Tree or Total Descent. A family history should place the members of the family in their historical, geographical, social and occupational contexts, and describe their activities and the lives they lived.

(ii) A journal published by the Institute of Heraldic and Genealogical Studies.

Family History Societies The SOCIETY OF GENEALOGISTS, founded in 1911, held the field alone in England except for one university society, until in the 1960s similar societies began to appear in the provinces. In the 1970s these proliferated, until nearly every county had one, and some more than one. These provincial societies hold monthly meetings addressed by knowledgeable speakers, issue journals (normally quarterly) with articles contributed by members, compile marriage and census indexes, and transcribe memorial inscriptions.

The emergence of societies in nearly all areas has radically changed ancestry research from being a hobby pursued in isolation, to one that is as sociable as any other spare-time pursuit. Their journals, which tend to be less scholarly than the organ of the Society of Genealogists, exhibit genealogy quite as much in its aspect of a leisure activity as in that of a branch of study. It is now common practice for a genealogist to be a member not only of his local society, for the sake of the lectures and discussion of problems with fellow members, but also of the society or societies in counties where his ancestors lived, for the benefit of what can be learnt from their journals and indexes, and arrangements for exchanged research.

For the names of these societies, *see* under their county headings: address enquiries should be sent c/o The Federation of Family History Societies, 31 Seven Star Road, Solihull, West Midlands B91 2BZ, marked 'Please forward' and enclosing a stamped self-addressed envelope. This Federation promotes and co-ordinates the activities of the societies.

A list of overseas family history societies can be found under EMIGRANTS.

Family Division, Principal Registry of the This registry houses all wills proved in England and Wales since 1858 inclusive, the year in which probate jurisdiction was taken out of ecclesiastical hands. Annual index volumes identify both testator and executor(s). Having found the index entry, the searcher can arrange to see the will and make brief pencilled notes, for which service a charge is made. Also, a photocopy of the will can be ordered. Letters of Administration are also indexed. Until 1870 they are shown in separate annual volumes; after that date, in the same volumes as the will. If the searcher is confident that a will was proved or Letters of Administration granted, the indexes may be used as a quicker method of finding a date of death than by a search of the civil registration Death Registers. The Registry is situated at Somerset House, Strand, London WC2. *See also* WILL.

Family Tree A summary, in chart form, of what is known about a male-line descent from a common ancestor; also called a tabular or drop-line pedigree. Early forms were designed like a tree, with the earliest ancestor at the trunk or root, and his descendants shown in the branches and twigs above, but it has long been the practice in the United Kingdom to set out the tree in reverse order, with the earliest known ancestor at the top and his descendants extending below him (*see* example on facing page). Sometimes, especially in America and Australia, trees are laid out horizontally with the generations proceeding chronologically from left to right.

A marriage is indicated by an = sign, then a vertical line drops from the marriage to the issue, who are linked to each other by a horizontal line, then with short drop-lines to each child's name, the eldest child being on the left and the youngest on the right. Illegitimate issue are indicated by a wavy drop-line, and probable but unconfirmed connections by broken lines. Beneath each name is shown, where known, the dates and places of birth/baptism, marriage and death/burial, employing the abbreviations b, bp, m, d and bur respectively, with c for *circa* (about) where the exact date is not known. Adopted children should have the fact noted, but should otherwise be shown as ordinary members of the family. The marriage details are usually shown under the wife's name, to leave room under the husband's for his occupation. The names of the wife's parents should also be shown. Because a family tree is a male-line descent, and space is usually limited, the spouse of a female member is usually entered below her name, together with the date and place of marriage, instead of beside her. Where space allows, other biographical details can be shown.

A tree can be embellished by the Arms, if any, of the family, and by those of any armigerous spouses. An alternative and appropriate decoration is an attractively drawn map of the family's ancestral area. Also, small photographs can be placed beside the persons' names. In a working tree it is useful to underline all surnames, or write them in capitals. This prevents confusion with Christian names and occupations.

An Extended Family Tree is one that shows the descendants from all sons to collateral branches. Such a tree can take up so much space that it will require to be rolled up or folded, and the names of brothers and sisters may have to be entered several feet apart. A more convenient and visually satisfying format is that of the 'stable-door' family tree, in which the most junior branch is charted on one sheet, from the earliest common ancestor of the family to the latest generation. Each more senior line is charted on a separate sheet of a shorter length, so that it can be laid on top of the other in such a way that descent from the common ancestor is seen to be continuous. As many sheets of appropriate length are then used as the branches of the family make necessary, and finally they can all be bound together along their left-hand edge in handy book form.

As mentioned above, abbreviations will be needed on a family tree for the ever-recurring words, born, baptized, married, died, buried, will made, probate granted, and *circa*. Single initial-letter abbreviations are of course the ideal, but three of the words start with the same letter. An attempt has been made to express 'born' by the letter z, a symbol of finality that tends to get interpreted as 'burial'. Usually people settle for bp and bur, but these take up too much space. This dictionary therefore suggests the following set of one-letter abbreviations:

b	= born	k	= killed
c	= *circa*	m	= married
d	= died	p	= probate
f	= funeral	w	= will made
x	= christened		

A word on two novelties in that list. In the twentieth century, cremation has become more common than burial, so an abbreviation that covers both (i.e. f) is now necessary. The letter x (really the Greek letter Chi) has for centuries

A typical, but fictitious, family tree.

BROWN   FAMILY

been the recognised abbreviation for Christ, as used in Xmas and Xopher, so x is the most appropriate one-letter abbreviation for christened.

It must be emphasised that a family tree is only a summary, useful as a visual aid; it is valueless unless confirmable by reference to the original documentary evidence on which it is based. Reference letters shown beside each statement take up too much room and are unnecessary if the transcripts of supporting evidence are kept in a loose-leaf binder in chronological order, thus making reference possible directly through the dates themselves.

For other methods of charting ancestry, *see* PEDIGREE; TOTAL DESCENT.

Family Tree Magazine An independently produced journal for ancestry researchers, founded in November, 1984, and appearing six times per year. It is popular in style and plentifully illustrated. Besides articles on

genealogical sources, it provides news of activities among family history societies and of new developments in the genealogical world. The magazine is published by Michael Armstrong, 129 Great Whyte, Ramsey, Huntingdon, Cambridgeshire PE17 1HP.

Family Trees and Histories Several lists of family histories already in print have been compiled and updated from time to time. The first of these was *The Genealogist's Guide*, by George W. Marshall, a work usually referred to by his name. It catalogues printed pedigrees of three or more generations. First published in 1879, it went through four editions by 1903 and was reprinted in 1967. In the days when the gentry were the only people actively interested in their family past, Marshall's work was rightly considered the best starting point for a genealogist. In 1953 appeared *A Genealogist's Guide*, by J.B. Whitmore, who brought the list down to that date and filled in gaps in the earlier one. Another book entitled *The Genealogist's Guide*, by G.B. Barrow, was published in 1977, and *A Catalogue of British Family Histories*, by T.R. Thomson, contains an Appendix bringing the list down to the date of the latest edition (1980).

A large number of family histories, in print, typescript and manuscript, can be consulted in the library of the Society of Genealogists, which also has a great collection of birth briefs and family trees.

For family trees already compiled, *see* NATIONAL PEDIGREE INDEX.

For research currently being carried out by other people, it is best to consult the family history society of the relevant county or area. Many of them issue lists of Members' Interests.

Farm (i) To work land.

(ii) To let out a process or task (e.g. the collection of a tax) for a fixed payment, leaving the 'farmer' to make what profit he can.

(iii) The rent or service paid for landholding. Also written as Ferm.

See also FARMER.

Farmer (i) One who rents and cultivates a farm.

(ii) One who collected taxes for a taxing authority in return for a fixed sum or rate per cent.

Farthing Originally the quarter of anything, but in time applied exclusively to a quarter-penny. Farthing land was a quarter of a yardland, which was an area of about thirty acres.

Father-in-law This expression was often used to mean what is now called a stepfather, i.e. a mother's second husband. The same also applies to mother-in-law, etc. On the other hand, a father-in-law is often found referred to as 'Father'.

Fealty The oral oath of allegiance to the king, required under the feudal system from every new tenant on his entry into occupation of land, and given at the same time as his homage to his immediately superior lord. The requirement continued longer for copyholders than for freeholders. When land was held by fealty alone,

i.e. not in combination with homage, no service to the lord was involved.

Federation of Family History Societies
This organisation was formed in 1974 to co-ordinate and assist the work of the growing number of family history societies in Britain. Its members are societies, specialising in family history, heraldry and associated disciplines, constituted in the British Isles; and associate membership is open to similar overseas societies and to those in the British Isles where the main interest is neither family history nor heraldry. The Federation issues *Family History News and Digest* twice a year, containing news of member societies and abstracts of articles (mostly from members' journals), and publishes booklet guides to the location of records useful to genealogists. Assistance is given in the formation of new groups in areas not already adequately covered, and national conferences are organised. The Federation advises members, commissions publications, makes representa-tions to official bodies and maintains a regular liaison with a number of interest-related organisations. Enquiries to the Administrator, 31 Seven Star Road, Solihull, West Midlands B91 2BZ, should be accompanied by a stamped self-addressed envelope. The address for United Kingdom book orders is Mrs N. Porter, 17 Fox Lea Road, Hayley Green, Halesowen, West Midlands B63 1DX. A letter to a member society of the Federation, if its address is not known, should be sent c/o the Federation and marked 'Please forward'. Member societies are shown under their county headings.

Fee The expression 'in fee' means 'hereditarily', and 'in fee male' means 'through male descent'. A Fee Simple was a freehold estate in land which passed at death to the common law heir. For Fee Tail, *see* ENTAIL. Fee Farm was a fixed annual rent charge payable to the king by chartered boroughs.

Feet of Fines The word 'fine' is derived from the Latin *finis*, meaning 'an end'. It came to mean a judgement or Final Concord regarding a title to land after a form of legal action, nearly always collusive, and intended to provide a record of title, often after a purchase. It was written out three times in the same words on the same side of a single sheet of parchment, two copies being written vertically and back-to-back, and the third along the foot of the sheet. The word 'Cyrographum' was sometimes written in large letters above the foot copy and between the other two, and the three copies were then cut apart along wavy lines and through the cyrograph. The back-to-back parts were given to the two parties, and the Foot was filed among the rolls of the Court of Common Pleas, now at the Public Record Office, Chancery Lane, London, under references CP.25 and 27. This procedure made forgery virtually impossible, and it was only abolished as late as 1834.

Until 1733 (except under the Commonwealth) the records were in Latin. The rolls, from 1182 to 1638, are arranged under counties. The date shown is that on which the writ summoning the parties to appear was due to be returned into court, and so gives only an approximate idea of the date of the actual agreement. The person whose right (*jus*) is admitted is the purchaser or recognised title-holder. A fine often contains a 'clause of warranty', in which certain persons, often relatives of the vendor or person of whom the land is held, warrant against him, i.e. pledge themselves to stand by the agreement if the title to the holding is questioned later. Other persons may be named as co-deforciants, but this is merely to bar any right they might claim in the future. Contemporary calendars are available for the period 1509-1798. For several counties the Feet of Fines have been printed. In many cases there also exist Notes of Fines, an additional record, and Concords, which are duplicates of the Fines.

Felony The word originally meant 'forfeiture', but was already, in feudal times, attached to any act for which forfeiture was the penalty. Later it came to mean offences for which the punishment included forfeiture of land and/or goods and chattels. The chief Common Law felonies were homicide, rape, larceny (i.e. stealing), robbery (i.e. theft with violence), burglary and similar offences. Other classes of crime were treason (the most serious), misdemeanour, and summary offence. Counter-

feiting, once classed as treason, was later made a felony.

Female Line Any line of ascent that runs through ancestresses. In a Total Descent chart, or birth brief, all lines but one — that of the father's father's father, etc. — will be female lines.

Feme A woman. A Feme Covert was a married woman whose husband was alive. A Feme Sole was a spinster, widow or divorced wife.

Feodary (i) A survey of the obligations of Crown tenants, i.e. the number of knights to be supplied, and so on.

(ii) The official responsible for enforcing such obligations. One feodary would normally cover several counties.

(iii) A person holding land on condition of fealty and service.

Feoffment The oldest form of the alienation (transfer) of land from one person to another. It was effected partly in writing and partly by a public act called Livery of Seisin. The existing owner took the owner-to-be on to the land, handed him a twig, a blade of grass, a clod or a piece of turf as a token, and stated the terms on which he handed over the land, e.g. in Fee Simple (*see* FEE). The new owner then turned everyone else off the land, thus asserting his rights as owner. The terms were put in writing in an Indenture of Feoffment, signed and/or sealed by both parties. It was endorsed on the back with a statement that the Livery of Seisin (the symbolic hand-over) had been carried out before witnesses, and without this endorsement the deed was worthless.

Feudalism The political and social system that developed as a result of the breakdown of government at the end of the Roman Empire. Its basis was the holding of land from a powerful local patron (vassalage), who afforded protection (known as benefice) in return. Under the Carolingians on the continent, the vassal relationship became extended to include the large landed proprietors and the king. In this form the institution was introduced into England by William the Conqueror. All the land of England was owned by the king alone. His nobles held their land of him in return for military service (*see* KNIGHT SERVICE), and lesser men held in turn from them on similar terms. The system in its pure form broke down from the need of King Edward I for an efficient military organisation. Money payments (*see* SCUTAGE) became general, and indentured fighting men took the place of tenants doing temporary service. Because of this, the system from the fourteenth century until the late fifteenth is known as 'bastard feudalism'.

Feudal Levy The troops raised for the king by his tenants-in-chief in accordance with their feudal obligations. Edward I found them inadequate in number for his Scottish and Welsh campaigns, and so took to recruiting men by means of indentures. The success of this method put an end to the feudal levy in practice, though the king's right to raise it remained in force.

Feudal Tenure *see* **Knight Service**

Fief The same as a fee held by military service. If its holder failed to perform the service, the fief reverted to the overlord. It could not be broken up without the overlord's consent.

Field (i) Arable land, as distinct from meadow and pasture.
(ii) A division of a building made by a low wall.
(iii) A heraldic term for the background of a coat of arms.

Fine (i) *See* FEET OF FINES.
(ii) The term 'fine' was also used for the sum of money paid, at the conclusion of an agreement, by the person favoured.

Fine Rolls These contain lists of payments made to the Crown for charters, writs, privileges and pardons. They also record the appointment of royal officials, and quote the orders sent to sheriffs, escheators and exchequer officers. The Record Commission has published the rolls of King John's reign, and extracts from those of Henry III's. Since then the Public Record Office has published many calendars covering the subsequent period.

Fire Insurance Companies In the early eighteenth century, several companies set up in the business of fire insurance. Their clients were, at first, London property owners, but provincial householders and businessmen soon followed suit. To each building insured, the company affixed a metal plaque bearing its trade mark, so that it could be identified as its liability. Some of these can still be seen *in situ*. The fire companies possessed their own fire engines, with which they endeavoured to keep their losses to a minimum.

The registers of several firms have been deposited at the Guildhall Library, London, and are in process of being indexed. These include the Sun Fire Office and the Hand in Hand, from 1710; the London Assurance, from 1720; and the Royal Exchange Assurance, founded in the same year but with surviving records only from 1773. For each property insured, the registers record the address and the owner's name and occupation. The passing of ownership on death to another member of the family is mentioned, and the exact location of the building is often made clear by reference to neighbouring properties.

Five Mile Act A statute of 1665 forbidding all clergymen ejected from their benefices under the *Act of Uniformity* to live within five miles of a corporate town. This was because nonconformity had been particularly strong in urban areas.

Flat Another term for furlong.

Flesher A butcher.

Fletcher A person who feathered arrows; commonly a maker of bows and arrows. The Fletchers' Company, one of the London Gilds, was founded in 1371.

Folio A sheet of parchment or paper which, in the making of a book, is folded to form several pages, which may be any number from four to sixteen.

Folkestone Family History Society *see* **Kent**

Foreigner This term was customarily applied

by townspeople to those, of English stock, who were not freemen of their city or borough.

Forest The word originally had nothing to do with woods. It designated an area, which would almost certainly be partly wooded, over which the king had rights of hunting and preserving game. The inhabitants of the area were subject to forest law, which restricted a number of what, elsewhere, were normal rights.
See also VERT AND VENISON.

Forthfare The passing-bell tolled in the parish church tower on the death of a local resident.

Fother An irregularly shaped piece of land in an open arable field.

Foundlings Sometimes called 'dropt children', these infants were usually left on the steps of a church, or in the porch or some other frequented spot, where they were fairly certain to be found. Some might have a note pinned to them, asking that they might be called by a particular Christian name. In most cases, such children were illegitimate.

The child had to be christened and given a surname by the church authorities, or whoever adopted it. Some were named after the spot in which they were found, e.g. Church, Porch, Churchstile, Bridge, or the name of the street. Some, especially in London, were given, either as Christian or surname, the name of the nearest saint's day or the name of the saint to whom the church was dedicated. The Christian name Moses was popular for those found in a basket, because the prophet Moses was found among the rushes. During the Puritan period, a girl foundling at Baltonsborough, Somerset, was given the names Misericordia Adulterina — an extreme example of the type of Christian names bestowed at that period.

In 1745 Captain Thomas Coram (*c.*1668-1751) opened his famous Foundling Hospital in Guildford Street, London, in accordance with a charter he had obtained in 1739. Outside the door was a basket suspended by a rope attached to a bell. When a child was placed in the basket, the bell rang and the gatekeeper came and collected it. At first the Hospital admitted any child who seemed to be under two months old and free from certain specified diseases. No questions were asked, and no attempt was made to trace the parents.

From 1756 the Hospital was given an annual grant by the government, and thereafter had to take in all children under one year in any state of health. The result was that in the following year, 3727 children were taken in and branches had to be opened at Ackworth in Yorkshire, Shrewsbury, Westerham in Kent, Aylesbury and Barnet. Poor parents brought dying children, in order to have them buried at the expense of the Hospital; thus of 14,934 children received in three years and ten months, only about 4400 lived to be apprenticed to trades. People in the provinces even set up a service of carrying illegitimate children to the Hospital in London at so much per head.

From 1760, indiscriminate intake was abandoned, and the government ended its grants in 1771, after which time the Hospital had to depend on charity. Later, children were taken in only if brought by their mothers, and the mothers had to show that they had been previously of good character and had been let down by the fathers. In Victorian times, foundling hospitals were thought to encourage immorality.

On admittance, the Foundling Hospital gave the child a number and a name. This name would be chosen by the hospital authorities regardless of any name left with the child. Infants requiring a wet-nurse were sent to one outside London for the benefit of their health, and were placed under the supervision of a doctor in the same locality. When weaned, the child would go into one of the branch hospitals, and would sometimes be transferred from one to another, perhaps because of age grouping. At about the age of eight, they would be apprenticed to husbandry at the expense of the Hospital (*see* APPRENTICES). Sometimes the parent who left the child attached a 'token' to identify it, in the hope that he or she might later be able to maintain it and would be able to claim it.

The parish records of the Overseer of the Poor and of the Constable contain mentions of what was done with the foundlings picked up and dealt with locally. The records of the Foundling Hospital are at the Greater London Council

Record Office. *See* GENERAL REGISTER OF BIRTHS.

Franchise (i) In the Middle Ages a franchise was an exemption from ordinary jurisdiction, such as that of a hundred court, accompanied by the privilege of a private jurisdiction or liberty (*see also* QUO WARRANTO).

(ii) Parliamentary franchise. The House of Commons was made up of county members, called knights of the shire; of town members, called burgesses; and of representatives of the universities, elected by university members.

From 1430 until the *Reform Act* of 1832, the franchise for electing county members was limited to those who held freehold estates to the value of 40 shillings per year or more; thus, while quite modest freeholders had the vote, large tenant farmers with no freehold did not. Also, owing to inflation, the number of 40 shilling freeholders in the counties increased greatly over the years. The Act of 1832 required anyone holding only a life interest in his freehold to be its actual occupant in order to be eligible for the vote, unless it had come to him by marriage or settlement, or was attached to an office; but those in possession of life freeholds at the time of the Act were allowed to retain their franchise.

However, the main function of the Act was not to restrict, but greatly to widen, the right to vote, which it extended to cover (a) those owning land worth £10 per year by any title, including copyhold and leases for sixty years; (b) those holding land worth £50 per year on leases for twenty years; and (c) tenants and other occupants paying rents of £50 per year. In 1867 the franchise was further extended and again in 1884 (rural voters), 1885 and 1918. In the last-mentioned year, women aged thirty and over were included, and in 1928 women were at last placed on the same footing as men. Until 1872, it is possible to ascertain the way in which many electors cast their votes (*see* POLL BOOKS).

In boroughs, the early system was quite different from the county franchise and much less uniform. The extent of each town's franchise depended sometimes on its charter of incorporation, and sometimes on custom, and as time went by the tendency was to reduce the number of freemen voters by charging ever-higher sums for the privilege of freedom of the borough. Very often the number of voters would be no more than a dozen. Over the centuries many boroughs decayed, and some disappeared altogether, but were still represented in Parliament. Other towns grew to a considerable size but were unrepresented. This inequitable distribution of the franchise was greatly reduced by the Act of 1832. Genealogists have also to thank that Act for a useful new set of location records — the Electoral Registers that listed all those entitled to vote.

Frankalmoign or Free Alms. In the Middle Ages, when land was granted in frankalmoign the only service required to be paid (apart from the TRINODAS NECESSITAS) was regular prayer for the souls of the donor, his family and descendants. Most of the medieval religious houses held their lands by this type of tenure. When military tenures were abolished in 1660, frankalmoign was expressly excepted and is the tenure by which the parish clergy and many church and charitable foundations still hold their land.

Franking of Letters A privilege claimed by Members of the House of Commons from 1660, and by the clerks of the Post Office. It was greatly abused until regularised by an Act of Parliament in 1764. Each peer and Member of Parliament was then allowed to send, each day, ten free letters not exceeding one ounce in weight, by signing his name in the corner of the outside of the folded letter (envelopes came later). Each Member could also receive fifteen letters per day. These privileged persons often signed letters for their friends, but in 1837 an attempt was made to restrict this practice. The franker was obliged not only to sign his name, but also to inscribe his address and post town, and the day of the month; and the letter had to be posted on the same or following day in a post town not more than twenty miles from the franker's home. In 1840, franking was abolished with the introduction of the penny post.

Franklin A substantial free tenant farmer in the Middle Ages. By the fifteenth century he was known by the term 'Yeoman'.
See also CLASS, SOCIAL.

Frankpledge The system by which every man was obliged to be a member of a group of ten or twelve, also called a Tithing, who were held corporately responsible for the good behaviour of one another. If a member of a frankpledge was accused of an offence and failed to appear to answer the charge, the members of his frankpledge were fined. A manorial View of Frankpledge was held periodically to ensure that all eligible men and growing boys were involved in such a group. Those in the household of some great man, who would be responsible for them, were exempted. By the fifteenth century the system was breaking down, but the name remained, signifying the Court Leet, of which it had previously been merely one function.
See also MANOR.

Free Alms *see* **Frankalmoign**

Freebench The right of a copyholder's widow to the whole of her late husband's land, either for life or until remarriage — the custom varied from one manor to another.
See also DOWER.

Freehold Originally land held on non-servile tenure, either for life or in Fee Simple or Fee Tail. It could be held either by knight service or in socage. Freeholders enjoyed security of tenure in perpetuity under the Common Law. At the Conquest, such tenure was particularly widespread in the former Danelaw.

Freeholders' Lists Also called Jurors' Lists. From 1696, rural vestries and urban corporations had to send to the Clerk of the Peace for their county, lists of the people within their jurisdictions who were eligible for jury service. These were men between the ages of 21 and 70 who owned freeholds worth at least 40 shillings per year. They were listed under the parishes in which they lived, but if their qualifying property was in another parish this was sometimes also stated. The annual value of their freeholds might be noted too, together with the owner's rank or occupation.

In 1825 the upper age of eligibility was reduced to 60, and the qualification revised to freeholds worth £10 per year, leaseholds for 21 years or more worth £20, rateability as householder at £20 (£30 in Middlesex), or occupation of a house with fifteen or more windows. At the same time the list of exempt occupations was extended. From 1832, freeholders' addresses were given on the lists, and the qualifying property specified.

The freeholders' lists provide a very useful location record for tracing the whereabouts of a family, and to some extent for establishing its economic status. The records are housed among the Quarter Sessions papers at the county record offices.

In 1873 a *Return of Freeholders* was published, covering the whole country.

Freemasons The origins of freemasonry are obscured in legend, but there is documentary evidence for the existence of masonic lodges in England in the Middle Ages. As with all other medieval gilds of free craftsmen, the early membership consisted of 'operatives' (masons by trade) and 'speculatives' (noblemen, gentry and members of other trades), who were 'accepted' as honorary members. In the course of time the lodges ceased to have any connection with the trade that gave them their name, and benevolence and fellowship became their main characteristic, with the acknowledgement of God as the Great Architect of the Universe. Meetings of members are carried out with an elaborate system of symbolic ritual. The lodges in various parts of the country were originally independent of one another, but in 1717 began to recognise the governance of a national Grand Lodge. In the same century the society spread, and lodges were formed on the Continent and in Asia and America. Since then, in some countries (notably France), the society has shed its religious character and become largely political. In England, members of the royal family have been freemasons, and some have been Grand Masters. If an ancestor is thought to have been a member, details of his date of entry and the name of his lodge can be obtained from the Secretary, The United Grand Lodge of England, Freemasons Hall, Great Queen Street, London WC2.

Freemen of the City of London Nearly all freemen of the City have become such in virtue

113

of being freemen of a City Gild (*see* LIVERY COMPANIES). On attaining company freedom, a man would automatically apply for the freedom of the City. He was then entitled to call himself 'Citizen' and, for example, 'Tallow Chandler'. A few distinguished persons have been granted honorary freedom in recognition of their achievements. Vouchers and indexes of freemen of the City from 1689 are kept by the Chamberlain of the City of London at the Guildhall, Gresham Street, London, and the apprenticeship enrolments are complete from 1786. Information can be obtained from the Office of the Chamberlain on payment of a search fee.

French Measles The illness now called German measles.

Friends, Religious Society of (Quakers)

In 1647, George Fox (1624-91), the founder of the Society of Friends, began preaching in the north of England and soon established a large following, mainly in Westmorland, north Lancashire and northwest Yorkshire. However, the Society incurred the hostility of many of the older sects from among whom their conversions were made.

The following key dates will be found useful in historical research.

1650   An Act of Parliament made the Friends liable to charges of blasphemy. A magistrate bestowed on them the nickname 'Quakers'.

1654   The earliest records of meetings began.

1650s   London Friends began the keeping of central records, particularly of 'sufferings', but also of committees.

1656   The first missionaries went to America.

1661   More than 4000 Friends were released from prison in a temporary relaxation of regulations, following the end of the Commonwealth regime.

1662   The *Quaker Act* enabled conventicles (unlicensed meetings) to be broken up.

1664   The first *Conventicle Act* strengthened the Act of two years before.

1666   The Society's system of organisation was established.

1668   The first Yearly Meeting was held in London.

1670   The second *Conventicle Act* made Quakers the prey of informers.

1672   The first *Test Act* required an oath of supremacy from all holders of public office. Quakers would not take any oath at all.

1673   The Society's Library was founded, which included MS records.

1675   The permanent standing committee of the Society was established; called the Meeting for Sufferings, and still so called.

1682   William Penn founded Pennsylvania as a Quaker state.

1689   The *Toleration Act* ended persecution for non-attendance at church; but Quakers still suffered for non-payment of tithes.

18th Century: Preparative Meetings were instituted for the management of local business. There were separate Men's and Women's Meetings.

1753   Quakers were exempted from Lord Hardwicke's *Marriage Act*, which restricted marriages to churches licensed for that purpose.

1794   A record repository was founded at Devonshire House, Bishopsgate, London.

1828-9   The repeal of the *Test Acts* allowed Quakers to affirm, and gave them freedom to hold public office.

1837   All known registers up to this date, some dating from the 1650s, were copied into Digests; and in 1840 the originals were deposited at the General Register Office.

1857   Registers discovered since 1840 were also deposited with the Registrar General. They are now all at the Public Record Office, Chancery Lane, London, under call numbers RG.6 and 8.

1926   The central records were moved to their present location at Friends' House, Euston Road, London NW1.

Some understanding of Quaker organisation is necessary for research. Each local congregation is called a Particular Meeting; it also has a meeting of discipline to manage its affairs, called a Preparative Meeting. All the Preparative Meetings in one district send representatives to make up a Monthly Meeting, an executive body for the area, in which all lands, meeting-houses, etc., are vested. The Monthly Meetings in turn send representatives to a Quarterly Meeting. At first the jurisdiction of these covered one county, but now some counties have merged. In spring, the Quarterly Meetings send representatives to the London Yearly Meeting, which is the executive body for the whole country.

Documentary records at Friends' House comprise the minutes of regular meetings, special meetings and committees, 'Suffering Books', correspondence, registers of births, marriages and deaths or burials, admission lists, collection lists, disownments, removal certificates, accounts, deeds and property records. The minutes, especially of Preparative and Monthly Meetings, cover a number of aspects of members' lives, including care of the poor, education, apprenticeships, discipline and, most important for genealogists, marriage. Permission to marry had to be obtained from the Monthly Meetings, which checked that both parties were free to marry and had their parents' consent. A bride or bridegroom from another district had to produce a certificate from his or her own Meeting, showing that they knew of no hindrance to the marriage. The ceremony itself was by the declaration of both parties in open meeting, and a certificate was signed by all adults present. Some Quakers who could not get permission 'married out', i.e. they married by the normal ceremony in a parish church.

Researchers should be aware that the Society uses its own dating system. The names of months and of days of the week are replaced by numbers. Before 1752, March is called First Month; April, Second Month; May, Third Month, and so on: after 1752, January is First Month. Sunday is First Day; Monday, Second Day, and so on through the week.

County records are in the custody of the Meeting that produced them, and in the care of a Custodian. The annual *Book of Meetings*, published by Friends' House, gives the names and addresses of all local Clerks, who will arrange contacts. Some county records have been deposited at Friends' House, and some at the county record offices.

The Library at Friends' House has a Digest copy of all the ancient registers, and each meeting has a Digest copy of its own. The central Digest is arranged geographically in Quarterly Meeting areas. Each register is divided into decennial sections, and in each section the entries are in alphabetical order of initial letters and in chronological order within each letter. Each entry carries a reference to the volume and page where it can be found in the original register. The Digests do not contain the names of witnesses. Removal Certificates were testimonials given on Friends' emigration to Pennsylvania. *Collection of the Sufferings* by J. Besse (1753) is indexed.

The Friends' Historical Society publishes a journal issued from their headquarters at Friends' House.

For further reading, see *Sources for Non-conformist Genealogy and Family History* by D.J. Steel (1973), and *My Ancestors were Quakers. How can I find out more about them?* (Society of Genealogists).

Furlong A piece of land formed by several parallel strips (selions), 220 yards long, lying in the open arable fields of a manor. Also, in some places, called a Shot or a Flat.

Fyrd The name of the local militia in Anglo-Saxon times. In emergencies it continued to be called out, even after the Conquest. It is likely that, as in later times, every able-bodied man was obliged to serve when required.

Gafol A rent, either in money or in land.

Gang Week A lay term for Rogationtide, immediately before Ascension Day, so called from the custom of 'ganging' round the parish to perform the perambulation of its bounds.

Gaol, Common Either a county gaol under the High Sheriff, or a city goal under the corporation, or a church gaol.

Gaol Delivery A judicial hearing of the charges against all prisoners awaiting trial in the area prisons. By a Commission of Gaol Delivery, the king appointed certain persons justices and empowered them to deliver his gaols at certain places of the prisoners held within them. This commission was at first issued to Justices in Eyre, but later to Justices of Assize and of Gaol Delivery. It ordered them to meet at a certain place and at a time which they themselves could appoint, when the sheriff of the county would bring all the prisoners of the area before them. The records are at the Public Record Office, Chancery Lane, London, under references JUST.ITIN.3 and PL.25.

Gate (i) Leas or pasture. As a suffix after cow-, horse-, ox-, sheep-, etc., it means the common right of pasture for that beast. A 'gated pasture' was one on which only a certain number of beasts was allowed to graze. (*See also* WASTE).

(ii) A road or way; an element often found in the names of ancient streets.

Gavelkind Derived from two Anglo-Saxon words meaning 'holding of a family', this term originally denoted a whole mode of tenure, but in time it became applied solely to one characteristic markedly different from the law of tenure over most of the country. This peculiarity was a local survival of a pre-feudal custom, by which a man's land was divided between all his sons instead of passing to his eldest son (as it did by the later feudal law). If he had no sons, it was divided between all his daughters; but not between both sons and daughters. However, if one of the man's sons predeceased him, having himself had only a daughter or daughters, then on the old man's death his land would be divided between his sons, and the deceased son's portion would go to his daughters, being his heirs.

This law survived in Wales, in Kent, and in pockets of the country elsewhere. In Wales it was abolished under Henry VIII, but in other places it continued until 1925. In Kent, gavelkind became the Common Law mode of land inheritance, and all lands held in socage were presumed to be partible unless proved to the contrary. Elsewhere in England, primogeniture was the Common Law, and if a claim of

partibility was made it had to be proved to be customary since 'Time Immemorial' (i.e. prior to the accession of Richard I in 1189).

The following list, not necessarily complete, of places outside Kent where gavelkind was the custom, was given by P.M. Thomas in *Genealogist's Magazine* Vol.15, No.2: Oswaldbeck Soke, Nottinghamshire, until 32 Henry VIII (his thirty-second regnal year); the fee of Pickering, Norfolk; the Soke of Rothelay, Leicestershire; the port of Rye and elsewhere in Sussex; several places in Shropshire; the manors of Monmouth, Usk and Trelleg, Monmouthshire; the two hundreds in Archinfeld, Herefordshire; Wareham, Dorset; Taunton Dean, Somerset; Kentish Town, northwest London.

Genealogist's Guide, The *see* **Family Trees and Histories**

Genealogist's Magazine The journal of the Society of Genealogists.

Genealogists, Professional *see* **Association of Genealogists and Record Agents**

Genealogists, Society of The Society was founded in 1911 by a small group of genealogists, mostly professionals, and at that time occupied one room in Fleet Street. However, it grew and moved to more spacious premises in Bloomsbury, and then in 1931 to occupy a whole floor at Chaucer House, Malet Street, London WC1. It is a limited company, classified as an 'Association not for profit'. By 1952 there were one thousand members. Again it outgrew its premises, and moved to a large house in Harrington Gardens, London SW3; and in 1984 it moved to still larger premises at 14 Charterhouse Buildings, London EC1M 7BA.

The President of the Society is HRH Prince Michael of Kent. The work of the Society is administered by an elected Executive Committee, and it employs, full-time, a Director of Research, a Secretary and a Librarian. From the thousand members of 1954 it has grown to over 6500 members, many of them resident overseas.

The main advantages of membership are: (i) access to the Society's magnificent genealogical library, which is still growing steadily, and to its card indexes, which contain about three million names; (ii) free subscription to *The Genealogist's Magazine*, which is published quarterly and contains useful articles on research, a list of the latest accessions to the library, and news of events likely to affect genealogists.

The most valuable research aids in the library are the copies of parish registers, some printed, some typescript and some in manuscript. Of the 11,000 ancient parishes of England there are now copies in the library of the registers — or of part of the registers — of over 5000. More marriage registers have been copied than those of baptisms and burials. Next in importance comes Boyd's Marriage Index, compiled by Percival Boyd. It covers about 2600 registers or part registers, and contains between six and seven million names. The library also contains indexes of eighteenth-century apprenticeships, of the wills of many probate courts, and of marriage licence records. There are numbers of local directories, professional directories, poll books, transcripts of memorial inscriptions, and publications of county historical societies. Where applicable, these are arranged under county headings. There are also school and university registers, works on palaeography, heraldry and surname origins, and a whole room is devoted to narrative family histories. The parish register copies, directories and poll books are catalogued, and there is a card index to the whole library. Copies of most of the reference books mentioned in this dictionary are on the library shelves. There is a Document Collection kept in box files, and a Great Index containing over three million references extracted from parish registers, memorial inscriptions, will indexes, Chancery suits and other records. The Society also has the International Genealogical Index microfiches for the whole country.

The Society's library is open from Tuesday to Saturday during the following hours: Tue., Fri. and Sat. 10 a.m. - 6 p.m , Wed. and Thurs. 10 a.m. - 8 p.m.

For subscription purposes, members are divided into Town Members and Country and Overseas Members. There is a common entrance fee for all members.

Non-members can use the library for either one hour, three-and-a-half hours, a whole day or a whole day and an evening, on payment of the appropriate search fee.

The Society's staff will undertake a certain amount of research, both in its own collection and elsewhere. Application should be addressed to the Director of Research at the above address.

Besides its quarterly journal and a number of specialist guides (mentioned under their subject headings), the Society publishes aids for the genealogist in the shape of charts, record cards and birth briefs.

See also BOYD'S MARRIAGE INDEX.

Genealogy The study of the descents of families and persons from an ancestor or ancestors. Genealogy takes several forms, but there are three main avenues of research. Firstly, the tracing of a male-line descent, leading to the compilation of a Family Tree showing male-line ancestors and ancestresses, and the ancestors' brothers and sisters. Secondly, the tracing of all male-line descendants of a common ancestor, leading to the compilation of an Extended Family Tree showing all collateral branches of a family. Thirdly, the tracing of all ancestors of a given person through male *and* female lines, leading to the compilation of a Total Descent chart.

Descents are traced from evidence provided by documents contemporaneous with the family events recorded in them (Primary Evidence). The techniques have been well developed, and most of the necessary records have now become readily available. Any lack of success is usually due to faulty record-keeping in the past, destruction or loss of records, movements of families from place to place, or the number of unrelated families of the same surname. Indexes of baptisms and marriages now in course of compilation will, when complete, greatly reduce the difficulty caused by family mobility. For the methods of genealogical research, see the Guide to Ancestry Research at the beginning of this book.

Genealogy has recently become a popular leisure pursuit, and has given rise to the formation of family history societies all over the country.

See also FAMILY HISTORY.

General Register of Births, Deaths and Marriages

By the *Births and Deaths Registration Act* and the *Marriage Act*, both of 1836, civil registration of births, deaths and marriages was begun on 1 July, 1837. For the first time, these events were entered in a single register for everyone in England and Wales.

The country was divided into 27 numbered regions, which were themselves divided into registration districts under the control of Superintendent Registrars, and sub-divided into sub-districts under Registrars. In 1851 there were 623 registration districts. Registration was compulsory, but at first there was no penalty for non-observance. Some parents failed (and some still do) to register their children's births, and some children have actually been registered twice under different forenames; but for deaths and marriages, registration is complete apart from occasional human error. The clergy have duplicate registration books for marriages, and no burial is permitted without a death certificate. When a duplicate marriage register book is full the clergyman has to pass it to his local registrar, but the latter also visits his local churches each quarter and makes copies of all marriage entries up to date. He maintains an index and, at the end of each quarter, the Superintendent Registrar of the district passes the duplicates to the office of the Registrar General in London. There they are all bound into volumes, and a separate quarterly index is compiled for each type of event. Marriages are indexed under the names of both parties. If the bride is a widow or divorcee, she is entered under the surname of her former husband.

The following dates are useful to bear in mind:

1852 Regional areas were altered and the number of them increased to 34 (*see* list below).

1866 The index of deaths began to show the age of the deceased. Also, all indexes from this date are printed or typed.

1874 Penalties came into force for failure to register births.

1911 From September of this year the mother's maiden name is shown in the index of births.

1912 The index of marriages shows the name of the spouse beside the one indexed.

1974 The General Register Office, which had been housed at Somerset House in the Strand, London, was moved to St Catherine's House on the east corner of Kingsway and Aldwych, where it is a section of the Office of Population Censuses and Surveys. The entrance is in Aldwych.

1980 Index volumes of deaths temporarily moved to Alexandra House, Kingsway.

Search Procedure The information supplied by the General Register Office is solely in the form of a certified copy of the original certificate. This can be applied for either by calling at the Office, searching the indexes and completing an application form, or by letter, giving sufficient information for the registration entry to be identified, and paying for it in advance.

Double-barrelled names are indexed in alphabetical order of the complete name, ignoring the hyphen; for example, the name Stone-Mogg will be found under S and after Stoneman. A guide leaflet (PSR.2) is available at St Catherine's House and can be usefully studied before a search.

Inside the entrance of the Office are racks containing application forms printed in red for births, and green for marriages. (Death indexes were until recently in a different building in Kingsway.) The searcher fills in the appropriate form with any particulars already known to him. He then proceeds further into the Office, where he will find rows of bookshelves containing quarterly indexes of births and marriages. The spine of each volume shows the year and quarter of the events indexed, and the initial letters of the surnames covered. The quarter is indicated by the name of its last month, so the volume for the first quarter of the year will show 'March' on its spine, and so on. If the researcher knows the exact date of the event he is looking for, he looks up the name in the relevant volume. Against it he will find a reference consisting of the name of the registration district, a volume number which is also the number of the region in which the registration district lies, and a page number. The name of the registration district will not necessarily be the same as that of the town or village in which the event took place. Usually it is the name of a large town in the district, but sometimes of the hundred or other area. If the district name is not familiar to the searcher, and so does not tell him in what part of the country it is, he can identify the region from the volume number by referring to the list at the end of this article. When there is more than one person of the same name in the index, the volume (region) number can help the searcher to decide which is the one he is looking for.

If the exact date of the event is not known, the researcher will have to search the volumes of several quarters or years around the most probable one. If he finds more than one person of the same name, he should note the references against them all and decide which is the most likely. He then enters its whole reference on the application form and indicates whether the certificate, when it is ready, is to be sent or called for. On the back of the form he can also enter details about the person sought. These are called checking points. If the certificate does not correspond with them the researcher will not receive a certificate, but will be refunded part of his payment. It is therefore very important that any such details given should be known to be absolutely correct.

If the searcher finds more than one index entry that could be the one he wants, he should fill in an application form for one of them in the usual way, with checking points on the back, and ask the cashier for a Reference Checking Sheet on which to enter the others. A charge will be made for each extra entry. A certificate will be issued for the first entry that corresponds with all the checking points. Fuller details about this multiple checking will be supplied by the cashier on form PSR.11.

The difficulty most likely to be encountered in searching the index is in the spelling of the surname, which may well differ from the one expected. Before making the search it is a good plan to think of as many variant spellings as possible. The most misleading variants are those that alter the first letter of the name. The letter H is liable to be dropped, or added, and the addition or omission of a final S or E is also common.

Another difficulty arises when there has been a change of forename after registration, or when a person has been commonly known by his or her second forename or a pet name. Unfortunately, too, the indexing is not faultless;

events that have been duly registered may have been omitted from the index, or one party to a marriage may have been indexed and not the other.

When the application form has been handed in and the fee paid, the applicant has to wait a few days before receipt of the certificate, either by calling for it at the General Register Office or by having it sent by post.

Birth Certificates A birth certificate supplies the date and place of birth, the name and sex of the child, the name and occupation of the father, the name and previous surname or surnames of the mother, and the name, description and address of the informant.

If the certificate shows not only the date but also the time of day of the birth, a multiple birth is indicated. The name or names of the other child or children can therefore be looked for in the same index volume, and will be recognised by having the same reference to district, volume and page.

Parents are allowed forty-two days in which to register a birth, so the registration of a child born at the end of March, June, September or December may appear in the index of the quarter following the birth.

Sometimes the child had not been named at the time of registration, in which case only 'Male' or 'Female' will appear in the index at the end of the list of named children of the same surname.

Sometimes the parent of a newborn child will have omitted to inform the registrar that the mother had been married before, so only one of her previous names will be shown on the birth certificate. If this is her maiden name, difficulty may be caused in finding the marriage certificate of the child's parents.

If the child was born out of wedlock, the father's name was usually omitted, but after 1875 a father who accompanied the mother to the registrar's office and admitted paternity could have his name entered on the certificate, in which case the birth would be indexed under both surnames.

Several children of exactly the same names may be registered in the same district in the same quarter. Even the father's name may match that shown on the child's eventual marriage certificate. So check against any other information that is known, e.g. the father's occupation, his address or the name of the mother. If none of these is conclusive, turn to the known brothers and sisters of the child and apply for their birth certificates in order to find a set with common parents — but consider the possibility of a second wife. In any case, it is wise, though expensive, to obtain birth certificates of all brothers and sisters. They may show changes of the parents' residence and the father's occupation.

Foundling children are listed after Z in the index.

Adopted Children's Birth Certificates The register of adopted children was started in 1927, and is indexed separately. The certificates show only the dates of birth and adoption, the names of the adoptive parents and the names they gave to the child. (*See also* ADOPTED CHILDREN.)

Marriage Certificates A marriage certificate supplies the date, place and rites of the marriage, both parties' names, ages (sometimes), marital status, occupations and addresses, the names and occupations of their fathers, and the names of the witnesses.

If the rites by which the marriage was celebrated were not those of the Church of England, eventual searches for the baptisms of the parties will probably have to be conducted in non-parochial registers.

When starting to search the marriage index, it saves time to note in advance the date of birth of the eldest child of the marriage, so that the search backwards can start from there. If the surnames of both parties are known, it pays to search for the more uncommon one. When it is found, the name of the spouse should then be looked up in the volume for the same quarter. There it must, of course, be accompanied by the same reference details. From 1911 onward, this checking of the spouse is unnecessary, as his or her name will be shown against the name you have found.

A divorced person is described as 'single person'.

Always treat any ages shown on a marriage certificate with caution. Often no exact age is given, just 'of full age', meaning 21 or over. The same information is sometimes more misleadingly stated just by the figure 21. Also, the

CERTIFIED COPY OF AN ENTRY OF BIRTH

CERTIFIED to be a true copy of an entry in the certi
Given at the GENERAL REGISTER OFFICE, LONDON, und

CERTIFIED COPY OF AN ENTRY OF BIRTH
The fee for this certificate is 40p.
When application is made by post a
handling fee is payable in addition.

CERTIFIED to be a true copy of an entry in the certifi
Given at the GENERAL REGISTER OFFICE, SOMERSET HOU

GIVEN AT THE GENERAL REGISTER OFFICE, LONDON

Application Number......*6724B*

DISTRICT					

Wisbech

Walpole St Peters in the *County of Norfolk*

5 Name, surname and maiden surname of mother	6 Occupation of father	7 Signature, description and residence of informant	8 When registered	9 Signature of registrar	10* Name entered after registration
Mary Wyatt formerly Baker	*Labourer*	*John Wyatt the Father Marsh Walpole St Peters*	*December 12th*	*John Bridgman Reg.*	

of a Register of Births in the District above mentioned.
of the said Office, the *28th* day of *February* 1980

Copies of nineteenth-century birth certificates. In the lower one, the absence of a father's name and occupation shows that the mother was unmarried.

Crown copyright, reproduced with the permission of the controller of HMSO

GIVEN AT THE GENERAL REGISTER OFFICE,
SOMERSET HOUSE, LONDON

Application Number......*AW 98383/72*

DISTRICT					

Sheffield

North Sheffield in the *county of York*

5 Name, surname and maiden surname of mother	6 Occupation of father	7 Signature, description and residence of informant	8 When registered	9 Signature of registrar	10* Name entered after registration
Mary Ann Bennett	—	*X The mark of Mary Ann Bennett Mother Union Workhouse Sheffield*	*Twentyfourth March 1844*	*W Hardcastle Registrar*	

of a Register of Births in the District above mentioned.
N, under the Seal of the said Office, the *13* day of *October* 19 *72*

121

Registration District___*Wisbech*___

1850___. Marriage solemnized at___*The Parish Church*___
in the *Parish* of_____ *West Walton*_____ in the___*County*

No.	When married	Name and Surname	Age	Condition	Rank or profession
91	May 14th	Edward Ulyat	Full age	Bachelor	Farmer
		Mary Anne Fisher	Full age	Spinster	—

Married in the___*Parish Church*___according to the *rites and Ceremonies* of the

This marriage was solemnized between us, { *Edward Ulyat* / *Mary Ann Fisher* } in the presence of us, { *Jno Thos Macdon...* / *Louisa Fish...* }

CERTIFIED to be a true copy of an entry in the certified copy of a Register of Marriages in the District

Given at the GENERAL REGISTER OFFICE, LONDON, under the Seal of the said Office, the 24th

CERTIFIED COPY OF AN ENTRY OF DEATH Given

REGISTRATION DISTRICT___*Wisbech*___

1866. DEATH in the Sub-district of___*Walpole Saint Peter*___in t

Columns :— 1	2	3	4	5	6
No.	When and where died	Name and surname	Sex	Age	Occupation	Cause of death
162	Third August 1866 West Walton	John Ulyatt	male	77 years	Agricultural labourer	General Dec... Certified

CERTIFIED to be a true copy of an entry in the certified copy of a Register of Deaths in the District ab...

Given at the GENERAL REGISTER OFFICE, LONDON, under the Seal of the said Office, the 24th day of

ENERAL REGISTER OFFICE, LONDON

Application Number.....4.73.0...D

	Norfolk		
6	7	8	
e time of marriage	Father's name and surname	Rank or profession of father	
e St Peters	Abraham Ulyat	Farmer	
alton	William Fisher	Farmer	

ished Church by Licence by me
D.P. Calliphronas

ntioned.

of ___ January ___ 19 78

ENERAL REGISTER OFFICE, LONDON.

Application Number.....5.1.7.1..4

County of Norfolk		
7	8	9
nature, description, and sidence of informant	When registered	Signature of registrar
The mark of hn Watson esent at death dept Walton	Fifth August 1866	William Winterton Registrar

ued.
19 80

---

residence at the time of marriage, especially that of the bridegroom, may be only a temporary one. The occupation of the bridegroom may be different from that in which he is known to have been engaged later in life. On some marriage certificates the father's name is omitted. This may mean that he was dead, or that he did not marry the mother. In other cases his name is given but not his occupation, and this usually means that he was dead.

Death Certificates A death certificate indicates the date, place and cause of death, the deceased's name, sex, age and rank or profession, and the name, description and address of the informant.

The main reasons for obtaining a death certificate are: (i) to ascertain the place and date of death for their own sake; (ii) to find out the deceased person's age as a clue to the year of his birth; (iii) to obtain his address in preparation for a search of the Census Returns.

From 1866 onward, the age of the deceased person is shown in the index. It is wise not to enter any known occupation on the application form, as this may have changed at some time. If the deceased died later than 1857, and is thought likely to have left a will, the date of death may be more quickly found by searching the Index of Grants of Probate at the Principal Registry of the Family Division (*see* FAMILY DIVISION.)

The person's place of death may not be his or her home address. Also, when the informant is not a member of the deceased's family, the age shown may be a mere guess. In any case, ages on death certificates should be treated with caution. If the informant is a coroner, the local newspaper should be searched for the report of an inquest.

Applications by post for certificates, including those for deaths, should be made to the General Register Office, St Catherine's House, Kingsway,

ABOVE Marriage certificate of Edward Ulyat and Mary Anne Fisher. The entry 'Full age' is frustrating, but all too common. BELOW Death certificate of John Ulyatt. Note the difference in spelling the family name here and on his relative's marriage certificate above, a difference that can safely be ignored. *Both documents: Crown copyright, reproduced with the permission of the controller of HMSO*

London WC2, with any *definitely known* information about the person. However, it is safest not to give an exact age or occupation — the former may be mis-stated on the certificate, and the latter may have changed since the time of your evidence. If any particular you supply does not match that on the certificate, you will be told the person cannot be found. If the exact date of the event (birth, marriage or death) is not known, the staff will make a search through five years. Fees for searches and certificates have to be paid at the time of application. The charge for an application made by post is much higher than for one made in person, even if it is sent on the official form after a personal search.

Index searching can be carried out at the local register office in the district where the event is thought to have taken place.

For the registration of the births, marriages and deaths of British persons abroad, *see* GENERAL REGISTER OFFICE *and* ABROAD, BRITONS.

General Registration Regions: 1837-51

I	West London
II	East London
III	Middlesex
IV	Surrey
V	Kent
VI	Bedfordshire, Berkshire (part of), Buckinghamshire, Hertfordshire
VII	Hampshire (part of), Sussex
VIII	Dorset, Hampshire (part of), Wiltshire
IX	Cornwall, Scilly Isles, Devon (part of)
X	Devon (part of), Somerset (part of)
XI	Gloucestershire (part of), Somerset (part of)
XII	Essex, Suffolk (part of)
XIII	Norfolk, Suffolk (part of)
XIV	Cambridgeshire, Huntingdonshire, Lincolnshire
XV	Leicestershire, Northamptonshire, Nottinghamshire, Rutland
XVI	Berkshire (part of), Oxfordshire, Staffordshire (part of), Warwickshire (part of)
XVII	Staffordshire (part of)
XVIII	Gloucestershire (part of), Shropshire, Staffordshire (part of), Warwickshire (part of), Worcestershire
XIX	Cheshire, Derbyshire, Flintshire (part of)
XX	Lancashire (part of)
XXI	Lancashire (part of), Yorkshire (part of)
XXII	West Riding (part of), East Riding (part of)
XXIII	West Riding (part of), East Riding (part of)
XXIV	County Durham, North Riding
XXV	Cumberland, Lancashire (part of), Northumberland, Westmorland
XXVI	South Wales, Herefordshire
XXVII	North Wales, Anglesey

General Registration Regions: 1852-1946 (August)

1a - 1d	Greater London
2a	Surrey, Kent
2b - 2c	Sussex, Hampshire (part of)
2d	Berkshire, Hampshire (part of)
3a	Middlesex, Hertfordshire, Oxfordshire, Buckinghamshire
3b	Bedfordshire, Cambridgeshire, Huntingdonshire, Northamptonshire
4a	Essex, Suffolk
4b	Norfolk
5a	Wiltshire, Dorset
5b	Devon
5c	Cornwall, Scilly Isles, Somerset
6a	Gloucestershire, Herefordshire, Shropshire

6b	Staffordshire, Warwickshire (part of), Worcestershire (part of)
6c	Warwickshire (part of), Worcestershire (part of)
6d	Warwickshire (part of)
7a	Leicestershire, Lincolnshire, Rutland
7b	Derbyshire, Nottinghamshire
8a	Cheshire
8b - 8e	Lancashire
9a - 9d	Yorkshire
10a	County Durham
10b	Cumberland, Northumberland, Westmorland
11a	South Coast Wales
11b	North Wales, Anglesey

The further changes to the list of districts for 1946 onward are not included, as they have little direct importance for most family history researchers.

General Register Office This section of the Office of Population Censuses and Surveys is situated at the junction of Kingsway (east side) and Aldwych, London, and is entered by the Aldwych doorway. It houses the General Register of Births, Deaths and Marriages, and also the following miscellaneous registers.

Marine Register Books Births and deaths of people of British nationality at sea since 1 July, 1837 (*see also* MERCHANT SEAMEN; SEA, BIRTHS AND DEATHS AT).

Air Register Books Births and deaths in UK-registered aircraft since 1949.

Army Chaplains' Returns Births, marriages and deaths of servicemen abroad, 1796-1880.

Army Returns of Births, Marriages and Deaths 1881-1955, abroad, but excluding the two World Wars (for which see below).

Army Regimental Registers Births, marriages and deaths abroad, 1761-1924.

Royal Air Force Returns Similar registers since 1920.

Consular Returns Information on births, marriages and deaths of British subjects in foreign countries since 1849, provided they were notified to Consular Officers.

Natal and South Africa Field Forces Deaths during the Boer War, 1899-1902.

Deaths abroad of Officers and Men in the Three Services (separate volumes) during the two World Wars.

Also, registers of deaths abroad in quite recent years.

The office is open from Monday to Friday, 8.30 a.m. to 4.30 p.m.

See also ABROAD, BRITONS for miscellaneous registers of births, marriages and deaths abroad, recently transferred from the General Register Office to the Public Record Office, Chancery Lane, London.

Generation Reckonings of what is meant by a generation in terms of years (i.e the period between the births of one male-line ancestor and the next) have varied in the past from twenty-five to thirty-three years, but all these appear to be underestimates. Some seem to assume what is now seen to be too low an age for men at marriage, and one recently published calculation of thirty years has been based on descents mainly through heirs and partly through females, thus confusing and reducing the generation gap. Peter Laslett of the Cambridge Group for the History of Population and Social Structure, has found that the average marriage age of an Elizabethan or Jacobean woman did not differ greatly from that in our own time. It was 'something like 24', and that of her bridegroom four years older at 28, so the average age of a husband at the birth of his eldest child would be 29. While this shows that the generation gap for the average median child must be several years greater, further demographic research is needed to establish a reliable figure. In the meantime, the following rule-of-thumb calculation will probably be found to be not far out in its result. The wife might go on bearing children until she was 42, and the husband 46, so that at the birth of his average median child he would be 36.5. As the intervals between children tend to lengthen as a woman grows older, this figure should be adjusted downward to, perhaps, 35, to find the median child. It is harder to say what upward adjustment should then be made to take account of second wives; probably only a few months. Thus, 35 would appear to be a good working figure. As it is an average, few families will correspond with it exactly.

Gentleman In the Middle Ages the word 'gentil' meant 'noble', but 'gentleman' came into use in the fifteenth century to signify a condition between baron and yeoman, or sometimes between knight and yeoman, after a statute of I Henry V (his first regnal year) had laid down that in certain legal documents the 'estate, degree or mystery' of the defendent must be stated. In 1429 the term *les gentils* was used in an Act of Parliament, of men having freehold property worth 40 shillings per year or more.

From the sixteenth century onward, the distinction between gentlemen and yeomen lay more in their way of life than in their relative prosperity. A gentleman did not work with his hands, so his household included personal servants; whereas the servants of a yeoman were his assistants on the land and in the dairy. A gentleman's son was often described as a yeoman while he was working his holding, pending inheritance of his father's lands. Members of the professions, i.e. army and naval officers and barristers, were regarded as gentlemen, some of them being entitled to the description 'Esquire'. For apprenticing a son to a London citizen a property qualification was required, so many gentlemen's sons entered the more profitable trades of the City. When a man, who during his working life was designated by his occupation (for example, tailor), retired, he would often then describe himself as 'Gentleman' as he was no longer gainfully employed.
See also CLASS, SOCIAL.

Gentleman's Magazine This magazine, known also as the *Monthly Intelligencer*, began publication in January, 1731. Its contents, modified comparatively little over the years, were then: A View of the Weekly Disputes and Essays in this Month (intellectual and literary), Poetical Essays, the Monthly Intelligencer (news day-by-day), Deaths, Casualties, Promotions, Ecclesiastical Preferments, Marriages, Bankrupts

and Accidents, Observations in Gardening, Foreign Affairs, Stocks, Prices of Grain and Goods, and Books Published.

General Indexes have been published for 1731-86 and 1786-1810 (two volumes); indexes of marriages for 1731-68; indexes of obituaries and biographies for 1731-80. Each volume also has its own index, but for names of persons they are reliable only for deaths and marriages. The obituaries section contains information of value to the family historian, and the Monthly Intelligencer and Foreign Affairs sections provide interesting background material. Announcements of deaths and marriages were usually culled from newspapers, which often contain more detailed information.

The magazine ceased publication in 1868. Complete series of the volumes can be found on the open shelves of the British Library and the Public Record Office, and the library of the Society of Genealogists has a set, though one with many gaps.

German A cousin german is a first cousin, i.e. the issue of an uncle or aunt. Brothers or sisters german are those having both parents in common.
See also SIBLINGS.

Gersum *see* **Gressom**

Gild, Craft In most of the older English towns, the master craftsmen were organised in craft gilds — associations of bakers, carpenters, mercers, shoemakers and others, whose origins date from the Middle Ages. The aims of such fellowships were to protect their members' interests, maintain prices, and exclude competition from non-members. The surviving records, to be found mainly in city record offices, are of the sixteenth to eighteenth centuries and consist of the following: *Minutes* of the meetings of the craft elders; *Ordinances*, which were the regulations laid down from time to time; *Accounts*, though it is seldom that all these are extant. For genealogists, the Accounts are the most useful, as the receipts include sums paid for admissions of apprentices and freemen (the names of masters are often mentioned), and amounts received for funeral obsequies at the burial of members deceased. They also supply, as do the Minutes and Ordinances, a wealth of background material about contemporary urban life.

Gild, Merchant A body of merchants whose members were drawn from a variety of occupations, authorised to regulate trade in their town. Their royal charter usually empowered them to hold their own courts, exempted them from the obligation to plead outside the borough, and acquitted them of toll on their goods when they traded elsewhere. Where merchant gilds existed, their records will be in the appropriate town archives.

Glebe The land held by a beneficed clergyman. Glebe Terriers describe the boundaries of such land, and mention the holders of lands adjoining. These are now usually to be found in county record offices.

Gloucestershire Since 1974 the southern parishes of the ancient county have been in the newly formed county of Avon. The Gloucestershire Family History Society and the Bristol and Avon Family History Society hold regular meetings and issue journals. Enquiries should be sent c/o The Federation of Family History Societies, 31 Seven Star Road, Solihull, West Midlands B91 2BZ, marked 'Please forward' and enclosing a stamped self-addressed envelope.

Record Repositories Gloucestershire Record Office, Worcester Street, Gloucester (tel: 0452. 21444); Bristol Archives Office, Council House, College Green, Bristol (tel: 0272.26031); The Cathedral Library, Gloucester; Gloucestershire and Cheltenham District Library, Clarence Street, Cheltenham.

Parish Registers and Indexes (*see* comment under COUNTY) Many of the 347 parishes have deposited their registers at the county record office (CRO). The Society of Genealogists has copies of many in its library. Boyd's Marriage Index covers 194 registers, plus extracts from some others. Pallot's Marriage Index covers 126, mainly from 1790 to 1812. A marriage index of the modern Bristol Diocese, 1754-1837, is being compiled by the Bristol and Avon Family History Society. The INTERNATIONAL GENEA-LOGICAL INDEX (IGI) contains an almost complete coverage of baptisms. The Bishops' Transcripts are at the CRO.

Marriage Licence Records These are at the CRO.

Wills before 1858 are at the CRO. Before 1541, Gloucestershire comprised the archdeaconries of Worcester and Hereford, so a few early wills can be found proved in the Consistory Courts of those dioceses. Bristol before 1542 was in the Diocese of Worcester, from 1542 to 1836 in that of Bristol, and from 1836 to 1897 in the Diocese of Gloucester and Bristol, so that many wills can be found at the Bristol Archives Office. As the whole county has always lain in the Province of Canterbury, wills could also be proved in the Prerogative Court of Canterbury.

Non-parochial Registers Sixty-four registers are at the Public Record Office (PRO), Chancery Lane, London, and the IGI covers a similar number.

Census Returns These are at the PRO, Portugal Street, London, and at the CRO. They are being indexed by the Bristol and Avon Family History Society.

Memorial Inscriptions Transcripts of over one hundred parishes are at the Society of Genealogists.

Heralds' Visitation Pedigrees have been printed for 1569, 1582, 1623 and 1682.

Goad A land measure of six yards. Another term for a rod, pole or perch.

Godparents The practice of giving a child three godparents (two of its own sex and one of the other) dates back to pre-Reformation times and was confirmed by the restoration of Anglican rites in 1661. In medieval England a spiritual relationship, or affinity, was held to exist between godparents on the one hand and godchildren and their parents on the other, so that marriage between them was forbidden. Godparents are almost certainly the second most powerful influence in the choice of a child's Christian name, which may be one reason why, in the sixteenth century, more than one child of a family is often found bearing the same name, though both were living.

Goodman The male counterpart of Goodwife. In the sixteenth and seventeenth centuries,

husbandmen and those of similar status were styled, for example, Goodman Smith, and addressed as 'Goodman'.
See also CLASS, SOCIAL.

Goodwife The female equivalent of Goodman. A woman below the status of those normally called 'Mrs', for example the wife of a husbandman.

Gore A triangular piece of arable land.

Gossip (i) A godparent (a corruption of 'Goodsib').
 (ii) A friend.
 (iii) A disseminator of personal news, or a rumour-monger.
 (iv) The talk of a gossip — rumour.

Grange (i) A centre of land cultivation belonging, until the Dissolution, to a monastery, but too far distant from it to be worked by the monks.
 (ii) Later, a barn.

Gravestones *see* **Memorial Inscriptions**

Green-sickness Anaemia.

Gressom (Gersum) The fine paid to a feudal superior upon entry into a holding.

Gretna Green Marriage *see* **Border Marriages**

Group, Archive *see* **Class, Archive**

Guardians of the Poor In 1834 the care of the poor was transferred from the parish to the Boards of Guardians newly constituted by the merging of parishes (for Poor Law purposes) into 585 Unions. Each Union was under the control of its own Board, consisting of parish representatives elected by the major rate-payers. The out-relief formerly given to the poor was restricted to cases of most serious need; for others, a spell in the Union's workhouse was substituted. Any previously existing work-houses in the area were disposed of. Workhouse inmates were segregated into seven groups, according to age and sex.

The records of the Unions include the following: *Minutes* of the Meetings of Guardians; *Rate Books* of the Overseers of the Poor of the parishes, who still had the Poor Rate to collect; the *Account Book of Workhouse Expenditure*; the Relieving Officers' *Accounts of Out-Relief*; the *Reports of Medical Officers* and *Reports of Undertakers*. Some Boards arranged for the emigration of their younger paupers (*see* EMIGRANTS). These records are at county or borough record offices.

Guide Books The publication of local guide books increased steadily from the middle of the eighteenth century, and by the end of that century some writers were specialising in that type of work, particularly for those resorts favoured by the gentry. In the nineteenth century, publishers followed suit by issuing uniform series of guide books, for example those of Black, Muirhead and Nelson. These supply useful information and background material for the family historian.

Guild *see* **Gild, Craft** *and* **Gild, Merchant**

Guildhall Library Located in Aldermanbury, London EC2, this library is one of the richest in genealogical material in the country, and comprises two sections: Printed Books, and Manuscripts. The collections in the latter section should not, however, be confused with the archives of the Corporation of the City of London, which are also housed at the Guildhall — not in the Library, but in the Record Office.

Printed Books During the Second World War, much of the Library's storage facilities, and up to 30,000 volumes, were destroyed by bombing. Now, however, in the new extension of the Guildhall the genealogist is able to enjoy comfort and service and a wide range of works of interest to him, including Phillimore's printed marriage registers and some exceptional collections of local directories, poll books and local histories. Also available are professional directories, school and university registers, the publications of the Historical MSS Commission and the Public Record Office, and many works of the record-publishing societies, including the Harleian Society's *Heralds' Visitations*.

Manuscript Collections This department includes a large number of city parochial records, such as vestry minutes, churchwardens' accounts, rate books and parish registers. Deposits from the City Companies are their apprenticeship books, freemen's books, minute books, ordinances and charters. The ward rate books are there, back to 1771, plus many earlier ones in separate collections. Also available is M.A.J. Jewer's *Guide to the Monumental Inscriptions of the City Churches.*

The Guildhall Library also has typed transcripts of a number of useful records, including the parish registers of all Sussex and parts of Surrey and London; Boyd's *Marriage Index* and *Index of Apprentices*; the *1695 Inhabitants of the City* by M.P.E. Jones, and *17th-Century London Inhabitants* by the Reverend T.C. Dale. There are also CMB (Christenings, Marriages, Burials) registers of British congregations in Europe and overseas, including marriage registers of chaplains licensed by the Bishops of London, 1816-1924.

The Library also has the International Genealogical Index for the whole country.

A booklet, *Guide to Genealogical Sources in Guildhall Library*, has been published by the Corporation of London.

H

Hair Powder An Act of 1795 required all persons, male and female, using hair powder to buy a permit. Registers of these permits sometimes survive in county record offices, usually giving the address of the purchaser. Such permits would be obtained by 'persons of quality' for themselves and their menservants.

Half-baptized A colloquial term meaning 'christened privately', i.e. not in church. The clergy were, and still are, instructed to warn parents 'that without … great cause and necessity they procure not their children to be baptized at home in their houses. But when need shall compel them to do so, then . . .' a very brief

form of private baptism was laid down. The necessity was the weak state of a baby which might cause it to die before it could safely be taken to church, in which case the parson was hurriedly sent for and would come to the house. 'Let them [the parents] not doubt but that the child so baptized is lawfully and sufficiently baptized and ought not to be baptized again'. However, if the child unexpectedly regained health it was required then to be 'received into the Church' at a church ceremony in the presence of its godparents and congregation.

Occasionally both ceremonies were entered in the register as baptisms. It seems likely, however, that private baptisms were one cause of the baptismal registers being the worst kept. In cases of extreme urgency the midwife used to perform the baptism.

Halfpenny A coin dating, like the penny, from Anglo-Saxon times. When sums of money are recorded in sixteenth- and seventeenth-century documents, using the symbols £-s-d (pounds, shillings, pence), a halfpenny may be shown as '½' or as 'ob' (the abbreviation for *obolus* or *obulus*, the Latin term for the coin).

Hall Until the late seventeenth century, 'hall' meant the main living-room of a house. Often part of its ceiling would be the roof of the building. A fireplace and chimney might be in the middle of the hall, the space behind them being for cooking; and above the kitchen-space would be the bedchamber or chambers, with stairs leading up to them. A house built in this way is now known as a hall-house. Any small private living-room leading off the hall was called a parlour. In the inventory of a yeoman's house of 1596, the contents of his hall were listed as: 1 table, 3 chairs, 7 stools, 1 bench, 1 long saddle (settle), 2 pewter candlesticks, 4 brass ditto, 18 platters, 3 salts, 7 kettles, 8 pans, 12 pothooks, irons, gallowtree (on which to hang a cauldron) and tongs.

Hallmoot Another name for a manor court.

Hamlet A small group of houses, separate from the main village of a parish but nevertheless part of the parish. A hamlet did not rank as a township, and so had no constable of its own.

Hampshire Formerly called the county of Southampton. Until 1974 it included the Isle of Wight, now a separate county. The Bournemouth area is now in Dorset. The Hampshire Genealogical Society has branches in the north of the county and in the Isle of Wight. It holds meetings at all of them, and issues *The Hampshire Family Historian.* Enquiries should be sent c/o The Federation of Family History Societies, 31 Seven Star Road, Solihull, West Midlands B91 2BZ, marked 'Please forward' and enclosing a stamped self-addressed envelope.

Record Repositories Hampshire Record Office, Southgate Street, Winchester (tel: 0962.63153); Isle of Wight County Record Office, Carisbrooke Castle, Newport, Isle of Wight; Southampton Civic Record Office, Civic Centre, Southampton; Portsmouth City Record Office, Guildhall, Portsmouth; Winchester Cathedral Library, The Cathedral, Winchester.

Parish Registers and Indexes (*see* comment under COUNTY) The registers of most of the 307 ancient parishes are in the appropriate record office. The Society of Genealogists has copies of about 200. Pallot's Marriage Index covers 119, from 1790 to 1812. Mrs A.M. Clench of 1 Bond Road, Southampton, has a marriage index for 1700-1837 covering the whole county, and a pre-1700 index in progress. For the Isle of Wight there is a marriage index at the island's Record Office, complete for 1780-1837, and with earlier years in progress. The INTERNATIONAL GENEALOGICAL INDEX (IGI) includes a number of registers of both counties. The Bishops' Transcripts, from 1780, are at the county record office (CRO), Winchester.

Marriage Licence Records These are at the CRO, Winchester. Indexes are in print.

Wills before 1858, proved in the Consistory and Archdeaconry Courts of Winchester and numerous Peculiar Courts, are at the CRO, Winchester. As the county lay in the Province of Canterbury, wills could also be proved in the Prerogative Court of Canterbury. The Society of Genealogists has indexes to some of the above wills.

Non-parochial Registers Sixty-one registers are at the Public Record Office (PRO), Chancery Lane, London, and the IGI covers a similar number.

Census Returns These are at the PRO, Portugal Street, London, and at the two CROs. The Hampshire Genealogical Society has a copy of the one for 1851, and an index in progress.

Memorial Inscriptions The Hampshire Genealogical Society has transcription in progress. The Society of Genealogists also has a number of transcripts.

Heralds' Visitation Pedigrees have been printed for 1530, 1575, 1622, 1634 and 1686.

The Hampshire Genealogical Society has published *A Guide to Genealogical Sources for Hampshire,* by F.H. and E. Edwards.

Hamsoken The offence of assaulting a man in his own dwelling.

Hanaper The department of Chancery to which fees were paid for the sealing and enrolment of charters.

Handwriting In Anglo-Saxon times, Latin documents were written in 'Caroline Minuscule', which derived its name from Charlemagne, in whose reign it appeared. Vernacular documents were written in a native script. After the Conquest most records were written in Latin, and many words were written in abbreviated form in conjunction with a system of explanatory signs above or below the line. In writing English, the same abbreviations and signs were used, as far as possible. The most common types of handwriting used from the twelfth to the sixteenth century are called Court Hands, or, less usually, Charter Hands. They were a cursive development of miniscule used in the law courts of Chancery, Exchequer, King's Bench and Common Pleas, and in each court the script had its own characteristics. However, the term Court Hand is used to cover the basic handwriting in which all records of this period were written.

There was another development from Caroline Minuscule, called Book Hand. It was not cursive and was reserved for the copying of liturgical manuscripts and learned and literary works.

By the late fifteenth century, although abbreviation continued, most of the associated signs had degenerated into meaningless

The Court Hand alphabet, from A. Wright's *Court Hand Restored*, based mainly on sixteenth- and seventeenth-century legal and chancery examples.

flourishes. However, they were not entirely discarded even after the reformation of handwriting in the mid sixteenth century.

This reformation took place partly owing to the more general use of paper, and partly to the secularisation of literacy. From 1570 onward, writing-masters published copybooks. These appeared in two scripts; Secretary Hand, which was based on Court Hand, and Italic or Italian Hand, which was an import from Italy. Not unnaturally — but unfortunately for researchers today — the less innovatory Secretary Hand proved the more popular, and it continued in use until late in the seventeenth century. Punctuation was little used until the eighteenth century.

From 1650 to 1660 Latin was abolished as the language of legal documents, but it was restored with the Restoration of the monarchy.

In the late seventeenth century, the Italic Hand was being more widely taught in schools, and by 1670 its use predominated. In this hand all abbreviations disappeared except superior letters (e.g. 12th), and the full stop (e.g. Nov.), which was introduced in 1703. In fact, Italic Hand is substantially the same as the one we use today. Secretary Hand is discussed under its own heading. Anyone familiar with it will have little difficulty in reading English in Court Hand.

For further study, see *Examples of Handwriting, 1550-1650*, by W.S.B. Buck, available from the Society of Genealogists; and *The Handwriting of English Documents*, by L.C. Hector.

Harkye The harvest supper. It derives from the first words, 'Hark ye', of the parson's announcement in church of the official end of the harvest. Also used in the form 'Harkey'.

Harleian Society A record-publishing society founded in 1869. It is best known for its numerous volumes of pedigrees of Heralds' Visitations of the English counties in the sixteenth and seventeenth centuries, but it has also published a great many parish registers, mostly of London, and six volumes of Musgrave's *Obituary prior to 1800*, culled from the *Scots Magazine*, the *European Magazine* and the annual and historical registers.

The address of the Honorary Secretary is Church Cottage, Thames Ditton, Surrey.

Hatchment The word is derived from the heraldic term, Achievement. It denotes a display of the arms and other heraldic insignia of a person on the occasion of his or her death. Originally this consisted of a man's actual helmet, shield and other accoutrements, but later it was confined to a pictorial representation of the achievement on a lozenge-shaped canvas, or board of wood. The custom was to hang the hatchment on the house-front of the deceased for a period of mourning, which might be as long as a year, and then transfer it to the interior of the parish church. Sometimes two were made, one for the house-front and the other for the church. The custom, which may have been imported from the Netherlands, was in vogue from the early seventeenth century to the mid nineteenth, and had not entirely died out in the 1920s. Many hatchments that used to hang in churches have now disappeared, owing to decay and church restorations.

The arms of an unmarried or widowed person were painted against a black background to denote mourning, but those of a married couple (i.e. with the arms of the husband 'impaling' those of his wife, or with his wife's arms on an escutcheon of pretence) had a particoloured background to indicate which party had died. If it was the husband who had died, the background behind the dexter side of the shield would be black; if the wife had died, the black would be on the sinister side. In each case the other side of the background would be white. (Dexter and sinister are the right and left sides of a shield respectively, as regarded by a person holding the shield from behind.)

When a hatchment was needed it was wanted at once, and heraldic artists often painted the arms of the local gentry on hatchments during their lifetime, so that when death came they had only to fill in the background.

For further reading, see *Hatchments in Britain*, edited by Peter Summers FSA.

Haybote The manorial right of tenants to cut wood for fences.

Hayward An official of the manor responsible for the maintenance of hedges.

Headborough Originally the head of a tithing

or frankpledge, but later the constable or deputy constable, according to the usage of the area, manor or parish.

Headland The space left at the end of a selion for the plough to turn on.

Health and Social Security, Department of This government department will forward letters to the last address in their records of any person sufficiently identified by their full name, any known address, date of birth or approximate age, and last known marital status. Enquiries should be addressed to Special Section A, Room 101B, Department of Health and Social Security, Records Branch, Newcastle-upon-Tyne. This service offers the best method of tracing relatives with whom one has lost contact.
See also MISSING PERSONS.

Hearth Tax The first Act imposing 'Hearth Money' came into force on 19 May, 1662, and the first collection was made at the following Michaelmas. It was managed by county and county borough authorities, and only taxable hearths were listed. The tax was levied upon all houses 'which are not worth in yearly value below Twenty Shillings and are not inhabited by Almsmen', and was two shillings per annum for each hearth or stove. Persons exempted were: those who paid neither Church nor Poor Rate; those inhabiting a house worth less than £1 per year, if they did not have any other property exceeding that value, nor an annual income of more than £10; charitable institutions, e.g. hospitals, almshouses and free schools; and industrial hearths, except for bakers' ovens and smiths' forges. The tax was payable by the occupier, not the landlord, and was assessed on the occupier's ability to pay. Attempted evasion of payment was punished by a prison sentence of up to one month.

1663 A new Act laid down that *all* hearths were to be included in the returns, including those that were exempt from the tax.

1664 From this Michaelmas until the next year, the collection was managed by Receivers appointed by the Treasury. The Lady Day assessment contains far more non-chargeable hearths than those of other dates and years. By the *Second Revisory Act of Collection*, all who had

more than two chimneys had to pay the tax. Landlords with poor tenants had to pay their tax for them. If a stopped-up chimney was discovered, it was charged double.

1666 From this Michaelmas, the tax was farmed on contract. Also, the collection of the Lady Day assessment was received by the farmers (*see* FARMER).

1669 The Treasury Receivers took over again. Most Receivers managed two or three counties.

1674-84 The collection was farmed out again.

1684-89 Collection was managed by a Commission appointed by the Treasury.

1689 The tax was abolished by William III as 'a great oppression to the poorer sort', and also because it allowed every man's house to be entered and searched by persons unknown. Also, the tax had never raised as much revenue as had been estimated. The last collection was for Lady Day of 1689.

The Hearth Tax Records consist of: the *Assessments*, of which very few survive; the *Payment Accounts* from the collection areas; the *Exchequer Duplicates* of the assessments, more complete and legible than the originals and the most useful source; the *Schedules of Arrears*; *Exemption Certificates* and *Miscellaneous Others*.

Some county record offices, including Devon, Kent, Essex, Lancashire, Lincolnshire (Kesteven and Lincoln only), Middlesex, Warwickshire and Westmorland, have Class I (Assessments), and some of the other Classes. Classes 2-6 are among the Exchequer Records at the Public Record Office, Chancery Lane, London. The Payment Accounts are under reference E.360. During the farmed periods of 1666-9 and 1674-84, and the Commission of 1684-9, no lists of names were returned to the government, so Hearth Tax Lists exist only for 1662-6 and 1669-74. Of these, the one for Lady Day, 1664, is the fullest. The lists provide a useful location record for the whereabouts of families within a county during the reign of Charles II. Printed lists are available for Bedfordshire, Cambridgeshire, Cheshire, Dorset, Oxfordshire, Shropshire, Somerset, Staffordshire, Suffolk, Surrey and Warwickshire.

Heir A person who, on the death of a relative,

133

was entitled to take over his freehold or copyhold land. Under the Common Law, the eldest son born in wedlock was the heir of his father. In the case of a copyhold, the inheritor was known as the 'customary heir', because he was so in accordance with the custom of the manor. In certain parts of southern England, different customs prevailed (*see* BOROUGH ENGLISH; GAVELKIND). If there were no sons, all the daughters were co-heirs.

Heling The coverlet of a bed, often mentioned in probate inventories.

Heraldic and Genealogical Studies, Institute of *see* Institute of Heraldic and Genealogical Studies

Heraldry The science of all that appertains to armorial insignia. One essential principle of heraldry is its hereditary character, though in its very earliest days, before the reign of Richard I, the arms of sons often differed materially from those of their fathers. However, from that reign onward, arms became numerous; they appeared on the seals of private families, and persisted unchanged in the same families from father to son. Arms had been first used for purposes of identification on the shields and banners of knights, and, from the reign of Henry III, on surcoats, which gave rise to the term 'coat of arms'. The evidence of their use survives on rolls of arms and on seals showing either shields or fully armoured men.

The principles of blazonry require a volume to themselves. We may, however, comment on the genealogical aspects of heraldry. These are bound up with the hereditary character of arms, which should render their use a valuable clue in the tracing of descents of gentry families. Unfortunately it must be recognised that mistaken or unauthorised use of arms, common at all periods from the fifteenth century onward, is all too often a cause of misdirected genealogical research. Misuse often arises from the erroneous idea that all people of the same surname, living in the same district, must be related. Another, more recent cause of misuse is to be found in the activities of firms selling representations of arms by employing the phrase 'arms associated with your surname'.

This tends to confusion, whereas the true and chief function of arms today is to distinguish one family from another when both bear the same surname.

Arms are obtainable solely by grant from the College of Arms, acting for the Earl Marshal, to an applicant and his heirs male. At the time of the grant the applicant registers the pedigree of those of his family known to him from personal experience. If he wishes to register earlier generations, the College will require to check the evidence, for which it will charge an additional fee. Thereafter, descendants of the grantee can register details of themselves for addition to the pedigree. If a genealogical researcher believes himself to be connected with an armigerous family, his best course is to apply to the College for whatever information it has about the family. As a precaution against needless expense, the researcher should first trace his line to some ancestor whom he believes to have used, rightly or wrongly, the arms in question.

Shields of arms themselves may contain genealogical clues. When an armigerous person marries the daughter of an armiger, he can display a shield with his own arms on the dexter half, 'impaling' his wife's arms on the sinister half. (Dexter and sinister relate to the right and left side, respectively, of a shield when held from behind.) If the wife is an heraldic heiress (i.e. if she has no surviving brothers or brothers' heirs) her husband can place her arms on a small shield in the centre of his own; this device is called 'inescutcheon'. For a descendant, an ancestress's arms will only appear on his shield if she was such an heiress, or became 'an heiress in her issue' owing to the subsequent extinction of her father's male line, in which cases her male-line descendants are entitled to quarter her arms on the shield with their own. If he has several heiresses in his male line, or if the arms of any of them were already quartered with those of ancestresses in their (female) lines, he may well have more than four quarters to deal with. In such cases the ancestresses' arms are arranged in rows after his own, with the most recently acquired one first, followed by any quarterings it had, and then by the next most recent, with its quarterings if any, and so on.

Officially, arms should, where the rule is

applicable, bear marks of 'cadency' to show whether the bearer is the eldest, second, third or fourth son of his father, but this rule is commonly ignored.

The descents of many armigerous families are to be found in the *Heralds' Visitation* volumes published by the Harleian Society, and in the many editions of Burke's two works, the *Peerage, Baronetage and Knightage* and the *Landed Gentry*; but the information shown there should be treated as secondary evidence that requires checking.

The Heraldry Society, founded under another name in 1947, has as its aims and objects to increase and extend interest in and knowledge of heraldry, armory, chivalry, genealogy and allied subjects. Its President is the Earl Marshal of England, and its Vice-Presidents and Council include a number of Kings of Arms, Heralds and Poursuivants. Membership is open to all. Meetings are held in London throughout the winter, and often elsewhere. There are also classes in heraldic art. The Society publishes a newsletter, *The Heraldry Gazette*, and a quarterly magazine, *The Coat of Arms*. The office of the Secretary is at 28 Museum Street, London WC1A 1LH.

See also ARMS, COAT OF; ARMS, COLLEGE OF.

Herd Used of a person, this meant a herdsman or shepherd.

Herefordshire The county is now joined to Worcestershire under their joint names. The Herefordshire Family History Society holds meetings and issues a journal. Enquiries should be sent c/o The Federation of Family History Societies, 31 Seven Star Road, Solihull, West Midlands B91 2BZ, marked 'Please forward' and enclosing a stamped self-addressed envelope.

Record Repositories County of Hereford and Worcester Record Office, Harold Street, Hereford (tel: 0432.65441); Hereford Cathedral Library, 5 St Peter's Street, Hereford; Hereford City Library, Broad Street, Hereford; National Library of Wales, Department of Manuscripts and Records, Aberystwyth.

Parish Registers and Indexes (see·comment under COUNTY) The registers of most of the ancient parishes have been deposited at the county record office (CRO). The Society of Genealogists

has copies of a few. The INTERNATIONAL GENEALOGICAL INDEX (IGI) covers a number of baptisms. There is a marriage index in the care of Mr B. Merrell, 39123, 252 W. Granger, Salt Lake City, Utah 84119, U.S.A. The Bishops' Transcripts are at the CRO.

Marriage Licence Records These are at the CRO, except for parishes in the Archdeaconry of Brecon and the Diocese of St David's, which are at the National Library of Wales in Aberystwyth.

Wills before 1858, proved in the following courts, are at the CRO:

> Episcopal Consistory Court of Hereford
> Consistory Court of the Dean of Hereford
> Peculiar (Pec.) Court of the Chancellor of Little Hereford
> Pec. Prebendary Court of Upper Bullinghope
> Pec. Prebendary Court of Moreton Magna

Those proved in the Consistory Court of the Archdeaconry of Brecon are in the National Library of Wales, Aberystwyth.

As the Archdeaconry was in the Diocese of St David's, and the whole county was in the Province of Canterbury, wills could also be proved in the Consistory Court of St David's (in the National Library of Wales) and in the Prerogative Court of Canterbury.

Census Returns These are at the Public Record Office (PRO), Portugal Street, London, and at Hereford Public Library.

Non-parochial Registers Eighteen registers are at the PRO, Chancery Lane, London. The IGI covers a similar number.

Heralds' Visitation Pedigrees have been printed for 1567, 1634 and 1683.

A survey of the county's genealogical material available in public libraries is contained in *West Midland Genealogy*, by A.H. Higgs and D. Wright, obtainable from the Honorary Treasurer, West Midlands Branch, Birchfield Public Library, Birchfield Road, Birmingham 20.

Heriot A fine payable by a villein, and later a copyholder, to his lord on inheriting copyhold land. Some freeholders, too, were liable to pay heriots. It was an early form of estate duty. In practice, it might take the form of the best beast of the new tenant.

Hertfordshire The Hertfordshire Family and Population History Society meets regularly and issues a journal. Enquiries should be sent c/o The Federation of Family History Societies, 31 Seven Star Road, Solihull, West Midlands B91 2BZ, marked 'Please forward' and enclosing a stamped self-addressed envelope.

Record Repository Hertfordshire County Record Office, County Hall, Hertford (tel: 0992.54242).

Parish Registers and Indexes (*see* comment under COUNTY) Almost all the registers are at the county record office (CRO). The Society of Genealogists has copies of them, and many are included in the INTERNATIONAL GENEALOGICAL INDEX (IGI), of which there is a copy at the CRO. At the CRO, too, is the Allen Index of Marriages, virtually complete for the county. The Bishops' Transcripts are at the CRO, except for those of the Bishop of London (very few) which are in the Guildhall Library, London.

Marriage Licence Records The CRO has these for the Archdeaconries of St Albans and Huntingdon (Herts. Div.). The Essex CRO has those of the Archdeaconry of Middlesex in Essex and Hertfordshire, as well as those for the Bishop of London's Consistory Court, which had jurisdiction in east Hertfordshire until 1730, and the same bishop's Commissary Court in Essex and Hertfordshire. The marriage licences of the Archdeaconry of Huntingdon (Huntingdon Div.) are at the Huntingdon Record Office. The Society of Genealogists has an index of St Albans Archdeaconry licences for 1584-1600/1.

Wills before 1858, proved in the following courts, are located as follows.

At the county record office:
    Archdeaconry Court of St Albans
    Archdeaconry Court of Huntingdon (Herts Div.)
At Huntingdon Record Office:
    Archdeaconry Court of Huntingdon (Hunts Div.)
At Essex CRO:
    Archdeaconry Court of Middlesex (Essex and Herts)
At the Dean and Chapter Library, St Paul's Cathedral, London:
    Peculiar Court of the Dean and Chapter of St Paul's

As the archdeaconries lay in the Dioceses of Lincoln and London, and in the Province of Canterbury, wills could also be proved in the Consistory Court of Lincoln, the Consistory and Commissary Courts (Essex and Herts) of London, and in the Prerogative Court of Canterbury.

Non-parochial Registers Forty-one registers are at the Public Record Office (PRO), Chancery Lane, London, and are covered by the IGI.

Census Returns These are at the PRO, Portugal Street, London, and at the Hertford Public Library.

Memorial Inscriptions The Society of Genealogists has a few transcripts, as has the family history society, and there is a large collection in the British Library.

Heralds' Visitation Pedigrees have been printed for 1572 and 1634.

Quarter Sessions The Hertfordshire Sessions have been calendared in a series of volumes.

The Hertfordshire Genealogist 1895-7, printed a number of records useful to the genealogist. Another useful aid is M.F. Thwaite's *Periodicals and Transactions Relating to Hertfordshire* (Herts Local History Council, 1959).

Heusire A customary payment made by the tenant of a manor to his overlord for the right to hold a manorial court.

Hide Originally land considered sufficient for the maintenance of one family, and therefore roughly what one eight-ox ploughteam could keep in cultivation. It would measure anything between 90 and 120 acres according to the type of soil and the lie of the land. Later, a tax-assessment unit.
See also CARUCATE; PLOUGH TEAM.

High Commission, Court of The highest ecclesiastical court in England. At the Reformation, Thomas Cromwell appointed in 1535 a council of ecclesiastics, ministers of state and lawyers, to deal with cases of heresy, but such appointments were of a temporary nature until, in 1565, the amount of work gave the commissions a permanent tenure, and they became known five years later as the High Commission.

The penalties imposed by the court were mainly the secular ones of fine and imprisonment. The court was resented by the increasingly influential Puritans because of its enforcement of the ritual and vestments of the Anglican rites. Also, defendants could be examined on an oath imposed upon them by the judge and so be compelled to convict themselves. The court was also disliked by the Common Law judges, and those judges appointed to the Commission soon ceased to attend. This was because of its mixed ecclesiastical and temporal character, and the infliction of non-ecclesiastical penalties. The opposition became political with the Puritans powerful in Parliament, and the court was abolished in 1641. It was restored by James II in 1686, but three years later was finally ended under William and Mary by the Bill of Rights.

Of the Commission's records that have survived, the majority are at the Public Record Office, Chancery Lane, London, in group SP, and the rest are held at the Borthwick Institute of Historical Research, a department of the University of York.

Highways, Surveyor of

The parish official responsible for the upkeep of the roads. The *Highways Act* of 1555 laid down that the main roads of each parish should be maintained by the unpaid labour of every householder, cottager and labourer of the parish, able to labour and being no hired servant, for four days per year (six days, after an Act of 1563).

The Act created the honorary parochial office of Surveyor of the Highways, two in each parish, to supervise the work within the parish bounds. They were selected by the Justices of the Peace from a short-list drawn up by the Vestry. They were expected to keep accounts and submit them to the Justices on the completion of their year of office, but very few accounts survive from before the *Highways Act* of 1691, which, among other improvements, authorised the raising of a Highway Rate. Farmers were often appointed Surveyors, because they had horses, carts and men available. Some Surveyors' accounts are still in the keeping of parish incumbents, but many have been deposited at county record offices. They may mention names in rate-lists and composition-lists, also names of those who were paid for working, and of those who paid because they were unable to perform their duties (defaulters). They also provide background information about parish life. In 1862, the duty of maintaining roads was passed to Highway Boards.

Hiring Fairs

Such fairs were held annually, usually in market towns, and sometimes as part of a general fair. Their purpose was to enable employers to find employees, and vice versa. The latter were mainly domestics, farm labourers and other artisans. They were hired for a year, when the engagement could be either terminated or renewed.

Both masters and servants would be attracted to the fairs from places miles away, and this is one cause of the mobility of families. An employer from fifteen miles east of the market town might well engage a servant from a similar distance to the west of it. If master and man were well suited, and the man found a wife locally, he would settle down and thus accomplish a personal migration of thirty miles for no reason obvious to his twentieth-century descendant. In fact, Census Returns show servants working at considerably greater distances from their homes.

Historical MSS, Royal Commission on

This body was appointed by royal warrant in 1869 with the task of locating, and making accessible to researchers, records in the private ownership of persons, families and institutions. The owners are approached for permission to inspect and edit their records, and then reports on them are published in the form of calendars, lists and edited texts. Well over 200 volumes of these reports have now been published, dealing with the papers of prominent families and institutions, counties and boroughs, Parliament, statesmen, admirals, generals and other important personages. Their contents are covered by an *Index of Personal Names* (down to 1957) and a *Topographical Index* (to 1911). Many historical records have been published in separate volumes, and annual *Lists of Accessions to Repositories* cover the material flowing into about 150 record offices.

The Commission also co-operates with record societies in the publication of local historical documents of wide general interest. In 1945, it was given the task of directing the newly instituted National Register of Archives. In 1958, the *Registers of Manorial Documents* (*see* MANOR) and of *Tithe Documents* (*see* TITHE) were transferred to the Commission from the Public Record Office. Since then it has been given the task of promoting and assisting the preservation of records. The principal officer of the Commission is the Secretary, and its offices are at Quality House, Quality Court, Chancery Lane, London WC2A 1HP.

Hitched Land A part of a common field used, in its fallow year, for special crops such as beans, peas and root vegetables. Sometimes the hitched land was part of the waste. Also called Hookland, or Hitchland.

Hocktide The second Monday and Tuesday after Easter. On Hock Monday the men, and on Hock Tuesday the women, of `the parish obstructed the roadway and bound passers-by with ropes until they ransomed themselves by contributing to the church dues and other 'pious uses'. Hence the expression 'in hock' (in pawn).

Hogsleas Pasture for pigs.

Holograph A document hand-written by the person who signed it, or in whose name it appears.

Homage (i) Acknowledgement by a freeholder of his feudal obligations to his overlord. A man often held land of more than one lord, and had to do homage to each of them, with his hands between the lord's, 'touching life and limb and earthly honour in what is honest and profitable, keeping his counsel to the best of his power, saving his faith to God and the king' (*see* FEALTY). But the lord of whom a man held his principal residence was his liege-lord, on whom the tenant could never sit in judgement and whom he must follow in war against everyone but the king. The liege-lord, on his side, was obliged to act as surety for his liegeman whenever necessary.

(ii) The jury of a manor court, sometimes also referred to as 'the twelve men'.

Honour A large estate held by a single lord, usually consisting of several scattered manors. Subtenants were obliged to attend the Honour Court.

Hookland *see* **Hitched Land**

Hospital (i) An institution for the temporary reception and treatment of sick persons. Before 1710 there were very few general hospitals in England, and they were intended for the poor. Although many were built in the nineteenth century, especially lying-in hospitals, the great majority of people continued until the twentieth century to be born and to die at home. London had only two general hospitals in the Middle Ages: St Bartholomew's in West Smithfield, founded in 1102 and refounded in 1547; and St Thomas's in High Street, Southwark, founded in 1213 and refounded by Edward VI. Guy's Hospital was founded by a wealthy bookseller in 1726. Early specialised institutions were Bethlehem, or Bedlam, Hospital for lunatics, founded in 1247; St Luke's Hospital for the incurably insane, 1732; and the Foundling Hospital (in the sense of hostel) for abandoned children, 1745.

(ii) A permanent retreat for the elderly or infirm. Among these were the Chelsea Hospital, 1690, for maimed and superannuated soldiers, and Greenwich Hospital for seamen, 1694.

These hospitals normally keep their own archives, from which details may be obtained on application, not only about patients but also about the surgeons who worked there and the apprentices who trained under them. When a patient died in hospital, his 'last reputed address' is sometimes given.

Housebote The right of a manorial copyholder to take wood for the purpose of house maintenance.

House-row The system in force in some parishes whereby some parish offices, such as that of constable, went annually by rotation from the occupier of one house to that of the next. Such a system was fair — some offices were unpopular — but often inefficient, since not all householders were equally suitable for the tasks to be performed.

House, White The dairy building on a farm.

Hudson's Bay Company One of the great Chartered Companies, it was founded by royal charter in 1670 as 'The Governor and Company of Adventurers of England Trading into Hudson's Bay'. It was granted all the land 'within the entrance of the straits commonly called Hudson's Straits', not already granted or belonging to others, and a monopoly of the trade there, which was almost exclusively in furs. Settlements were established on the rivers of Rupert's Land, and furs were obtained chiefly by means of barter with the Indians. In the early years enormous profits were made, which attracted competition from the French, who were also in the northern territories of America. During the next century, when England and France were at war, this competition developed into military hostilities, and several of the Company's forts were captured by the enemy. However, they were restored on the return of peace and the profitability of the Company was not seriously disturbed.

When France finally ceded her Canadian lands to Britain in 1763, more serious competition arose from the founding, by British settlers, of the North-West Fur Company to exploit the ceded areas. In 1812, the Hudson's Bay Company sold land to Lord Selkirk with the aim of bringing in Scottish settlers to consolidate its rights. This led to open warfare between the companies, which was finally brought to an end by their merger in 1821. By this time the large-scale slaughter of animals and the consequent increase in the volume of trade brought about a slump in the price of furs. In 1869, the Company ceded its lands to the Canadian Government; but it still remained a trading company. Its historical records are in Canada, with microfilm copies at the Public Record Office, Kew. Requests for permission to search should be made to Hudson's Bay & Annings Ltd, 77 Main Street, Winnipeg, Manitoba R3C 2RI.

Hue and Cry When a felony was committed, the victim, or a witness, had to raise the alarm by shouting — raising a hue and cry — and all within earshot had to come to his aid in securing the guilty person. However, if the latter succeeded in crossing the parish boundary, the responsibility for his capture passed to the township to which he had fled. Failure to raise the hue, or to report the offence to the tithingman (*see* TITHING), made the person so negligent liable to a fine. Anyone who raised a hue falsely was likewise fined.

Huguenots This name for French Protestants is said by one authority to be a nickname bestowed by a Catholic preacher, from the practice of the Protestants of Tours to assemble by night under the gate of King Hugues. By others, it is thought to be a corruption of the German *eidgenossen* (confederates united by oath), a league of Swiss Protestants. It was already in popular use by 1560, and has since come to cover Walloons and other Protestant refugees from Spanish persecution in the Low Countries.

The first French communities were followers of John Calvin. They increased rapidly after a synod held in 1559, and there followed the series of internal French Wars of Religion which gave rise to some Protestant emigration and culminated, during a period of apparent reconciliation, in the Massacre of St Bartholomew in 1572, which caused many Huguenots to flee to Protestant countries, including England. When Henry of Navarre came to the throne, French Protestants were granted religious and political freedom by the *Edict of Nantes*, 1598. However, the Catholic Church kept up the pressure against the Huguenots and eventually on 18 October, 1685, Louis XIV revoked the *Edict of Nantes* and caused the greatest flood of emigration by Protestants of all classes to England and elsewhere.

When a Huguenot settled in England, he would apply for either Naturalization or Denization, and become a member of one of the numerous Huguenot churches in the country. Except for the large community in Spitalfields, east of London, who retained their French character for some time, the settlers' descendants were soon absorbed into the social life of their new homeland. The earliest Huguenot ecclesiastical register is that of their church in Southampton, dating from 1567. Those of congregations in London and other large towns soon follow.

The researcher into Huguenot ancestry

should turn first to the many volumes of *Proceedings, Church Registers, Returns of Aliens,* and other records published by the Huguenot Society since its foundation in 1885. Especially helpful are: Volume 10 (in 4 parts), *Returns of Aliens in London, 1523-1603;* Vol. 8, *Denizations and Naturalizations of Aliens in England, 1509-1603;* Vols 18, 27 and 35, *Letters of Denization and Acts of Naturalization for Aliens in England, 1603-1800;* and Vol. 30, *Oaths of Naturalization* (late seventeenth century).

Many of the French surnames have become anglicized in spelling, or even translated. The registers of baptisms, marriages and burials outside London were deposited with the Registrar General in 1858, but are now at the Public Record Office, Chancery Lane, London. They have been published by the Huguenot Society.

For further research, the library of the French Protestant Church of London, in Soho Square, and the joint library of the French Hospital de la Providence and of the Huguenot Society at University College, London, contain many records, and these are listed in the *Huguenot Society Proceedings*, Vols 14, 18 and 13 respectively. The Secretary of the Huguenot Society of London is Mrs I. Scouloudi, 67 Victoria Road, London W8 5PH.

For further reading, see *Sources for Nonconformist Genealogy and Family History*, by D.J. Steel (1973).

Humberside A county formed in 1974 out of south-east Yorkshire and north Lincolnshire. *See also* LINCOLNSHIRE; YORKSHIRE.

Hundred Until Tudor times, this was an administrative subdivision of a county, probably so named from its having originally contained either a hundred families, a hundred fighting men or a hundred hides. Jurisdiction was supposed to be vested in the county's sheriff, but many hundreds got into private hands. In either case, a bailiff, to whom the profits were sub-let, held a Court Baron and Court Leet every few weeks. They dealt with minor offences such as trespass, obstruction of the highway and assizes of bread and ale.

Presentments of these offences were made by a reeve and four men from each township in the hundred. If these representatives failed to appear, their township was amerced. From the thirteenth to the fifteenth century a special court was held after Easter and Michaelmas, called the sheriff's tourn, the main object of which was to check that the system of frankpledge was being observed. Hundred courts, much decayed since Tudor times, lost almost all their functions after the *County Courts Act* of 1867. Of its few remaining duties, that of repairing damage caused by rioters was taken from them in 1886. Surviving records are to be found in county record offices.

Hunt, Hugh *see* **Recovery Rolls** *and* **Roe, Richard**

Huntingdon's Connexion, Countess of Selina Hastings, Countess of Huntingdon (1707-91) was left a wealthy widow in 1746. Already a member of a Methodist society, she now threw herself into the Calvinist branch of that movement. In 1751 she appointed its leader, George Whitefield, her chaplain. Under his tutelage she poured money into the movement, built chapels at Bath, Brighton, Tunbridge Wells and other resorts of the upper classes, and employed chaplains, all regularly ordained Anglicans, to serve them. In 1756 she founded the Tottenham Court Chapel in London.

At this time Methodism was still a movement within the Church of England, but its followers were much divided and in 1763 a Plymouth preacher was ordained by dissenting clergy and set up an Independent church there (*see* CONGREGATIONALISTS). The London chapels, too, were registered as Independent, and in 1767 Lady Huntingdon founded a theological college at Trevecca in Breconshire to train young men of Calvinist persuasion for the universities and eventual ordination. Whitefield died in 1770, and in 1779 there came a general break with the established church and the founding of a movement organised nationally on the same lines as the Presbyterians. By this time the Countess's followers had become known as Lady Huntingdon's Connexion. Sixty years after her death they had upwards of one hundred chapels, and their services were still conducted according to the rites of the Church of England. Their registers are deposited at the

Public Record Office, Chancery Lane, London, in group RG.

For further reading, see *Sources for Nonconformist Genealogy* (Methodists), by D.J. Steel (Phillimore, 1973).

Huntingdonshire The county of Huntingdon was absorbed into Cambridgeshire in 1974. A family history society was formed in the summer of 1985, with the intention of publishing a journal and joining the Federation of Family History Societies. Enquiries should be sent to Mrs K. Wright, 14 Horseshoe Way, Brampton, Cambridgeshire PE18 8TN, enclosing a stamped self-addressed envelope for the reply.

Record Repository Cambridge County Record Office (Huntingdon Branch), Grammar School Walk, Huntingdon (tel: 0480.52181).

Parish Registers and Indexes (*see* comment under COUNTY) Many of the registers are at the county record office (CRO), and the Society of Genealogists has copies of some of them. There is a marriage index in the care of T.P.R. Layng, 39 Gogmagog Way, Stapleford, Cambridge, and Pallot's Marriage Index covers six parishes, mostly 1790-1837. The Bishops' Transcripts are at the CRO. The INTERNATIONAL GENEALOGICAL INDEX (IGI) includes a few.

Marriage Licence Records These are at the CRO.

Wills before 1858, proved in the following courts, are at the CRO:

> Commissary Court of the Bishop of Lincoln and Archdeacon in the Archdeaconry of Huntingdon
> Peculiar (Pec.) Court of Brampton
> Pec. Court of Buckden
> Prebendal Court of Stow Long
> Prebendal Court of Leighton Bromsgrove

As the county lay in the Diocese of Lincoln until 1837, and then in that of Ely (*see* CAMBRIDGESHIRE), and always in the Province of Canterbury, wills could also be proved in the Consistory Courts of those dioceses, the Archdeaconry Court of Ely and the Prerogative Court of Canterbury.

Non-parochial Registers The registers of eleven chapels are at the Public Record Office (PRO), Chancery Lane, London, and the IGI covers a few.

Census Returns These are at the PRO, Portugal Street, London, and at the CRO.

Memorial Inscriptions The Society of Genealogists has transcripts from thirty churches.

Heralds' Visitation Pedigrees have been printed for 1613.

Protestation Oath Returns 1641/2, have been printed in Vol.5 of the Transactions of the Cambridgeshire and Huntingdonshire Archaeological Society.

Husbandman The term may be used in several ways. When it describes an occupation it could apply to a man of any status who was engaged or interested in husbandry (i.e. the cultivation of the land); but it was also used to designate a status, in which sense it usually applies to a small-holder, who might also have to work on the land of larger owners to maintain himself (i.e. one below the status of a yeoman). *See also* CLASS, SOCIAL.

Husting, Court of Derived from a Saxon word meaning 'house of trial', it was the name of courts held in London, Winchester, York and some other cities. In London it was a lay court of the Corporation of the City, and was held annually at the Guildhall before the mayor and aldermen. Its records are at the Corporation of London Record Office, Guildhall, Gresham Street, London EC2. Wills relating to London property could be proved there, and conveyances of real estate could be enrolled for permanent evidence. The Corporation's record office has a name index of vendors and purchasers.
See also LONDON AND MIDDLESEX.

Hutch A chest or cupboard. A term often found in inventories.

The wavy line at the top of the medieval document ABOVE identifies it as an indenture. *British Library MSS Dept.*

I

Immigrants By this term is meant foreigners settling in England since the Norman Conquest. Of these, the largest single community was made up of the French and Walloon Protestants of the seventeenth and late sixteenth centuries, who are dealt with under the separate heading of HUGUENOTS.

Those immigrants who could afford to obtain Acts of Naturalization are covered by the records of those Acts in Parliament Rolls at the Public Record Office (PRO), Chancery Lane, London (C.65), and the greater number who obtained Denization are covered by Letters Patent recorded in Patent Rolls (C.66 and 67), followed by Close Rolls (C.54) for the period 1844-73. They are indexed in the printed *Index to Rolls of Parliament, Calendar of Patent Rolls* and *Letters and Papers, Henry VIII* (HMSO). For aliens entering under the Stuart kings, refer to *Calendars to the State Papers* for that period, and also the *Calendar of Treasury Papers, 1557-1728.*

Chancery Original Denizations, 1751-93 (C.97) are indexed in the Chancery class list on the search room shelves; and *Home Office Patents for Denization for 1804-43* (HO.4) are also enrolled on the Patent Rolls, where they were indexed.

Immigrants fleeing from the French Revolution can be found in the *Bouillon Papers* (HO.69), *Unbound Papers* (PC.1.), *Foreign Office Miscellanea* (FO.95) and *War Office In Letters* (WO.1). Those who were assisted by the French Refugees Relief Committee are recorded in *Treasury Papers* (T.93). From 1793 onward, the Home Office became responsible for aliens and, from 1844, for the granting of naturalization. For these, there is an *Index to Names: Certificates of Naturalization, 1844-1900* (HMSO), with class references to the original records. For 1836-52, the certificates issued to aliens (HO.2) are arranged under ports of arrival and record arrival date, nationality, last country visited, occupation and signature. For indexes to these, see HO.5, Vols 25-32. There are also passenger lists made by the ships' masters, but these are unindexed and so should be consulted only after the immigrant has been found in the certificate records. For later periods, see the *Index to Denizations, 1801-73*, and *Index to Memorials for Denizations and Naturalization, 1835-44*, available at the PRO. From 1792, aliens had to register their names, addresses and occupations with the Quarter Sessions of their county. The registers will be found at county record offices. A free leaflet, *Immigrants, Documents in the Public Record Office*, is available at the PRO.

Impertinent This expression, often found in Chancery proceedings, means 'irrelevant'. If a defendant's answer was reported for 'impertinence' it meant that it failed to answer the plaintiff's complaint.

Impropriate As a verb, this means to annex an ecclesiastical benefice to a corporation or lay person as their private property. The Great Tithe would be payable to such person, and the care of the parish would be in the hands of a vicar.

As a noun, an impropriate signifies such a benefice.

Incumbent The holder of a benefice; for example, the rector or vicar of a parish. In applying to a parson for a parish register search, or for permission to make a search oneself, it is generally advisable to address the envelope to 'The Incumbent', because Crockford's *Clerical Directory* (*see* CLERGY), like all directories, is inevitably partly out of date on the day it is published and the parson may well have left the parish. If the envelope has been addressed to him by name it will be forwarded to his new address and have to be forwarded back to the new incumbent at the original addressee's expense. At best, this causes delay and can even mean that the enquiry never reaches the new parson. A stamped, self-addressed envelope should be enclosed.

Indenture A deed executed between two or more parties and written out in as many copies as there were parties — all on one sheet of parchment or paper. An 'indented' or wavy line was drawn between the copies, sometimes with the word 'Chirograph' written through it, and the sheet was then cut into parts along the line. The copies could later be identified as tallies when brought together. The term is now used of any sealed agreement, and particularly for a contract of apprenticeship.

See also CHIROGRAPH; DEED POLL; FEET OF FINES.

Independents *see* **Congregationalists**

India Office Library and Records These comprise the archives and collections of the East India Company and the India Office, both now defunct, and cover the period from 1600 to 1947. The Office has published *A Brief Outline to Biographical Sources*, which is essential to the researcher. The India Office Library and Records are housed at Orbit House, Blackfriars Road, London SE1.

See also EAST INDIA COMPANY.

Infangnethef The right of a manor or borough court to judge a thief caught within its area of jurisdiction.

Infant Mortality The incidence of death among children of less than one year old. Even until late in the nineteenth century the proportion of deaths in the first year of life was very high. There were certain obvious causes, such as deficiencies in, or absence of, plumbing and other aspects of domestic hygiene, the feeding of babies with unsuitable foods, and the lack of pre- and post-natal trained care. But some modern researchers believe that strong parental affection for babies, regarded today as almost instinctive (especially in mothers), is a social phenomenon that has evolved during the last 250 years, at different rates among different classes, and that infant deaths in the past were largely due to what would now be regarded as neglect. Country mothers were often kept busy outdoors for much of the day, leaving their babies unattended: such infants were obviously at considerable risk. And even the practice of stopping a baby's crying by violent shaking survived among European peasant communities into the age of scientific observation. Middle-class people often put their newly born babies out to nurse for two years. The christening of weakly infants as 'creature', and the baptizing of later children with the same names as earlier ones who had predeceased them, are practices quoted as evidence of lack of parental feeling.

In earlier times, the term 'infant' designated a child under eight years of age.

Ing A common meadow in manorial land.

Inghamites A small nonconformist sect founded by Benjamin Ingham (1712-72), whose wife was Lady Margaret Hastings, sister-in-law of Lady Huntingdon (*see* HUNTINGDON'S CONNEXION, COUNTESS OF). Ingham's group was founded in 1754 when he and his followers broke away from the Moravians. A year later they had a large number of followers, mostly in Yorkshire and Lancashire, and broke away from the Church of England, within which they, like the Moravians, had previously been internal societies. Ingham became influenced by the ideas of the Scottish Sandeman sect, and this caused the break-up of his own group in 1763; some becoming Methodist, where Ingham himself had begun, some Sandemanian, and some Baptist. However, a few societies remained loyal. In 1814 they amalgamated with the Daleites of Scotland, and the church still survives today in Yorkshire, Lancashire and Cumbria. In 1840, eight Inghamite baptismal and burial registers were deposited at the General Record Office, and these are now at the Public Record Office, Chancery Lane, London, in group RG.

For further reading, see *Sources for Nonconformist Genealogy and Family History*, by D.J. Steel (1973).

Ink The medium in which virtually all of the genealogist's information is made available to him. It used to consist of oak-galls, sulphate of iron, gum-arabic and water, often made up at home from private recipes of varying value. Such ink was liable to turn yellow and fade in the course of time, through decay of the vegetable matter, leaving only rust and peroxide of iron, though it could be restored by 'the careful application of an infusion of galls'. On the other hand, the fading of a manuscript may also be due to the paper on which it was written having been made from inferior rags and with an excess of chlorine in the bleach. Faded writing can be more easily read under ultra-violet light, and lamps of this kind are often available at record repositories. On the introduction of steel nibs in the nineteenth century, the composition of ink had to be changed to eliminate acid constituents.

Inn A house that provided overnight accommodation, as distinct from a tavern or ale-house, though all these would offer beer for sale, drawn by 'tapsters'. The bedroom accommodation in a large inn was looked after by an employee called a 'chamberlain'. Records of inns and innkeepers can be found among Quarter Sessions papers because the keepers had to be licensed by Justices of the Peace and to give recognizances for the proper running of their houses. Title deeds, where extant, will give the names of previous owners. The names of many inns have been changed from time to time, and signs for the King's Head are not always repainted with a portrait of the same king.

Innage Enclosed cultivation of portions of manorial arable land during its fallow year. *See also* HITCHED LAND.

Innocent A CHRISOM child.

Inquisition Post Mortem In 1235, Henry III created regional officials called Escheators, who, on the death of any tenant-in-chief in their area holding lands in fee, were to take possession of the deceased's lands and summon juries of free local men in the neighbourhood, to give details, on oath, about the lands and their value, the services by which they were held, the date of the deceased owner's death, and the identity and age of the heir. The escheator then sent his report to the royal Court of Chancery, with a copy to the Exchequer. After 1540, in relevant instances, another copy went to the Court of Wards and Liveries.

If the heir was a minor, the king became his guardian and disposed of him in marriage, meanwhile taking the revenues of his lands. If he was, or when he became, of age, the lands were delivered to him on payment of a relief. This procedure continued to operate until Knight

Service, which was its basis, fell into disuse and was finally abolished in 1662.

The documents created by this procedure were as follows:

The *Writ of Diem Clausit Extremum* ('he has closed his last day') from the Court of Chancery to the escheator, instructing him to make the inquisition. Sometimes the escheator acted without a writ.

The *Inquisition Post Mortem*, the escheator's report to the Court.

A *Writ of Mandamus* issued when there was a delay between the death and the first writ, to discover who had been taking the revenues of the lands in the meantime.

A *Writ ad Melius Inquirendum* issued to amend a first report, if thought desirable.

A *Writ Que Plura* issued if it was found that some lands had been omitted from the return.

A *Writ of Devenerunt* issued if the heir died while a minor.

A *Writ De Dote Assignanda* issued when the return showed that a widow could claim dower.

There are separate series of records for the Palatine Counties, as they had their own chanceries.

The action subsequently taken is reported in a *Writ of Livery*, filed with the Close and Fine Rolls at the Public Record Office (PRO).

All these documents are in Latin. The Chancery series is less legible than those of the other two courts. The records enable a link to be established between two or more generations or brothers, and also provide the date of the tenant's death and the age of the heir.

The records are at the PRO, Chancery Lane, London, and calendars of Inquisitions Post Mortem (IPM) have beeen published covering the period Henry III to Edward III, and for Henry VII, with indexes for later reigns. For the missing period, there is a *Calendarium* (Record Commissioners), giving tenants and their lands. Some local record societies have published more detailed calendars for their areas. The PRO references are C.133-142 for the Chancery records, and E.149 and 150 for those of the Exchequer.

Inquisition Quo Warranto *see* **Quo Warranto**

Inquisitor A person appointed to report on any shortcomings of parishioners so that they could be 'presented' at the next Archdeacon's Court.

Instance Suit *see* **Ecclesiastical Court**

Institute of Heraldic and Genealogical Studies The Institute was founded in 1961 to make provision for training, study and research in family history. It maintains a School of Family History as well as organising other courses, both by lectures and correspondence, in genealogy. Its library, of many thousands of books, is open to visitors. *Family History*, the journal of the Institute, appears usually in six numbers per year, containing articles on heraldry, genealogy, family history and related subjects. The Institute is also the publisher of a valuable series of maps of English and Welsh counties for genealogists, showing parochial boundaries, commencement dates of extant parish registers, and areas of probate jurisdiction. Other useful publications are maps showing the census and registration regions and districts for 1837-51 and 1852-1947, a bibliography, and numerous leaflets. The address of the Institute is Northgate, Canterbury, Kent.

Intercommon Pasture land shared by adjoining parishes.

International Genealogical Index (IGI) This Index contains over 30 million baptismal entries from parish and non-parochial registers all over England, together with a smaller number of marriages. These have been compiled and computerised by the Genealogical Department of the Church of Jesus Christ of Latter Day Saints, situated at Salt Lake City, Utah, U.S.A.

The index is arranged under counties, and the entries are listed in alphabetical order of surnames, which are grouped under spellings decided on by the compilers, but the original spellings are cross-referenced. The surnames themselves are arranged in alphabetical order of forenames, and, where several forenames are the same, in chronological order. The forenames are arranged in alphabetical order of their original spelling or abbreviation. Marriages are

	Name	FATHER MOTHER OR SPOUSE	1	2	DATE	TOWN, PARISH
1	ULYAT	JOHN ULYAT/ELIZABETH	F	C	12JAN1760	TIMBERLAND
2	ULLIOT, ABRAHAM	ROBERT ULLIOT/MARY	M	C	05NOV1749	WADDINGTON
3	ULYAT, ABRAHAM	JOHN ULYAT/ELIZ.	M	C	12DEC1762	TIMBERLAND
4	ULYAT, ABRAHAM	JOHN ULYAT/ELIZ.	M	C	05MAY1765	TIMBERLAND
5	ULLYAT, ABRAHAM	ABRAHAM ULLYAT/LEVINA	M	C	23SEP1807	HOLBEACH
6	ULYAT, ABRAHAM	ABRAHAM ULYAT/MARY	M	C	12DEC1813	KYME
7	ULYATT, ABRAHAM	REBECCA GREEN	M	M	22MAY1832	HOLBEACH
8	ULLIOT, ALICE	JOHN MIDLETON	W	M	03MAY1671	MABLETHORPE, SAINT MARY
9	ULLYETT, AN	CHRISTOFER ULLYETT/AGNIS	F	C	15FEB1629	HOLBEACH
10	ULLIATE, ANN	JOH ULLIATE/ANN	F	C	06OCT1686	BILLINGWAY
11	ULLYET, ANN	JOHN ULLYET/DEBORAH	F	C	04APR1734	ORBY
12	ULLYATT, ANN	JOHN ULLYATT/MARY	F	C	08JUL1748	GRANTHAM
13	ULYATT, ANN	WILLIAM WATSON	W	M	11FEB1782	SURFLEET
14	ULYEAT, ANN	JOHN ULYEAT/ANN	F	C	05JUN1785	ANCASTER
15	ULITT, ANN	SAMUEL TURNBULL	W	M	21OCT1799	MOULTON NEAR SPALDING
16	ULYATT, ANN	ABRAHAM ULYATT/MARY	F	C	16JUL1809	KYME
17	ULIATT, ANN	EDWARD ULYATT/SARAH ANN	F	C	11JUL1830	KIRTON IN HOLLAND
18	ULLYATTE, ANNE	WILLIAM FENWICKE	W	M	08DEC1597	ADDLETHORPE
19	ULLYET, ANNE	JOHN ULLYET/ANNE	F	C	18JAN1699	ORBY
20	ULLYETT, ANNE	JOHN ULLYETT/JANE	F	C	23MAY1730	ORBY
21	ULYAT, ANNE	JOHN ULYAT/ELIZ.	F	C	01NOV1754	TIMBERLAND
22	ULYATE, CALAMANA	ROBERT BRIGGS	W	M	12AUG1788	GRANTHAM
23	ULLYET, CATHARINE	JOHN ULLYET/DEBORAH	F	C	15AUG1732	ORBY
24	ULYATT, CATHARINE	WILLIAM BONNER	U	M	06MAY1832	BOSTON
25	ULYETT, CATHERINE	THOMAS ULYETT/CATHERINE	F	C	02SEP1821	KYME
26	ULLYATT, CHARLES	ABRAHAM ULLYATT/SARAH	M	C	17JUN1798	HOLBEACH
27	ULYATT, CHRISTOPHER	JOHN ULYATT/SARAH	M	C	22JUN1817	KYME
28	ULLIAT, COLLIMANA	WM ULLIAT/COLL.	F	C	25JAN1764	GRANTHAM
29	ULLIOTT, CONSTANCE	WILLIAM ULIOTT/CONSTANCE	F	C	05JUL1738	GRANTHAM
30	ULLYET, DEBORAH	JNO. ULLYET/DEBORAH	F	C	18DEC1737	ORBY
31	ULLYET, DOBSON	JOHN ULLYET/DEBORAH	M	C	09JAN1739	ORBY
32	ULLYET, DOBSON	JOHN ULLYET/DEBORAH	M	C	07NOV1740	ORBY
33	ULLYETT, DOBSON	WILLIAM ULLYETT/FRANCES	M	C	27JUL1813	HOGSTHORPE
34	VLYET, EDWARD	WILLM VLYET/	M	C	14JAN1590	TATHWELL
35	ULLIOT, EDWARD	ROBT. ULLIOT/	M	C	01JAN1630	GRANTHAM
36	ULLIOT, EDWARD	THO. ULLIOT/SARAH	M	C	22JAN1681	GRANTHAM
37	ULLIOT, EDWARD	WM ULLIOT/JANE	M	C	01JUN1707	GRANTHAM
38	ULLIOTT, EDWARD	JOHN ULLIOTT/ELIZABETH	M	C	26DEC1712	SOUTH ORMSBY
39	ULYATT, EDWARD	ABRAHAM ULYATT/MARY	M	C	16JUN1809	KYME
40	ULLYAT, EDWARD	ABRAHAM ULLYAT/LEVINA	M	C	17JAN1810	HOLBEACH
41	ULYATT, EDWARD	THOMAS ULYATT/CATHERINE	M	C	20JUN1824	KYME
42	ULLYETT, EDWARD BRADSHAW	/MARY ULLYETT	M	C	11JUN1817	HOGSTHORPE
43	ULYATT, EDWARD WOODS	THOMAS ULYATT/JANE	M	C	11FEB1827	SWINESHEAD
44	ULYAT, EDWD.	JANE PEARS	M	M	16JAN1753	BOSTON
45	ULLIOT, ELIZ.	WM ULLIOT/ANNE	F	C	17SEP1699	GRANTHAM
46	ULITT, ELIZ.	JOHN ULITT/MARY	F	C	13NOV1727	GRANTHAM
47	ULYET, ELIZ.	JOHN ULYET/CATHARIEN	F	C	29MAY1731	BOSTON
48	ULLYETT, ELIZ.	DOBSON ULLYETT/MARTHA	F	C	01FEB1788	ORBY
49	ULLIAT, ELIZABETH	JOHN ULLIAT/	F	C	06JAN1633	GRANTHAM
50	ULLYETT, ELIZABETH	THOMAS ULLYETT/ELIZABETH	F	C	27AUG1703	ORBY-IN-THE-MARSH
51	ULLIOT, ELIZABETH	ABRA. ULLIOT/ELIZ	F	B	05AUG1725	WADDINGTON
52	ULIOTT, ELIZABETH	WILLIAM ULIOTT/CONSTANCE	F	C	12MAR1733	GRANTHAM
53	ULLIOTT, ELIZABETH	JOHN ULLIOTT/ELIZABETH	F	C	06DEC1734	SOUTH ORMSBY
54	ULLYET, ELIZABETH	HENRY ULLYET/MARY	F	C	06MAY1739	ORBY
55	ULLIAT, ELIZABETH	ROBERT ULLIAT/MARY	F	C	08JUL1744	WADDINGTON
56	ULYAT, ELIZABETH	JOHN ULYAT/ANN	F	C	01MAY1745	BICKER
57	ULYAT, ELIZABETH	JOHN ULYAT/ELIZABETH	F	C	11OCT1752	TIMBERLAND
58	ULYAT, ELIZABETH	RICHARD GOULDING	W	M	26NOV1761	KYME
59	ULYAT, ELIZABETH	ABRAHAM ULYAT/LYDIA	F	C	18OCT1796	SUTTON SAINT EDMUND

A microfiche page of the International Genealogical Index (first six columns only). *Courtesy Church of Jesus Christ of Latter-Day Saints*

indexed under the names of both parties. The coverage of any given parish is not necessarily complete, and in many cases consists only of extracts.

The information is laid out as follows.

Column 1 gives the names of the person. *Col.2.* the parents of a person baptized, or the spouse of a person married. *Col.3.* the sex, abbreviated to M = male, F = female, H = husband, W = wife. *Col.4.* the type of record, abbreviated to B = birth, C = christening, M = marriage. *Col.5.* the date of baptism or marriage, but not of birth. *Col.6.* the name of the parish of record. *Cols.7, 8 and 9* dates on which Mormon ceremonies were carried out following the discovery of the names, with code letters for the temples concerned. The word 'Cleared' means that the entry is in the process of being checked. 'Infant' means that there is reason to suppose that the person died before the age of eight. Illegitimate children who died as infants are not included in the index. *Cols.10 and 11,* headed 'Batch' and 'Serial Sheet', give coded references to further information available at Salt Lake City. If the third digit from the front is less than 4, the whole register has not been indexed.

The IGI is the most helpful of all finding aids because of its wide range, although, in all counties, many parishes have yet to be included. If a name corresponding to the one sought is found in the file, the same should then be looked up in the original parish register both to check its correctness and to obtain any additional information given there, such as occupations and names of witnesses. The index is published on microfiche, of which new sets with additional entries are issued from time to time. Many county record offices, public libraries and family history societies have the microfiche and the equipment for viewing them. Details of their whereabouts are contained in a booklet, *Where to find the International Genealogical Index* (1984), obtainable from J.S.W. Gibson, Harts Cottage, Church Hanborough, Oxford OX7 2AB. In most counties, either the county record office or the family history society will have a set.

Interred An expression sometimes meaning 'buried without Christian rites'; used, for example, of excommunicates or unbaptized persons.

Intestate A person was intestate when he died without having made a will. Unless his estate was small, and the inheritance undisputed, the next-of-kin would need to apply for Letters of Administration to administer it.

Inventories Among probate records, the inventory is a list of the movable effects of a deceased person, sometimes expressly called for by the Probate Court, especially in the case of intestate persons whose next-of-kin were applying for Letters of Administration. The list had to be drawn up and signed by two reputable neighbours of the deceased. Such inventories, almost all required during the period 1529-1750, give a fascinating glimpse into a person's lifestyle. His household goods were listed, often under the headings of each named room (i.e. the hall, parlours, chambers, shops (workshops), etc.), and include furnishings, plates and drinking vessels, bedclothes, personal clothes, tools and stock in trade, as well as anything stored in the barn, animals and growing crops, with the estimated value of each item. Debts, credits and leases were also listed, but the law on what should be included differed from time to time. The tools and stock in trade often give a truer indication of how the deceased earned his livelihood than the description he gave of himself in his will; e.g. gentleman, yeoman, husbandman, etc. Larger pieces of equipment might be regarded as fixtures and therefore omitted. His wife's property would be excluded from the list, even when she had predeceased him. Because inventories were usually compiled by unscholarly neighbours, and the spelling was apt to follow the phonetics of the local dialect, they are often difficult to read.

Many records are held at county record offices, and at the Borthwick Institute at the

---

OVERLEAF An inventory of the goods and chattels of William Thatcher, yeoman, of Chertsey, Surrey, who died in 1625. After mentioning the value of his wearing apparel and the money in his purse, all his household possessions are listed room by room: the hall (the main living-room), the chamber over the parlour, the cheeseloft, the chamber over the hall, the garret, the kitchen, the bolting house (where flour was sifted), the milk house, and the loft over the kitchen; then his pewter and linen; and finally the farm equipment and animals. Only the parlour seems to have been overlooked. The value put upon his belongings came in all to £247.16s.4d. *Crown copyright: PROB.205*

An Inventory of all the goods Cattell
and Chattells of William Thatcher late
of Godlestone, in the parish of Shortesgrin the
Countie of Surrey yeoman deceased praised
by Edward Rogers theelder John Myddest &
Henry Cooke the second day of Anno 1625
in manner & forme followinge (vizt)

Imprimis the wearinge apparrell
of the deceased and money in his house .... iiij li

In the Hall

Item one table & a paire of trestells
one Cubbord, one forme, forme ioyned &
stooles and a Cradle .... xviij ..... s

In the Chamber over the parler

Item one ioyned beddsteddle one fetherbed
two fether boulsters, two pillowes, two
blanketts, one Coverlett, one paire of sheete
three Chests & one wooden Chaire .... liij iij li

In the Chese lofte

Item one olde Chest & one other
one table
Chest thirteene Cheeses, twelve yarde of
wollen Cloth, eightene pounde of lynen
yarne, one Iavelin with other small thinge .... iij li

In the Chamber over the hall

Item one ioyned bedd stedd one fetherbedd
one fether boulster, one strawbedd, two
blanketts one Coverlett & one paire of
sheets, one trundle beddstedd, one flockbedd
two fether boulsters, one blankett one Coverlett
one paire of sheets and three Chests .... iiij li

In the Garrett

Item One sack of wooll and one
lynnen wheele .... xvj ..... s

In the Kitchen

Item two brasse pott, one brasse
possnett, one Chafer, one skillett two brasse
kettells, one Cauldron, three spitts and one
frminate .... iij li

148

And one yron dripping pann, one gridyron
two paire of pott hooks, two paire of pott hangers
one fryenge pann, one warmeing pann
one mortar & pestle, two paire of Childyrens
and one trevett

In the boultinge house

Item one kneadtrough, one saltrough
one boultinge hutch, one cheesepresse, one
olde cubbord, one little table, with other timber

In the milkehouse

Item fowre cheesemoats & followers
eight boulles, one kever, seven firkins, with
other wooden vessells & timber

In the lofte over the kitchen

Item of rye & wheate, fifteene bushells
and two bushells of Malte

Pewter

Item five & twenty platters pewter
dishes, one bason, five sawcers, fowre
saltsellers, three pottingers, one dozen of
spoones, two candlestickes & one chamber pott

Lynen

Item three paire of sheete, fowre table
clothes, one dozen of napkins & three hand
towells

Item one longe cart, one dunge carte
one plough, one paire of harrowes with other
implements of husbandry

And two kyne, one steere & three weaninge calfes
And three olde horses
And seven & forty sheepe & tenn lambes
And five hogge & three shotes, three weaninge piggs
And one goose & a gander, five hens
five henns and a cocke

And corne upon the ground
And one lease of a close of land
And five stalles of bees

Debtes sperat and desperat

Sum total
bona Invent

University of York. Those for the Prerogative Court of Canterbury are at the Public Record Office, Chancery Lane, London, under PROB.2-5 and 31 (PROB.4. is only partly indexed). Inventories are occasionally found among Chancery proceedings and other records.

For further reading, see *Probate Inventories — a glossary of Household, Farming and Trade Terms* (Derbyshire Record Society).

Irvingites The popular, but not accepted, cognomen of the Catholic Apostolic Church in which Edward Irving (1792-1834) played a prominent role. He was ordained by Presbytery at Annan, Scotland, in 1822, and became minister of the Caledonian Church, Hatton Garden, London. His sermons attracted influential supporters but his theology was viewed with suspicion by the London presbytery, and when his followers began to claim the gifts of tongues and prophecy, they excluded him. In 1833 he was deposed by the Presbytery of Annan but re-ordained by his new Catholic Apostolic Church, which was led by twelve 'apostles' and six 'prophets'. Churches were founded in London, and elsewhere in England, the increase in followers being helped by their not having to separate themselves from the churches of their former allegiance. The rites of their ceremonies were very different from the plain services of other nonconformist bodies, being based on those of the Greek Orthodox and Roman Catholic Churches, and in time even the presence of a statue of Buddha was not considered inappropriate. The registers of nine churches (five from London) were deposited with the Registrar General in 1840, and are now at the Public Record Office in group RG.

For further reading, see *Sources for Nonconformist Genealogy and Family History*, by D.J. Steel (1973).

Isle of Wight A county formed in 1974. Formerly in HAMPSHIRE.

Italic Hand *see* **Handwriting**

J

Jews (in England) During the Roman occupation, there was almost certainly a small number of Jewish traders in Britain.

1066 An organised Jewish community came over with William the Conqueror, mainly from Normandy.

*c.*1100 From this time, the Jews in England were *servi camerae regis* (serfs of the Royal Chamber). All their money and effects belonged to the king, and he could resume them at any time. Jews were not allowed to engage in agriculture or wholesale or retail trade, but were encouraged in money-lending because usury was forbidden to Christians by the Church. From time to time royal tallages of enormous sums were levied on the Jewish community, which had to be paid from among its members. Their numbers probably varied between 3000 and 10,000, but at one time the taxation of the Jews produced about one-seventh of the total revenue of the Crown. From time to time, massacres of Jews took place, especially when a crusade was being prepared or after some unexplained child murder. The smaller barons, who were the chief debtors of the Jews, would organise riots with the aim of killing their creditors and destroying their IOUs.

1290 By this time, tallages had finally impoverished the Jews to a point at which they were of no further use to the king; so Richard I expelled them from England, and later from his Norman possessions. For nearly 400 years their entry into England was considered illegal, though a few did come in, some of them very distinguished persons, including doctors to the royal household.

*c.*1500 Refugees from Mediterranean countries, where they had been suffering under the Inquisition, gained illegal access into England. The influx consisted mainly of those who had been expelled from Spain in 1492 and had settled in Portugal, where they had been forcibly baptized in 1497, but had secretly adhered to their own religion.

1655   At this time, there were about 140 secret Jews (Marranos) in England. Cromwell wanted to make Jewish entry into the country legal, because Jews had been a great help in the commercial success of the Netherlands, England's chief trade rival, but the Church and the City prevented it. However, two High Court judges gave it as their opinion that there was no law prohibiting the entry of Jews, and this was sufficient to start a slow immigration, nine-tenths of it from Mediterranean countries. These immigrants were called Sephardim. They were largely importers-and-exporters, wholesalers, ship's chandlers and ship owners, some of them wealthy and armigerous. Only about one-tenth of the newcomers were Ashkenazim, very poor Yiddish-speaking people from Germany, Poland and Russia, but gradually the East Europeans came to outnumber the Sephardi community, and still do today.

1663   The Sephardi synagogue in London started keeping records, in Portuguese.

1680   There were about 2000 Sephardim in London.

1722 & 1735   There were two more influxes of Jewish refugees from the Inquisition.

1760   The Board of Deputies of British Jews was formed to undertake political, social and administrative tasks on behalf of Jews.

1841   The *Jewish Chronicle* began weekly publication in London.

1870   The Anglo-Jewish Association was formed. Membership was — and is — by invitation to prominent Jews. Its functions tend to duplicate those of the Board of Deputies.

1880 & 1905   There were influxes of Ashkenazim from Russian pogroms.

1930s   Refugees came to England from the persecutions of Jews under the Nazi regime in Germany.

1962   A committee called Anglo-Jewish Archives was formed, under the joint auspices of University College, London, and the Jewish Historical Society of England, to record, collect and preserve archives.

1975   There were about 400,000 Jews in Britain, of whom 270,000 lived in Greater London. Less than half of the total descend from ancestors who were in this country in 1880.

There are about 375 synagogues in England. Sixty-one per cent of British Jews belong to a synagogue, but a much smaller proportion is in regular attendance. The synagogues are grouped in various denominations. The United Synagogue consists of 81 London synagogues and is in the central Jewish tradition. The Federation of Synagogues comprises 42 synagogues in London and is right-wing. The Union of Orthodox Hebrew Congregations has 42 small London synagogues and is extreme right-wing. The Liberal Synagogues and the Reform Synagogues are recently formed left-wing groups, numbering about 45 congregations over the whole country.

The names and addresses of the synagogues, and of the cemeteries maintained by some of them, are listed in the *Jewish Year Book*, published by The Jewish Chronicle Ltd. It also lists most other Jewish organisations.

Most Jewish synagogues retain their own records, some of which are in Hebrew, but those of the United Group are deposited at the headquarters of the United Synagogue, Woburn House, Upper Woburn Place, London WC1. Those of defunct congregations may be in the Anglo-Jewish Archives (see below). The civil and religious marriages of Jews are performed at the same time in the presence of a Marriage Secretary appointed by the Board of Deputies of British Jews, as a deputy to the Superintendent Registrar. The Reform groups appoint their own Marriage Secretaries.

The archives of the Board of Deputies of British Jews (Jewish Board of Deputies) are in a poor state in the cellar of the Board's premises at Woburn House. Those of the Anglo-Jewish Association are in the Anglo-Jewish Archives, Mocatta Library, University College, London WC1. The Association itself is at Woburn House. The Archives also contain the records of many other organisations.

The Jewish Historical Society of England has, among other records, a collection of Anglo-Jewish genealogies bequeathed to them by Sir Thomas Colyer-Fergusson, Bart., which it keeps at the Jewish Museum, Woburn House. The Secretary of the Society can be contacted care of University College, London WC1. The Society has published (1949) Arthur Arnold's index of all ascertainable wills and Letters of Administration of Jews in the Prerogative Court of Canterbury, under the title *Anglo-Jewish Notabilities*.

The marriage registers of the Spanish and Portuguese Synagogue of London, Bevis Marks, London EC3 (1687-1837), have been published as *Bevis Marks Records II*. They show the parents of both parties.

The early issues (from 1941) of the *Jewish Chronicle*, 25 Furnival Street, London EC4 (telephone 01.405.9252) have been subject-indexed. Sometimes Jews can be found among the baptismal, marriage and burial entries of Church of England parishes, especially, in London, those of St Dionis Backchurch, St Katherine Cree, and St Helen's Bishopgate.

For further reading, see *My Ancestor was Jewish. How can I find more about him?*, available from the Society of Genealogists.

See also IMMIGRANTS.

Joined In inventories, pieces of wooden furniture are sometimes described as joined, or joint. This means 'carpentered'. A joined table is distinct from one consisting of a board resting on a trestle.

Joint Enfeoffment The settlement of a property on a husband and wife jointly. Such an arrangement made it possible to avoid the lord's rights of relief and wardship, if the husband predeceased his wife.

Jointure A fixed yearly sum payable to a widow out of her husband's freehold, either for life or until she remarried. She had a right to this payment, if she wished, instead of a dower.

Journeyman A day labourer. The *Statute of Artificers* of 1563 laid down the journeyman's hours of work as being, in summer, from, at or before 5 a.m. until between 7 and 8 p.m., with not more than 2½ hours off for breakfast, dinner and drinking; and in winter from dawn till dusk. Unlike apprentices and employees engaged on a longer-term basis, most journeymen lived away from their work. The term has no connection with travelling. In London, journeymen employed under licence by freemen had themselves to be freemen until 1750. Indexed licence books for 1750-1845 are at the Corporation's Record Office, Guildhall, Gresham Street, London EC2, showing names of journeymen and masters.

Jurors' Lists *see* **Freeholders' Lists**

Jury of Presentment By an ancient custom confirmed at the Assize of Clarendon in 1166, twelve respectable men of the hundred and four similar men from each vill were liable for bringing suspected offenders before the justices and sheriff of the county in the hundred court.

Justices of the Peace Originally called Keepers of the Peace, these magistrates were appointed by a commission under the Great Seal, to keep the peace within a stated jurisdiction. The justices first acquired their name, and the power to try major offences, under a statute of 1361. On appointment they gave their services without pay. In order to exclude men too poor to be suitable, a statute of 18 Henry VI (his eighteenth regnal year) requires that each justice should hold lands to the value of £20 per annum. This amount was raised to £100 clear of all deductions, in 1744. Parish constables and other parochial officials were responsible to Justices of the Peace for the satisfactory performance of their duties. The justices enforced the law in their county and tried cases before a jury at Quarter Sessions. Between sessions, justices could meet together in Petty Sessions to settle very small matters. They are named in the Quarter Session rolls, but not all the justices in the commission were obliged to be present at every court.

K

Kelly's Directories This series of local directories started in 1799 with a volume for London, and has since covered all the counties and large cities of England, outlasting all their competitors. New editions of the county volumes appeared roughly every eight years until 1939, and city volumes were published rather more frequently. Their contents in the nineteenth century expanded in line with those of other local directories. The earliest contained the names and addresses of commercial concerns, then those of the more prosperous private householders were included, and finally of all householders. In the 1930s and 40s, as more and more private people owned telephones and so had their names and addresses in the free Post Ofice Telephone Directories, Kelly's sales were seriously affected. However, the firm now publishes British Telecom's directories and manufacturers' guides. A copy of each publication since the beginning is kept at Kelly's Directories Ltd, Dorset House, Stamford Street, London SE1, where they may be consulted on payment of a search fee. Many of the volumes can also be seen at county libraries, the Guildhall Library in London, and the Society of Genealogists.

Kent The Kent Family History Society, North-west Kent Family History Society, Folkestone Family History Society, and Woolwich and District Family History Society, all hold regular meetings and issue journals. Enquiries should be sent c/o The Federation of Family History Societies, 31 Seven Star Road, Solihull, West Midlands B91 2BZ, marked 'Please forward' and enclosing a stamped self-addressed envelope.

Record Repositories Kent County Archives Office, County Hall, Maidstone (tel: 0622.671411); South-east Kent Branch of Kent Archives Office, Folkestone Central Library, Folkestone; Cathedral Archives and Library, and City Record Office, The Precincts, Canterbury (tel: 0622.63510); Greenwich Town Clerk's Department, Town Hall, Wellington Street, London SE18; Greenwich Borough Archives, 90 Mycenae Road, Blackheath, London SE3; Diocesan Registry, 9 The Precincts, Canterbury; Kent County Library, Springfield, Maidstone; Archives and Local History Department, Lewisham Library, 170 Bromley Road, London SE6; Gravesend Public Library, Gravesend; Institute of Heraldic and Genealogical Studies, Northgate, Canterbury.

Parish Registers and Indexes (*see* comment under COUNTY) The registers of most of the 400 ancient

parishes have been deposited, mostly at the county record office (CRO), with a few at other repositories mentioned above. The Society of Genealogists has copies of about half of them. There is a marriage index for east Kent, 1813-37, in the care of M.J. Gandy, 64 Oakleigh Park North, Whetstone, London N20; and one for west Kent, 1780-1812, in the care of S.G. Smith, 21 Homefield Close, Swanley. The INTER-NATIONAL GENEALOGICAL INDEX (IGI) covers a large number of baptisms. The Bishops' Transcripts for the Rochester Diocese are at the CRO, Maidstone; those for the Canterbury Diocese at the Cathedral Archives; and those for the Peculiars of the Arches, Shoreham and Croydon, at Lambeth Palace Library. The House of Lords Record Office has Bishops' Transcripts of 98 parishes for 1640-2, with modern copies at the Institute of Heraldic and Genealogical Studies.

Marriage Licence Records Those for the Diocese of Canterbury are in the Cathedral Library; those for the Diocese of Rochester at the CRO; and those for the Peculiars at Lambeth Palace Library. There are some indexes at the Society of Genealogists' library.

Wills before 1858, proved in the following courts, are at the county record office:

> Consistory Court of Canterbury
> Archdeaconry Court of Canterbury
> Consistory Court of Rochester
> Archdeaconry Court of Rochester ·
> Peculiar Courts

After 1846, wills for the extreme northwest corner of the county were proved in the Consistory Court of London. As the Dioceses of both Canterbury and Rochester lay in the Province of Canterbury, wills could also be proved in the Prerogative Court of Canterbury. The Society of Genealogists has indexes to the Consistory and Archdeaconry Courts of Canterbury.

Non-parochial Registers The registers of 112 chapels are at the Public Record Office (PRO), Chancery Lane, London. Nearly as many are covered by the IGI.

Census Returns These are at the PRO, Portugal Street, London, and at the County Library, Maidstone.

Memorial Inscriptions There are transcripts from a large number of churches at the Society of Genealogists, and several hundred at the Institute of Heraldic and Genealogical Studies. The family history societies are extending the coverage.

Heralds' Visitation Pedigrees have been printed for 1530, 1574, 1592, 1619-21 and 1663-8.

Kent Archaeological Society has made a number of historical records of the county available in print.

King's Bench, Court of

One of the three courts that evolved from the Curia Regis (King's Court) of the Norman and early Plantagenet kings, the others being the Courts of Common Pleas and Exchequer. It had become separate by the reign of Edward I, with the function of trying cases affecting the king himself and magnates privileged to be tried only before the king (Coram Regis) or, in his absence abroad, by his Council. It also corrected the errors of other courts. After the civil wars of Henry III it tried criminal cases (the Crown Side), but in time came to deal also with civil suits (the Plea Side). The records are at the Public Record Office, Chancery Lane, London; of the Crown Side under references KB.1-4, 6-13, 18-19, 30-32, 35; of the Plea Side, KB.20-29, 33, 36. The Placita Coram Rege Rolls (KB.27), 1 Edward I to 13 William III (their first and thirteenth regnal years, respectively) contain entries of all proceedings in the Court of King's Bench. The Judgement Rolls record suits between private persons.

King's Evil

Scrofula; a disease of the lymphatic glands, once thought to be curable by a touch from the king's hand. Accounts of the origin of this idea in England differ widely; W.E. Tate ascribing it to the time of Saint Edward the Confessor (and others to Edward III) inheriting the power from Saint Louis IX of France. Originally the king used to wash the diseased parts and present the sufferer with a penny, but Henry VII and his successors did no more than touch the afflicted persons during the course of a special church service, after which they were presented with the 'touch-piece', which by then was a gold angel pierced for hanging round the

neck. Charles II gave a gold medal worth ten shillings. The last monarch to touch for the King's Evil was Queen Anne.

Each applicant for the royal touch had to bring a certificate from the incumbent and church-wardens of his or her parish, that the suffering was genuine and the touch had not been administered before. The issue of such certificates was usually noted in the parish records. Most of the touchings were performed in London, for which afflicted people came from all over the country, but when the king was on a visit to a subject he sometimes touched sufferers in his host's parish.

Kitchen

Until the sixteenth century, the kitchen of a house was almost always a building separate from the dwelling house itself, because of the fire risk; but when brick chimneys were introduced, it was brought indoors and became the area at the back of the chimney base, which stood fairly centrally placed in the hall on the ground floor.
See also HALL.

Knight

Knights were the fighting men, fully equipped, who followed the Conqueror into England and were rewarded by grants of land (knights' fees) which they held either directly from the king or, more often, from his barons, in return for Knight Service. The knight's male descendants served as squires (esquires) in their teens, and were dubbed when they came of age. However, in the course of a few generations, actual military Knight Service became separated from the holding of land, by the practice of division and sub-infeuding of knights' fees between smaller land-holders. This led to the commutation of service by a money payment, called Scutage (shield-money), with which funds the king was able to employ paid fighting-men. In 1224, at a time when more than half the holders of knights' fees were paying for exemption from service, Henry III issued them a summons either to take up knighthood or be fined for refusal, which was probably a device for bringing in additional funds. The holder of a knight's fee who did not take up knighthood remained an esquire all his life, and so the style of (e)squire became permanently attached to the social class of gentry, and especially land-holding gentry, in spite of efforts to give it a more limited technical connotation later on (*see* ESQUIRE).

Bereft of all hereditary connection, knighthood became a purely personal honour, the reward at first for military, and later, for any other kind of service. The knight was, and is, styled 'Sir', followed by his forename.

It was only the abolition of feudal tenure in 1646, confirmed in 1662, that ended the obligation (since 1306) of a landholder worth £40 per annum to take up the privilege of knighthood, though it had long been a dead letter, but Charles I tried to extract fines from all such men who would not accept knighthood. Lists of the men involved in this Distraint of Knighthood are at the Public Record Office, Chancery Lane, London, under reference E.178/7154, grouped under counties.

From the early crusades onward, special orders of international knighthood were instituted, including the Knights Hospitallers of the Order of St John of Jerusalem, the Knights Templar, and others in Europe. The earliest English order was that of the Garter, founded in 1343 by Edward III, an enthusiast for the principles of chivalry. It was followed at the end of the same century by that of the Bath, and in course of time by a number of others. An ordinary knight who had not achieved the rank of knight banneret (*see* BANNERET, KNIGHT) was called a knight bachelor and was entitled to a forked pennant.

A register of knights has been maintained at the College of Arms since 1622. New knighthoods are reported in the *London Gazette*, and living knights are listed in the volumes, issued from time to time, of both Burke's and Debrett's *Peerage, Baronetage and Knightage*. W.A. Shaw's *The Knights of England* (1906) lists knights from 1257 onward.

Knight Service The military tenure by which freehold land was held under the feudal system of the Middle Ages. From the Conquest, all the land of England was owned by the king and he enfeoffed all of it, except his own royal demesnes, to earls, barons and lesser men in return for their liability for military service. The service required was based upon the 'constabularia' of ten knights. An important tenant-in-chief might be expected to provide one or more of these units, and lesser men, half of one. To obtain such knights for the king's service, the tenants-in-chief sub-infeuded some of their manors to gentlemen in return for the necessary obligation. The sub-infeuding process then continued downwards to a lord of a single manor, representing only a fraction of a knight's fee, which was therefore paid in money (*see* SCUTAGE). The total number of knights' fees was between five and six thousand.

Knight Service consisted of active military service in the field, if called upon, for forty days per year, bringing arms, armour and horse as laid down. It also involved castle ward (guard duties) at his immediate lord's chief castle for a fixed number of days per year. Certain other obligations were also involved, including (i) a relief paid on succeeding to his land; (ii) wardship, the liability of an heir who was a minor to become a ward of his lord (*see* WARDS AND LIVERIES); (iii) marriage (unless bought off), the liability of an heir (if a minor) to be given in marriage by his lord, the same also applying to an heiress or a widow.

The principle of knight service remained until 1662.

Knight of the Shire A Member of Parliament elected on the county vote; not necessarily, indeed seldom, a knight in rank. The term was a survival into the nineteenth century from the medieval early days of Parliament, when knights were selected to represent the smaller gentry of the countryside.

Knobstick Wedding The wedding of a pregnant single woman to the putative father-to-be, under pressure from the parish vestry. The churchwardens attended to see that the ceremony was performed, and the name is derived from their staves of office.

Knocknobbler A parishioner given the responsibility for driving dogs out of church, if they were a nuisance. Also called a dog-whipper.

Kymnell A wooden trough or tub, used in kneading dough and in home brewing, a utensil often listed in inventories.

L

Lairstall A grave inside a church.

Lambeth Palace Library Founded in 1610 by Archbishop Bancroft as a public library, it is now administered by the Church Commissioners. For single searches, application should be made in advance, in writing, to the Librarian at the address given below.

The records most generally useful to genealogists are the marriage licence records of the Faculty Office and Vicar General's Office, and the probate records of the Court of Arches and of the Peculiars of the Archbishop of Canterbury in the Peculiar Deaneries of the Arches (London), and — to a lesser degree, because all the records are not here — of Shoreham (Kent) and Croydon (Surrey). There are also a great number of documents originated by the spiritual and temporal functions of the Archiepiscopate.

The address is Lambeth Palace Library, Lambeth Palace, London SE1. The separate library entrance is by a door in the long wall in Lambeth Palace Road.

Lambrequin *see* **Mantling**

Lammas Commonly said to be the festival of the wheat harvest, celebrated, before the 1752 change in the calendar, on the first of August and afterwards on the thirteenth. The name is often said to originate from loaf-mass. However, Dr Johnson, in his dictionary, derived it from Latter-math (a second mowing), which would appear to have agricultural practice in its favour, since all the hay should be in by Lammas while it would still be too early for all the wheat. Lammas land was land enclosed and held in severalty until Lammas, and then thrown open to the beasts of the manor for grazing. There was once an old saying, 'at latter Lammas', meaning 'never'.

Lancashire Since 1974 the ancient county has been divided into Lancashire, Greater Man-

chester, and Merseyside. Furness has been transferred to Cumbria, and the county's southern border to Cheshire. Manchester and Lancashire Family History Society, Lancashire Family History and Heraldry Society, Liverpool and District Family History Society, all hold regular meetings and issue journals. Enquiries should be sent c/o The Federation of Family History Societies, 31 Seven Star Road, Solihull, West Midlands B91 2BZ, marked 'Please forward' and enclosing a stamped self-addressed envelope.

Record Repositories Lancashire Record Office, Bow Lane, Preston (tel: 0772.58347); Greater Manchester County Record Office, 56 Marshall Street, Ancoats, Manchester; Liverpool Record Office, Brown Library, William Brown Street, Liverpool 3 (tel: 051.207.2147); Wigan Record Office, Leigh Town Hall, Leigh (tel: 0942.672421); Manchester Central Library, Archives Department, St Peter's Square, Manchester (tel: 061.236.9422); John Ryland's University Library of Manchester, Oxford Road, Manchester; Chetham's Library, Manchester 3; Rochdale Public Library, Esplanade, Rochdale; Salford Archives Centre, 658-62 Liverpool Road, Irlam, Manchester; Merseyside County Archives Service, 64-66 Islington, Liverpool.

Parish Registers and Indexes (*see* comment under COUNTY) Of the ancient parishes, virtually all have now been deposited at the appropriate record office. The Society of Genealogists has copies of more than one hundred of them. The INTERNATIONAL GENEALOGICAL INDEX (IGI) includes many of them. Both the Manchester and Lancashire Family History Society and the Lancashire Family History and Heraldry Society have copies of the IGI and are compiling marriage indexes. The Beckett Index (J.D. Beckett, 34 Eastwood Drive, Droylesden, Manchester) covers Bolton, Bury, Middleton and Prestwich, from 1754 to 1800. There is also a Greater Liverpool Index, in the care of H. Culling, 11 Lisburn Lane, Liverpool L13 9AE. The Bishops' Transcripts are almost all at the county record office (CRO), but those of the Peculiar of the Dean and Chapter of York are at the Borthwick Institute, at the University of York.

Marriage Licence Records Those for the Archdeaconry of Chester (south of the River Ribble) are at the Cheshire Record Office; those for the Archdeaconry of Richmond at the CRO; and those for the Peculiar Court of the Dean and Chapter of York are at the Borthwick Institute.

Wills before 1858, proved in the following courts, are at the CRO:

> Episcopal Consistory Court of Chester
> Consistory Court of the Commissary of the Archdeacon of Richmond (Western Deaneries)
> The Manor Courts of Halton, Nether Kellet, Slyne with Hest, and Skerton

Those proved in the following courts are at the Borthwick Institute:

> Peculiar Court of the Dean and Chapter of York
> Exchequer Court of York
> Chancery Court of York

Rochdale Public Library has abstracts of 2400 wills and Letters of Administration, 1553-1810, relating to local people.

As the diocese lay in the Province of York, wills could also be proved in the Prerogative Court of York and the Prerogative Court of Canterbury. Indexes of wills, 1545-1837, have been printed by the Lancashire and Cheshire Record Society.

Non-parochial Registers The registers of 252 chapels are at the Public Record Office (PRO), Chancery Lane, London. The IGI covers about one hundred.

Census Returns These are at the PRO, Portugal Street, London, and at the CRO. The University of Lancaster has those for the county north of the River Ribble. Some libraries in Manchester and Liverpool hold returns for those cities.

Memorial Inscriptions The Manchester and Lancashire Family History Society has transcription in hand. The Society of Genealogists has some transcripts.

Heralds' Visitation Pedigrees have been printed for 1533, 1567, 1613 and 1664-5.

Record Publishing Societies Lancashire and Cheshire Record Society; Lancashire Parish Record Society; Chetham Society.

Lance (i) A long spear for use by a horse soldier.

(ii) A medieval army unit consisting of a knight or man-at-arms, two archers, a swordsman and two pages armed with daggers. The term 'Lance-Corporal' derives from this body.

Land Another name for a selion; i.e. a strip of ploughland within a furlong in the open arable field of a manor.

Landed Gentry, Burke's This series of volumes, appearing at irregular intervals, began as Burke's *History of the Commoners*, but changed its title with the volume of 1846 to *A Genealogical and Heraldic Dictionary of the Landed Gentry*. The volumes contain constantly updated paragraph pedigrees of the landed and county families of Great Britain, accompanied by representations of their arms. In the course of time many families have sold their estates, but continue to be included in Burke as 'formerly of ...'. In each volume the main pedigrees section is preceded by essays of genealogical interest. The most recent edition, the eighteenth, appeared, by innovation, in three volumes, each listing families in a separate alphabetical order.

Landgable A nominal rent payable to their lord by borough tenants on burgess tenure.

Land Registration *see* **Enrolled Deeds**

Land Tax The Land Tax was first regularly imposed in 1697, on an assessment made in 1692. A quota was fixed for each county, and local assessors were left to allot appropriate amounts to each parish and, within the parishes, to each taxpayer. At first movable property and salaries were taxed too, but because of the difficulty of assessing them it was soon decided to confine assessments to real estate, some offices of profit, tithes, and some buildings. The early records of collection were defective in compilation, and very few survive. In time, anomalies arose, leaving rural areas too heavily taxed compared with the new industrial districts. In 1772 the returns were altered to incorporate a list of all the occupiers of land in each parish. From 1780, duplicates had to be lodged with the Clerk of the Peace, so that they could be used to establish the qualifications of parliamentary voters. In 1782 a further column was added to show the proprietor of each building. These deposited records are available down to 1832.

From 1772, the tax was normally levied at the rate of four shillings in the pound, and in 1798 landowners were allowed to buy themselves out of the liability by a lump sum of fifteen years' purchase, but until 1832 the names of 'exonerated' owners continue in the lists. By the end of 1815 about one-third of the land had been thus redeemed.

From 1826, until the tax was abolished in 1832, an additional column describes the property on which the tax is levied.

Documents consist of *Assessments* and *Returns*. The former show the assessed value of the land; the Returns, the amounts actually collected. Sometimes the columns are unheaded, and this can be misleading because some clerks reversed the columns for proprietors and tenants. Comparison should be made with previous or subsequent years. The property shown does not necessarily indicate the tenant's abode, much less the proprietor's. Most of the returns were drawn up annually, but some quarterly, and in the latter case the tax shown is a quarter of the annual rate. 'Exonerated holdings', from 1798 until about 1815, were usually listed at the end of the parish return.

The records from 1780 are in county record offices, usually in annual volumes or 'bundles', with the parishes grouped in Hundreds. Not all start from the same date, and there are often gaps. Some assessments and minutes of commissioners' meetings are to be found among parish records.

The tax records are a useful aid in finding the whereabouts of a householder, once his county is known. The researcher who cannot find his family among the Land Tax records of a given county should refer to a series of volumes at the Public Record Office, Kew, under reference IR.23. These contain a copy of the Land Tax assessments for the whole country for the year 1798, and show proprietors, occupiers and sums assessed but no details of the properties, nor are sub-tenants or sharing tenants shown. The volumes are arranged by counties, Hundreds and parishes, with sub-divisions for boroughs

and hamlets, and so provide an excellent location record for people needing to find their family's whereabouts at the turn of the century.

The Federation of Family History Societies has published a booklet guide, *Land Tax Assessments, c.1690-1950*.

Lanspesado A rank in the militia, equivalent to lance-corporal.

Larceny Stealing. Grand larceny (a felony) was the theft of goods above the value of twelve pence from the owner's house; not from the person, or by night. It was a capital crime. Petty larceny was the theft of goods to the value of twelve pence or less, and the punishment was imprisonment or whipping. The distinction between grand and petty larceny was removed in 1827.

Latin, Medieval Before 1733, except for the period 1651-60, Latin was the compulsory language of legal documents and often, by the writer's choice, of other records. It is, therefore, a stumbling block for researchers who have not studied classical Latin at any level, and even to some extent for those who have, because texts of the Middle Ages and the sixteenth and seventeenth centuries employ Latin words for things and ideas that did not exist in classical times. Furthermore, they were written in a system of abbreviations that require practice to read. Fortunately, certain aids are available, the most important of which is Eileen A. Gooder's *Latin for Local History*, a textbook of grammar for beginners, using, as examples, words and phrases helpful to local historians and genealogists, and giving translations of frequently consulted records. It is intended to be used in conjunction with B.H. Kennedy's *Shorter Latin Primer*, but is very effective on its own.

A second aid is R.E. Latham's *Revised Mediaeval Latin Word-List* (Oxford, 1965), listing non-classical meanings occurring in English and Irish documents between the fifth and sixteenth centuries. A third is C.T. Martin's *The Record Interpreter* (Kohler & Coombes, 1979). This contains a medieval Latin word-list, lists of abbreviations and of the Latin names of places, bishoprics, surnames and Christian names. The vocabulary at the end of Eileen Gooder's book contains only a tiny portion of the words in the two other word-lists, but is helpful because they are specially selected.

Because genealogical research involves only a comparatively small number of Latin records, the vocabulary required is not large; the same words and phrases are met with again and again. Parish registers, the records most frequently consulted, were often written in Latin until about 1625, or even later, so a vocabulary of the words and phrases likely to be found in them is given under the entry PARISH REGISTERS. Translations are also supplied under ACTS OF ADMINISTRATION, CHRISTIAN NAMES, MANOR and PROBATE.

Latten An alloy of copper and zinc, yellow in colour, used for a variety of household plates, dishes and vessels, and for monumental brasses in churches.

Latter Day Saints The members of the Church of Jesus Christ of Latter Day Saints are commonly known as Mormons, from the Book of Mormon on which the beliefs of the Church are based. One of its tenets encourages its followers to discover the names of their ancestors. The assistance given to their researches by the Church's Genealogical Society, with headquarters in Salt Lake City, Utah, U.S.A., in the form of microphotography of historical records, indexing and computerisation, has been of enormous assistance to all British genealogists. The two most notable of their aids has been the microfilming of the British Census Returns, and the creation of a consolidated International Genealogical Index (IGI) of a large number of English baptismal registers, and some marriages. Copies of the Census Returns on microfilm, and of the IGI on microfiche are now available to the public at most county record offices: many public libraries have their local Census Returns, and a number of family history societies have the IGI.

In the library at Salt Lake City, further data are available to local searchers. A list of these searchers can be obtained from the Genealogical Department, Church of Jesus Christ of Latter Day Saints, 50 East South Temple Street, Salt Lake City, Utah 84101, U.S.A.

Law Day The day on which a manor Court Leet, or view of frankpledge, was held. Often used to refer to the court itself.

Law Merchant Commercial law administered in borough courts. In detail it varied from town to town.

Lawyers As is the case with other professions, details of the careers of lawyers, both barristers and solicitors, are to be found in an annual printed publication, the *Law List*, which has appeared since 1775. For barristers there are also the printed registers of the four Inns of Court, namely Lincoln's Inn, the Middle Temple, the Inner Temple and Gray's Inn. The Inner Temple's register covers only admissions of an early period, but information can be obtained from the Librarian, Inner Temple, London EC4.

The Inns of Court were founded as schools of common lawyers in the fourteenth century. By the sixteenth century they were attracting not only men intending to practise law, but also the sons of the nobility and gentry, who attended them as an alternative to the two Universities, since a knowledge of law was useful in the management of their estates and also in any political ambitions they might have.

There were also Inns of Chancery, Staple Inn and Barnard's Inn (affiliated to Gray's Inn), Clifford's Inn and Clement's Inn (affiliated to the Inner Temple), New Inn (affiliated to the Middle Temple), and Thavie's Inn and Furnival's Inn (affiliated to Lincoln's Inn). These were originally preparatory colleges for younger students, who might later go on to an Inn of Court, but who often ended their studies there and became either solicitors acting for clients in the equity court of Chancery, attorneys licensed in the Common Law courts, or proctors in the ecclesiastical and admiralty courts. Inns of Chancery no longer exist. Details of articles of clerkship, and admissions of both types of lawyers from 1729, are to be found at the Public Record Office, Chancery Lane, London, in the records of the Court in which they practised. These are indexed. They include the names and addresses of fathers and of the lawyers to whom the clerks were articled.

For further reading, see *Tracing Your Ancestors*

at the PRO, by J. Cox and T. Padfield (HMSO, 1983).

Lay Subsidy By the end of the thirteenth century, land was no longer the only indication of a person's wealth, so a new tax, called Lay Subsidy, was levied on movables. Assessors were appointed for each district and they appointed local collectors. Not every house-holder's name is to be found in the returns, because some were too poor to be taxed and clerical properties were assessed and taxed separately; hence the name Lay Subsidy (*see* CLERICAL SUBSIDY). Certain items of property necessary to a person's livelihood were exempted; e.g. a knight's armour and riding horses, and a merchant's investment capital. So it is not possible to deduce with any certainty a taxpayer's relative prosperity.

At the head of each roll, the rate of tax is mentioned. This may be a tenth, twelfth, fifteenth or twentieth, depending upon the need of the Crown at the time. Sometimes two rates are indicated, in which case the larger fraction applies to urban populations and those who lived on the ancient demesnes of the Crown, and the smaller one to country folk. The two categories are usually listed separately on the roll.

From 1334, for two centuries, the rolls of personal names cease and only place names are listed, but in course of time the relative economic conditions of localities changed, so the Great Subsidy of 1542-5 lists all people over 16 years of age with income from land or with taxable goods worth £2 per annum, or with annual wages of £1 or more. Later subsidies, which continued to the end of the seventeenth century, give less detail.

The original Lay Subsidy Rolls are at the Public Record Office, Chancery Lane, London, in class E.179, and are catalogued in the List and Index Society series. Many county lists have been printed by record publishing societies. These are accompanied by explanatory articles.

Laystall A place for rubbish, dung, etc.

League This measure of distance cannot be relied on to be either the medieval 1½ miles, or

the present 3 miles. It differed from one part of the country to another.

Leas Meadowland. Also called 'lease'.

Lease and Release A procedure for transferring land from one party to another without the necessity of enrolment. The intending new owner first took a lease of the property for one year, which could be done by a deed that did not need to be enrolled. Then, a day later, the vendor conveyed the reversion of the lease to the purchaser, which, being only a right, could be transferred without livery of seisin or enrolment on a court roll, since possession did not pass as a result. This method of conveyance remained popular until the *Statute of Uses* was repealed in 1845. The records (*see* TITLE DEED) consist of two documents, the Lease and the Release.

See also BARGAIN AND SALE; ENROLLED DEEDS.

Leasehold Tenure Such tenure could be for a term of years, for life, for up to three lives, or at the will of the landlord. Land available for such leases was mainly either demesne land or land reclaimed from the waste, or a copyholder's holding that had reverted to the lord through the extinction of his family. In leases for three lives (not necessarily of three generations) the names of the three persons had to be recorded, and it has been suggested that this is one reason why a man would christen more than one of his sons with the same name.

Lecturer A clergyman without a benefice, employed to preach. Not all beneficed clergy were able or licensed to preach. Instead, they used to read from *The Book of Homilies,* but by the beginning of the seventeenth century con-gregations were not satisfied with this practice and so subscribed funds to employ a lecturer, usually on an annual basis.

RIGHT Few churchyard memorials provide so much biographical material as this; and on the back are shown the name, birthplace in France, and date of death of the soldier's wife. *Photo: John Mennell*

TO THE HONOURED MEMORY
OF
SERJEANT WILLIAM LAWRENCE
(OF THE 40TH REGIMENT FOOT)
WHO AFTER A LONG AND EVENTFUL LIFE
IN THE SERVICE OF HIS COUNTRY
PEACEFULLY ENDED HIS DAYS AT STUDLAND
NOVEMBER 11TH 1869
HE SERVED WITH HIS DISTINGUISHED REGIMENT
IN THE WAR IN SOUTH AMERICA 1805
AND THROUGH THE WHOLE OF THE PENINSULAR WAR 1808-1813
HE RECEIVED A SILVER MEDAL AND NO LESS THAN TEN CLASPS
FOR THE BATTLES IN WHICH HE WAS ENGAGED
ROLEIA   VIMIERA   TALAVERA
CIUDAD RODRIGO
BADAJOZ
(IN WHICH DESPERATE ASSAULT BEING ONE OF THE VOLUNTEERS
FOR THE FORLORN HOPE HE WAS MOST SEVERELY WOUNDED)
VITTORIA PYRENEES NIVELLES
ORTHES   TOULOUSE
HE ALSO FOUGHT AT THE GLORIOUS VICTORY OF
WATERLOO
JUNE 18TH 1815

While still serving with his Regiment during the
Occupation of Paris by the Allied Armies
Serjeant Lawrence married Clotilde Clairet
at St Germain en Laye who died Sep 26th 1853
and was buried beneath this Spot

ABOVE Members of the Essex Society for Family History playing their part in the nationwide project to record every memorial inscription in the country.
Photo: Martin Reed

RIGHT A plain gravestone, with plain lettering, nevertheless gives information about three generations of the Wheeler family in the nineteenth century.

FACING PAGE An eighteenth-century Burial Register contains several items of information useful to family historians. *Courtesy Chertsey Parish Church*

IN MEMORY OF
GEORGE WHEELER
WHO DIED DEC 10TH 1814
AGED 58 YEARS.
ALSO OF
SARAH WIFE OF THE ABOVE
SHE DIED AUG 24TH 1836
AGED 78 YEARS.
ALSO OF
THOMAS WHEELER
GRANDSON OF THE ABOVE
HE DIED NOV 19TH 1845
AGED 33 YEARS.
ALSO OF
ANN WHEELER MOTHER OF
THE ABOVE NAMED THOS WHEELER
SHE DIED MAY 24TH 1847
AGED 68 YEARS.
ALSO OF
THOMAS WHEELER
SON OF GEORGE AND SARAH
HUSBAND OF ANN AND FATHER
OF THOMAS ABOVE NAMED.
HE DIED AUG 11TH 1852
AGED 65 YEARS.

October.

3.d — Sarah Bauldwin Bur.d —

5.th — Henry Chapman Bur.d —

6.th — Rebecca Gammage Bur.d —

9.th — Mary Fuller Bur.d (by the Parish)

23. — William Barnett Bur.d

26.th { Ann Webb (a Pair travellers Child) Bur.d
{ Thomas Bauldwin (from Workhouse) Bur.d

29.th — Richard Hart Bur.d

d.o { Thomas Field (an Inf.t) Bur.d by the Parish)

30.th — Barbara Smith Bur.d

November. —

4.th — James Carter (from Workhouse) Bur.d

13.th — Patience Puss Bur.d (by the Parish)

29. th { M.rs Ann Rowe (from London) Bur.d
{ M.rs Mary Gordon Remov.d from Marybonne & Bur.d

30.th — Henry Crockford Jun.r Bur.d

December.

9.th — John Stevens (an Inf.t) Bur.d

16.th { Alice Freeman Bur.d (by the Parish)
{ Ann Blake (an Inf.t) Bur.d

19.th — Sarah Moore Bur.d

26.th — William Russell (from Workhouse) Bur.d

28.th — Mary Benham Bur.d —

y 12th of July 1752

At a Vestry called and held in the Vestry Room
of the Parish of Lingfield It was Unanimously
Agreed by all present to proceed immediately
to y° Building of a House for the Reception
of Such persons who shall at Any time be Seiz'd
with the small pox or Other pestilential Distemper
And that the Officers do forthwith prepare Estimates
of the Charges of the Said Building to be laid
before the Parishoners at the next monthly Meeting

At a Vestry called and held in the vestry Room
of the parish of Lingfield the 21st of Octobr 1753
It was then Unanimously Agreed to give Robt Bristy
the Sum of Three pounds Tenn Shillings P Annm
for the house and Orchard which he now holds by
Lease on Lingfield Common During the Term
of his Lease for the Use of a pest house,
Exempt and free from all Taxes.

Jn° Stanford
William Hother } Church Wardens

John Brister } Overseers
Abraham Hale }

Geo: Lee.
Tho: Exeter
Tho. Underhill
Rich: Agate

Landlords	Land & Houses	Occupiers	Rents	Rents	Taxes
			£	£ s	£ s d
Wm Larkin	Brot forward		52		
Do	House Row Same	Wm Hagley	4		
Do	Do Do	Jno Chamberlain	4		
Do	Do Do	Jno Smith	4	64	3 4 -
Margt Toms	Late ye 3 Compasses Ale house	Widw Dakers	12		
Do	Here hill Street	Bn Denham	5	17	- 17 -
Mr Pechell	House, Garden & c and Stables	Comte Woronzow	80		
Do	House Do	Jno Willis	5		
Do	Do adjoining Do	Do	3		
Do	1 Acre of Land East Bancroft	Wm Salter	3	91	4 11 -
Benjn Fox	Ground under hill	late Pechell	to be let out		
Do	House	Do Hosier Esqr	40		
Do	Do Do	Mr Rives	40		
Do	Do Do	Countess of Darby	120	200	10 - -
Joshua Jebb Esqr	House on ye Hill	Lion Darell Esqr	110	110	5 10 -
Fras Watkins	The Ivy house and Land on ye hill	Himself	27	27	1 7 -
Thos Skinner	House & Garden on the Common	Lady Eglinton	23		
Do	Land adjoining do	Jas Wizard	10	33	1 13 -
Late Wm Sewle	House & Garden	P Tucke Esqr	35		
Do	Land near Do	Thos Cope	8	43	2 3 -
The Trustees of the Marshalsea Prison	Two houses, Coach house & Stables on the Hill	Drake Esqr	47	47	2 7 -
Danl Grose	House on ye Hill	Himself	20		
Do	Coach house, and Stables on ye Common	Do	5	25	1 5 -
					32 17 ~

LEFT A page from the Vestry Minute Book of Lingfield, Surrey, recording, first, the decision to build a pest house for the parish, and, at the next meeting, to rent a building for it instead. A pest house was not exclusively, as is popularly supposed, a hospital for plague sufferers.

ABOVE A page from a Land Tax record, showing the owners and occupiers of properties in a parish. The order of the columns is not necessarily the same in all records, and sometimes the headings are omitted, creating uncertainty as to who are owners and who occupiers, but generally the most numerous 'ditto' entries appear in the owners (or landlords) column. *Courtesy the Surrey Record Office*

ABOVE Part of a seventeenth-century Northamptonshire Lay Subsidy record shows the names of all parishioners except those too poor to be taxed; whether they were assessed on their lands (*in terris*), or on their goods (*in bonis*); the taxable value of their estate; and the tax levied. The most prosperous residents have their status mentioned, e.g. knight, esquire, gentleman. *Crown copyright, E179/159/422*

RIGHT A Sussex squire's estate accounts in the reign of Queen Anne throws light on the livelihood not only of the landowner, but also of the local farm labourers and craftsmen. This page of 'Moneys disbursed' records payments to 'Comer the taylor for making a coat, John Henley for curing my cow, Mr Edwards for reading prayers, Henry Barrett for looking after my clocks for one year'.

170 7/8

                             li   s   d

	li	s	d
February ye 7th To Goodman Duley for four quarters of Peas	05	12	00
for shirts and handkerchiefs	05	13	06
To Mr Garland ten pounds	10	00	00
To Goodman Knight for ordering my fruit trees att Street	00	11	09
To Comes ye Taylor for making a coat	00	09	00
for one dozen of Teal	00	06	00
for pockett money	00	10	00
for taken my oyletts	00	02	06
Given to Mr Clarke	09	01	06
To Tho: Parker for Letters and other things	09	01	06
To Mr Challenor ye Taylor	20	00	00

March ye 5			
To Will: Boys collector for ye first and second quarterly payments for ye Queens Tax ffowing Wood lands lying in Arlington due att Michaelmas last past	01	16	04 1/2
To John Henley for curing my Cow	00	08	06
for pockett money	00	10	00
My Expences with Mr Medly	02	00	00
for one years poor Tax to ye Parrish of Wilington	00	12	06
for birds seed	00	02	06
given to Goodman Adnis	00	07	06
Given to Mr Edwards for reading prayers	04	06	00
for one years Water scots for my land lying in Wilington due att July last past	01	02	00
To Franchfield of Wilmington for 12 Bushells of horse Beans	02	02	00
To Everett for Looking after my Cocks for one year due att Lady day next	00	07	00
To Tho: ffittness for Cleaning the Arms	01	03	00
To Goodman Rawcond for eighteen days work a setting wood	00	08	00
To Will: Obin for one years Wages due on Lady dey	05	15	00
To Peter Morphant for altering my Wigg	02	10	00
To Mr Coppard for a Bill for Candles	08	02	09

April ye 3th To Philip Rutland for Wood			
To Philip Rutland for Looking after my Woodlands att Street	01	10	00
for one years poor Tax for my land lying in Jevington due att Lady last past Collected by Tho: ffearn att ye rate of one shilling p pound	00	15	00
To him Likewise for one years Church Tax for ye same parish	00	05	00
To Nathaniel Harrison for a coach poale	00	05	06
for one years poor Tax for ye Parish of Tullington att Record	03	07	00
A Bill to my Gardener for things he bought for me	00	15	00
for Pockett money	00	10	00
To John Walter for two short Wiggs	06	10	00
To Goody Beck for Weeding in ye Garden	00	08	06
To Will: Whinnick for seven young hogs	01	16	00
To Mrs Snatt and Mrs Peckham for halfe one years Interest for two 200 due on ye 22 December last past	06	05	00
To Philip Rutland for Looking after my Rose and Gardens att Street	13	00	00
To Goodman Tranquire for twenty two days work	01	02	00
for one years Looking after Burrells Wife	00	18	00
for Pockett money	01	00	00
To Will: Rose Sadler a Bill of	03	08	06
for pockett money	01	11	06
for leding att my wods	00	15	00
for Michaell	00	07	00
given to Goody Ayden	00	10	00
To George ffornish	10	00	00
for two quarterly payments of ye Queens Tax for my wood Lands lying in Hailshame due att Lady day last past	00	12	09

every ſticuler Member of the Veſtry doe indeauor to ſ
ſeſt and diſorders of or in the ſiſh and to prſent it at a publike m
mody
all theſe orders be entred in a booke and that euery member of the
triche his name there unto /

Mr Cooper	Will: Daniell	Johnſobes
	Maugh villaſour	Robert Clarke
	bo: preaſon	ohn Clarke
	Humfry Chapman	
		Wm Whitworth
		Henry Daulton
		Robert Preſon
		Leary Amy
WH Hoskins		Eraſmus Cullin
John motſ		Lngeud recth
iam wouldham		will Hiccote
arris Caſh		John Toltw
beſſmworth		
iam		
n Burlace		Geo Keggett
bo: Purtonſ		ickſon Lanſey
arge F Rotta		homas
harles Carter		amuel
daurl Deſon		Charles Crayler
Harus /		

A The Friars
B S. Loyes
C Alhollowes Stre
D S Cuthbers
E Lyme kilne
F Sfull Lane
G S. Tears
K S. Peters Grene
L Bendroußs Lane
M Duck Lane
N Larke Lane
P Hill Lane
Q S. Cuthbers
R Pick Plat
S Castle Hill
T Castle Lane
V High Stre
X S. Paulis
Y Moate Hall
Z The Schole
1 Castle Lane
2 Rea Lane
3 will Stre
4 shops Choppyn
5 silverstrete
6 Scone Lane
7 Poultry market
8 Fish Raunes
9 The Brid.
10 Bridge Stre
11 S. Maryes
12 Potters Stre
13 Cardewell stret
14 S Thomas Stre
15 S. Iohn Baptist
16 Cardwell Stbre
17 S Iohns Church

Changes in urban street names can make an ancestral
house hard to locate. This plan of Bedford by John
Speed, 1600, supplies all the names of that period.

LEFT Ancestral autographs. In 1654, the rector and vestry
men of St Olave's Southwark signed their vestry book.
Only one man, George Kettle, made his mark.

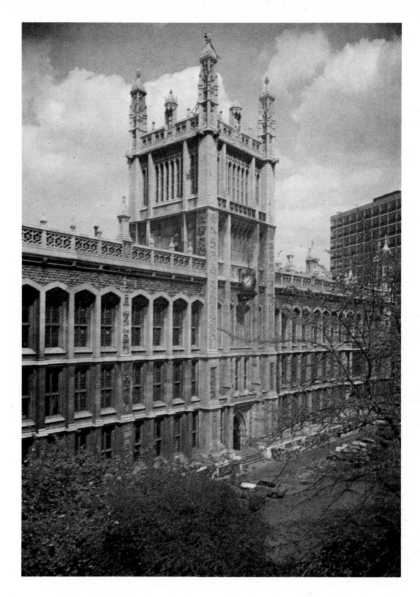

A contrast in styles. On the LEFT the main entrance to
the new Public Record Office, nicknamed 'Fort
Ruskin', in Ruskin Avenue, Kew, Middlesex. ABOVE
The Tower and Searchers' Entrance at the Public
Record Office, Chancery Lane, London, opened in
1856 (*Crown copyright*). The division of records
between the two buildings is given in the entry under
Public Record Office.

One hundred years separates the illustrations ABOVE and LEFT. The engraving, published in the *Illustrated London News* of 1875, shows the Search Hall of what is now called the Principal Registry of the Family Division, Somerset House. The photograph LEFT (*Copyright Skyline Publications Ltd*) shows how little things have changed.

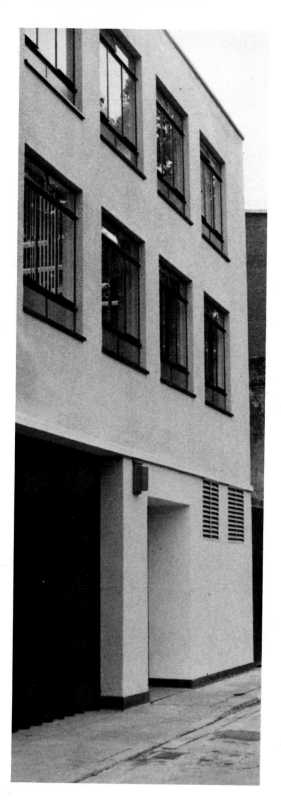

LEFT The Society of Genealogists, 14 Charterhouse Buildings. This centre of ancestry research stands near the junction of Aldersgate Road, Goswell Road and Clerkenwell Road, London, with the Barbican (on the Metropolitan and Circle lines) as the nearest Underground station. *Photo: Family Tree*

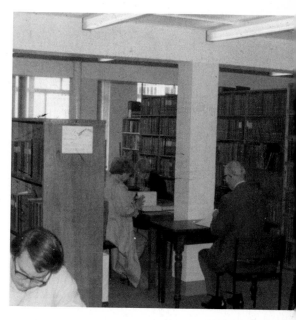

ABOVE The Upper Library of the Society of Genealogists. This section contains family history volumes, professional and service directories, apprentice lists, registers of schools and universities, Boyd's Marriage Index, marriage licence records, will indexes, works on nonconformist bodies, heraldry and the peerage, also deposited MS documents. *Photo: Family Tree*

MARRIAGES REGISTERED IN OCTOBER, NOVEMBER AND DECEMBER 1912.

Names of persons married.	District	Vol.	Page.
Rout, Emmeline	Tuck	Willesden	3 a	550
— Frederick C.	Bales	Bethnal G.	1 c	318
— Hannah	Mason	Stockton	10 a	154
— James W.	Smith	Boulcoate	9 d	351
— Walter H.	Bonds	Poplar	1 c	1032
— William H.	Wolfe	Blything	4 a	2530
Routcliffe, Bertie J.	Gardner	Kingsbridge	5 b	484
Routen, Ernest	Beal	Melton M.	7 a	699
Routh, Charles	Sidebottom	Burnley	8 e	542
— Harold	Ray	Wakefield	9 c	14
— William H.	Turner	Steyning	2 b	599
— Willie	Tunnington	Leeds	9 b	827
Routledge, Ada M.	Owens	Conway	11 b	881
— Albert A.	Hollis	Brighton	2 b	563
— Elizabeth	Kershaw	W. Derby	8 b	990
— Ernest	Taylor	Rochdale	8 e	146
— Florence H.	Dipple	Camberwell	1 d	1665
— Frederick C.	Hucklebridge	Kensington	1 a	311
— Herbert W.	Wright	Stockton	10 a	109
— Jane A.	Nicholson	Leeds	9 b	763
— Mary C.	Grey	Gateshead	10 a	1714
— Mary E.	Marschall	W. Derby	8 b	963
— Robert	Wilson	Carlisle	10 b	976
— Thirza	Ripkin	Prestwich	8 d	527
Routley, Henry	Rowe	Williton	5 c	593
— John	Vaughan	Williton	5 c	622
— Maud E.	Charlton	Birmingham	6 d	325
— Stanley H.	Anneley	Wandsworth	1 d	1137
— Walter H.	Folwell	Atherstone	6 d	952
Rover, Ethel M.	Burton	W. Ham	4 a	306
Row, Edith F.R.	Quarman	Pancras	1 b	264
— Ellen L.	Rutherford	Newcastle T.	10 b	112
— Henry C.	Mountjoy	Lancaster	8 e	1430
— Jane W.	Jameson	Sunderland	10 a	1174
— John W.	Mitchell	Paddington	1 a	4
— Lucy L.T.	Stephens	Bodmin	5 c	147
— Mary A.	Jefferies	Bristol	6 a	474
Rowan, Ada	Booth	Ecclesall B.	9 c	902
— Arthur	Sprague	Islington	1 b	516
— Catherine	Donovan	Salford	8 d	223
— Francis M.	Musk	Wandsworth	1 d	1292
— George	Lindsay	Liverpool	8 b	132
— Jessie	Beaumont	Staines	3 a	57
— Joseph	Nolan	Liverpool	8 b	154
— Lily	Oates	Ecclesall B.	9 c	785
— Sarah	Cromwell	Ormskirk	8 b	1441
— William	Hymns	Southwark	1 d	220
— William H.	Buckley	Ecclesall B.	9 c	700
Rowberry, Charles	Twigg	Stourbridge	6 c	312
— Frank	Willis	Ledbury	6 a	1067
— Laurie S.	Pearn	Swindon	5 a	23
Rowbotham, Alice L.	Hewson	Horncastle	7 a	1315
— Andrew	Lucas	Devonport	5 b	786
— Arthur H.	Salt	Stoke T.	6 b	443
— Fred	Haley	Salford	8 d	84
— Fred V.	Frost	Hayfield	7 b	1923
— Harry	Furney	W. Bromwich	6 b	1665
— John	Ellison	Stockport	8 a	86
— Sarah	Hall	Aston	6 d	640
Rowbottom, Alice M.	Pizzey	Pontefract	9 c	223
— Annie	Gregory	Worksop	7 b	119
— Ethel	Hemp	Glossop	7 b	1901
— Harry B.	Hill	Huddersfield	9 a	796
— Henry	Dougall	Swansea	11 a	2225
— Hetty	Heath	Atherstone	6 d	959
— Jane	Ashworth	Salford	8 d	80
— John W.	Davidson	Sculcoates	9 d	552
— Joseph	Taylor	W. Derby	8 b	920
— Mary E.	Smales	Wakefield	9 c	66
— Mary E.	Hudson	Nottingham	7 b	849
— Richard T.	Lowe	Wigan	8 c	93
— Thomas L.	Walker	Birkenhead	8 a	1135
Rowbury, Beatrix M.	Meek	Hereford	6 a	1187
Rowcliffe, Alice M.	Parsons	Edmonton	3 a	1012
Rowcroft, James H.	Haylett	St. Olave	1 d	521

Names of persons married.	District	Vol.	Page.
Rowcroft, John	Nightingale	Preston	8 e	1058
Rowden, Arthur	Stoneman	Totnes	5 b	365
— Charles	Mortimer	Farnham	2 a	256
— Edith	Pitts	Totnes	5 b	361
— Emma	German	Tiverton	5 b	962
— Frederick S.	Douglas	Medway	2 a	1697
— Mary	Lowden	Lewisham	1 d	2251
Rowdon, Ernest J.	Clark	Wandsworth	1 d	960
Rowe, Albert A.A.	Cross	W. Ham	4 a	536
— Albert J.	Palmer	Holborn	1 b	1495
— Albert J.	Beckett	Alverstoke	2 b	1291
— Albert J.	Miles	Cardiff	11 a	951
— Alice	Bourne	Devonport	5 b	811
— Alice L.M.	Ward	Medway	2 a	1484
— Alice M.E.	Cole	Liskeard	5 c	111
— Annie A.T.	Wilmott	Chorlton	8 c	1192
— Annie F.	Luff	Edmonton	3 a	854
— Annie H.	Routley	Williton	5 c	593
— Annie M.	Burgess	Aston	6 d	416
— Annie V.	Poohin	Newton A.	5 b	262
— Augustus L.G.	Eldridge	Bamford	4 a	2254
— Betsy	Whitear	St. Geo. East	1 c	549
— Catherine	Henfrey	Todmorden	9 a	545
— Cecil	Weeden	Strood	2 a	1435
— Charles	Nock	St. Geo. H. Sq.	1 a	1092
— Charles W.	Anthoney	Derby	7 b	1356
— Clara V.	Smith	Plymouth	5 b	600
— Dolly	Young	Willesden	3 a	599
— Edith	Moore	Southwark	1 d	321
— Edith	Patey	Plymouth	5 b	551
— Edith	Alexander	Newcastle T.	10 b	286
— Edith D.E.	Simons	Wandsworth	1 d	1356
— Edward	Pearson	Guisbro	9 d	1163
— Edward A.	Giles	Southwark	1 d	323
— Eliza	Plant	Barnsley	9 c	475
— Eliza M.	Rowe	Bethnal G.	1 c	390
— Elizabeth A.	Andrew	E. Preston	2 b	765
— Elizabeth J.	Sweeney	Lambeth	1 d	724
— Elizabeth J.	Shire	Axbridge	5 c	1154
— Ellen	Burton	Walsingham	4 b	825
— Emily	Broadbent	Haslingden	8 e	362
— Emily M.	Retallick	Falmouth	5 c	347
— Ethel	Woods	Ipswich	4 a	2375
— Ethel E.M.	Smart	Warminster	5 a	345
— Florence	Allen	Birmingham	6 d	164
— Florence M.	Davidson	Chorlton	8 c	1391
— Florence F.	Skellam	Wolstanton	6 b	185
— Frances L.	Wright	W. Derby	8 b	1025
— Frank H.	Pursse	Hackney	1 b	878
— Fred C.	Allen	Chelmsford	4 a	1245
— Frederick	Rowe	Bethnal G.	1 c	390
— Frederick	Wilson	Alverstoke	2 b	1265
— Frederick	Balls	Pancras	1 b	79
— Frederick A.J.	Ferns	Salford	8 d	13
— Frederick B.	Gibbs	Blything	4 a	2575
— Frederick C.	Allen	Chelmsford	4 a	1245
— Frederick H.	Durrant	Erpingham	4 b	171
— Frederick J.	Cope	Aston	6 d	788
— Frederick T.	Harries	Haverfordwest	11a	2708
— George	Keeble	Swansea	11 a	2188
— George	Trewartha	Redruth	5 c	409
— George H.	Tyler	Bedwellty	11 a	157
— Gwladys	Griffiths	Llanelly	11 a	2361
— Harold T.	Sear	H. Hempstead	3 a	1695
— Henry	Sadler	King's N.	6 c	998
— Henry E.	Ridge	Wolstanton	6 b	221
— Herbert	Matthews	W. Ham	4 a	32
— Herbert	Whitaker	Leeds	9 b	973
— Ida	Paul	Lincoln	7 a	1271
— Isaac C.	Hutchings	Bridport	5 a	939
— Isaac J.	Dean	Devonport	5 b	728
— James	Dexter	Brentford	3 a	307
— James	Figures	King's N.	6 c	816
— James H.	Holman	Redruth	5 c	457
— Janie	Frey	Pancras	1 b	193

The photograph TOP RIGHT shows family historians searching the index volumes at the General Register Office. ABOVE A page of the General Register Marriage Index for the last quarter of 1912. In earlier years, there was no helpful second column to show the name of the spouse. *Both illustrations: Crown Copyright.*

The illustration RIGHT shows a marriage licence allegation of 1750, made at the office of the Dean and Chapter of St Paul's. *Courtesy Guildhall Library. Photo: Godfrey New Photographics*

The sixth day of December 1750

Which day appeared personally Thomas Harper of the parish of St Gregory London in the County of aged Twenty Three years or therabouts and a Batchelor and alledged that he intendeth to marry with Ann West of the parish of St Gregory aforesaid in the County of aged Twenty four years and a Spinster

And that he doth not know or believe that there is any lawfull Let or Impediment by reason of any precontract Consanguinity Affinity or other just Cause whatsoever to hinder the said intended marriage Of the Truth of the premisses he made Oath and prayed Licence for them to be married in the Cathedrall Church of St Paul London

Daniel King Deputy Master M Allen Mayor

Thomas Harper

Sworn before me

And: Coltee Ducarel Surrogate

Granite Mountain Records Vault, Utah, U.S.A., where
the Church of Jesus Christ of Latter-Day Saints stores
the master negatives of their microfilmed genealogical
records. *Courtesy Church of Jesus Christ of Latter-Day
Saints*

Leicestershire Since 1974 Rutland has been a part of Leicestershire. The Leicestershire Family History Society holds regular meetings and issues a journal. Enquiries should be sent c/o The Federation of Family History Societies, 31 Seven Star Road, Solihull, West Midlands B91 2BZ, marked 'Please forward' and enclosing a stamped self-addressed envelope.

Record Repositories Leicestershire Record Office, 57 New Walk, Leicester (tel: 0533.554100); Leicestershire County Library, Thames Tower, Navigation Street, Leicester; Leicester Museum, Archives Department, New Walk, Leicester.

Parish Registers and Indexes (*see* comment under COUNTY) Nearly all registers have been deposited at the county record office (CRO), and the Society of Genealogists has copies of nearly 200. There is a marriage index complete for 1801-37 at the CRO. PALLOT'S MARRIAGE INDEX covers 107 parishes for 1790-1837. The INTERNATIONAL GENEALOGICAL INDEX (IGI) includes baptisms from nearly all the registers; there is a copy at the CRO. The Bishops' Transcripts are at the CRO.

Marriage Licence Records These are at the CRO. The Society of Genealogists has several indexes to them, down to 1748.

Wills before 1858, proved in the following courts, are at the CRO:

> Bishop's Commissary Court and Archdeaconry Court
> Prebendal Court of St Margaret and Chapelry of Knighton
> Commissary Court of the Manor of Rothley
> Commissary Court of the Manor of Evington
> Commissary Court of Groby

As the county lay in the Diocese of Lincoln and Province of Canterbury, wills could also be proved in the Consistory Court of Lincoln and the Prerogative Court of Canterbury.

Non-parochial Registers Fifty-seven registers are at the Public Record Office (PRO), Chancery Lane, London, and the IGI covers most of them.

Census Returns These are at the PRO, Portugal Street, London, and at the CRO.

Memorial Inscriptions There is a large number of transcripts at the Society of Genealogists, and the family history society has further transcription in hand.

Heralds' Visitation Pedigrees have been printed for 1563, 1619 and 1683.

Letters and Papers of the Reign of Henry VIII A published calendar of miscellaneous documents, in many volumes. It is very full and for most purposes makes reference to the originals unnecessary. It contains much useful biographical material.

Letters Close *see* **Close Rolls**

Letters Patent *see* **Patent Rolls**

Levant Company The Worshipful Company of Merchants of England Trading to the Levant Seas was founded in 1581, though it acquired its name a little later. It became, however, commonly known as the Turkey Company as the lands it traded with were then parts of the Ottoman Empire. In 1606, the Company was granted a virtual monopoly of that trade in the shape of considerable reduction in excise duty. Unlike the East India Company, it did not trade as one organisation; its members, who had to be Freemen of the City of London, operated as independent merchants but under rules laid down by themselves corporately. By the Turkish Government it was seen as the commercial and diplomatic agent of the English Crown, and was granted a commercial treaty known as the capitulations; but, unknown to the Turks, the British ambassador's salary and expenses were paid by the Company, not by the Crown. The Company had factories (trading stations manned by factors) at Aleppo (the largest), Constantinople, Smyrna, Cairo, Iskanderun (Alexandretta), Larnaca in Cyprus, Angola, Tripoli and Acra. In each, one of the factors was appointed Consul to represent its interests with the local authorities.

In 1753, agitation in London against the Company's monopoly was successful in throwing membership open to anyone who would pay an entrance fee of £20. However, British trade with the Levant was already in decline and the Seven Years War, 1756-63, made conditions still more difficult. The Company's monopoly trade with the Levant was finally ended in 1825. The records are at the Public Record Office, Chancery Lane, London, under reference SP.105.

Lewd Contemptible, profligate; but it can also mean 'lay', as in 'layman'.

Lewis's Topographical Dictionary *A Topographical Dictionary of England* (1831, 1833 and 1849) and *A Topographical Dictionary of Wales* (1833, 1849), both by Samuel Lewis, describe in a number of volumes every town and village in the country, giving brief historical details of each. Its great value to genealogists is that it states whether a place is a parish in its own right, or, if not, in which parish it lies.

The England editions of 1831 and 1833, and the Wales edition of 1833, also show in what ecclesiastical probate jurisdiction a place is situated. References to 'townships' mean civil parishes.

All information of genealogical value has been extracted from these volumes and published separately as *A Genealogical Gazetteer of England* (compiler, Frank Smith) by the Genealogical Publishing Company of Baltimore, U.S.A.

Lex An entry, made in the margin of the minutes of a legal suit, indicating that either the defendant or the plaintiff was to go to 'wager of law'; i.e. his statements were to be vouched for by a number of neighbours.

Leywrite A fine due from a medieval villein to the lord of his manor, if his unmarried daughter became pregnant. It was to compensate for the depreciation of her manorial value.

Libel The written case of a plaintiff in an ecclesiastical court.

Libertate Probanda, Writ of de If a villein absconded from his manor but was caught and reclaimed by his lord on a *Writ of de Nativo Habendo*, he himself was entitled to a *Writ of de Libertate Probanda* allowing him to remain free until his lord had succeeded in proving his claim in a royal court.

Liberty A manor, or group of manors, or other area lying outside the jurisdiction of the sheriff, and having a separate Commission of the Peace. Also called a 'soke'.

Licence to Pass Beyond the Seas This was an early form of passport issued between the late years of Elizabeth I and 1677. The records consist of registers of soldiers taking the oath of allegiance, before serving in the Low Countries, 1613-24; people going abroad, mainly to Holland, in the period 1624-37; and passengers to New England, Barbados and other colonies, 1634-9 and 1677. The last class has been printed in J.C. Hotten's *Original Lists of Persons Emigrating to America, 1600-1700*. The original records are at the Public Record Office, Chancery Lane, London, under class E.157.

Liege *see* **Homage**

Linch *or* **Linchet** The strips of grassy turf between two pieces of arable land in a common field.

Lincolnshire The north of the ancient county is now in Humberside. The Family History Section of the Society for Lincolnshire History and Archaeology holds regular meetings and issues a newsletter. Enquiries should be sent c/o The Federation of Family History Societies, 31 Seven Star Road, Solihull, West Midlands B91 2BZ, marked 'Please forward' and enclosing a stamped self-addressed envelope.

Record Repositories Lincolnshire Archives Office, The Castle, Lincoln (tel: 0522.25158); Lincoln Central Library, Free School Lane, Lincoln.

Parish Registers and Indexes (*see* comment under COUNTY) Most of the 627 ancient parishes have deposited their registers at the county record office (CRO). The Society of Genealogists has copies of over one hundred. The family history society has compiled a marriage index of Lincoln city parishes. Pallot's Marriage Index covers 72 parishes, 1790-1837. The INTER-NATIONAL GENEALOGICAL INDEX (IGI) has baptisms from most registers and there is a copy at the CRO. The Bishops' Transcripts are also at the CRO.

Marriage Licence Records These are at the CRO.

The Society of Genealogists has indexes of the early periods.

Wills before 1858, proved in the following courts, are at the CRO:

> Consistory Court of Lincoln
> Archdeaconry Court of Stow
> Court of the Dean and Chapter of Lincoln
> Manorial Court of Kirkstead
> Peculiar Courts of Caistor, Corringham, Heydown, Kirton in Lindsey, Louth, Bishops Norton, Sleaford, and Stow in Lindsey.

As the county lay in the Province of Canterbury, wills could also be proved in the Prerogative Court of Canterbury.

Non-parochial Registers The registers of 62 chapels are at the Public Record Office (PRO), Chancery Lane, London. The IGI covers a number of them.

Census Returns These are at the PRO, Portugal Street, London, and at Lincoln Central Library.

Memorial Inscriptions There are transcripts of a number of burial grounds in the library of the Society of Genealogists, and the family history society has transcribed others.

Heralds' Visitation Pedigrees have been printed for 1563-4, 1592, 1634 and 1666.

The family history society has published *Genealogical Sources in Lincolnshire*.

List and Index Society
A society formed to print lists and indexes of records in the Public Record Office. They are not to be confused with the volumes of the Index Library, published by the British Record Society.

Literacy
Reading and writing were already being taught in the Middle Ages to boys attending Grammar and English Schools; and Professor F.R.H. Du Boulay has reckoned that in the fifteenth century about 30 per cent of the population, taking both sexes into account, could read but not necessarily write — a proportion increasing to about 40 per cent by 1530. In the middle of the sixteenth century, literacy was increased by the publication of copybooks both in Secretary and Italic hands (*see* HANDWRITING).

From 1754 onward, the proportion of the population that was literate has been calculated mainly from the number of people who subscribed their signatures to their marriage entries in parish registers, instead of 'making their mark'. In the year 1857, all except 28 per cent of bridegrooms signed their certificates and all except 39 per cent of women. However, it has been found from other sources that some of those who authenticated their certificate with a mark certainly could write. Perhaps their mark had become their customary 'sign manual'. Conversely, a written signature at that period did not necessarily indicate that the signatory could write anything else.

Liverpool Family History Society *see* Lancashire

Livery
(i) The giving and taking of possession; called 'livery of seisin'. A manorial copyholder who was alienating his holding would deliver a rod or wand to the lord of the manor or his steward as a sign of surrender of the tenement, and the lord or steward would deliver the rod to the new tenant, both actions taking place in the presence of other tenants called upon to witness the 'act of livery'. In the case of freeholders, the delivery was made with a piece of turf or a clod of earth, or the ring of the door, direct to the new owner. By the *Real Property Act*, 1845, such transactions could be carried out by deed alone, without livery.

(ii) Release from wardship.

(iii) A uniform worn in the Middle Ages by squires and pages as a sign of allegiance to their knight or nobleman. It usually bore upon the left sleeve the patron's heraldic badge (*see* MAINTENANCE). From Henry VII to the beginning of Charles II's reign, the keeping by magnates of retainers in livery was made subject to royal licence, which had to be paid for. By the eighteenth century, livery in the sense of a special dress had become a prerequisite provided by a private employer to certain of his servants, such as footmen and coachmen, and usually took the form of an out-dated and colourful costume. Those menials who wore it were addressed by their Christian names, but the more senior servants, such as the butlers and ladies' maids, who wore an approved form of contemporary dress, were spoken to by their surnames.

(iv) For the liveries worn by members of London Gilds, *see* LIVERY COMPANIES.

Livery Companies The Gilds of the City of London, the earliest of which were in existence in the twelfth century. From the reign of Edward III they were incorporated by royal charter, and they became known as livery companies from their assumption of a distinctive dress or livery.

An ordinance of Edward II required all Freemen of the City to be members of one or other of the gilds, and it became the practice for all gild freemen to become freemen of the City. The original function of the gilds was to regulate trade and traders in their particular mystery (a word originating in 'mistery' from the Old French *metier*, an occupation), but by the end of the sixteenth century London trades and crafts had outgrown their old form of organisation, and new trades had been introduced. The companies were becoming wealthy charitable institutions whose members were not necessarily connected with the occupations indicated by the gild name. A linen-draper might, for instance, be a member of the Fishmongers' Company, and it was possible for a man to be described in one document as 'William Brown, hosier', and, equally correctly, in another as 'William Brown, Citizen and Merchant Taylor', the latter description indicating that he was a freeman of the company named and of the City of London, but saying nothing about how he earned his livelihood. The gilds continued for some time, however, to be closely linked with the constitution of the City's government, and the restrictions of trade in the City to freemen lasted until the end of the eighteenth century.

Freedom of a company could be obtained by one of three methods: (i) by servitude, after apprenticeship to a freeman of the company (*see* APPRENTICES); (ii) by patrimony, being the son of a freeman of the company; (iii) by redemption, i.e. by buying the freedom of a company. On gaining his company's freedom, the new member immediately applied for, and obtained, the freedom of the City (*see* FREEMEN OF THE CITY OF LONDON). From a company's freemen were recruited the liverymen, a privileged middle rank from whose numbers the Court of

Assistants, the governing body of the company, was elected. This, in turn, elected the Master, Wardens and Renter Wardens for the ensuing year. Liverymen were enfranchised to vote for the Lord Mayor and for Members of Parliament for the City of London. A man could be a freeman of more than one company, or change from one to another. The charitable work of the City companies can be seen in the schools that owe to them their foundation and support. The following is a list of the present Livery Companies.

Air Pilots*	Glass-Sellers
Apothecaries	Glaziers
Armourers and Brasiers*	Glovers
Bakers	Gold and Silver
Barbers	Wire Drawers
Basketmakers	Goldsmiths**
Blacksmiths	Grocers
Bowyers	Gunmakers
Brewers	Haberdashers*
Broderers*	Horners
Brown-Bakers	Inn Holders
Butchers	Ironmongers*
Carmen	Joiners
Carpenters	Leathersellers*
Clockmakers	Loriners*
Clothworkers*	Masons
Coachmakers	Master Mariners*
Combmakers	Mercers*
Cooks	Merchant Taylors
Coopers	Musicians
Cordwainers	Needle Makers
Curriers	Painter Stainers
Cutlers	Parish Clerks
Distillers	Patternmakers
Drapers*	Paviors
Dyers	Pewterers
Fan Makers*	Plaisterers
Farmers*	Playing Card Makers
Farriers	Plumbers
Fellowship Porters	Poulters
Feltmakers	Saddlers
Fishmongers	Salters*
Fletchers	Scientific Instrument
Founders	Makers*
Framework Knitters	Scriveners
Fruiterers	Shipwrights
Gardeners	Silk Throwsters
Girdlers	Skinners*

Spectacle Makers
Stationers**
Tallow Chandlers
Tin Plate Workers
Tobacco Pipe Makers
Turners
Tylers and Bricklayers
Upholders

Vintners*
Watermen
Waxchandlers
Weavers
Wheelwrights
Woodmongers
Woolmen

The records of the above, or microfiche of them, are deposited at the Guildhall Library, except those marked *. Those marked ** have deposited part of their records. The Pinmakers' records are in the Egerton series of the MS Department of the British Library. The records of the Linen Drapers' Company have disappeared. The Guildhall Library has a number of published histories of the London Livery Companies, and has itself published a *Guide to the Archives of the Livery Companies and related Organisations in Guildhall Library*.

Local Historian, The A journal founded as *The Amateur Historian* in 1952 to publish articles on documentary sources and related subjects, for spare-time researchers into local, family and institutional history and archaeology. In 1961 it was presented, by its proprietor, to the Standing Conference for Local History as its official organ. In 1968 its name was changed to *The Local Historian*. Over the years, the articles, originally addressed to amateurs, have become increasingly scholarly, reflecting the growth in interest in local history taken by universities since the 1950s.

Local History An ancestor's home town or village as it was in his lifetime is one context into which the family historian needs to set him. The history of the counties and smaller districts of England has been an object of study since the sixteenth century, and since then local histories have been published in increasing numbers and are available in public reference libraries in their own areas. In 1899, work on *The Victoria History of the Counties of England* was begun and has been progressing, with set-backs caused by two wars, ever since.

The destruction of ancient buildings in England caused by bombing in the Second World War, gave rise to a great surge of interest

in local history in the late 1940s and the 1950s, and many local history societies came into existence at that time. In 1948 the Standing Conference for Local History was formed, with members representing one hundred historical bodies, including the Society of Genealogists. In 1961 it adopted the quarterly journal, *The Amateur Historian*, as its official organ and, in 1968, changed its title to *The Local Historian*. The Standing Conference has now been reconstituted as the British Association for Local History, and today most local history societies are members.

The Association issues a number of pamphlets for the guidance of local historians. Information about societies researching in any particular area can be obtained through the British Association for Local History, The Mill Manager's House, Cromford Mill, Matlock, Derbyshire DE4 3RQ.

London and Middlesex Much of the northern part of the ancient county of Surrey is now in London, and London is the home of the Society of Genealogists, the organisation for all genealogists tracing British descent. Area societies situated in the capital are: Central Middlesex Family History Society, North Middlesex Family History Society, West Middlesex Family History Society, East of London Family History Society, and the City of London Family History Group. They all hold meetings and issue journals. Enquiries should be sent c/o The Federation of Family History Societies, 31 Seven Star Road, Solihull, West Midlands B91 2BZ, marked 'Please forward' and enclosing a stamped self-addressed envelope.

Record Repositories General Register Office, Office of Population Censuses and Surveys, St Catherine's House, 10 Kingsway, London WC2 (tel: 01.242.0262); Public Record Office (PRO), Chancery Lane, WC2 (tel: 01.831.6541); PRO, Ruskin Avenue, Kew, Surrey (tel:01.876.3444); PRO, Portugal Street, WC2 (tel: 01.405.3488); Lambeth Palace Library, Lambeth Palace Road, SE1 (tel: 01.928.6222); House of Lords Record Office, Houses of Parliament, SW1 (tel: 01.219.3074); Principal Registry of the Family Division, Somerset House, Strand, WC2.

British Library, British Museum, Great Russell Street, WC1 (tel: 01.636.1544); British Newspaper Library, Colindale Avenue, NW9 (tel:

01.200.5515); Greater London Council Record Office, 40 Northampton Road, EC1 (tel: 01.633.5000); Corporation of London Record Office, Guildhall, Gresham Street, EC2 (tel: 01.606.3030); Guildhall Library, Aldermanbury, EC2 (tel: 01.606.3030); Dean and Chapter, St Paul's Cathedral, EC4.

Westminster Library, Buckingham Palace Road, SW1 (tel: 01.730.0446); Minet Library, Knatchbull Road, SE5 (tel: 01.733.3279); Shepherds Bush Library, Uxbridge Road, W12; Lewisham Public Library, The Manor House, Old Road, SE13; Shoreditch Library, Pitfield Street, N1; Dr Williams's Library, 14 Gordon Square, WC1; Southwark Local Studies Library, 211 Borough High Street, SE1 (tel: 01.403.3507); Society of Friends, Friends' House, Euston Road, NW1; India Office Records and Library, Orbit House, Blackfriars Road, SE1.

National Army Museum, Royal Hospital Road, SW3; National Maritime Museum, Park Row, SE10; Imperial War Museum, Lambeth Road, SE1; Historical Manuscripts Commission and National Register of Archives, Quality House, Quality Court, Chancery Lane, WC2.

Parish Registers and Indexes (*see* comment under COUNTY) Nearly all parish registers have been deposited either at the Greater London Record Office or the Guildhall Library, but some at local libraries. The Society of Genealogists has copies of about 200. Boyd's Marriage Index covers 163 parishes and institutions, some only extracts. Pallot's Marriage Index covers 235 registers, mostly from 1800 to 1812 or 1837. The Society of Genealogists has the Middlesex marriage index of grooms, 1812-37, covering 46 parishes outside the City not included in Boyd or Pallot. It also has the City of London Burial Index. The INTERNATIONAL GENEALOGICAL INDEX (IGI) treats over 200 parishes. Copies are at the Society of Genealogists, the Mormon Stake Library in Exhibition Road, Kensington, and the Guildhall Library. The Bishops' Transcripts, mainly from 1800, are at the Guildhall Library.

Marriage Licence Records Those of the London Diocese are at the Greater London Record Office, with indexes from 1700 at the Guildhall Library. That library also has the marriage licence records for the Royal Peculiar of St Katherine by the Tower, and the Peculiar of the Dean and Chapter of St Paul's. The records of the Faculty Office and Vicar General's Office are at Lambeth Palace Library, as are those of the Peculiar Deanery of Croydon and the Peculiar of the Dean and Chapter of Westminster.

Wills before 1858, proved in the following courts are located as shown.

At the Greater London Record Office:
   Consistory Court of London
   Commissary Court of London (London Div.)
   Archdeaconry Court of Middlesex (Middx Div.)
   Archdeaconry Court of Surrey
   Commissary Court of Surrey

At the Guildhall Library:
   Archdeaconry Court of London
   Peculiar Court of the Dean and Chapter of St Paul's
   Royal Peculiar of St Katherine by the Tower

At the Corporation of London Record Office:
   Court of Hustings

At Lambeth Palace Library:
   Peculiar Courts of the Deaneries of the Arches and of Croydon

At Westminster Library:
   Royal Peculiar of the Dean and Chapter of Westminster

As South London (formerly Surrey) lay in the Diocese of Winchester, wills could also be proved in the Consistory Court of Winchester (*see* HAMPSHIRE). As London, Middlesex and Surrey all lay in the Province of Canterbury, wills could also be proved in the Prerogative Court of Canterbury.

Non-parochial Registers The registers deposited at the Public Record Office (PRO), Chancery Lane, include not only those of non-conformist chapels but also those of Greenwich, Chelsea and the Holborn Lying-in Hospitals, the Chapel Royal and Somerset House Chapel, and also clandestine marriages. The IGI covers many such registers for this area.

Census Returns These are at the PRO, Portugal Street.

Memorial Inscriptions The Society of Genealogists has some transcripts. Those from many City churchyards have been printed in P. Rushen's

The Churchyard Inscriptions of the City of London (1910), and those inside the churches in M.A.J. Jewer's *Guide to the Monumental Inscriptions of the City Churches.*

Heralds' Visitation Pedigrees have been printed for London, for 1568, 1633-4, 1664, 1687; and for Middlesex, for 1634 and 1663.

Lists of Londoners include: *The 1695 Inhabitants of the City*, by M.P.E. Jones, and *17th Century London Inhabitants*, by T.C. Dale, both at the Guildhall Library. The Society of Genealogists has Boyd's *Index of London Citizens*, mainly seventeenth century.

Record Publishing Societies: London Record Society; London and Middlesex Archaeological Society; London Topographical Society.

London Gazette This official publication first appeared under that name on Monday, 5 February, 1665/6, and for long was issued each Tuesday and Friday but now appears daily. It publishes official church, civil, naval, military and legal appointments and promotions, including those of the militia, and advertisements relating to the formation and dissolution of business companies and partnerships; settlements of estates and claims, and other financial and legal matters appertaining to private persons and corporate bodies, including bankruptcies and insolvent debtors. In 1787 half-yearly indexes were commenced, one relating to official government news such as State Intelligence and appointments and promotions, and the other to the remaining matters mentioned. The Guildhall Library, London, has a complete set of the *Gazette*, though some of the early indexes are missing. The set in the British Library is indexed only from the year 1803.

For further reading, see *A History of the London Gazette, 1665-1965*, by P.M. Handover.

Lord Lieutenant In 1551, the control of the militia forces of the country was placed in the hands of newly created officials known as the king's lieutenants. As these officials were almost always noblemen, they came to be known as 'lords lieutenant'. At first the lieutenant was commissioned only for some special occasion, such as a threat of invasion or rebellion, but in

time tended to be appointed until notice to the contrary, and so the post became nearly permanent, in some counties even hereditary, until in 1662 the *Militia Act* regularised it as personal and permanent.

The lieutenant was responsible for musters and beacons, and was allowed to appoint deputies as well as a provost marshal and muster master. After a reorganisation of the office in 1757, minute books were kept by a Clerk to the Lieutenancy, some of which are extant. From 1797, the danger of invasion by the French threw many responsibilities upon the Lord Lieutenant, calling for the keeping of detailed minutes and returns. These include nominal lists of militiamen, their available implements for constructing makeshift defences, supplies of flour, emergency baking facilities and available transport. The Lieutenancy records are kept at the county record office.

Lorimer *or* **Loriner** A word, and surname, derived from the Old French *lormier* (the rein of a bridle). A maker of bits, spurs and metal mountings for bridles and saddles; hence, a saddler.

Lot A church rate.
See also SCOT.

Lot-Meadow A portion of the manorial meadow that was held in severalty, but subject to annual re-allotment.

Lug A land measure of six yards; another term for a rod, pole or perch.

Mainpast The surety of good behaviour from the head of a household for those in it, as part of the security system of tithing.

Mainport A due payable, in some parishes, to the rector by poorer householders in lieu of certain tithes. It usually consisted of loaves of bread.

Mainprise The committal of a person, who might otherwise be imprisoned, into the friendly custody of someone (his 'mainpernor') who had given security that he would be forthcoming at a certain time and place. Unlike bail, of which it is a special obsolete form, mainprise forbade the mainpernor to put the person under physical constraint.

Maintenance The keeping by a landed magnate, mainly in the fourteenth to sixteenth centuries, of a retinue of followers, usually in a badged livery. From Henry VII's time, such a privilege was allowed only under royal licence. In the fourteenth century some of these bands of men were little better than gangs, robbing their patron's smaller neighbours, seizing their lands and giving false witness against them in law suits. In return, the lord supported his followers in legal disputes, by force if necessary. The system was known as Badge and Maintenance.

Manchet Best quality wheaten bread.

Manchester, Greater A metropolitan county formed in 1974 out of a part of LANCASHIRE.

Mandamus, Writ of An order to a public officer to carry out his duty. From the Latin, 'we command'.

Manor For 500 years after the Conquest the manor, an agricultural estate, was the unit of local government. Its head was the lord of the manor (literally a landlord, not necessarily a titled person), who held the estate from the king either directly or through one or more mesne lords. Typically the inhabitants of the early manor were villeins, bound to the land, and one or more freeholding franklins. Over a large part of England the typical estate contained a village with a church, and agricultural land consisting of two, or more usually three, large arable fields in which the inhabitants held scattered strips. The lord's own demesne might be in scattered strips or in a consolidated block, tending more to the latter as time went by. The land near the local stream was the meadow, where grass was grown for hay, and the less lush grassland was the permanent pasture for the beasts of the manor. There would usually also be some woodland.

Each villein's tenement (his holding) entitled him to a certain number of strips of arable land, and grazing for a certain number of cattle and sheep.

The organ of manorial administration was the manor court, a periodic meeting of the tenantry, presided over by the lord of the manor or his steward. The courts met regularly, at intervals laid down by the custom of the manor that might be anything between six weeks and six months. The procedure was judicial, but the matters dealt with were both judicial and administrative. Each court had two aspects: the Court Baron, originally for free tenants but which, by the sixteenth century, administered the agriculture of the manor, the lord's and tenants' rights and duties, changes of occupancy, and disputes between tenants; and the Court Leet, originally for villeins but which, by the sixteenth century, was also called the View of Frankpledge and covered the election of officials and what would now be called police matters (for example, maintenance of the lock-up, disturbances of the peace, and so on).

Custom governed everything and checked the rights and duties of both the lord and the tenants. The principle was, 'Justice shall be done by the lord's court, not by the lord'. The steward (*seneschallus*), who might be a neighbour of some substance and legal training and similarly responsible for several manors in the district, convened the court and usually presided over it. All tenants were bound to attend and the procedure (recorded in Latin) was as follows:

Election of the jury (*juratores*) or homage (*homagium*) and their swearing in. Anyone who refused to serve was fined.

Consideration of excuses for absence, called essoins (*essonia*), and absences without a valid excuse (*defalte*). These defaulters were punished by a fine.

At one annual court there would be the election of officials for the ensuing year. The steward's manager, the bailiff (*ballivus*), was appointed by him, but the rest of the officials were elected. They were the reeve (*praepositus*), the chief representative of the tenants and the bailiff's opposite number; the hayward (*heiwardus*); the beadle (*bedellus*); the constable (*constabulus*); the ale-taster and two affeerors (*afferatores*). The function of the last-named was to assess the amount of each fine imposed by the court. If the culprit was amerced (*in misericordia*), he had to pay no more than the minimum laid down by the custom of the manor.

Transfers of property (*alienationes*) and other matters were raised and dealt with, and orders (*precepti*) issued. There was often an adjournment for a midday meal. By the eighteenth century there was usually only one court, the Court Leet having lost its functions to the parish Vestry and the Justices of the Peace.

Besides the regular courts there were two special ones, held when the lordship of the manor changed hands, either by sale or inheritance. The first was a Court of Recognition, or *Curia Prima*, at which the new lord became formally 'seized' of the services of the tenants and received their recognition as the new lord. They made him a symbolic money payment and all renewed the oaths of fealty that they had first taken when entering into their tenancies. The record of this court listed the tithes due on the lord's lands and also those on the copyholders'. Secondly, A Court of Survey was summoned either just before or just after a change of lordship. Its purpose was to list all the lands of the manor and the customary dues by which the copyhold tenants held their lands.

The origins of the manorial court are lost in antiquity, but treatises on procedure were being written as early as the thirteenth century. Most of the tenants held land by villein (unfree) tenure, but there were always some freeholders too. As the feudal system decayed and villein services became commuted for money, their tenure became known as copyhold, because on entry into their tenancy they were given a copy of the court's record of the fact as their title deed. The early court rolls were written in Latin, but under the Commonwealth, English was introduced. However, after the Restoration, Latin became again the language of the rolls, persisting in many manors until 1733. A 'reputed manor' was an estate administered on manorial lines but having no freehold tenants.

During the nineteenth century the holding of manor courts gradually came to an end, and in 1925 copyhold tenure, almost extinct, formally ended in accordance with the *Law of Property Acts*, 1922 and 1924.

The records of a manorial estate consisted of:

The Court Rolls The minutes of the court, written by the steward's clerk and kept by the steward or the lord himself. For the genealogist, these are the most useful.

Jury Verdicts (self-explanatory)

The Valor A record of financial values.

The Rental Details of rents due and paid.

The Custumal Intended for permanent reference, a description of the customary rights and duties of the lord and tenants.

The Terrier A description of the whereabouts and size of the lord's and each tenant's lands within the manor.

The Extent A document that could include any or all of the information in the above-mentioned records.

The court rolls record changes of occupancy of copyhold lands, and, in some manors, of freehold land, giving the names of the late and new owners. As these were usually father and son, it is sometimes possible to trace several generations of a family from court rolls. When the new occupant came from outside the manor, his place of origin was usually given. From these, dates of death can also be established. When a tenant died, his will, or an extract from it, might be quoted in the court roll. Sometimes this is the only surviving record of the will. Even a new freehold tenant had to pay the lord a relief, a small sum of money for taking up his tenancy; so there is some record of freeholders, too. The copyholder paid a fine and swore fealty, i.e. to pay the customary dues and observe the ancient rules of the holding with regard to his animals, etc. Disputes between tenants often reveal the names of members of a family hitherto unknown, or serve to confirm or disprove hypotheses based on parish registers.

Since 1926, all manorial records have had to be reported to the Master of the Rolls, as also have any changes in their ownership and custody. The Historical Manuscripts Commission maintains a *Manorial Documents Register*, which takes the form of two series. The first, arranged under parishes, shows the names of the manor or manors in each parish; the second, arranged under manors, shows the last-known whereabouts of the manorial records. In perhaps a

121

The Manor of Ebbisham in the County of Surry } to wit

The Court Leet or View of Frank pledge of Ricarda Parkhurst Widow Lady of the said Manor holden for the same on Monday the 26th Day of Octr. in the 8th year of the Reign of our Sovereign Lord Geo. the 3. by the Grace of God of Great Brit. France & Ireland King Defender of the Faith &c & in the year of our Lord 1767 & Before Peter Prevost Gent Steward there.

Essoigns to wit None at this Court

Constable of Ebbisham — Thomas Butcher appears & Nothing presents

Constable of Woodcote — John Wheatley appears & Nothing presents

Headborough of Ebbisham — Wm Lamb appears & nothing presents & pays 3s. 4d. according to anct. Custom

Headborough of Woodcote — Robt. Steer jun. appears & Nothing presents & pays 3s. 4d. according to anct. Custom

Aletasters — Francis Peake & Peter Kempsell — Nothing present

Common Drivers — Geo: Fox & William Adams — Nothing present

The Inquest for our Sovereign Lord the King

John Eastland first sworn

Robt Wrench	Wm Holland	John Yalden
Henry Reeve	Jno Lewis Jaquet	Henry Harris
Rich: Hubbard	John Hopkins	Jas Greenhouse
John Winchester	John Halswell	Benj: Furness

(sworn)

The Election of Officers.

Constable of Ebbisham — James Buggs is duly elected Constable of Ebbisham for the year ensuing

Constable of Woodcote — Geo: Peters is duly elected Constable of Woodcote for the year ensuing & is sworn.

Headborough of Ebbisham — John Soveland is duly elected Headborough of Ebbisham for the year ensuing & is sworn

Headborough of Woodcote — Thos. Davis is duly elected Headborough of Woodcote for the year ensuing & is sworn.

Aletasters — Joseph Philips & Wm Mansell are duly elected Aletasters for the year ensuing & Wm Mansell is sworn

Common Drivers — Edward Stone and Jas Griffin are duly elected Common Drivers for the year ensuing & Edwd. Stone is sworn.

The first page of the record of the Court Leet or (more usually, 'and') View of Frankpledge of the Manor of Ebbisham, Surrey, held on 26 October, 1767, showing the names of the jurors and out-going and newly elected officers of the manor. *Surrey Record Office*

The Manor of
Ebbisham in the } to wit
County of Surry

The Court Baron of Ricarda
Parkhurst Widow Lady of the said Manor holden
in & for the same on Monday the 26.th Day of Octr. in
the 8.th Year of the Reign of our Sovereign Lord George
the 3.d by the Grace of God of Great Britain France &
Ireland King Defender of the Faith &c and in the year
of our Lord 1767 By Peter Prevost Gentleman Steward
there.

Plaints to wit — None at this Court

Homage to wit — John Eastland Foreman Sworn

Robt. Wrench }
Wm. Woollard } Sworn
John Yelden }
John Hopkins }

At this Court it is attested and inrolled by the Steward there
that on the 1.st day of July 1760 Joseph Shaw of Ebbisham in the County
of Surry Esq. Admor. of the Goods & Chattels Rights & Credits of his
Father Joseph Shaw late of Ebbisham af.d Esq. deced. Did acknowledge
to have had & received of & from John Eastland of Ebbisham afored. Barber
the Sum of £400. in full payment & Satisfaction of & for all principal &
Int. Monies due to him as Admor. of his sd. Father upon or by Virtue of
a certain Condl. Surrender bearing date the 3.d day of June 1729 & made
by the sd. John Eastland of certain Copyhold Messes. Tenemt.s & Heredit.s held
of this Manor To the Use of the sd. Joseph Shaw deced & his heirs for securing
the payment of £150: & Int. at the Times & in manner therein ment.d
and also upon or by Virtue of a further Charge made at a Court Baron
holden in & for this Manor on the 21.st day of Oct.r 1729. whereby the sd.
Premes. were charged by the sd. Jn.o Eastland with the paymt. to the said
Joseph Shaw deced of the further Sum of £50. & Int. And also upon
or by Virtue of a certain other Condl. Surrender bearing Date the 8.th day of
May 1732 and made by the said John Eastland of a certain Piece or
Parcel of Copyhold Ground held of this Manor To the Use of the said —

A record of the Court Baron held for the Manor of Ebbisham on the same day as the Court Leet shown on the facing page. As it illustrates, the Court Baron dealt with legal matters arising from the holding and transferring of properties within the manor. *Surrey Record Office*

187

majority of cases, the solicitors of manorial families are still the custodians of the rolls, but many have been deposited at county record offices. The Public Record Office, the British Library, Birmingham Reference Library and the Shakespeare Library, Stratford-on-Avon, also have considerable deposits. Unfortunately the majority of manorial records has failed to survive.

For further reading, see *Manorial Records*, by P.D.A. Harvey (British Record Association, 1984), and 'Manorial Documents', by A. Travers, in *Genealogists' Magazine*, Vol.21, No.1.

Mantling A short cape, depicted in a heraldic achievement as held on the helmet by a wreath of twisted silk (the torse), and flowing around the shield of arms. Its edges are usually slashed for decorative purposes. The outside and the lining are normally depicted in the two main tinctures of the arms. The purpose of the cape was to protect the metal helmet from becoming over-hot in the sun of Palestine. It was also deadening to a sword-cut, and could entangle an opponent's sword. Also called a lambrequin.

Manuel Rente The money paid for a commuted feudal service.

Manumission The act of a feudal lord that gave a villein his freedom.

Maps It can sometimes be important to know the lie of the land around an ancestor's home. The nearest neighbouring town or village as the crow flew may not have been the quickest to reach. Hills might intervene, or bridges over the local river might be few and far between. Contacts between neighbours would be governed by such considerations, and also by the whereabouts of the market town, where people needed to gather at regular intervals to buy and sell. The market town was not always the obvious one, because charters were often ancient and a town's importance could alter with the centuries. Where a bride and bridegroom were of different parishes not very close together, the local market may have been the cause of their meeting: 'Where are you going to, my pretty maid?' 'I'm going to market, sir,' she said. The study of old maps may provide

possible explanations for family migrations. Many town street plans exist from the seventeenth century, and a careful comparison of one with the local rate assessments may make it possible to pinpoint an ancestral home. The maps that form part of a parish's Tithe Redemption Award and Enclosure Award are an absolute must for identifying a family's home site in the mid nineteenth century. Ordnance Survey maps, which began to appear from 1805, can be found at county record offices. The old directories and guide books that can be found in some libraries often contain county maps. David & Charles Publishers have reprinted early nineteenth century Ordnance Survey maps, but with the later railways inserted.

Estate maps can be found in the deposited records of landed estates, and sometimes in church terriers and the records of the Ecclesiastical Commissioners.

A valuable modern aid is provided by the County Parochial Maps published by the Institute of Heraldic and Genealogical Studies. They show the position and shape of each pre-1832 parish, the date from which its registers survive, whether deposited, IGI index, whereabouts of copies, and the ecclesiastical probate jurisdictions in which it lay.

For further reading, see *County Atlases of the British Isles published after 1703*, Vol.I, by D. Hodson (Tewin, 1984).

Maritagium A gift to a daughter on her marriage.
See also DOWRY.

Mark A money of account worth 13 shillings and 4 pence, but never minted as a coin.

Market A gathering of vendors of goods and services for sale. The right of a town or village to hold a weekly market was granted by the sovereign and had to be paid for. Originally, markets were held on Sundays but were moved to weekdays in the thirteenth century. In the sixteenth century many village markets closed down, unable to compete with more popular ones in nearby towns, or with those in villages more favourably placed. Market day attracted people from surrounding villages, some to sell their goods, some to buy, and some for social gatherings. When an entry in a marriage register shows that the partners came from different parishes, the district's market may well have been the means of bringing them together.

Marque, Letters of In time of war, the Lord High Admiral received a special commission from the sovereign to grant letters of marque. Issued to a private ship-owner or commander, letters of marque empowered him to fit out an armed vessel or vessels for the purpose of harassing the enemy. Such ships, called privateers, were usually employed to capture the enemy's merchant ships.

Marquess The peerage title next in dignity after a duke, and before an earl. The first English marquess was Robert de Vere, Earl of Oxford, created Marquess of Dublin by Richard II in 1385. The function of lords marchers, or margraves, on the continent was to guard the borders of a kingdom; and the lords of the marches of Scotland and Wales were termed marchiones from early times; but that authority, by then already a dead letter, was formally abolished by Henry VIII. The title is often spelt in the French way, marquis. The wife of a marquess is a marchioness.

On the creation of a dukedom, a marquisate has sometimes been granted at the same time, to provide a second title to be borne by courtesy during the duke's lifetime, by his heir. Except for formal purposes, a marquess and marchioness are referred to as Lord and Lady (So-and-so), and their children are termed Lord and Lady before their Christian names.

Marriage Certificate *see* **General Register of Births, Deaths and Marriages**

Marriage Horizon The term coined by demographers to express the radius within which a certain percentage of extra-parochial marriage partners lived; e.g. 90 per cent of partners from outside the parish came from within a radius of fifteen miles — the marriage horizon.

Marriage Index An index, compiled for genealogical purposes, of marriages in a certain area, usually a county, using information culled from parish registers, bishops' transcripts and marriage licence records. It is one of the most valuable of location records, providing a short cut to finding the whereabouts of a family at a given period. The first index to be compiled was Pallot's Marriage Index, mainly of London and Middlesex marriages. This was followed by Boyd's Marriage Index of sixteen counties and two miscellaneous series. Neither of these covers every parish nor, in many cases, the whole period of a register. During recent years many family history societies have been indexing the marriages of their counties, and some are already complete. Information from most of them is open to non-members of the societies (*see under* county headings). Some counties are indexed under the names of both parties; others of bridegrooms only. Each entry shows the name of the spouse, the parish of marriage and the date, or at least the year, of marriage. If present progress is maintained it should not be many years before all recorded marriages in England are indexed. When information is sought, attention should not be confined to one particular marriage; those of all people of the same surname should be extracted, unless the name is very common. Regarded as clues to a family's whereabouts, the marriages of women are more helpful than those of men, because there has always been a tendency for weddings to be held in the bride's parish. Any marriage found in an index should be looked up in the original register for additional information, such as the names of witnesses, the bridegroom's occupation and the parties' parishes of residence, also to check that no indexing error has been made.

The Federation of Family History Societies has published *Marriage Indexes*, a booklet on how to find, use and compile them; and *Marriage, Census and Other Indexes for Family Historians*, by J.S.W. Gibson.

Marriage Licence Records From the early sixteenth century, people intending to marry were able to avoid the inconvenience of banns

OVERLEAF London in 1832. Seventy years before Kingsway, the present mecca of genealogists, came into existence.

189

by obtaining a marriage licence. The inconveniences included delay and publicity, and besides this, well-to-do people felt it undignified to invite every Tom, Dick and Harry in the parish to object to their marriage. The result was that most people who could afford the fee married by licence. Later, dissenters objected to their banns being called in a parish church.

The licence was normally obtained from the chancellor or surrogate of the diocese in which one of the parties lived, and in which the marriage was to be celebrated; but application could be made to the Vicar-General of the Archbishop of the province. If the parties lived in different dioceses, they had to apply to the Vicar-General. If they lived in different provinces they applied to the Master of Faculties of the Archbishop of Canterbury. In fact, the Archbishop of Canterbury could issue a licence to any couple in England. If the wedding was to be performed in a diocese other than that of either of the parties, a special licence had to be obtained, either from the Faculty Office of Canterbury or the Registry of York, or the Vicar-General of Canterbury. Licences could also be obtained from certain deans and chapters and archdeacons within their jurisdiction, and also from the Ordinary or presiding authority of certain peculiars, provided both the parties lived within them.

To obtain a licence, one of the parties, normally the bridegroom, had to make a formal statement called an allegation, including an oath that there was no lawful impediment to the marriage.

If either of the parties was under age, the application had to be accompanied by the consent of his or her parent. The bridegroom brought a friend with him and they might (jointly until 1823) be required to enter into a bond to forfeit a sum of money, if the proposed marriage was found to be contrary to Canon Law. Sometimes the name of the friend was fictitious, and sometimes the bridegroom was not one of the two bondsmen.

The licence was issued to the applicant for delivery to the clergyman performing the ceremony. It cannot be taken for granted that a marriage licence always meant a marriage — there is always the possibility that the engagement was broken off. Also, the marriage did not always take place at the church, or any of the churches, named.

Marriage licence allegations and bonds are usually to be found at diocesan registries and county record office (*see under* county headings). The licences themselves were issued to the bridegrooms and have normally not survived. Some records include a register of licences issued, with the names of the bondsmen. Both the Canterbury Vicar-General's and the Faculty Office records are in the library at Lambeth Palace, the residence of the Archbishop of Canterbury, and can be seen by appointment with the librarian. For these, the following indexes have been printed:

Faculty Office
    1545-75 in Harleian Society Volume 24.
    1632-1714 in British Record Society Volume 23.
    Extracts 1632-1869 in further Harleian Society volumes.

Vicar-General
    1660-94 in Harleian Society Volumes 23, 30-34.
    1694-1709 in typescript; 1801-3 on cards by the Society of Genealogists.

The Federation of Family History Societies has published a useful booklet, *Bishops' Transcripts and Marriage Licences, Bonds and Allegations, a Guide to their Location and Indexes*, by J.S.W. Gibson.

The Society of Genealogists has a collection of abstracts and indexes and has published a guide to them.

Marriage Registers *see* **Parish Registers**

Meadow An area where grass was grown for a hay crop. After Lammas, the hay having been cut, the beasts of the manor were driven into the meadow, which was then used as pasture during the ensuing autumn, winter and spring. Meadows were often on low-lying ground near a river or stream, where they might be subject to flooding, in which case they were called wet meadows or meads. A water-meadow was one that was deliberately 'floated', i.e. flooded. A dry meadow was one not liable to flooding. Lot meads or meadows were common grassland, of which the crop each year was allotted to a manorial tenant by lot.

Mechanic A journeyman engaged in one of the lower forms of handicraft.

Medals The War Office's campaign medal rolls are at the Public Record Office, Kew, under call number WO.100. Citations are published in the *London Gazette*.
See also DOMESTIC CLUES.

Meer A boundary, often a bank or hedge, between fields or furlongs, but sometimes one requiring to be marked out by meer-stones. These stones were liable to require replacing each year after being disturbed by cattle grazing on the stubble. Alternative spelling, mere.

Membrane A sheet of parchment. It was customary to sew several sheets together end to end, to form a roll. Parchment is made from the skin of an animal. The flesh-side, the inner side of the roll, was called the face and carried the main written entry; the outer, hair-side, was the back or dorse.
See also VELLUM.

Memoranda Rolls These contain notes of matters arising during the auditing of the sheriff's accounts, and in the daily course of Exchequer business. Of greater interest to genealogists are the private deeds enrolled upon them to ensure permanent record, also details of lands and goods forfeited to the Crown, enclosure awards, and offences against statutes regulating trade or industry. The rolls, of which the later ones are actually in volumes, cover the period from 2 Henry III (his second regnal year) to 1959. They are in two series, which to some extent overlap, those of the King's Remembrancer and of the Lord Treasurer's Remembrancer. Like other Exchequer records they are at the Public Record Office, Chancery Lane, London. Their call number is E.159.

Memorial Inscriptions These inscriptions are conventionally termed 'monumental'. The oldest surviving inscriptions are on brasses and around effigies inside churches. The majority record peers, knights, gentry and church dignitaries, but generally they provide little information. Gravestones of this period are very few and often bear no wording.

In the sixteenth century, the custom spread of burying the gentry and more prosperous merchants within the church building, and the number of memorials on the church walls and floor increased accordingly. However, an interior memorial does not necessarily mean that the deceased was buried in the church; the clergy objected to church burial, and even many distinguished clerics are interred in churchyards. Burial ground monuments are of many kinds: wooden deadboards, vertical headstones, footstones, horizontal ledger stones at ground level, table tombs, box tombs, cylindrical bale tombs, mummy stones, oven tombs, etc. After the Reformation, crosses on memorials were considered papistical, and fell out of use.

In the seventeenth century, the oldest churchyard inscriptions, except for those of wealthy people, were probably all engraved on wooden boards supported by wooden posts. Few have survived, and most are no longer legible. The oldest headstones date from the middle of that century. As canals made transport cheaper, memorials of stone and slate came within the means of less affluent people, and so greatly increased in number; but local sources of material were always the most commonly used, and the carving was by local craftsmen. Members of a parish's most prosperous families tended to be buried in the southern, sunny side of the churchyard, and paupers and unbaptized babies on the northern, but in some places sections of the churchyard were allocated to specific areas of the parish. Excommunicates and suicides were often denied churchyard burial. The favourite gravestone ornaments of this century were skulls and bones, hourglasses, scythes and inverted torches.

In the eighteenth century, angels' heads and urns tended to replace the more grisly symbols of death, and it was in this century that monumental inscriptions became the most informative — and the most fulsome.

The inscriptions of the nineteenth century are less wordy, and simple crosses drove out classical decoration. Down to the middle years of the century, it was customary to have the.

headstone inscription on the side away from the grave, but later it became usual for the wording to appear overlooking the grave.

Memorial inscriptions tend to give more information than the bald entries in the parish register, but they are more prone to error because normally a stone cannot be put in place until about a year after the death, to allow the earth to settle. Details should therefore be checked with the registers. They often indicate places and dates of birth, former places of residence, occupation, the name of a married woman's husband and that of her father. If the death was violent, the fact may be stated. Sometimes a man's occupation may be indicated by engravings of the tools of his trade. Coats of arms — if correctly used — can link the deceased with ancestors and descendants, and distinguish his family from others of the same name. Plaques in churches often commemorate members of local families who died overseas, especially officers on active service and servants of the great chartered companies. Many gravestones and tombs commemorate more than one person, and mention their relationship to each other.

Churchyard stones are best studied with the light at an angle to throw shadows into the incisions. A stiff brush may be necessary to remove surface growth. Dates are particularly liable to become difficult to read; a worn 4 can look like a 1. The whole inscription should be transcribed and any heraldic insignia copied. If a plan is made to copy all the inscriptions of a churchyard for the benefit of other people, the incumbent should first be consulted — the job may have been done already and, in any case, it would be discourteous not to. To prevent duplication, checks should also be made with the Society of Genealogists and the county family history society. Most of the county societies are at work transcribing the inscriptions of the burial grounds of their area, so an approach to the appropriate one may make a visit to the churchyard unnecessary. The Society of Genealogists, in addition to the copies of inscriptions held in their own library, has Tucker's card index of memorial inscription copies held elsewhere. Many of such transcripts are in the British Library, local reference libraries and county record offices. Transcripts

of inscriptions made at cleared burial grounds are at the Public Record Office, Chancery Lane, London, under reference RG.37.

For further reading, see *Monuments and their Inscriptions*, by H.L. White, and *Monumental Inscriptions in the Library of the Society of Genealogists, Part I: Southern England*, both available from the Society. Also, *Notes on Recording Monumental Inscriptions*, by John Reyment.

Merchant Gild *see* Gild, Merchant

Merchant Seamen Records of men in the merchant service were kept by the Board of Trade and are now at the Public Record Office, Kew.

Ship's Muster Rolls These (under reference BT.98) list all members of the crew. The keeping of them was obligatory on ships' masters from 1747, but the early ones no longer exist except for Dartmouth vessels (from the beginning), and Liverpool and Plymouth vessels (from later in the century). The rolls returned at other ports survive for the nineteenth century down to 1851.

Agreements and Crew Lists, Series I (BT.98) From 1835 the masters of ships owned by a British subject and engaged on a foreign voyage, and of British-registered ships of 80 tons or more on coastal trade or fishery, had to carry a written agreement with every member of the crew, stating his wages, the capacity in which he was serving and the nature of the voyage. Also required was a list of all men carried. At the end of the voyage the agreements were delivered to the Registrar General of Shipping and Seamen. Since 1861 only a sample of 10 per cent of these records has been preserved, as *Series II* (BT.99).

Agreements and Crew Lists, Series III (BT.100) are for famous ships, such as the *Titanic, Lusitania*, etc.

Agreements and Crew Lists, Series IV cover fishing vessels of less than 80 tons, but again only a 10 per cent sample has been kept. They date from an Act of 1883. A list of merchant service officers was first published in 1869.

Register of Seamen From 1835 a register was kept of all seamen. For 1835-6 it occupies five volumes, in alphabetical order, entitled *Register of Seamen, Series I* (BT.120). A *Series II* (BT.112), with an alphabetical index (BT.119), covers the period 1835-41.

Register Tickets, to be held by every seaman, were introduced in 1844. The applications for these give the man's date and place of birth, date of first going to sea, capacity in which he served then and thereafter, and any service in the Royal Navy. Tickets were abolished in 1854. The *Register of Seamen's Tickets* (BT.113) has an alphabetical index (BT.114). The *Register of Masters' Tickets* is under BT.115. On the ending of tickets a new *Register of Seamen, Series III* (BT.116) was started, listing men alphabetically and giving age, place of birth, voyage, ship, and port of departure. However, this register was ended in 1856.

Masters' and Mates' Records Voluntary examinations for men intending to become masters or mates were introduced in 1845, and an Act of 1850 made them compulsory for foreign-going ships. In 1850 the same was applied to home trade vessels. Registers were kept of the certificates of competency issued, showing name, place and date of birth, and date and place of certificate issue. The records are: *Certificates of Competency, Masters and Mates, Foreign Trade* (BT.112); *Certificates of Service, Masters and Mates, Foreign Trade* (BT.124); *Certificates of Competency, Masters and Mates of Steamships, Foreign Trade* (BT.123); *Certificates of Competency, Masters and Mates, Home Trade* (BT.125); *Certificates of Service, Masters and Mates, Home Trade* (BT.126); *Index to the Registers* (BT.127).

Engineers' Records Certificates of competency and service were begun for engineers in 1862. The records are: *Certificates of Competency, Engineers* (BT.139); *Certificates of Service, Engineers* (BT.142); *Index* (BT.141).

Colonial Records Certificates issued to the above categories at colonial ports are registered in *Certificates of Competency, Masters and Mates, Colonial* (BT.128), and *Certificates of Competency, Engineers, Colonial* (BT.140). They are indexed in BT.127 and 141.

Fishermen Certificates for skippers and mates of fishing vessels were introduced by an Act of 1883. For Competency the reference is BT.129;

for Service, BT.130; and for the Index, BT.138.

Apprentices The Act of 1835 authorised the indenturing of apprentices. There is an *Index of Apprentices* (BT.150), and five-yearly specimens of indentures under BT.151 and, for fishing boats, BT.152.

Other records of seamen are:

Registers of Wages and Effects of Deceased Seamen (BT.153) from 1851. They show cause, date and place of death, and are indexed in *Indexes to Seamen's Names* (BT.154).

Registers of Deaths of British Nationals at Sea (BT.159) beginning in 1888.

For details of passengers, *see* PASSENGER LISTS.

Lloyd's Marine Collection is at the Guildhall Library, London. Among its records of vessels are the captains' registers for 1868-1947. These show their date and place of birth, certificate number, date and place of examination, vessels in which they served, and date of death. There are also voyage records of ocean-going vessels, 1740-1970.

There is a collection of Trinity House Petitions at the Society of Genealogists. These are appeals for relief from poverty-stricken merchant seamen and their widows, dating from 1780 to 1854. Certificates of baptism, marriage and death are often enclosed.

A free leaflet, *Records of the Registrar General of Shipping and Seamen* is available at the Public Record Office.

Merchet The payment due to the lord of the manor from a villein, on the occasion of the marriage of the latter's son or daughter. In some places it only applied if the marriage was to someone outside the manor.

Mere (i) As an adjective, sheer, unalloyed, pure.

(ii) A boundary. Within a manor, boundaries might be marked out by mere-stones or posts.

Merrybegot An illegitimate child.

Merseyside A metropolitan county formed in 1974 out of the Liverpool area of LANCASHIRE.

Mese Another term for messuage.

Mesne Lord In the feudal hierarchy, a lord in the middle; i.e. the lord of a manor who held (was the tenant) of a superior lord, but was himself the superior lord of a lord holding one or more of his manors. The pronunciation and significance of the word are as in 'meantime'. *See also* MANOR; TENANT-IN-CHIEF.

Messuage A dwelling-house with the ground around it and any outbuildings. A capital messuage was that of the lord of a manor, or of any other large residential property. Also sometimes referred to as a 'mese'.

Methodists The Methodist movement began in 1738, when John and Charles Wesley set out to revive a sense of spirituality and inner holiness in worship. At first, they preached to church congregations and religious societies; then their followers formed themselves into 'societies' and met at members' houses. In 1739, George Whitefield, an associate of the Wesley brothers when they were at Oxford, began to preach in the open air, and the Wesleys followed his example. They accepted the nickname 'Methodist', which had been mockingly bestowed upon them at Oxford. Although they remained members of the established church, they built supplementary preaching-houses (Wesley) and tabernacles (Whitefield), and these became grouped into Circuits under a Circuit Chapel.

In 1741 the followers of Whitefield, who were Calvinists and believed in predestination to heaven or hell, separated from those of the Wesleys, who were Arminian and held that salvation was open to all true believers. During the eighteenth century both sects continued to be called Methodists. Wesley travelled the whole country and his following grew greatly. In 1778, Wesley's Chapel in City Road, London, was founded, with its own graveyard and burial register. By 1784, Methodist clergy were being barred from Anglican churches, so they invoked the *Toleration Act* and became, officially, Dissenters. From then on they took less care to arrange their meetings at times that did not conflict with Church of England services, but the baptisms of their children were still performed and registered in church.

Charles Wesley died in 1788 and John Wesley in 1791. The movement continued to grow but, in the following decades, it was subject to an almost constant state of change, as a succession of sub-denominations developed and split off from the main body. In 1797 a sect called the Methodist New Connexion was founded. It gave its laity more control over its affairs, and by 1837 it had thirty circuits, each with its own register.

In 1807, a small group called the Independent, or Quaker, Methodists left the main body, and in the following year the followers of Hugh Bourne were expelled from the Burslem Circuit and built their first chapel at Tunstall. In 1812 they adopted the name of Primitive Methodists and expanded, especially in the industrial towns of the north. Three years later, the Bible Christians (O'Bryanites) broke away in the southwestern area of England. In 1818 a Metropolitan Wesleyan Registry of Births and Baptisms was begun in London, from duplicate certificates sent in by the circuits.

The movement continued to divide. In 1827 the Protestant Methodists became a separate body, wanting more rights for ordinary members against the Annual Methodist Conference. In 1833, the Independent Methodists took the name of the United Churches of Christ, and in 1836 the Wesleyan Methodist Association was formed, with the same aim of lay members' rights.

In 1837, the Methodists obeyed the call to deposit their registers with the General Registrar. They sent 856, of which the oldest is one of 1738 in London. However, a higher proportion of Methodist registers escaped deposit than was the case with other denominations, though some have since gone to county record offices.

1932 saw the Wesleyan Methodists, Primitive Methodists and the United Methodist Church combined to form the Methodist Church.

Baptismal registers belonged to circuits and were originally stored in the circuit chapel, but circuits sometimes altered their borders, so a genealogist should be ready to search neighbouring circuits' registers. Also, the circuit boundaries of the various sects were not the same. Burial registers are rare, and membership rolls are scattered among various collections. From 1778 onward, the various sects issued magazines which contain biographies, death notices and obituaries. An index to those of 1778-1839 has been published in Volume 9 of the *Proceedings of the Wesley History Society* (founded 1897).

The largest deposits of registers are at the Public Record Office, Chancery Lane, London, under references RG.4/4677-80, RG.5/162-207, and RG.8; others are in county record offices. The Methodist Archives and Research Centre, 23-35 City Road, London EC1, have non-deposited registers, especially of defunct societies, and much other historical material, including the *Minutes of Conference,* which contain biographies of ministers. The Super-intendent Ministers of Circuits still have a number of registers and some eighteenth-century membership rolls, but sometimes depute local ministers to house them.

Some useful addresses for researchers are: The Archivist, Methodist Missionary Society, 25 Marylebone Road, London NW1 (for records of overseas missions); the Wesley Historical Society, The Manse, St Keverne, Helston, Cornwall; the Independent Methodist Churches Historical Society, Providence Independent Methodist Church, Albert Road, Colne, Lanca-shire; the Wesleyan Reform Union Record Office, 123 Queen Street, Sheffield, Yorkshire.

Each of the thirty-one Methodist adminis-trative areas has an archivist, and the Connexional Archivist at the Property Division of the Methodist Church, Central Buildings, Oldham Street, Manchester M1 1JQ, will supply the name and address of the Methodist archivist of any named district. If the regional records have not been found in the appropriate record office, the Methodist Archivist for the area may know where they are.

For further reading, see *My Ancestor was a Methodist: How can I find more about him?,* available from the Society of Genealogists; and *Sources for Nonconformist Genealogy and Family History,* by D.J. Steel (1973).

Michaelmas The feast of St Michael the Archangel, celebrated on 29 September, is a quarter-day on which rents and rates became due. Many tenancies and other agreements also date from Michaelmas. It was the custom to have Michaelmas goose for dinner, as the birds were

considered to be in their prime at that time of year. Michaelmas is also the name of one of the four law and college terms.

Middle Ages A modern term used to designate the period between the ancient world of the Roman Empire and the modern age ushered in by the Renaissance, the Reformation, and the development of national states. As applied to England, the period may be said to have begun with the departure of the Roman army in A.D. 410, and to have ended gradually during the late fifteenth and early sixteenth centuries. At one time, the year 1485 was used as a convenience to represent its end with the death of the last Plantagenet king, but that date ignores many complex factors.

In the past, the Middle Ages were known as the Dark Ages, to signify the period between the disappearance of the classical culture of the ancient world and its revival in the fifteenth century, but now that term is applied in England to the obscure period from the departure of the Romans to the beginning of documented history under the Anglo-Saxon kings.

Middlesex *see* **London and Middlesex**

Mile In early times a variable distance, of which the sixteenth-century average was 2140 yards. The standard mile of 1760 yards was laid down in the year 1593.

Militia A body of men enrolled for emergency military service, on a local basis. From Anglo-Saxon times there was an obligation on every grown male to defend his country, or at least his county. The *Assize of Arms* in 1181, the *Statute of Winchester* in 1285, and other decrees, laid down what weapons each man must keep, according to his means and status. In the Middle Ages, the force in each county was raised by the sheriff, but in Tudor times it became the responsibility of the lieutenant, later known as the Lord Lieutenant.

In 1558 two Acts were passed revising each man's responsibilities for providing arms, armour and horses. The men of the nation were divided into ten groups. Those with incomes of £5-£10 per year had to have a coat of plated armour, a steel cap, a longbow with arrows, and either a bill or a halberd. Men with an annual income of £10-£20 had to find the same, but with a harquebus instead of a bill or halberd, and a morion instead of a cap. Additional armour had to be supplied by the gentry, and the scale of requirements went on up to the men worth £1000 per year or more, who had to provide 16 horses, 80 suits of light armour, 40 pikes, 30 longbows, 20 bills or halberds, 20 harquebuses and 50 steel caps or helmets. People with property in two places were usually only assessed on one. In addition to the above rates, if a man's wife wore velvet kirtles or silk petticoats, he had to provide a light horse with its armour and harness.

From time to time, all the men liable for services were called, with their arms, to musters; and from 1570, men who were both fit and keen underwent regular training in small units. Consequently it became the custom to distinguish, in muster certificates, between trained and untrained men, and so arose the Trained Bands, almost the equivalent of later territorial units. In Stuart times, in some places, the more prosperous gentry raised their own volunteer forces. One problem in that age, when firearms were replacing halberds and bills, was to ensure that all such arms brought to the musters had the same bore and used the same type of powder. The aim was to create an exact or perfect militia. In the horse militia, the gentry served as cuirassiers or pistoliers, armed with pistols, while the 'best yeomen' served as carbines or dragoons, armed with a small harquebus. When, in 1798, the danger of invasion by the French seemed acute, the militia was increased and its organization made more rigorous. By this time the cavalry units were known as Yeomanry, to distinguish them from the infantry who were still called the Militia, Volunteers or Fencibles. (For information on developments during the Napoleonic Wars, *see* LORD LIEUTENANT.) All appointments and promotions of officers in the Yeomanry, Militia and Volunteer corps are published in the *London Gazette*. Early militia records can be found in the Public Record Office, Chancery Lane, London, in classes E.36, 101 and 315, also SP.1, 2, 10, 12, 14, 16 and 17. Late eighteenth-century and nineteenth-century records are in HO.51, and WO.13 and 68 (at the PRO, Kew), with some also among lieutenancy records at the county record offices.

The Public Record Office has issued a free leaflet, *Militia Muster Rolls, 1522-1640*.

Milkhouse Another name for a dairy, which was also sometimes called a white house. An inventory of 1596 lists the following contents of a yeoman's dairy: 10 cakes of butter, 3 cheeses, 6 cheese vats, wooden bowls and a cheese press.

Ministers' Accounts These records, more fully named *Bailiffs' and Ministers' Accounts*, are the accounts of revenue and expenditure in the management of crown lands, including those taken temporarily into the king's hands. Those of the latter are sometimes supplemented by earlier accounts rendered to the manorial lords but appropriated by the royal agents, or ministers, for their guidance. An understanding of these accounts calls for some knowledge of farming and handicraft techniques, and the vocabularies, often local, belonging to them. The records are at the Public Record Office, Chancery Lane, London, under *Special Collections*, and are indexed in *Lists and Indexes*, Vols.5, 8 and 34.

Misdemeanour An offence less serious than a felony.

Misprision of Treason Any offence akin to treason, but not so serious. Concealment of a treasonable act was a common example and came to be a synonym for it.

Miss A style of address that only came into respectable use for unmarried women in the early eighteenth century. In the late seventeenth century it had been an abbreviation for 'mistress' (concubine), whereas all women of the status corresponding to the men known as Mr were called Mrs (Mistress), whether married or single. The marriage announcements in the *Gentleman's Magazine*, from its inception in 1731, use the style 'Miss' for spinster brides, but unmarried women of mature years were still called Mrs as a mark of respect.

Missing Persons In 1885 the Salvation Army set up a bureau, the main purpose of which was to find relatives with whom their enquirers had lost touch. It was known at that time as Mrs Booth's Inquiry Agency. The service is still in considerable demand. However, enquiries are not pursued if it is felt that they might cause pain, and no addresses are divulged without the consent of the persons concerned. A modest fee is charged for these searches. The present full name and address of the bureau is, The Salvation Army Missing Persons Bureau, 110 Middlesex Street, London E1 7HZ.

For another method of contacting living members of one's family whose whereabouts is unknown, *see* HEALTH AND SOCIAL SECURITY, DEPARTMENT OF.

Mobility of Families The migration of families from one part of the country to another in pre-industrial England is now recognised to have been considerable. In a number of areas it has been found that about half the rural population died in a parish other than that in which it had been born, though most movement was within a ten-mile radius and almost all of it within twenty miles. However, the migrant with a large town in his mind's eye was prepared to travel further, and it may be said that the larger the town, the greater its drawing power, with London attracting people from all parts of the country.

The most mobile sections of the population were young people who moved to the type of work where they would 'live-in', notably to domestic and farm service (*see* HIRING FAIRS), and to trade apprenticeships. Conversely the least mobile were men in the senior line of farming families, both freehold and copyhold; and the larger the farm, the more settled the family. The evidence for mobility is derived from census returns, memorial inscriptions, settlement papers, wills and depositions in ecclesiastical courts. It seems to have reached a peak in the period around 1600. After declining during the seventeenth century, mobility increased again in the eighteenth, and even more in the nineteenth, as the Industrial Revolution developed.

Mock of the Church The name applied to the breaking of a betrothal after the calling of banns. Often penalised by the churchwardens with a fine.

Modus More fully known as *Modus Decimandi*, this was a commutation of tithes in kind by money payment.

Month's Mind A memorial service for the dead, performed a month after the death. Legacies for the provision of candles for this ceremony were often mentioned in pre-Reformation wills.

Monumental Inscriptions *see* **Memorial Inscriptions**

Moravians After the death of John Huss in 1415, some of his followers in Bohemia and Moravia (now Czechoslovakia) founded religious societies, and in 1728 three Moravian missionaries came to London and Oxford and introduced their mode of worship into England. It flourished, particularly in London, and in 1738 John and Charles Wesley joined the movement and became its leaders. However, two years later they broke away and founded their own Methodist Society.

In 1742 the Congregation of the Unity of Brethren was founded, which was the beginning of the Moravians as a separate sect in England, though they tried to keep close to the established church. They were also close in thought to the Methodists. Societies were founded in the industrial areas of Yorkshire, the villages around Bedford, and in Derbyshire, north Cheshire, south Lancashire and Wiltshire.

Moravian groups were of three types:

Societies The most numerous. Although they had their own minister and a meeting-house, the members took Communion in their parish churches. Some churches even kept special seats for the local Moravians.

Congregations These were a higher organisation, but they were few and small. In 1747, of the 1200 members in Yorkshire, only 62 were in Congregations.

Settlements A still higher order of permanent residential communities, living under austere discipline and trying to be economically self-sufficient. They had separate quarters (choirs) for married couples, bachelors, and spinsters. There were four of these Settlements: Fulneck in Yorkshire, Fairfield in Lancashire, Ockbrook in Derbyshire, and Bedford.

In 1749 the Moravians were recognised by Parliament as a Protestant Episcopal Church, but they were obliged to license their rooms as dissenters' chapels. In 1754 their first English 'bishop' was appointed, although the organisation of the movement was similar to the Presbyterian. The term 'bishop' became a mere mark of respect.

By 1800 there were about twenty-four Congregations in the British Isles, but many more Societies, mainly in London, Bristol, north Wiltshire, Berkshire and Yorkshire. As the leaders of the movement were German, the minutes of their meetings were often written in that language, or at least in German script. This tended to hold the movement back, as also did their reluctance to proselytize: they went only where they were invited. However, they were highly respected and were the first to engage in foreign missions.

In the 1830s the rise of the Oxford (high church) Movement led to the Moravians finally breaking with the Church of England.

Moravians' registers cover baptisms, burials and, at Fetter Lane, London (from 1741), Fulneck (1749/50) and Bedford (1743), marriages, After 1754, all marriages had to be performed in parish churches, but they were also recorded in the Moravian registers. The same useful duplication applies to burials, except where the Moravians had their own burial ground. Often such entries include a note of the place of birth. In the period before 1752 the dates are given in both Old Style and New Style, owing to the continental nature of the movement (*see* CALENDAR). People often travelled from far away to join a Settlement, and sometimes the entries for members of one Congregation would be made in the register of a neighbouring one. Some people are described in the registers as Non-Moravians, presumably because they were only members of a Society. Baptismal entries normally include the date of birth and the father's occupation.

Registers are either at the Public Record Office, Chancery Lane, London, in group RG, or with the local Congregations. Those of some

defunct Congregations are at the Moravian Church House, 5 Muswell Hill, London NW10. Other records available to searchers are the *Congregation Book*, with valuable personal details about members; the *Congregation Diary*, recording church services, movements of members, relations with outside bodies, and obituary notices; and *Minutes of the Conference of Elders*, recording applications for membership. These are with the Congregations. The short-lived General Registry of Births, started in 1747 by the College of Arms, has entries contributed by Moravians.

For further reading, see *Sources for Nonconformist Genealogy and Family History*, by D.J. Steel (1973).

Morion A seventeenth-century helmet with a defensive ridge and a brim.

Mormons *see* Latter-Day Saints

Mort d'Ancestor Cases of *mort d'ancestor* were claims to be the heir of a previous owner of a property.

Mortmain The first legislation affecting the conveyance of land to the 'dead hand' of perpetual religious bodies was incorporated in a re-issue of *Magna Carta* in 1217. In 1279, the *Statute of Mortmain*, more properly called *De Viris Religiosis*, sought to control such conveyances and to protect the rights of the king and mesne lay lords. The statute forbade alienation in mortmain without a licence, on pain of resumption of the land by the immediate lord. Before a licence was granted, an enquiry was made by the local escheator as to what lords were involved. These enquiries were called *Inquisitions ad quod dampnum*. Licences to donate lands held *in capite* (direct grant from the king) were usually refused.

In 1391 a statute extended the mortmain laws to gilds, fraternities, municipal corporations and perpetual offices, and enforced the completion of conveyances by trustees. An Act of 1736 forbade the conveyance by will of land to all perpetual bodies.

Inquisitions ad quod dampnum are at the Public Record Office. There is a calendar, but this gives very little of the information in the original.

Patent Rolls at the Public Record Office include grants of licences (refer to the printed *Calendars of Patent Rolls*). Close Rolls at the Public Record Office give details of disputes about the legality of alienations (refer to the printed *Calendars of Close Rolls*).

Mortuary (i) A payment by a parishioner to the rector or vicar on the occasion of a death in the family; originally the family's second best animal, but commuted, under Henry VIII, to a money payment graded according to the estate of the deceased. Those under the value of ten marks were exempt.

(ii) A building to which the dead are brought, awaiting burial or identification.

Mote A meeting for discussion; as in WARDMOTE.

Motto A sentence or phrase, usually either pious or defiant, which appears on a scroll as part of an heraldic achievement. The mottoes of English families are customarily worded in either Latin, Norman-French or English, regardless of their date of origin.

Mr An abbreviation for Master, and originally so pronounced. Harrison, in his *Description of Britain* (1577), refers to 'Master, which is the title that men give to esquires and gentlemen'. In the seventeenth century it was a courtesy title for any man of respectable status.
See also CLASS, SOCIAL; ESQUIRE; GENTLEMAN; GOODMAN.

Mrs The courtesy title for women of the status corresponding to that of men addressed as Mr, but throughout the seventeenth century applied both to married and unmarried women, and even through the eighteenth century to spinsters of mature age, as a mark of respect.
See also MISS.

Muniment A title deed, or evidence of rights or privileges. A muniment chest for containing such documents is often an article of furniture in the houses of landed families.

Muster Certificates Also referred to as Muster Rolls. The word muster originally meant a display, in this context a display of men, horses and equipment, but soon became attached to the men and appurtenances themselves. A muster certificate is an account of those who presented themselves with their accoutrements at a parade called to show the county authorities who and what arms were available in each Hundred for purposes of defence.

To the musters came all men between 16 and 60 under the rank of baron, with the arms and armour prescribed for them (*see* ARRAY, COMMISSION OF *and* MILITIA). This inspection was called a 'general muster'. From 1573 there were efforts to train the fit men, who were liable to be called together in smaller units for drill in what were called 'special' or 'particular', or even 'private' musters.

In normal times, musters were probably held at least once every three years, but there was no regularity. In times of danger there might be two in one year, and special musters in perilous times might be held daily. The order would pass down from the Commissioner for Musters in each county (the Lieutenant, after 1571), through his deputy, to the Justices of the Peace, the high constable of each Hundred, and then to the petty constable of each parish, with lists of the men and arms expected. From the 1570s it became normal to classify them into trained and untrained.

The general muster usually covered two days, separated by an interval. At the first, the men and arms were inspected and any absences or defects were ordered to be made good before the second muster. The deputy lieutenant, or a Justice of the Peace, presided with a clerk to note results. After a short service the men were sorted into 'choice men', 'men of the second sort' and 'men unable to keep the country'. Each man received a day's pay. On the second day, absentees and men who did not bring their arms were liable to ten days' imprisonment or a fine of forty shillings. The Pioneer Corps, for less active men, had to bring picks and shovels for digging ramparts and trenches. Additional armour had to be brought, not only by the more affluent residents but also by local government bodies such as counties, corporate boroughs, livery companies and parish vestries.

Muster certificates were often badly written and some were never sent in to the Secretary of

State. Some show all healthy males between 16 and 60, others only trained men and pioneers, and some only the number of men for whom there was adequate equipment. The best returns, where they are extant, are those for 1569 and 1573. For the first nine years of James I's reign, musters and training fell into abeyance, but they were resumed in 1612 when a Spanish invasion was expected. The vogue for Artillery Grounds, or Gardens, sprang up for military practice, artillery then meaning not cannons, which were ordnance, but any missile weapon, such as a bow or musket.

The sources for sixteenth century musters are the State Papers (SP) at the Public Record Office, Chancery Lane, London, with others in class E.101; and the *Lansdowne MSS* at the British Library. After 1600, rolls can be found in the lieutenancy papers at county record offices, the British Library, and the Bodleian Library.

Muster certificates are valuable location records, but it must be borne in mind that they do not necessarily cover all the menfolk. Evasion was evidently easy. The updating on some rolls can be helpful in showing people's movements, deaths and approximate ages.

For further reading, see *The Elizabethan Militia, 1558-1638*, by Lindsay Boynton (1971).

Mynge The phrase 'in mynge and undivided' in connection with arable lands in the common fields of a manor, meant 'intermingled and unenclosed'.

Mystery A handicraft or trade. A mystery play was acted by the craftsmen's gilds.

N

Nabob (i) An Indian provincial governor. A corruption of Nawab.

(ii) In the eighteenth century, an East India Company factor who had returned to England with a display of wealth, and often with one or more Indian servants. Anyone who returned

with less than fifty or sixty thousand pounds was unkindly called a 'chicken nabob'.

Naked A note made in a burial register when the corpse was unshrouded and the coffin unlined. This was sometimes the case with a poor family who could not afford the expense of a woollen shroud, nor the payment of a fine for using any other type of cloth. It was caused by the *Act for Burying in Woollen*, passed in 1660 and reinforced in 1678, to support the woollen trade by making it an offence to wrap corpses or line coffins in any material other than wool. The only bodies exempt were those of people who had died of plague.

Namesake *see* **One-name Society**

Narrative Pedigree *see* **Paragraph Pedigree**

National Army Museum This institution was founded by royal charter in 1960 to portray the history of the British Army, including the Volunteers, East India Company's army, Indian Government Services and Colonial Forces, but it has also a Department of Records with a Reading Room, for which a Reader's Ticket is required.

The Department of Records houses four main collections: (i) books, including the *Army List, India List*, regimental histories and journals, campaign histories, biographies and bound volumes of periodicals; (ii) manuscripts, including the letters, journals and papers of a number of military commanders in several wars, and the manuscripts formerly belonging to the Royal United Service Institution; (iii and iv) prints and photographs of persons and places, including some of the very earliest military photographs. There is also a biographical index of officers of the East India Company and Indian Army.

The Museum is situated in Royal Hospital Road, Chelsea, London SW3.

National Pedigree Index A card index started in 1976, registering the existence, owners and whereabouts of pedigrees. It is planned as a central clearing-house of pedigrees of three generations or more, researched or being researched, in order to avoid duplication of work already done and to put researchers in touch with one another. Compilers of pedigrees are encouraged to register the results of their researches (not depositing their pedigrees), and enquiries are welcomed on payment of a search fee. All correspondence must enclose a stamped self-addressed envelope or international reply coupon. Inclusion in the Index does not in any way authenticate pedigrees. Letters should be addressed to The National Pedigree Index, c/o Society of Genealogists, 14 Charterhouse Buildings, London EC1M 7BA.

See also WHITMORE, J.B..

National Register of Archives Founded in 1945, on the proposal of the British Records Association, the National Register is a branch of the Historical Manuscripts Commission, charged with making a complete survey of all archives (except those of central government) in England, Wales and the Channel Isles, including even those of private families and clubs.

The Register consists of two card indexes: one topographical, under parishes and boroughs, recording the whereabouts of archives, their nature, scope, date, etc.; the other a rough working index of subjects and persons. The personal names indexed are only those of some fame, even if only local. Two useful subject headings are Family History and Heraldry. Archives listed are not necessarily open to inspection by enquirers.

The contents of surveyed collections are detailed on report forms, and copies of these are sent to the archive owner, the local record office, and the national libraries. Most county archivists are official representatives of the Register. Some county record offices have made systematic searches for archives in their areas.

Each year HMSO publishes, for the National Register of Archives, a *List of Accessions to Repositories*; also an occasional *Bulletin*.

Enquiries should be addressed to The Registrar, National Register of Archives, Quality Court, Chancery Lane, London WC2 (tel: 01.242.1198). A search room is open to students from Monday to Friday each week. Normally an appointment is necessary.

Nativo Habendo, Writ of de A writ that

could be issued by a feudal lord demanding that a sheriff hand over a villein who had fled from his manor.

See also VILLEIN.

Naturalization Before 1844, aliens could become naturalized British subjects only by private Act of Parliament. The records of these Acts can be consulted at the House of Lords Record Office and are indexed in Part XIII of the *Index to Local and Personal Acts*. From 1844, naturalization could be granted by a certificate from the Home Secretary, and the records are at the Public Record Office, Chancery Lane, London, under Group HO. Many aliens never troubled to apply for naturalization. By marrying English women and begetting children born in Britain, their families automatically acquired British nationality.

Neck Verse *see* **Benefit of Clergy**

Negative Proof The discovery of a baptismal entry of a person of the same name as a sought-for ancestor cannot, by itself, be assumed to have solved the problem of the ancestor's baptism or parentage. Until recent times, the range of choice for Christian names was small, so that many people in the same neighbourhood bore identical Christian names and surnames. If there is no independent evidence that the entry found refers to the person sought, then an effort must be made to find whether there is any other entry of the same name. The registers of all the parishes and non-parochial chapels within a fifteen-mile radius of the 'parish (or parishes) of indication' should be searched. The parish of indication can be any or all of the following: the parish in which the family was later living; the one stated to be the person's birthplace (e.g. in a census return); the parish of the entry already found.

In addition, an effort should be made to discover whether the person named in the entry died or married under such circumstances as to eliminate him from consideration. Only if such searches fail to throw doubt on, or disprove, the identification is it reasonably safe to conclude that the entry found is the one sought. The general principle is — if an identification is unconfirmed, try to disprove it.

Neif A female villein.

Nephew Until the end of the seventeenth century this word meant a grandson, descendant or kinsman.

New Jerusalemites The Swedenborgians' New Church was founded in London in 1788 by a group influenced by the ideas of the Swedish theologian, Emanuel Swedenborg (1668-1772). Churches were soon established in many parts of England, but especially in Lancashire. In 1837-40 their well-kept registers were deposited with the Registrar General and are now at the Public Record Office in Group RG, but duplicates, made at the same time as the originals, are at Church Headquarters, 20 Bloomsbury Way, London WC1, with other archives of the Church.

For further reading, see *Sources for Non-conformist Genealogy and Family History*, by D.J. Steel (1973).

Newspapers The earliest English newspaper appeared in 1622, and the first with domestic news in November 1641 after the freeing of the press by the abolition of the Court of Star Chamber. Newspapers proliferated during the Civil Wars, but in September 1655 all were suppressed except *Mercurius Politicus* and *The Publick Intelligencer* (1655-60). The *London Gazette* actually started on 16 November, 1665, though it was called the *Oxford Gazette* until 5 February, 1666/7. It has been published ever since as the government's official organ. The *Gazette* was, for twelve years, the only newspaper permitted, but press censorship was abolished in 1693, and then several London and provincial weekly newspapers began publication. In 1702 came the first English daily newspaper, *The Daily Courant*, and *Lloyd's List* started in 1726, at first weekly then twice weekly.

In the eighteenth century the outstanding daily was the *Public Advertiser*, earlier called the *General Advertiser* (and for a time *The London Daily Post*). Other important papers were, *The Morning Chronicle* (1769-1862), *Morning Herald* (1781-1869), *Morning Post* (seventeenth to twentieth century), *The Times* (1788-today, and indexed, but founded in 1785 as *The Daily Universal Register*), *Morning Advertiser* and

Examiner. Their main function was to report Parliamentary debates, but *Advertisers* were connected with business and carried numerous advertisements.

The first provincial newspapers were the *Worcester Postman* (1690) and *The Lincoln, Rutland and Stamford Mercury* (1693).

The first tax on newspapers, from 1712, was one penny on a whole sheet and a half-penny on a half sheet. In 1756 it was raised to 1½ pence, in 1789 to 2 pence, 1798 to 2½ pence, 1804 to 3 pence, and in 1815 to 4 pence less 20 per cent. From 1831 to 1835 hundreds of newspapers appeared without tax stamps in spite of prosecutions. They were of a sensational and revolutionary character.

At the beginning of the nineteenth century the provincial press consisted of less than one hundred journals, with a minimum of local news; but after 1836 the local press came into its own, carrying both national and local news. Thanks to Bulwer Lytton, M. Gibson and Richard Cobden, the tax on newspapers had in that year been reduced to one penny, and in 1855 it was abolished. Many newspapers began in this period, including *The Daily Telegraph*. In 1836 the circulation of newspapers rose from 39 million to 122 million. The railways, the telegraph and automatic printing machines all helped to promote their production and distribution.

The British Library has a catalogued collection of early newspapers at the British Museum. Called the Burney Collection, after Dr Charles Burney, it is arranged chronologically and not by separate newspapers. Other papers of the seventeenth and eighteenth centuries are listed in the *General Index* under their titles. The *Thomason Tracts*, also in the British Library, include newspaper items which are listed separately in the catalogue. Newspapers, national and local, since 1800 are at the British Newspaper Library in Colindale, Middlesex, but the building was bombed during the war and parts of the collection were destroyed. The card index should first be consulted to find what newspapers, for what districts and dates, are available. On the open shelves are indexes for births and marriages from certain East Anglian newspapers. Newspaper publishers themselves usually retain copies of past issues. Public libraries, too, often have files of old newspapers. At the Public Record Office are a number of colonial newspapers in a Colonial Office series, running from the mid 1820s to the mid 1850s. The Bodleian Library, Oxford, has a collection of newspapers from 1622 to 1800.

The Times Tercentenary Handlist of English and Welsh Newspapers, 1620-1920 lists all known newspapers of the period. This can be found at county libraries. Palmer's *Index to The Times* has appeared quarterly from 1791, but the births, marriages and deaths are not included. The main reference libraries have a copy.

See also HARLEIAN SOCIETY.

Niece Until the seventeenth century, this word meant a descendant, either male or female; but occasionally it was used to mean any younger relative.

See also NEPHEW.

Nisi Prius When a date was fixed for a trial at one of the central courts, the note *nisi prius* ('unless before') was often added, meaning that if the appropriate County Assizes were held first, the case should be heard there. Unless there was a good reason for the case to be tried in a central court, it was usual to fix a date falling after the next Assize.

Noble A gold coin, first minted in 1351 and valued at 6 shillings and 8 pence. On one side it bore the image of the king, Edward III, in a ship, and on the reverse a floriate cross. Edward IV added a rose to the ship (from which it was called a rose-noble) and raised its value to 10 shillings. At the same time, he introduced a new coin, the angel, valued at 6 shillings and 8 pence.

Nonconformists People of English Protestant denominations other than that of the established Church of England. Also called Dissenters. For their records and history, *see* under the names of the various denominations. *See also* NON-PAROCHIAL REGISTERS; RECUSANT ROLLS; WILLIAMS'S LIBRARY, DR.

Non-parochial Registers These are the records of baptisms and burials, plus a few marriages, maintained by religious bodies other than the Church of England. For details of the registers of any particular denomination, *see* under the name of that denomination, and under WILLIAMS'S LIBRARY, DR.

1837 With the founding of the General Register of Births, Deaths and Marriages, marriages in nonconformist meeting-houses were permitted from July, 1837. Existing non-parochial registers of England and Wales, including some of foreign churches, were called in by a specially appointed commission, and 3630 congregations complied, sending in about 7000 registers. The Roman Catholic bishops refused to authorise the depositing of their registers, and the Jews, College of Arms, Quakers, the non-denominational Bunhill Fields burial ground of the City of London, and the East India Company (for marriages in India) also refused. However, schedules were made of the registers of the three last-named.

1840 In accordance with the *Non-parochial Register Act* of this year, the surrendered registers were deposited in the care of the General Register Office. The denominations affected were: Baptists, Independents, Presbyterians, Scottish churches in England, the Methodists of the Wesleyan, New Connexion and Primitive persuasions, the Bible Christians, Inghamites, Moravians, Lady Huntingdon's Connexion, Calvinistic Methodists, Swedenborgians, foreign Protestant churches and some cemeteries. Some Roman Catholic registers from the north of England were deposited.

1841 The Quakers surrendered some of their registers.

1857 About 300 more registers were sent in by the above-mentioned denominations, by the Chelsea, Foundling and Greenwich Hospitals, and by Bunhill Fields burial ground, and these were authenticated and deposited in the following year.

1859 The List and Index Society published, in its Volume 42, *The General Register Office List of Non-parochial Registers, Main Series*, and the *Society of Friends Series*. It includes about 8800 registers. The dates shown in it for the foundation of congregations and the commencement of registers are not all correct. The first register entry was not necessarily for the first ceremony.

1961 The deposited registers were transferred from the General Register Office to the Public Record Office, Chancery Lane, London, in classes RG.4-8.

Some non-parochial registers have come to light since 1857 and are housed either by the denominations' historical societies, or at county record offices. Most of the chapels that were in existence at the beginning of the nineteenth century no longer exist, and many of their records are lost.

For further reading, see *Sources for Nonconformist Genealogy and Family History*, by D.J. Steel (1973).

Norfolk The Norfolk and Norwich Genealogical Society (FHS) holds meetings, issues a journal and publishes historical records. Enquiries should be sent c/o The Federation of Family History Societies, 31 Seven Star Road, Solihull, West Midlands B91 2BZ, marked 'Please forward' and enclosing a stamped self-addressed envelope.

Record Repositories Norfolk and Norwich Record Office (CRO), Central Library, Norwich (tel: 0603.22233); Muniment Room of the Dean and Chapter, The Cathedral, Norwich; Borough Record Office, Town Hall, Great Yarmouth; Town Hall, King's Lynn.

Parish Registers and Indexes (*see* comment under COUNTY) Many of the 691 ancient parishes have deposited their registers at the CRO, and the Society of Genealogists has copies of about 22 in its library. Boyd's Marriage Index covers 146; Pallot's Marriage Index covers 138, from 1790. The INTERNATIONAL GENEALOGICAL INDEX (IGI) treats a similar number. The FHS has a marriage index for Norwich in hand. The Bishops' Transcripts are at the CRO.

Marriage Licence Records These are at the CRO. The Society of Genealogists has indexes of some early periods.

Wills before 1858, proved in the following courts, are located at the CRO:

Consistory Court of Norwich
Archdeaconry Court of Norwich
Archdeaconry Court of Norfolk

Peculiar (Pec.) Court of the Dean and Chapter of Norwich
Pec. Court of Castle Rising
Pec. Court of Great Cressingham
Court of the City of Norwich

As the county lay in the Province of Canterbury, wills could also be proved in the Prerogative Court of Canterbury. The Society of Genealogists has indexes to some of the above courts.

Non-parochial Registers Those of 70 chapels are at the Public Record Office, Chancery Lane, London, and the IGI covers a similar number.

Memorial Inscriptions The FHS has transcribed those from about one hundred churchyards, and the Society of Genealogists has a few transcripts.

Heralds' Visitation Pedigrees have been printed for 1563, 1613 and 1664.

Norman-French language Brought into England at the Norman Conquest, it was maintained by schools because it was the tongue of the royal court, the upper classes and, with Latin, of literature. As late as the seventeenth century it was also the language of oral argument in the courts of law. English did not become the literary language of the country until the mid fourteenth century. The first post-Conquest king to speak English as his native tongue was Henry IV. In 1487 Anglo-Norman ceased to be the language of the operative parts of Parliamentary statutes. Only the sentence 'la Reine le veult', giving the Queen's consent, and (in theory) 'la Reine s'avisera' ('the Queen will think about it') remain today.

Northamptonshire In 1974 the Soke of Peterborough was transferred to CAMBRIDGE-SHIRE. The Northamptonshire Family History Society (FHS) holds regular meetings and issues a journal, *Footprints*. Enquiries should be sent c/o The Federation of Family History Societies, 31 Seven Star Road, Solihull, West Midlands B91 2BZ, marked 'Please forward' and enclosing a stamped self-addressed envelope.

Record Repositories Northampton Record Office (CRO), Delapre Abbey, Northampton NN4 (tel:

0604.62129); Northampton Central Library, Abington Street, Northampton.

Parish Registers and Indexes (*see* comment under COUNTY) Of the 292 ancient parishes, most have been deposited at the CRO. The Society of Genealogists has copies of about 50. Pallot's Marriage Index covers 20, from 1790. The INTERNATIONAL GENEALOGICAL INDEX (IGI) treats rather more. The Bishops' Transcripts are at the CRO.

Marriage Licence Records These are at the CRO.

Wills before 1858, proved in the following courts, are at the CRO:

Consistory Court of Peterborough
Archdeaconry Court of Northampton

The following are at Lincolnshire CRO:

Peculiar (Pec.) Court of Gretton with Duddington
Pec. Court of Nassington

As the county lay in the Diocese of Lincoln until 1541, early wills could be proved in the Consistory Court of Lincoln. The county has always lain in the Province of Canterbury, so wills could also be proved in the Prerogative Court of Canterbury.

Non-parochial Registers The registers of 52 chapels are at the Public Record Office (PRO), Chancery Lane, London, and the IGI covers a similar number.

Census Returns These are at the PRO, Portugal Street, London, and at the CRO.

Memorial Inscriptions The Society of Genealogists has transcripts from a few churches.

Heralds' Visitation Pedigrees have been printed for 1564, 1618-19 and 1681.

Northampton Record Society has made a number of historical records available in print.

Northumberland Newcastle-upon-Tyne is now in the new county of Tyne & Wear. For Northumberland and Durham Family History Society (FHS), *see* DURHAM.

Record Repositories Northumberland County Record Office, Melton Park, North Gosforth,

Newcastle-upon-Tyne NE3 (tel: 0632.362680); County Record Office of the Metropolitan County of Tyne & Wear, 7 Saville Place, Newcastle-upon-Tyne 1; City Archives Office, 7 Saville Place, Newcastle-upon-Tyne 1.

Parish Registers and Indexes (*see* comment under COUNTY) Of the 96 ancient parishes nearly all the registers are now at the Northumberland County Record Office (CRO). The Society of Genealogists has copies of more than half of them in its library. Boyd's Marriage Index covers 84 parishes, and Pallot's Marriage Index covers fifteen, for 1790-1812. The INTERNATIONAL GENEALOGICAL INDEX (IGI) treats almost the whole county. The Bishops' Transcripts are at the Department of Palaeography, University of Durham.

Marriage Licence Records These, too, are at the Department of Palaeography, University of Durham.

Wills before 1858, proved in the following courts, are located as shown:

Consistory Court of Durham, *see* DURHAM.
Consistory and Chancery Courts of York, for clergy possessed of *bona notabilia*, *see* YORKSHIRE.
Peculiar Court of the Archbishop in Hexhamshire, 1593-1602, at the Borthwick Institute of Historical Research, based at the University of York.

As the county lay in the Province of York, wills could also be proved in the Prerogative Courts of York and Canterbury.

Non-parochial Registers The registers of 52 chapels are at the Public Record Office (PRO), Chancery Lane, London, and the IGI covers rather more.

Census Returns These are at the PRO, Portugal Street, London, at the two county record offices, and at Newcastle Central Library.

Memorial Inscriptions About two-thirds of the ancient churchyards have been covered by the FHS. The Society of Genealogists has copies of about fifty.

Heralds' Visitation Pedigrees have been printed for 1615 and 1666.

The Surtees Society and the Newcastle Society

of Antiquaries have made a number of historical records available in print.

Notes and Queries A magazine described as 'a medium of intercommunication for literary men, artists, antiquaries and genealogists, etc.' It began publication in November, 1849, and continued until 1962. Its volumes, a store-house of curious items of historical and genealogical information, are available in a number of public libraries and at the Society of Genealogists.

Nottinghamshire The Nottinghamshire Family History Society (FHS) holds regular meetings and issues a quarterly journal. Enquiries should be sent c/o The Federation of Family History Societies, 31 Seven Star Road, Solihull, West Midlands B91 2BZ, marked 'Please forward' and enclosing a stamped self-addressed envelope.

Record Repositories Nottinghamshire Record Office (CRO), County House, High Pavement, Nottingham (tel: 0602.54524); Archives Department, Nottingham Central Library, Sherwood Street, Nottingham; Department of MSS, University Library, University Park, Nottingham; Nottinghamshire County Library, Trent Bridge House, Fox Road, West Bridgford; Southwell Minster Library, Southwell.

Parish Registers and Indexes (*see* comment under COUNTY) Of the 220 ancient parishes, virtually all the registers are at the CRO, and the Society of Genealogists has copies of about 200. The FHS has a marriage index in hand; and Pallot's Marriage Index covers 168 registers, mostly from 1790. The INTERNATIONAL GENEALOGICAL INDEX (IGI) treats over 200 registers. The Bishops' Transcripts are at Southwell Minster Library, and on microfilm at the CRO.

Marriage Licence Records These are at the University MSS Department. The Society of Genealogists has indexes from 1754.

Wills before 1858, proved in the following courts, are at the CRO:

Archdeaconry Court of Nottingham
Manorial Courts of Dale Abbey, Edwinstowe, Gringley-on-the-Hill, and Mansfield

Peculiar (Pec.) Court of the Vicar of Kinoulton
Pec. Court of the Chapter of the Collegiate Church of Southwell

As the county lay in the Diocese of York, wills could be proved in the Consistory Court of York, and as it lay in the Province of York they could also be proved in the Prerogative Courts of York and Canterbury.

Non-parochial Registers The registers of 48 chapels are at the Public Record Office (PRO), Chancery Lane, London, and the IGI covers a similar number.

Census Returns These are at the PRO, Portugal Street, London, and at the County Library.

Memorial Inscriptions The FHS has transcription in hand, and the Society of Genealogists has a few transcripts.

Heralds'Visitation Pedigrees have been printed for 1530 and 1662-4.

Novel Disseisin, Writ of A claim of recent dispossession.

Numbered Houses Until the middle of the eighteenth century, houses in town streets were identified by overhanging signs, a custom that survives today for public houses. However, in 1708 the houses in Prescot Street on the south side of the Tenter Ground in Goodman's Fields, London, were given numbers; and in the period 1721-7, Fire Insurance Company records show that two insured houses, one in Ropemaker's Alley and one in Burr Street, had numbers, which implies that those streets were numbered. Cornhill in the City of London also had numbers early in that century.

In 1762 it was ordered that all overhanging signs in London and Westminster be removed. Even so, the local directories of the 1760s show that only about thirty houses were numbered (of which six were in Prescot Street); another seventeen in the Inns of Court and Chancery were almost certainly staircase numbers. Then an Act of Parliament of 1767 authorised the numbering of houses in the City and its liberties, and Westminster and neighbouring parishes followed suit. The directory of 1770 showed three-quarters of the capital's houses as numbered, a practice that soon spread to provincial towns. At first, many streets were numbered consecutively up one side and down the other, but the alternative practice of putting odd numbers on one side and even numbers on the other eventually prevailed. However, some streets are still numbered in the old way. In many, the numbering has been changed from time to time, making the accurate identification of properties difficult, and in country districts the house numbers can be those in the estate books, and not consecutive at all.

Numerals Until the end of the seventeenth century, figures were normally written in Roman numerals. These were shown as: j, ij, iij, iiij, v, vj, vij, viij, ix, x, l, c, d, m, etc. The j took the place of i when it was the last (i.e. right-hand) figure of the numeral; the v and x usually appeared as written in Secretary Hand (*see* HANDWRITING).

Until the end of the first half of the sixteenth century, dates were indicated by the REGNAL YEAR of the sovereign. After about 1560, it became usual to add the year of the Christian Era, which, except when written in words, was always shown in Arabic numerals.

Nuncupative Made by word of mouth only; an expression used to designate wills that were neither written nor signed nor sealed by the deceased. They are more fully described under WILL.

Oath ex officio mero A statement on oath required by an ecclesiastical court from an accused person, not because of an accusation against him but at the pleasure of the court. A great cause of discontent with ecclesiastical courts.

Obeisance In sixteenth- and seventeenth-century records this word can mean Jurisdiction.

Obit A mass for a deceased person celebrated on the anniversary of his death; often mentioned in pre-Reformation wills.

Octave An eight-day period, beginning with the festival day (e.g. Monday to Monday). The term derives from the Latin word for eight, but it was customary, in measuring a period of time, to include the first day (or year) as well as the last. Sometimes written as *utas*.

Office Suit *or* **Ex Officio Suit** An action brought against a person in an ecclesiastical court by the court itself, and not by another party.
See also ECCLESIASTICAL COURT.

Official The deputy of a diocesan bishop or archdeacon to act in judicial matters. In that capacity he would preside over the ecclesiastical court. The Official Principal was the deputy of an archbishop (*see* VICAR GENERAL). Mention of the Official by name is often made in probate acts.

One-name Societies Genealogists tracing families with fairly uncommon surnames often note all references to persons of the name, in case there is a common ancestor. This has led to the formation of a number of one-name societies and correspondence groups.

In 1975, under the auspices of the Federation of Family History Societies, Mr Frank Higinbottam started a *Register of One-Name Studies*. Its purpose was to act as a clearing house by recording the names and addresses of persons or societies specialising in research on all bearers of a single surname, so that enquirers could be referred to them. The Register covers: (i) constituted societies in the UK; (ii) family correspondence groups in the UK; (iii) individual researchers specialising in one surname; (iv) overseas groups. News of the register attracted wide interest, and resulted in the recording of a considerable volume of one-name research. Persons and societies specialising in certain names have formed a Guild of One-Name Studies, and the names registered are listed twice a year in *Family History News and Digest*, published by the Federation of Family History Societies. The address of the Guild's Registrar is c/o Box 6, 14 Charterhouse

Buildings, Goswell Road, London EC1M 7BA. He will supply an up-to-date register, and answer reply-paid enquiries on the registered names and their variants.

Oral Family History The first step in genealogy — provided the start has not been left until too late — is to get elderly relatives talking about long-deceased members of the family whom they once knew personally, or heard talked of. Use a tape-recorder if one is available, provided it does not inhibit the flow of recollections. Failing that, start by drawing up, with their help and on a large sheet of paper, a family tree of the generations they knew, so that the facts revealed can be quickly noted under each name. Try to obtain as many as possible of the items essential on every family tree, i.e. dates and places of births, marriages and deaths, occupations and spouses. Afterwards, write up your notes in narrative form under the heading 'Conversation with . . .', together with the date. Ask your informant to check it, and it will almost certainly inspire additional remembrances. Do not confine your enquiries to one relative. Each one will add something to the record, and their accounts may not agree. Ancestral legends will be repeated, 'It was always said that our family . . .'. Such tales may have a core of fact within an accumulation, over the generations, of unconsciously added romance. As much of the oral information as possible should be checked against documentary evidence.

The Oral History Society, Sociology Department, University of Essex, Colchester CO4 3SQ, issues a journal, *Oral History*.

For further reading, see *Oral Evidence and the Family Historian*, by Lawrence Taylor.

Orator In legal documents a plaintiff or complainant referred to himself as 'your orator', i.e. petitioner; from a Latin word meaning 'prayer'.

Ordeal A medieval method of deciding a legal suit. For knights, ordeal was by combat ('appeal of battle'); for freemen, by fire; and for villeins, by water. In both the latter, success for the defendant was more frequent than failure. The practice fell into discredit at the end of the twelfth century, but continued to be used in criminal cases until it was abolished by papal decree in 1212.

Ordinary (i) In civil law, an official who had jurisdiction in his own right, not by deputation. In canon law, an ecclesiastical judge.

(ii) A bishop's appointee to a prison. It was he who heard condemned criminals read the Neck Verse (*see* BENEFIT OF CLERGY) and, if they failed, prepared them for death.

(iii) A public eating-house.

(iv) A collection of coats of arms classified by charges, of which the earliest was Cotgrove's *A Roll of Arms Compiled in the Reign of Edward III, 1337-40*, edited by Sir Harris Nicholas in 1829. A later one is Papworth's *Ordinary of British Armorials*.

Orphans Young children left orphaned by poor parents fell on the charity of their parish, and evidence of them will be found in the accounts of either the churchwardens or the Overseers of the Poor, now mostly deposited at county record offices. After 1835, Poor Law Guardians set up and administered orphanages, the records of which are also at county record offices. In due course all such children were apprenticed to trades or husbandry (*see* APPRENTICES). In the nineteenth century, some were shipped in parties overseas. Some institutions for homeless children were founded by wealthy benefactors, and for information on these *see* BARNARDO'S HOMES, DR and FOUNDLINGS. Not all orphans were poor; in 1540 the Court of Wards was formed to appoint and supervise guardians for children whose deceased fathers had held land of the king in chief. Such minors were a source of profit to both the king and their guardians.

See also WARDS AND LIVERIES, COURT OF.

Outfangthef The right to summon local people to court, charged with committing theft outside the court's jurisdiction.

Outlawry The punishment for anyone who either fled from justice, or refused to appear in court to answer for a transgression. The term means exclusion from all benefits and from protection of the law. From the Conquest until Tudor times an outlaw might be lawfully killed by anyone who met him, but if he was captured alive his fate was in the king's hands. To make a defendant aware of his summons to court, three Writs of Capias would be issued against him and, failing his appearance, a Writ of Exigend requiring the sheriff to call on him in five successive courts. If he still did not appear, the judgement of outlawry was pronounced. Outlawry entailed the forfeiture of goods and chattels, and the forfeiture of lands to the Crown for a year and a day, after which time they escheated to the superior lord. Women could not properly be outlawed, because they were not sworn to the law by taking the oath of allegiance in the Court Leet, so they were said to be waived.

Overseer of the Poor

An honorary parochial post. Before the Reformation the care of the poor was the responsibility of the Church, i.e. of the monasteries and the parish clergy. In fact, one-third of the parson's tithes were intended to be given by him to the poor. When the monasteries were dissolved, the problem of relieving poverty became acute, and the clergy were ordered to collect alms for poor people. An Act of 1572 created Alms Collectors and Super-visors of the Labour of Rogues and Vagabonds in each parish. People who would not give alms voluntarily could be compulsorily assessed. In 1597 the two offices were combined under the title of Overseer of the Poor, an official whose appointment required the approval of the Justices of the Peace.

By the great *Poor Law Act* of 1601, churchwardens became ex-officio Overseers of the Poor, together with those approved by the Justices. One of their number was appointed executive officer of the Overseers and looked after the funds raised by parochial rates. From 1691, the Overseer was obliged to keep a record of his disbursements and distribution of clothing, etc. His rate books list the sums collected from parishioners according to the value of their properties. In 1772 an Act was passed enabling parishes to buy or rent premises for workhouses, and to employ a workhouse-keeper. From 1790, such work-houses had to submit to inspection by Justices of the Peace.

In 1834, parochial responsibility for the poor was ended. Parishes were amalgamated for such purposes into Poor Law Unions, governed by elected Poor Law Guardians with a property qualification. At national level the system was controlled by Poor Law Commissioners.

See also BASTARDY; RATE BOOKS; SETTLEMENT.

Oxfordshire

Since 1974 the county includes the northern part of the ancient county of Berkshire. The Oxfordshire Family History Society (FHS) holds regular meetings and issues a journal, *The Oxfordshire Family Historian*. Enquiries should be sent c/o The Federation of Family History Societies, 31 Seven Star Road, Solihull, West Midlands B91 2BZ, marked 'Please forward' and enclosing a stamped self-addressed envelope.

Record Repositories Oxford County Record Office, County Hall, New Road, Oxford; Department of Western MSS, Bodleian Library, Oxford (tel: 0865.44675); University Archives, Bodleian Library, Oxford; Oxford Central Library, Oxford.

Parish Registers and Indexes (*see* comment under COUNTY) Most parishes have deposited their registers at the Department of Western MSS of the Bodleian Library, and the Society of Genealogists has copies of over 200. Pallot's Marriage Index covers sixteen, mostly from 1790 or 1800. The FHS has published a marriage index of the City of Oxford, 1813-37, and has coverage of the rest of the county in hand. The INTERNATIONAL GENEALOGICAL INDEX (IGI) includes about 200 registers, and the Bodleian Library has a copy. The Bishops' Transcripts are at the Department of Western MSS of the Bodleian Library.

Marriage Licence Records These, too, are at the Department of Western MSS of the Bodleian Library.

Wills before 1858, proved in the following courts, are at the Department of Western MSS of the Bodleian Library:

> Consistory and Archdeaconry Courts of Oxford
> Archdeaconry Court of Berkshire
> Peculiar (Pec.) Courts of Banbury, Dorchester, Longford, Monks Risborough, Thame,

Cropredy, Harley and Harnton, and the Dean and Canons of Windsor in Wantage Manorial Court of Sibford

Wills proved in the Court of the Chancellor of the University are in the University Archives, Bodleian Library.

As the county lay in the Province of Canterbury, wills could also be proved in the Prerogative Court of Canterbury.

Non-parochial Registers The registers of 26 chapels are at the Public Record Office (PRO), Chancery Lane, London. The IGI covers a similar number.

Census Returns These are at the PRO, Portugal Street, London, and at Oxford Central Library.

Memorial Inscriptions The Society of Genealogists has transcripts from a few churchyards, and the FHS has transcribed about one hundred.

Heralds' Visitation Pedigrees have been printed for 1574-5, 1634 and 1668.

The Oxfordshire Record Society has made a number of historical records available in print.

Oxgang One-eighth of a ploughland. Also called a bovate.

Oyez and Terminer, Commission of Sometimes written 'determiner'. Originally an order 'to hear and decide' a specific case reported to King's Bench, but in the late thirteenth century, when Commissions of Eyre were being less frequently issued, the king empowered justices of the royal courts to hear all charges of felony in the provinces. By the sixteenth century, the Commission was usually combined with one of Gaol Delivery.

P

Palaeography The study of the rules of old handwriting, scribal practices and conventions, and the peculiarities associated with specific places and periods, resulting in the ability to identify writers and to date and place the provenance of a document from the evidence of the script. A word often misused in genealogical circles to mean merely the study of how to read old handwritings.

See also HANDWRITING; SECRETARY HAND.

Palatine Counties Counties over which Norman magnates and their successors possessed royal rights and jurisdiction, the word 'palatine' meaning 'pertaining to a palace', or 'to a high officer of a palace'. The original counties were those along the Welsh and Scottish borders, ruled by the Earls of Chester, Shrewsbury and Hereford, and the Prince Bishop of Durham.

In granting English manors to his chief followers, the Conqueror's policy was to scatter each earl's lands over the whole country, which had the dual effect of identifying their interests with those of the country and of preventing their acquiring undue power in any one area. However, for reasons of national defence he made exceptions along the country's borders; hence the unusual concentrations of power in the palatine counties.

Palimpsest (i) A sheet of parchment or paper that has been written upon twice, the first writing having been erased to make room for the second.

(ii) A memorial brass that has been taken up and engraved on the reverse side with another figure.

Pallot's Index of Marriages and Births This index was begun in 1818 by a firm of record agents specialising in chancery work and intestacy cases, and was continued by their successors, among whom were Messrs Pallot & Co. It was finally purchased for the Institute of Heraldic and Genealogical Studies. The index of marriages in London's parish registers was augmented by London births and obituaries, culled from the *Gentleman's Magazine*, and by English marriages, births and deaths overseas. Unfortunately nearly all records except the London marriages were destroyed during the Second World War. What remain are the marriages of 101 of the 103 ancient parishes of the City of London, of many Middlesex parishes, and a variable number from registers of other counties. There are also about 30,000 baptisms from a small number of London and provincial registers.

A catalogue is available, listing the parishes included. Enquiries should be addressed to the Institute of Heraldic and Genealogical Studies, Northgate, Canterbury.

See also under county headings.

Palmer A wandering religious votary who had visited the Holy Land, and carried a branch of palm in token thereof. Not the same as a pilgrim, since the latter was making one particular journey, whereas the palmer was a constant and homeless traveller.

Pannage (i) The right to feed pigs in the woods of a manor.

(ii) A payment made for that right.

Papers The term for a punishment of a convicted offender by exhibiting him, perhaps in a pillory, with papers pinned to him specifying his offence.

Paragraph Pedigree Also called a Narrative Pedigree. The system of setting out a family descent in indented and numbered paragraphs. This is the system employed in Burke's *Peerage* and *Landed Gentry*. For showing a number of collateral lines, it is the method most economical of space, but it does not have the merit of instant clarity.

Parcenary A type of tenure of Norman origin by which a younger brother held his fief of the elder, and the elder of the superior lord.

Parchment *see* **Membrane** *and* **Vellum**

Parish A township or group of townships under the administration of a single priest who was originally paid by tithes on the produce of the parochial area, and who was under the supervision of a bishop. In England, parishes date back to before the Conquest, being first mentioned in AD 970, but did not appear in their full form until the second half of the fourteenth century. The Tudor monarchs found parishes a more practical instrument of local government than the manor, and began to place civil responsibilities on them, of which the most important was the care of the poor. In the south of England, ecclesiastical parishes served adequately as civil parishes, but in the north and west the larger parishes had to be divided into two or more civil parishes, each centering on a chapel of ease.

During the seventeenth century the parish in its civil aspect gradually replaced the manor as the unit of local government. In the early nineteenth century the great increase in population, and the growth of new industrial towns, forced the sub-dividing of many ecclesiastical parishes and the building of additional churches; and by 1851 the total number of churches and chapels had risen to 13,854.

Parish Registers Before the Reformation, some monasteries noted births occurring in the leading local families, but there was no standard, countrywide system for keeping such records. In 1536 an attempt was made to start parish registers, but it finally became effective only as a result of a mandate of 5 September, 1538. The registers were to be entered up weekly, and were often kept on loose sheets of paper, so it is not surprising that only about 800 registers still exist from as early as 1538. In 1555 and 1557, under Mary I, bishops were required to see that the sponsors were named in baptismal entries, but this ceased under the next reign. In 1598, Queen Elizabeth approved an order of 25 October, 1597, that registers be kept in parchment books and that all the old register entries be copied into such volumes. The clergy were, however, given the option of starting from 1558 (the beginning of the Queen's reign), so a number of registers now start from that date. The paper originals have nearly all disappeared. In the transcription, errors naturally crept in. From 1598, copies of all entries had to be sent annually, at Easter, to the bishop's registry (*see* BISHOPS' TRANSCRIPTS).

Parish registers, once kept in church vestries, are now being deposited in increasing numbers at the county record offices. For lists of these, consult *Original Parish Registers in Record Offices and Libraries* and its Supplements (Local

Population Studies). Also, thousands of registers have been copied and can be consulted in the library of the Society of Genealogists. A *National Index of Parish Registers*, in several area-volumes, has been published by Phillimore.

Parish incumbents are entitled to charge for allowing a search to be made in their registers. Fees for searches made by the incumbent are by agreement.

Baptismal Registers In some early registers, christenings, marriages and burials are all entered on the same pages, in chronological order. Usually the three were kept in the same book but in separate parts; sometimes on alternate pages. In these cases the dates shown on the cover do not necessarily apply to the christenings. Entries up to 1598 or 1603 are usually neatly written because they were deliberately copied, as mentioned above. After that the handwriting degenerates. In the sixteenth and early seventeenth centuries, entries are often in Latin (see below).

Between 1645 and 1660 many people did not have their children baptized because of their disapproval of the changed rite under the Commonwealth. This is unfortunate, because under that regime the date of birth was ordered to be entered in the christening register, and also the parents' names. On 22 September, 1653, the duty of registration was transferred by the 'Barebones Parliament' from the clergy to an official called the Parish Register (or Registrar, as we should say now), elected by the ratepayers. A fee of one shilling had to be paid, which proved another disincentive, and, to make matters worse, the registers were very laxly kept at this period. After the Anglican Restoration of 1660, many of the unchristened babies were baptized as older children.

Towards the end of the seventeenth century, many children were being baptized by dissenting ministers and so were not officially recorded. Because of this, in 1694 notification of birth to the Anglican incumbent was made compulsory under penalty of a fine. A tax was charged for registration, plus a fee of six pence to the incumbent, even if no baptism took place. Many clergy ignored this order, and in 1706 it was revoked.

During the late seventeenth century and all through the eighteenth, baptisms were often perfomed at home, and these sometimes went unregistered. However, occasionally a child's christening might be entered twice in the register — once for his or her private baptism at home, and again on public reception into the church. On the whole, christening registers have been less reliably kept than those for marriages and burials.

A later deterrent to the registration of baptisms, especially of poor children, was a tax of three pence levied between 1783 and 1794.

As a result of George Rose's Act of 1812, separate printed baptismal books were started from 1 January, 1813, and there were spaces in these for entering the names, and places of residence, of the parents, and the occupation of the father. Illegitimacy was always mentioned, and in such cases the fathers' names were given only if paternity was admitted. Foundlings were often christened with the name of the saint to whom the church was dedicated, or of the street in which they were found.

Civil registration of births began on 1 July, 1837 (*see* GENERAL REGISTER OF BIRTHS, DEATHS AND MARRIAGES). In June of that year, owing to some misunderstanding of the *Civil Registration Act*, there was, in some places, a rush of unchristened people to undergo baptism before 1 July, and many of these will have been adults. When civil registration began, no penalties were exacted for non-observance, and in consequence there are some omissions. Baptismal registers therefore continue to be of use until 1874, when fines were prescribed for non-registration.

It was a common custom for a young wife to return to her mother for her first confinement, so the baptism of the eldest child of a marriage will often be found in the register of the mother's parish.

Marriage Registers Before 1929, a girl could marry at the age of 12, and a boy at 14, but a parent's consent was required. Since that date the lower age limit for both has been set at 16.

An Act of 29 September, 1654, took marriages out of the hands of the clergy and gave them as a responsibility to the Justices of the Peace.

A baptismal register page from the sixteenth century. *Chertsey Parish Church*

Vicesimo nono die mensis eiusdem Sepultus fuit Thomas [?] page

Decimo quarto die mensis Decembris Sepulta fuit Johanna vxor
Thome Tickner /

Decimo nono die eiusdem mensis Sepultus fuit Richardus Dean

№ 2   [Secundo Anno Regni Elizabeth]

Nono die mensis Januarij baptizata fuit Maria filia Joh̄is Rogers

Vicesimo die eiusdem mensis baptizata fuit Johanna filia Willmi
Stranger /

Vicesimo secundo die mensis ffebruarij baptizata fuit Anna filia
Henrici Cheman /

Vicesimo quarto die eiusdem mensis baptizatus fuit Willmus filius
Richardi Cooke /

Primo die mensis marcij baptizatus fuit Joh̄es filius Nicholai
Turowe /

Decimo Septo die eiusdem mensis Sepulta fuit fflorentia filia [?]

Vicesimo quinto die mensis eiusdem baptizata fuit Elizabeth filia
Richardi Eliott generosi /   Anno Dni 1560

Septo die mensis Aprilis Sepulta fuit Johanna Chennell vidua

Octavo die eiusdem mensis Sepultus fuit Willmus Mingell /

Vicesimo primo die mensis maij baptizaverant Willmus Lange et
Margareta Tixford /

Vicesimo Tertio die mensis Maij baptizatus fuit Georgius filius
Georgij Ingilmore /

Vicesimo quinto die mensis eiusdem Sepultus fuit Richardus Cooke

Vicesima die mensis eiusdem Sepultus Thomas Stone /

Quarto decimo die eiusdem mensis baptizatus fuit Thomas filius
Joh̄is Stone /

Vicesimo nono die mensis eiusdem Sepulta fuit Anna Rogers vidua

Primo die mensis Julij Sepulta fuit Johanna Lange vidua

Vicesimo primo die mensis Julij baptizata fuit Dorothea filia [?]

January y' 3'

3	Ann y daughter of William Hammilton baptized.
7	Elizabeth y daughter of John May baptized.
12	Elizabeth y daughter of Zachariah ffloodgate baptized.
28	Ann the daughter of John Riggs baptized.
Eodem	Elizabeth y daughter of Ann Wellelove (a bastard) baptized.
Eodem	Edward the son of Edward Goddard baptized.
31	Mary the daughter of John Adams baptized.

ffebruary y' 11th

11	Ann Allenby y daughter of Sarah Mullen (a bastard) baptized.
Eodem	Hannah the daughter of Robert Hurst baptized.
18	Sarah y daughter of Joseph Peirson baptized.
25	William the son of William Cutt baptized.
28	William y son of William Mitchel baptized.

March y' 2'

2	Benjamin y son of Benjamin Digsby baptized.
Eodem	Ann y daughter of Nathaniel Novell baptized.
4	John the son of Thomas Huntingford baptized.
7	Mary y daughter of John Light baptized.
8	Mary y daughter of Thomas Ranbly baptized.
9	Jacob y son of Jacob Sizeman baptized.
Eodem	John the son of Mr John Millest baptized.
Eodem	Joel and Isaac twins of John Goring baptized.
10	Jane y daughter of Daniel ffeild baptized.
11	George the son of John Tyler baptized.
Eodem	Mary y daughter of Daniel Beard baptized.
15	Richard y son of William Edmead baptized.
22	William the son of William Atfeild baptized.

April y' 22d 1739

22	John y son of John Southy baptized.
Eodem	Jane y daughter of John Smith baptized.
23	John y son of Joseph Hammilton baptized.
25	Jacob y son of John ffeild baptized.
29	James y son of John Sedgwick baptized.

216

LEFT Baptismal register entries of 1739, and RIGHT a baptismal register page for 1831. Illegitimate children were always entered as such. *Chertsey Parish Church*

BAPTISMS solemnized in the Parish of _Chertsey_ in the County of _Surrey_ in the Year 18_31_

When Baptized.	Child's Christian Name.	Parents Name. Christian.	Surname.	Abode.	Quality, Trade, or Profession.	By whom the Ceremony was performed.
1831. Sept. 11th Born Aug. 10th No. 49.	Charles	Benjamin & Mary	Thorn	Chertsey	Carpenter	R Coulthard offg. Curate
Sept. 11th Born Aug. 23rd No. 50.	Eliza	Henry & Harriett	Monk	Chertsey	Labourer	R Coulthard offg. Curate
Sept. 11th Born Aug. 18th No. 51.	Albert	George & Susannah	White	Chertsey	Tailor	R Coulthard offg. Curate
Sept. 15th Born Aug. 9th No. 52.	Sarah	Isaac & Caroline	Hyde	Chertsey	Labourer	R Coulthard offg. Curate
Sept. 16th Born Aug. 15th No. 53.	Richard	Ann Illegitimate	Chandler	Chertsey		R Coulthard offg. Curate
Sept. 18th Born Aug. 21st No. 54.	Emma	Richard & Sarah Celia	Paice	Chertsey	Labourer	R Coulthard offg. Curate
Sept. 25th Born Aug. 26th No. 55.	James	Richard & Sarah	West	Chertsey	Labourer	R Coulthard offg. Curate
Sept. 25th Born Aug. 28th No. 56.	William	Richard & Jane	Smithers	Chertsey	Labourer	R Coulthard offg. Curate

However, these civil marriages were disapproved by many of the more devout, and such couples might get themselves married by their parish clergy, or even by ejected Anglican clergymen, in which case the ceremonies would not be registered. Also at this time, some contiguous parishes were combined for registration purposes to enable them to employ a joint Parish Register (Registrar). On the other hand, some marriages at this time, and also later, were registered in two places — the parish where they took place, and the parish of residence of one of the parties. During the Interregnum, registration was very laxly carried out, but at the Restoration in 1660 marriage and its registration by the clergy were resumed and entries became more regular. Civil marriages already contracted after market-place banns were legalised, and the children of such marriages legitimised. Between 1698 and 1703, taxes were charged on the registration of marriages, and this led to gaps in the record for poorer families.

Until 1754, marriage by affirmation before witnesses, but without ecclesiastical rites and unregistered, was nevertheless recognised as valid by the law, but Lord Hardwicke's *Act for the Better Preventing of Clandestine Marriages*, effective from 25 March, 1754, instituted marriage register books separate from those for baptisms and burials. It also required banns books to be kept. Entries showed marital status and parishes of residence, and had to be signed by both parties and by witnesses. They follow a prescribed, usually printed, form. Also, marriages had to be performed in licensed buildings, which were always the churches and chapels of the Church of England. From this law only Quakers and Jews were exempted.

The *Stamp Act* of 1783 (effective 1 October) charged a duty of three pence on all registrations, with the same result as the earlier tax. It was repealed in 1794. Between 1795 and 1820, parochial registration is said to have virtually collapsed.

In 1813, George Rose's Act introduced new columnar forms for the registers, giving the incumbent less freedom for adding his own, often useful, pieces of information, but ensuring the recording of the bridegroom's occupation, the marital status of both parties and their parishes of residence, with signatures of the parties and witnesses.

From 1837, when civil registration began, marriages could once more be performed in Roman Catholic and Nonconformist houses of worship, but had by law to be carried out in the presence of a registrar. Parish marriage registers are now kept in duplicate, the second copy being sent at the end of each quarter to the District Superintendent Registrar, who sends it to the Registrar General.

There has always been a tendency for marriages to take place in the parish of the bride, rather than that of the bridegroom, but sometimes in neither. In the last case, the researcher should look for a marriage licence mentioning a specific church, and, failing that, a marriage entry in the parish register of the market town nearest to the couple's homes.

Until about 1642 there were 'close seasons' of the year when few marriages took place. These were: Advent to St Hilary's Day (13 January), 41-47 days; Septuagesima to Low Sunday, 10 weeks; Rogation Sunday to Trinity Sunday, 3 weeks.

Over the years the form of the marriage entry has changed a good deal, but the researcher is likely to come across three main types: *Early* 'John Smith and Jane Brown, nupt.' (but some sixteenth-century entries made no mention of the bride); *After 1754* 'John Smith, of Mansfield, nailer, aged 28 years, bachelor, and Jane Brown, of Belper, aged 25, spinster', plus the signatures or marks of both parties and the witnesses; *From 1813* 'John Smith, nailer, of the Parish of Mansfield in the County of Nottingham, bachelor, and Jane Brown, of this Parish, spinster, were married in this church by Banns/Licence with the consent of James Brown, this fifteenth day of August in the year 1820, By me, John Austen, Rector. In the presence of Mary Smith, John Jones. Signed (by the parties and witnesses).'

Marriages after 1 July, 1837, are more easily found in the General Register, which contains copies of the register entries.

The marriage register of a Surrey parish for the years 1609-21. The first three entries are written in Secretary Hand, the rest in an angular form of Italic (see HANDWRITING). *Courtesy Guildford Muniment Room*

Anno Domi 1609.

Richard Robinson ⎫ were married the 25th Day of
Joan Akingam ⎬ Septemb.

John Bishow ⎫ married the 2th Day of October
Anne Hawmon ⎬

Anno Domi 1610.

Edward Humphrie ⎫ were married the 24th day of June. Anno
Sarah Woode ⎬

Anno Domi: 1611.

Anno Domini. 1611 et
Regis Jacobi 9°.

1. George Steere and Joane Smalpeece were married in the Parish Church of
St Saviours in Southwarke the 17th day of Aprill. Anno Domi: 1611
2. John Bixley of Capell and Marie Terill were married the 22th of April
3. John Weller and Elenor White were married the 28th of Aprill
4. John Woden and Margerie Steere widdow were married the 29th of July
5. John Aunsell of Horsham & Elioner Gardiner widdow were married Octob

Anno Domini. 1612.

Anno Dom: 1612. et
Regis Jacobi 10°.

1. Thomas Demet of Horne & Margaret Milles were Maried Maii 11
2. William Constable of Capell & Susan Willet were married July 27.
3. Thomas Mathew of Charlewode & Elizabeth Francis were married August 23
4. Robert Chatfeilde and Agnes Gardener were married Septemb: 2

Anno Dom: 1613.

Anno Dom: 1613. et
Regis Jacobi 11°.

1. Thomas Lifford and Elizabeth Elliot were married Maii 9°.
2. Richard Taylour, and Elizabeth Rossie were married Junij 13°.

Anno Dom: 1614.

Anno Dom: 1614. &
Regis Jacobi 12°.

1. Thomas Genner of Leigh and Margerie Kerrington widdow were married Maii
2. James Edwardes of Reigate & Elizabeth Mischwoke widdow were Maried Jul

Anno Dom: 1615.

Anno Dom: 1615. et
Regis Jacobi 13°.

1. John Constable of Capell & Susan Wonham were married July 3.
2. Philip Forrell of Heild & Elizabeth Richman were married July 16.
3. Henrie Penfolde & Margaret Tepsell were married Janua 10°.

An: Dom: 1616.

Anno Dom: 1616. et
Regis Jacobi 14°.

1. Henrie Swan of Ockley & Elizabeth Edwards widdow were married Maii 29.
2. Thomas Dimocke & Lydia Dudley were married Septemb: 1°.
3. Thomas White & Katherine Francis were married Februa: 23.

Anno Dom: 1617. et
Regis Jacobi 15.

1. Edward Chatfeilde of Worth & Joane Daniel were married July 14.

An: Dom: 1618.

1. William Wright & Marie Brooker were married Maii 17.
2. John Smith & Hester Robinson were married Maii 20.
3. Walter Longast & Margaret Nie widdow were married Junij 23.

An: Dom: 1619.

1. Mathew Bishop & Sarah West were married Sept: 21°.

An: Dom: 1620.

1. Nicholas Ch..

Marriage register entries written in Latin, as shown
ABOVE, are unusual at such a late date as 1720. By 1770,
entries are recorded in a printed book RIGHT. Of the
contracting parties on page 109, only Isaac Collins and
Sarah Pais could write their names. *Chertsey Parish
Church*

Nº 105.

John Curtis   of [this] Parish
and Ann Roberts   of [the]
same   were
Married in this [Church] by [Banns]
this Fourth   Day of October   in the Year One Thousand Seven Hundred
and Seventy eight   by me   Ste. Miller [Minister]
This Marriage was { John Curtis his Mark X
solemnized between Us { Ann Roberts her Mark X
In the { William Roberts his Mark X
Presence of { Wm Touch

Nº 106.

Thomas Fletcher   of [this] Parish
and Mary Wells   of [the]
same   were
Married in this [Church] by [Banns]
this Nineteenth   Day of October   in the Year One Thousand Seven Hundred
and Seventy eight   by me Cuthebert Potter   [Minister]
This Marriage was { Thomas Fletcher his Mark X
solemnized between Us { Mary Wells her Mark X
In the { Richard Brown
Presence of { Wm Touch

Nº 107.

Isaac Collins   of [this] Parish
and Sarah Pais   of [the]
same   were
Married in this [Church] by [Banns]
this 25th   Day of October   in the Year One Thousand Seven Hundred
and Seventy eight   by me   Ste. Miller [Minister]
This Marriage was { Isaac Collins
solemnized between Us { Sarah Pais
In the { William Pais
Presence of { Wm Touch

Nº 108.

Benjamin Adams   of [this] Parish
and Ann Farley   of [the]
same   were
Married in this [Church] by [Banns]
this 25th   Day of October   in the Year One Thousand Seven Hundred
and Seventy eight   by me   Ste. Miller [Minister]
This Marriage was { Benjamin Adams his Mark X
solemnized between Us { Ann Farley her Mark X
In the { John Gray
Presence of { Wm Touch

Before 1754, marriages are usually found in the same books as baptisms and burials, and can sometimes be found starting, upside down, on the last page of the book. Single entries may be mixed with those of baptisms and burials. Pages may have been bound in the wrong order, giving a wrong impression of date at first sight. Where the registers show gaps, the Bishops' Transcripts should be consulted.

A few parishes have espousal books recording betrothals. Until the early seventeenth century a betrothal was considered to have almost the validity of a marriage, and this may sometimes account for a first child being born 'rather early' after the marriage.

Before 1835, marriage with a deceased wife's sister was legal but against the canons of the Church, so some clergy would not perform the ceremony. Such marriages were 'voidable' but not 'null and void'. The 1835 *Marriage Act* recognised such marriages already contracted as legal, but from then on they were illegal until the *Deceased Wife's Sister Marriage Act* of 1907. *See also* BANNS OF MARRIAGE; ESPOUSAL.

Burial Registers Entries seldom identify the deceased, but the burial of a child is sometimes indicated by implication in the addition of the father's name (e.g. 'Martha, daughter of James Smith'), though such an entry may refer to a spinster living with her father. Early burials are often to be found entered among christenings and marriages, but are sometimes in separate sections of the same volume, and sometimes in separate volumes. Some incumbents only registered burials by Anglican rites, which excluded suicides, excommunicates, executed criminals and unbaptized children. Burials of still-born babies were seldom recorded.

After the *Toleration Act* of 1689, Nonconformist, Roman Catholic and Jewish cemeteries were opened, so that not all burials after that will be in the parish records. In any case, relatives were free to choose any parish for their burials, and everyone had the right of sepulchre in the parish in which he died. Occasionally the social status of the deceased is shown by the title, Mr, Mrs or Dame. Acts of 1666 and 1678 encouraged the wool trade by laying down that bodies were not to be buried wrapped in anything but wool, and a relative had to make an affidavit before a

justice, or, failing him, a clergyman, within eight days of the funeral, stating that the law had been complied with. In some parishes, at the conclusion of the burial service, the clergyman asked, 'Who makes the affidavit?' The making of a satisfactory reply was indicated in the register by the word Affidavit, or an abbreviation. Some parish incumbents recorded the affidavits in separate books. The Act was repealed in 1814, but by then was virtually a dead-letter.

Half of all burial entries are for infants, so that if a child is christened with the same name as his father, and there is a burial entry of the same name within a year of the christening, it is probably the child, not the father, who had died (*see* CHRISOM). During the periods 1694-1706 and 1783-94, when taxes were payable on registration, burials often went unregistered, though sometimes the incumbent obtained the relevant information from the undertaker or the coffin plate and made the entry without charge. Burials are more conscientiously recorded than baptisms, but less so than marriages. Those of infants were particularly liable to be omitted.

From 1 January, 1813, in accordance with George Rose's Act of 1812, burials had to be entered in separate books, under printed headings. These required the recording of the deceased's age and abode, so making the register much more useful to genealogists.

Parochial Registers and Records Measure 1978. As from 1 January, 1979, the following are the regulations laid down regarding parish registers.

> They are the property of the parochial church council of the parish concerned. Their custody is the responsibility of the incumbent, or, during a vacancy, of the churchwardens. However, parishes are required to deposit in a diocesan record office all records completed over one hundred years ago, unless they particularly wish to keep them, in which case they must conform to the following conditions: (a) the bishop must be asked for and give his consent; (b) the records shall be inspected every six years; (c) the records shall be kept in the church in a

---

RIGHT Page from a nineteenth-century burial register. *Chertsey Parish Church*

BURIALS in the Parish of _Chertsey_

in the County of _Surrey_   in the Year 18_29_

Name.	Abode.	When buried.	Age.	By whom the Ceremony was performed.
Mary Goring No. 1089.	Chertsey	Dec.ʳ 19ᵗʰ	67	C Pembroke Curate
Mary Gray No. 1090.	Chertsey	Dec.ʳ 19ᵗʰ	45	C Pembroke Curate
William Thomas White No. 1091.	Chertsey	Dec.ʳ 18ᵗʰ	3 months	C Pembroke Curate
Rebecca Baker No. 1092.	Chertsey	Dec.ʳ 27ᵗʰ	74	C Pembroke Curate
Charlotte Smith a foundling No. 1093.	Chertsey	Dec.ʳ 27ᵗʰ		C Pembroke Curate
Mary Moore No. 1094.	Chertsey	Dec.ʳ 28ᵗʰ	33	C Pembroke Curate
No. 1095.				
No. 1096.				

fire-proof and rust-proof cupboard, humidity and temperature of which must be checked once a week; (d) access for people wishing to see the registers is to be provided 'at all reasonable hours'; (e) fees may be charged for inspecting the registers. These fees are laid down in the Ecclesiastical Fees Order from time to time. At present, where a register is still in the custody of the incumbent, the following charges may be made to anyone undertaking his own search: £3 for the first hour, or part thereof; £2 for each subsequent hour. If an incumbent is asked to make a search on an enquirer's behalf, the fee should be agreed in advance.

The clergy are bound by certain other regulations:

The incumbent must supply certificates if requested. He is not legally bound (a) to permit the photographing of records, (b) to supply certificates on postal application, though this is normally done on payment of the appropriate fee, (c) to make searches on behalf of an enquirer, though he may consent to do this for such remuneration as may be agreed.

The most extensive catalogue of parish registers is the *National Index of Parish Registers*, mentioned above. A useful booklet with several supplements, listing 'Original Parish Registers in Record Offices and Libraries', is obtainable from Local Population Studies, Tawney House, Matlock, Derbyshire.

Latin Words and Phrases found in Parish Registers

Latin	English
ambo	both
annoque predicto	of the year aforesaid
baptizatus(-a) erat *baptizabatur* Abbrev: *bapt.*	was baptized
coelebs	bachelor
copulati sunt	were married (see also below)
creatura Christi	child of Christ (who died unnamed)
cum contione Abbrev: *cum cont.*	with a sermon
de hac parochia *de hujus parochie*	of this parish
die	on the ... day
dominus(-a) Abbrev: *dom.*	lord or sir (lady or dame)
duxit	led (in marriage). The word is then followed by the bride's name.
ejus	his or her (of him or her)
eques	knight
ex hac eadem parochia	of this same parish
filius(-a) Abbrev: *fil.*	son (daughter) The word is then followed by the parent's name in the genitive.
filius(-a) populi *filius(-a) vulgi* Abbrev: *fil. pop.*	bastard son (daughter) of a harlot
gemelli(-e)	twins (twin girls)
in comitatu Abbrev: *in com.*	in the county (of)
innuba	unmarried (woman)
juxta Christi	according to Christ (i.e. in a year starting 25 March)
in matrimonia *juncti sunt*	were joined in matrimony
mensis	of the month
meretrix	harlot
miles	knight
nothus	bastard
nupti fuerunt Abbrev: *nupt.*	were married
obiit Abbrev: *ob.*	died
parochie Abbrev: *par.*	of the parish (of)
per bannos	by banns
per licentiam Abbrev: *lic.*	by licence
puella	spinster
renatus(-a)	baptized
sepeliebatur *sepultus(-a) erat*	was buried Abbrev: *sep.*

solutus (-a)	bachelor (spinster)
stylo Angliae	in the style of England (i.e. in a year starting 25 March)
ut dicitur	as is said
ut fertur	(of a putative father)
uterque	both
uxor Abbrev: *ux.*	wife
viduus (-a) Abbrev: *vid.*	widower (widow)

Examples:

Johannes Smith, coelebs, parochie
John Smith, bachelor, of the parish of

Chertsey, et Anna Wilkes, soluta, de hac
Chertsey, and Anne Wilkes, spinster, of this

parochia, nupti fuerunt per licenciam.
parish, were married by licence.

Note that in baptismal entries the Latin names of the parents are in the genitive case, to mean 'of'. In the example given above, the parents Robertus et Maria Brown have their endings changed to -i and -e. Latin entries in a parish register do not mean that the persons were called by the Latin names shown. Robertus et Maria were Robert and Mary to their friends and relations. *See also* CHRISTIAN NAMES.

Parliamentary Papers Apart from the Bills and Acts of Parliament, there are four important classes of papers that constitute the records of Parliament. These are:

Command Papers Those laid before Parliament by government departments or *ad hoc* bodies such as royal commissions. They date from the reign of Charles I.

House Papers Those ordered by either House itself, dating from 1626. The best known of these are the Protestation Oath Returns of 1641/2.

Act Papers Those compulsorily laid before Parliament under the terms of an Act, dating from 1669.

Petitions These are the papers of greatest interest to family historians, since they were laid before Parliament by private individuals, groups of individuals, trade, local and other bodies, and bear the signatures or marks of at least the chief petitioners. They date from 1601. Because of the fire that destroyed much of the British parliamentary buildings in 1834, the seventeenth-, eighteenth- and early nineteenth-century papers of the Upper House are all that survive. They are available at the House of Lords Record Office in the Victoria Tower of the Houses of Parliament.
See also ACTS OF PARLIAMENT.

Parlour A ground-floor room off the hall for day-time use, including the entertainment of guests but not for meals. Sometimes used as a room for sleeping in when necessary.

Parochyn A parishioner.

Passenger Lists Lists of people leaving the United Kingdom by sea, other than the ships' crews, had to be supplied by commanders to the port officers. They were then sent to the Board of Trade for statistical purposes and passed finally, from 1890, to the Public Record Office, where they are to be found at Kew under BT.27, arranged under years, ports of departure and ships. They give each passenger's occupation, age and port of destination.

From 1906, there are helpful *Registers of Passenger Lists* (BT.32) showing, under each port, the names of ships and months of departure, with exact departure dates from 1920. But before 1908, registers exist only for Southampton, Bristol and Weymouth. For the period 1840-70, the American Customs House copies of lists of passengers to the United States are in the Fiscal Section, General Records Division, National Archives, Washington DC. For the period after 1907, *Manifests of Aliens arriving in the U.S.A.* are in the Library of Congress, Washington DC.
See also EMIGRANTS.

Passports Passports were not compulsory for travellers from the United Kingdom before the First World War. The *Register of Passports* at the Public Record Office, Kew (FO.610) begins in 1795 and is entered up in chronological order. There are *Indexes of Names* (FO.611) for the periods 1851-62 and 1874-98, when the Register ends. There is evidence that when a family or married couple travelled, the husband alone (being the applicant) was noted in the Register. Modern book passports with descriptions and photographs of the holders were introduced in 1921. For seventeenth-century travellers, *see* LICENCE TO PASS BEYOND THE SEAS.

Patent Rolls These comprise the registered copies of Letters Patent issued by the royal court of Chancery during the period 3 John to 9 George VI (their third and ninth regnal years, respectively). The original letters were issued 'open', with the Great Seal pendant from the foot. They dealt with national affairs (such as treaties); grants and confirmations of liberties, offices, privileges, lands and wardships to private persons and public bodies; charters of incorporation; licences for the election of bishops; and creations of nobility. The Rolls are at the Public Record Office, Chancery Lane, London, under reference C.66.
See also CHARTER; CLOSE ROLLS.

Patronymic A surname derived from that of a father or ancestor; e.g. Johnson, FitzWalter.
See also SURNAMES.

Peculiar An area within an archdeaconry but outside the jurisdiction of the archdeacon, and mostly of the bishop too. There were over two hundred such 'peculiar' areas and courts, mostly arising from properties of church dignitaries which lay within the dioceses of other bishops. They were the probate jurisdiction of either an archbishop, a bishop, a dean and chapter, dean, sub-dean, rector, vicar, or lord of a manor.

The area of a peculiar might be anything from a single township within a parish, to a parish or even a scattered group of parishes. The powers were taken from some of them by Acts of Parliament during the first four years of the reign of Queen Victoria, and in 1858 all probate powers were transferred from ecclesiastical to civil jurisdiction. Their probate records are now mostly to be found at the county record office of the county in which they were situated.
See also WILL.

Pedigree A term for charts showing the descents of human beings and pure-bred horses and dogs, but not with the same meaning in each case. The pedigree of an animal shows its descent from all known sires and dams, and so corresponds to the chart for human beings

known as either a Birth Brief, Total Descent or Blood Descent. A pedigree of a human being shows male-line descent, and is a synonym for the more popular term Family Tree.
See also NATIONAL PEDIGREE INDEX; PARAGRAPH PEDIGREE.

Peerage Under the Norman and early Angevin kings, all tenants-in-chief had the duty of attending the King's Court (*Curia Regis*). When a court was to be held, a general summons was issued, via the sheriffs, to the tenants-in-chief in each county. In time it became the custom to issue personal writs of summons to the larger land-holding barons and high ecclesiastics, thus distinguishing them above the rest. This arrangement was codified in *Magna Carta*. At first, however, the king felt no obligation to summon a baron just because he or his predecessor had been called to a previous court or Parliament, but gradually the 'greater barons' came to be summoned regularly and their heirs likewise, thus constituting an hereditary peerage.

From the reign of Richard II, any new peerage was formally conferred by Letters Patent, but writs of summons to Parliament continued to be sent out until they were abolished under Henry VIII. A patent defined the peerage and its mode of descent, mostly to direct male descendants by primogeniture, whereas the older peerages-by-writ descended to heirs general, i.e to females in the absence of heirs male (*see* ABEYANCE).

The peerage now consists of five ranks: Duke, Marquess, Earl, Viscount and Baron, and can be either of England, Scotland, Ireland, or the United Kingdom. Only a limited number of peers of Scotland and Ireland have the right to sit in the House of Lords.

Details of peers and their living relatives have been published periodically since 1713 in Debrett's *Peerage and Baronetage*. A later series, Burke's *Peerage, Baronetage and Knightage* (from 1826) gives paragraph pedigrees of all living peers and baronets, the information having been supplied by the persons themselves. The most reliable account of peerages, current, extinct, dormant and in abeyance, is to be found in the *Complete Peerage* (1887), edited by George Edward Cokayne. The full title is *The Complete Peerage of England, Scotland and Ireland, Great*

Britain and the United Kingdom, Extant, Extinct and Dormant. Addenda to this work to the present day are held at the House of Lords Record Office, reference Hist.Coll.116.

For further reading, see *A Dictionary of British Peerages*, by F.L. Leeson and C.L. Parry (1984).

Penance A penalty that could be imposed by the Church as a punishment for faults. Before the Reformation a penance might be the repetition of certain forms of devotion (such as Paternosters or Ave Marias), the payment of a sum of money, pilgrimage, fasting or flagellation, but after the Reformation the usual penalty was the Declaration Penance. This might be imposed as a result of the fault having been presented at an ecclesiastical visitation, or before an ecclesiastical court. It took the form of the reading of a statement containing an admission of the fault, a recognition of its sinfulness, penitence, and a prayer to be forgiven and helped never to fall into the same sin again. The guilty person had to stand up in church in the presence of the congregation and read it, clad in a white sheet but bare-headed, barefoot and bare-legged, and with a white wand in his hand. The incumbent of his parish then had to send in to the Registrar's office a certificate, signed by himself and the two churchwardens, stating that the penance had been duly performed. Certificates also survive to the effect that the offender was a person of sufficiently good general character to warrant the imposition of a private penance, i.e. one carried out before the incumbent and churchwardens, instead of before the congregation.

Perambulation A procession around the parish bounds was customarily carried out by the clergy, parish officers and schoolchildren at Rogationtide (the Monday, Tuesday and Wednesday before Ascension Day), or on Ascension Day (Holy Thursday) itself. The day of the perambulation was called Gang Day. Small boys were ceremonially beaten over boundary stones to impress their location upon their memories, and so ensure that their location would be passed on to future generations.

Perpetual Calendar A calendar for ascertaining the day of the week at any date. The following chart and its key cover the period 1500-1999.

The Perpetual Calendar consists of two parts, the Calendar and the Key. To find the day of the week on which a certain date fell, look up the year in the key and note the letter assigned to it. Then turn to the calendar and find that letter in the left-hand column. Look along the same horizontal line until you come to the column for the month you want. There, two days of the week are shown, one above the other. Above the calendar are shown the dates of nine 'Days of Each Month', in two rows, one above the other. The weekdays named under each month in the calendar fall on these dates; the upper ones on those in the upper row, and the lower ones on those in the lower. If the date in the month you are looking for is one of those shown, then it will fall on the corresponding weekday shown. If your date is not shown, find the date closest to it in the 'Days of Each Month', then count one or two days forward or backward until you come to the day you seek. The following example will make the procedure clear.

Example You want to know the day of the week on which 22 July 1572 fell. In the key you find that the letter against 1572 is E-. In the calendar, run your finger horizontally along from E- to the July column, where you will find Tuesday in the upper position and Friday in the lower. Then refer to the 'Dates of Each Month' and you will see that the 22nd (the date you want) is one of those shown in the upper row; so, that date corresponds with the weekday of July in the upper position, namely Tuesday. The 22 July, 1572, fell on a Tuesday.

If you had wanted 24 July, which is not shown among the 'Dates of Each Month', you would pick the nearest date — the 25th in the lower row. As that corresponds to the day in July shown in the lower position (Friday), then the 24th would be the day before, i.e. Thursday.

See pages 228 and 229-30.

Personalty Movable property that, on the death of the owner, did not in Common Law pass to the heir. It includes cattle, chattels, furniture, money, debts, investments and leases. It was always bequeathable by testament.

Days of Each Month: 1 8 15 22 29 / 4 11 18 25

	Jan	Feb	Mch	Apr	May	Jun	Jul	Aug	Sep	Oct	Nov	Dec
A	Su W	W S	W	Sa	M	Th	Sa	Tu	F	Su	W	F
A–	Sa Tu	Tu F	Sa	Tu	Th	Su	Tu	F	M	W	Sa	M
B	Sa Tu	Tu F	Tu	F	Su	W	F	M	Th	Sa	Tu	Th
B–	F M	M Th	F	M	W	Sa	M	Th	Su	Tu	F	Su
C	F M	M Th	M	Th	Sa	Tu	Th	Su	W	F	M	W
C–	Th Su	Su W	Th	Su	Tu	F	Su	W	Sa	M	Th	Sa
D	Th Su	Su W	Su	W	F	M	W	Sa	Tu	Th	Su	Tu
D–	W Sa	Sa Tu	W	Sa	M	Th	Sa	Tu	F	Su	W	F
E	W Sa	Sa Tu	Sa	Tu	Th	Su	Tu	F	M	W	Sa	M
E–	Tu F	F M	Tu	F	Su	W	F	M	Th	Sa	Tu	Th
F	Tu F	F M	F	M	W	Sa	M	Th	Su	Tu	F	Su
F–	M Th	Th Su	M	Th	Sa	Tu	Th	Su	W	F	M	W
G	M Th	Th Su	Th	Su	Tu	F	Su	W	Sa	M	Th	Sa
G–	Su W	W S	Su	W	F	M	W	Sa	Tu	Th	Su	Tu

Key to Perpetual Calendar, 1500-1999

1500 D-	1550 E	1600 E-	1650 F	1700 F-	1750 G	1800 E
1 C	1 D	1 D	1 E	1 E	1 F	1 D
2 B	2 B-	2 C	2 C-	2 D	2 Sp	2 C
3 A	3 A	3 B	3 B	3 C	3 G	3 B
4 F-	4 G	4 G-	4 A	4 A-	4 F	4 G-
5 E	5 F	5 F	5 G	5 G	5 E	5 F
6 D	6 D-	6 E	6 E-	6 F	6 C-	6 E
7 C	7 C	7 D	7 D	7 E	7 B	7 D
8 A-	8 B	8 B-	8 C	8 C-	8 A	8 B-
9 G	9 A	9 A	9 B	9 B	9 G	9 A
1510 F	1560 F-	1610 G	1660 G-	1710 A	1760 E-	1810 G
1 E	1 E	1 F	1 F	1 G	1 D	1 F
2 C-	2 D	2 D-	2 E	2 E-	2 C	2 D-
3 B	3 C	3 C	3 D	3 D	3 B	3 C
4 A	4 A-	4 B	4 B-	4 C	4 G-	4 B
5 G	5 G	5 A	5 A	5 B	5 F	5 A
6 E-	6 F	6 F-	6 G	6 G-	6 E	6 F-
7 D	7 E	7 E	7 F	7 F	7 D	7 E
8 C	8 C-	8 D	8 D-	8 E	8 B-	8 D
9 B	9 B	9 C	9 C	9 D	9 A	9 C
1520 G-	1570 A	1620 A-	1670 B	1720 B-	1770 G	1820 A-
1 F	1 G	1 G	1 A	1 A	1 F	1 G
2 E	2 E-	2 F	2 F-	2 G	2 D-	2 F
3 D	3 D	3 E	3 E	3 F	3 C	3 E
4 B-	4 C	4 C-	4 D	4 D-	4 B	4 C-
5 A	5 B	5 B	5 C	5 C	5 A	5 B
6 G	6 G-	6 A	6 A-	6 B	6 F-	6 A
7 F	7 F	7 G	7 G	7 A	7 E	7 G
8 D-	8 E	8 E-	8 F	8 F-	8 D	8 E-
9 C	9 D	9 D	9 E	9 E	9 C	9 D
1530 B	1580 B-	1630 C	1680 C-	1730 D	1780 A-	1830 C
1 A	1 A	1 B	1 B	1 C	1 G	1 B
2 F-	2 G	2 G-	2 A	2 A-	2 F	2 G-
3 E	3 F	3 F	3 G	3 G	3 E	3 F
4 D	4 D-	4 E	4 E-	4 F	4 C-	4 E
5 C	5 C	5 D	5 D	5 E	5 B	5 D
6 A-	6 B	6 B-	6 C	6 C-	6 A	6 B-
7 G	7 A	7 A	7 B	7 B	7 G	7 A
8 F	8 F-	8 G	8 G-	8 A	8 E-	8 G
9 E	9 E	9 F	9 F	9 G	9 D	9 F
1540 C-	1590 D	1640 D-	1690 E	1740 E-	1790 C	1840 D-
1 B	1 C	1 C	1 D	1 D	1 B	1 C
2 A	2 A-	2 B	2 B-	2 C	2 G-	2 B
3 G	3 G	3 A	3 A	3 B	3 F	3 A
4 E-	4 F	4 F-	4 G	4 G-	4 E	4 F-
5 D	5 E	5 E	5 F	5 F	5 D	5 E
6 C	6 C-	6 D	6 D-	6 E	6 B-	6 D
7 B	7 B	7 C	7 C	7 D	7 A	7 C
8 G-	8 A	8 A-	8 B	8 B-	8 G	8 A-
9 F	9 G	9 G	9 A	9 A	9 F	9 G

Year		Year		Year	
1850	F	1900	G	1950	A
1	E	1	F	1	G
2	C-	2	E	2	E-
3	B	3	D	3	D
4	A	4	B-	4	C
5	G	5	A	5	B
6	E-	6	G	6	G-
7	D	7	F	7	F
8	C	8	D-	8	E
9	B	9	C	9	D
1860	G-	1910	B	1960	B-
1	F	1	A	1	A
2	E	2	F-	2	G
3	D	3	E	3	F
4	B-	4	D	4	D-
5	A	5	C	5	C
6	G	6	A-	6	B
7	F	7	G	7	A
8	D-	8	F	8	F-
9	C	9	E	9	E
1870	B	1920	C-	1970	D
1	A	1	B	1	C
2	F-	2	A	2	A-
3	E	3	G	3	G
4	D	4	E-	4	F
5	C	5	D	5	E
6	A-	6	C	6	C-
7	G	7	B	7	B
8	F	8	G-	8	A
9	E	9	F	9	G
1880	C-	1930	E	1980	E-
1	B	1	D	1	D
2	A	2	B-	2	C
3	G	3	A	3	B
4	E-	4	G	4	G-
5	D	5	F	5	F
6	C	6	D-	6	E
7	B	7	C	7	D
8	G-	8	B	8	B-
9	F	9	A	9	A
1890	E	1940	F-	1990	G
1	D	1	E	1	F
2	B-	2	D	2	D-
3	A	3	C	3	C
4	G	4	A-	4	B
5	F	5	G	5	A
6	D-	6	F	6	F-
7	C	7	E	7	E
8	B	8	C-	8	D
9	A	9	B	9	C

Peterborough and District Family History Society *see* **Cambridgeshire**

Petitions *see* **Parliamentary Papers**

Petty Sessions Courts of summary jurisdiction held by two or more Justices of the Peace, and, later, by a stipendiary or metropolitan police magistrate, for trying lesser offences or as a preliminary enquiry in indictable offences. In 1828, Courts of Quarter Sessions were empowered to create Petty Sessions districts. Few records exist for Petty Sessions, but some Minute Books are to be found in county record offices and borough record offices.

Photographs *see* **Domestic Clues** *and* **Portraits**

Physicians Practitioners of physic had, like midwives, to be licensed by the ecclesiastical authorities, so mentions of their names are to be found in the records of ecclesiastical courts and visitations. By the eighteenth century the physician was usually a graduate, and so can be found in university registers. Medical degrees were not always awarded as a result of study, they could often be bought. In the capital, the Royal College of Physicians of London was founded in 1518, and its Annals contain records of the members. The College has published several volumes, known as *Munk's Roll*, on the lives of its Fellows and Licentiates, but not of ordinary members. The fourth volume, from 1826 onward, deals solely with Fellows.
See also APOTHECARIES; DOCTORS, MEDICAL; SURGEONS.

Piece, Record *see* **Class, Archive**

Piepoudre, Court of By the charter granting a market or trade fair, the grantee was obliged to hold a court to maintain order therein. The court was presided over by the lord or his steward, often with a jury of market traders. The cases dealt with were those of false measures, inferior quality of goods, pilfering and assault; felonies were usually excluded. The courts disappeared with other feudal jurisdictions. The name is thought to derive from the French, *pieds* *poudreux*, meaning 'dusty feet', the nickname applied to an itinerant trader.

Pightle A small, irregularly shaped piece of arable land.

Pigs On the manor, pigs had to have their noses ringed from Michaelmas until Christmas to prevent them grubbing up the soil. Owners who failed to ring them were fined by the manor court. The woodland or copse of a manor was the feeding ground for the tenants' pigs.

Pike A weapon, used by the rank and file soldier or militia-man, consisting of a long wooden shaft capped at one end by a flat steel point.
See also BILL.

Pinder The person responsible for rounding up stray animals and confining them in the pound, or pinfold, of the manor or parish.

Pipe Rolls The annual accounts rendered to the Exchequer by the sheriffs, arising from their function as the king's agents in the shires, and entered up each Michaelmas by the Exchequer clerks. The oldest are those for 1120-30, and from 1155 they survive as a continuous series down to the 1830s. The Rolls will be found in the Public Record Office, Chancery Lane, London, under reference E.372.

The farm of royal lands was removed from the accounts in 1284 and transferred to the newly constituted Rolls of the Bodies of Counties. A number of Pipe Rolls have been published by the Pipe Roll Society. The name is derived from the fact that when the parchment membranes are rolled up they resemble pipes. The succession of tenants-in-chief can be traced from the Pipe Rolls.

Place-names The names of most English towns and villages date from the settlement of Anglo-Saxon invaders in the fifth and sixth centuries, or from that of Scandinavian invaders in the ninth and tenth; but those of Cornwall, out of reach of the invaders, are mainly Celtic in origin. Most place-names derive either from a natural physical feature of the location (e.g. Byfleet — by the stream), from the first settler or

settlers (e.g. Hastings — the Hastingas tribe), or from the settlement (e.g. Hickleton — Hicela's homestead).

Place-names form one of the main sources of family surnames and can show where an ancestor once lived (*see* SURNAMES). Some place-names have had the surname of medieval local landowning families added to them, e.g. Yardley Hastings in Northants and Tarrant Gunville in Dorset. Other local landlords of the Middle Ages are indicated by such place-names as Abbots Langley, Kings Langley, Huish Episcopi (of the bishop), and the like.

For further reading, see the county volumes of the English Place-name Society, and the *Oxford Dictionary of Place-names* by E. Ekwall.

Plague Although the term 'plague' was once used for any killing epidemic, it is now usually confined to bubonic plague, carried by fleas on the black rat. Incidence of plague in England was frequent from the seventh century onward, but the most devastating was the Black Death, which killed about one third of the population in 1347-50. Records of plague in the provinces are rare. Epidemics can be inferred from marked increases in the number of burials registered, but other mortal diseases, such as sweating sickness, may have been responsible. In seventeenth-century London there were out-breaks of plague in 1603 (33,000 deaths), 1625 (35,417) and 1636 (10,400), and the Great Plague of 1665 (68,596). After that there were no further severe outbreaks owing to the elimination of the black rat in England by the brown.

For further reading, see *A History of Epidemics in Britain*, by C. Creighton (1891-4, reprinted 1965).

Plea (i) An action at law between parties.

(ii) The presentation of a case, either for the prosecution or for the defence. Certain types of plea bore special names; for example, the primary plea for the prosecution was known as First Plea (in an ecclesiastical court), the Declaration (in Common Law courts), the Bill of Complaint (in equity courts), Articles (in criminal cases), Libel (in a court of Instance), and Allegation (in testamentary cases). In all causes, subsequent pleas were called Allegations.

Plea Rolls These are records of actions brought under the Common Law. They cover actions heard in the Curia Regis (King's Court) and in the courts that grew out of it, namely the courts of Common Pleas, King's Bench and the Exchequer; also of other Common Law courts.

The records begin in the reign of Richard I and end after the *Judicature Act* of 1873. They are written on parchment membranes (rotulets) stitched together at the top, sometimes with more than 500 membranes in one 'bundle'. Many private deeds are also recorded (enrolled) on the rolls. The earliest Curia Regis rolls are being printed in full, and the Selden Society has published extracts in their *Select Pleas*. Some Eyre Rolls have been printed or calendared by local record publishing societies. (The rolls do not include actions in the court of Chancery and other courts of equity, where the procedure differed from that of the Common Law courts.) The Plea Rolls of the above mentioned courts are at the Public Record Office, Chancery Lane, London. Plea Rolls of the City of London, preserved at the Guildhall, have been calendared and published down to 1482 under the title *Calendar of Plea and Memoranda Rolls* (Cambridge University Press).

Ploughland The area of land that could be cultivated in a year, using a single oxteam. *See also* CARUCATE; HIDE; PLOUGH TEAM.

Plough Monday The day when work was resumed after the twelve days of Christmas.

Plough Team Eight oxen constituted a plough team in East Anglia and Lincolnshire, but not always elsewhere. In Cheshire the terms 'carucate' (Latin *caruca*) and 'hide' were used interchangeably for the area of land capable of being ploughed by one team in a year (i.e. a ploughland), but in some other counties a hide could contain several carucates.

Plurality *or* **Pluralism** The simultaneous holding by a person of more than one benefice with care of souls; a practice always officially discouraged. By a canon of 1703, dispensation for pluralism could be permitted only to a graduate M.A. who was also a public and sufficient licensed preacher. It also required that

he reside a reasonable time each year in both benefices, and that they should be not more than thirty miles apart. But this rule was often either ignored, or evaded by committing the second benefice to the parson *in commendam*, i.e. by committing it to his charge temporarily.

Police Until early in the second quarter of the nineteenth century, the maintenance of law and order was in the hands of parochial constables, assisted in towns by watchmen and responsible to Justices of the Peace.

In London in the early eighteenth century there was at first one police office, at Bow Street, with a magistrate in charge of the 'Bow-Street Runners'. Henry Fielding, the novelist, was the magistrate in 1753, and his recommendations led to the setting up of more police offices, each with magistrates, clerks and a handful of constables. This was in addition to the constables of the London parishes. In 1829 Sir Robert Peel's *Act for Improving the Police in and near the Metropolis* separated the police from the magistrates and placed them under police commissioners, a step strongly opposed in many quarters as an infringement of civil liberties. Later, the City of London appointed its own commissioner and policemen. In 1829 and through the reign of William IV, 171 cities, boroughs and towns followed London's example, but in the countryside law and order was largely maintained by voluntary associations for catching and prosecuting felons, organised and supported by contributions from private persons and organisations. It was the *Rural Constabulary Act* of 1839 that empowered the appointment, by Quarter Sessions, of chief and petty constables. In 1856, county forces became compulsory. The policing of the country was the responsibility of the Home Office, and the records are at the Public Record Office, Chancery Lane, London. The term 'police', when used in nineteenth-century railway records, means 'signalmen'.
See also CONSTABLE.

Poll Books On 10 April, 1696, a bill intended to prevent irregularities in parliamentary elections by biased returning officers received the royal assent. One provision was that the officers should be obliged, if requested, to

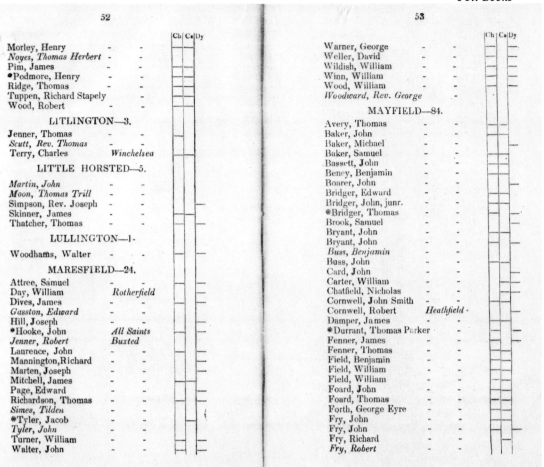

Poll Book page. The horizontal strokes in the three columns show which two candidates each freeholder voted for. *Courtesy Guildhall Library*

deliver to any member of the public a copy of the poll, showing how the electors had voted, 'at a reasonable charge for writing the same'. Soon after this, returning officers allowed Poll Books of county elections to be published as a commercial venture by local printers. Such books were usually in demand only when the result of the poll had been close. Poll Books could also be published for borough parliamentary elections, but as the members of borough electorate were often no more than a dozen or so, urban polls could often be published in local newspapers.

Poll Books continued to appear until and including the General Election of 1868. Their end was owing to the introduction of the secret ballot, which was first operated at a by-election on 17 August, 1872. Not all Poll Books are for the election of members of parliament; some have been published for elections of county coroners.

The information published in the books is not uniform. Names and votes are always given and sometimes the addresses and occupations of the voters and the nature of their qualifying freeholds. The list is usually arranged under parishes and/or hundreds. A Preface giving an account of the candidates and their opinions is sometimes included. A comparison of these with the way in which an ancestor voted can reveal his opinions on the issues of his day. From 1832, Electoral Registers are also available, but record only entitlement to vote.

The Institute of Historical Research, Senate House, University of London, has over 500 Poll Books. The British Library, London Guildhall and Bodleian Libraries also have large numbers. Smaller collections are at the Society of Genealogists, county record offices and reference libraries. County record offices may also have the original MSS of unpublished lists. The Society of Genealogists has issued a catalogue of its own Poll Books.

For further reading, see *A Handlist of British Parliamentary Poll Books*, by John Sims (University of Leicester, 1984).

Poll Tax A tax levied on the population per head. It was imposed three times during the fourteenth century. In 1377 the rate was one groat (fourpence), but regular beggars and children under 14 were not included. In 1379 and 1381 the tax was graded socially, but after 1381 only aliens were taxed per head until another general poll tax was levied in 1513. The tax was imposed again on people over 16 in 1641, 1660, 1666, 1677 and 1694. The last poll tax was in the year 1698. The London returns for 1694 have been printed. The records are at the Public Record Office, Chancery Lane, London, under reference E.179.

Pontage A local tax or toll levied for the maintenance of a bridge.

Poor Law The system of public relief of the poor laid down by Acts of Parliament since the original great *Poor Law Act* of 1601. The care of the poor was then placed in the hands of the parish, where it remained until the 'New Poor Law' replaced the 'Old Poor Law' in 1834. The responsibility was then removed to Poor Law Unions (of several parishes) administered by Boards of Guardians of the Poor. The records created by the working of the Poor Law sometimes enable the descent of a really poor family to be more easily traced than that of a more prosperous one.

For the various aspects of the Poor Law administration, *see* BADGE-MAN; BASTARDY; GUARDIANS OF THE POOR; OVERSEER OF THE POOR; SETTLEMENT; WORKHOUSES.

Population The population of England at the time of Domesday has been accepted to be about one and a quarter million. Estimates of the figures for the fourteenth century, which

embrace the drastic reduction caused by the Black Death, vary greatly, as indeed do all figures for the period before the first population census of 1801. The following figures, drawn from various sources, provide a rough guide. After 1200 they include Wales.

1086	1,100,000
1345	3,800,000
1377	2,350,000
1400	2,100,000
1500	2,250,000
1600	4,500,000
1700	5,250,000
1750	6,407,000
1801	8,892,536
1851	17,927,609
1901	32,527,843

To estimate the population of a parish, a good rule of thumb is to count the householders listed in a Lay Subsidy Roll, add about one-third (some say one-quarter) of that number for poorer householders exempt from taxation, double the total to include the womenfolk, and double again to include the children. The Local Population Studies Society, 17 Rosebery Square, Rosebery Avenue, London EC1, issues a journal, *Local Population*.

For further reading, see *The Population History of England, 1541-1871*, by E.A. Wrigley and R.S. Schofield (1981).

Porail *or* **Poverail** The poor, as a class.

Portion The money brought by a bride to her husband.

Portraits Portraits of ancestors are among the most treasured relics of the family past, whether they are life-size, full-length oil paintings or fading cigarette-card-size, head-and-shoulders photographs. If the sitter is known for certain, his or her name should be written on the back, so that the knowledge will be passed on with the picture. If the name is a probability deduced from evidence of provenance, vague oral tradition, costume or apparent age of the sitter, the clues should be noted alongside the probable name. All portraits should be photographed (or re-photographed) so that the copy can be filed in the same way as transcripts of documentary evidence. Original photographs should remain in any album in which they have been passed down. Portraits can be dated from the evidence of costume and hairstyle (the latter being more reliable), and from the apparent age of the sitter; for professional photographers there is also the evidence of the photographer's name and address, which can be checked from local directories. If a painting appears to be a good one, the artist may be identifiable either by the experts at the National Gallery in Trafalgar Square, London WC2, or by those of the auctioneers' firms, Christie and Sotheby, also in London but with regional offices throughout England. The latter two will also value them for insurance purposes. If the painter is sufficiently well known to have had his biography written and works catalogued, a reference to the catalogue, often appearing as an appendix to the biography, may lead to the identification of the sitter. Portraits are sometimes mentioned in wills, when the subject is usually named.

Posnet A small iron pot often mentioned in inventories.

Pound An enclosure, erected by local authority, for confining cattle and other beasts that were trespassing or straying. A pound overt was open overhead, and a pound covert was roofed over or entirely enclosed, like a stable or byre. Also called a pinfold.
See also PINDER.

Precisian Another term for PURITAN.

Prelatist A mid seventeenth-century term of denigration used by Presbyterians and Independents to designate anyone, of the Anglican persuasion, who wished to preserve the episcopal hierarchy of the Church of England and the use of the *Book of Common Prayer*.

Prerogative Courts The courts of the Archbishops of Canterbury and York, which took precedence over those of bishops. As courts of probate they had to be applied to for the proving of wills of any testator who left *bona notabilia* ('considerable goods') in more than one diocese. They could also be used for proving any will leaving property in their province, since it

was always open to an executor to apply to a higher court than was necessary.

The Prerogative Court of Canterbury, being that of the Primate of All England, could prove wills of testators anywhere in England, Wales, the Isle of Man and the Channel Isles. The records of the Canterbury Court (known as PCC) are at the Public Record Office, Chancery Lane, London, and those of York (PCY) at the Borthwick Institute at the University of York.

The Society of Genealogists has a consolidated slip index of PCC wills of the second half of the eighteenth century. Information from it is supplied on payment of a fee, but publication of this index is in progress.

Presbyterians English nonconformity began as a Puritan movement, within the Church of England, to bring ritual and organisation nearer to Lutheran and Calvinistic forms by abolishing bishops, archdeacons, deans and chancellors. Most Puritans wanted parish clergy to be elected presbyters and their wider organisation to be by committees called presbyteries; but they wished to remain within the established church. The Presbyterians grew in influence and formed the majority in Charles I's early parliaments. The movement was strongest among the middle classes in the towns, and it became the established church of the country in 1647, under the Commonwealth, until it was overthrown at the Restoration. In 1653, civil registration was introduced, which discouraged the starting of nonconformist registers.

On the Restoration of the monarchy, the *Act of Uniformity* required the clergy to accept the *Book of Common Prayer* and to be ordained by bishops. Presbyterian clergy who refused to conform were ejected from their livings. They retained many supporters from their congregations in conventicles. Quarter Sessions records show prosecutions. In 1664, the *Conventicle Act* forbade such assemblies, and in the following year the *Five-Mile Act* forbade dissenting clergy to come within five miles of corporate towns, which was where dissent was strongest. Bunhill (Bonehill) Fields Burial Ground was opened just outside Moorgate, London, and was used mainly by dissenters. Between 1672 and 1674 the *Declaration of Indulgence* allowed conventicles and dissenting teachers to operate if they were licensed.

In 1689 the *Toleration Act* fully recognised conventicles, and this gave rise to the building of over one thousand meeting-houses in the next twenty years. As they were not allowed to have any central or regional links, they were Independent in organisation. This brought the Presbyterians and Independents closer together, and their conventicles sometimes shared or exchanged names. The sects opened burial grounds and began keeping burial registers. Previously, deaths had been recorded in parish registers because burials had taken place in parochial churchyards.

In 1691, Presbyterians and Independent ministers in London combined under the name of the United Brethren. Sometimes one congregation would have two ministers, one of each denomination, but in 1694 the London Union broke down.

In 1695, Church of England incumbents were ordered to register the births (not baptisms) of dissenters in their parishes, either in their registers or in separate books; so the word 'born' in a parish register may be a clue to dissenting parents. As in the Church of England, the baptism of dissenters' children at home became common and lasted for one hundred years.

In 1702, 'The Three Denominations' (Presbyterians, Independents and Baptists) united under a combined General Body of Protestant Dissenting Ministers. The practice of keeping registers now became more general, though far from universal. Bunhill Fields burial register began in 1713, but was kept very negligently until 1786.

In 1719, the Three Denominations split up. Presbyterians fell under the influence of Unitarianism. Some of their ministers became Unitarians and carried their congregations with them. Sometimes they moved to other meeting-houses; sometimes the Presbyterian loyalist minority had to move. At this time the practice of dating register entries with the New Style New Year (*see* CALENDAR) became common with dissenters, ahead of the official change in 1752.

In 1742/3, a body of Protestant Dissenting Deputies set up a General Register of Births for the children of dissenters all over the country, because of the failure of so many ministers to keep registers. It was located at the library bequeathed to the movement by Dr Daniel Williams (*c.*1643-1716), a prominent and wealthy Presbyterian minister.

Before 1754, fewer marriages were performed in Presbyterian meeting-houses than in those of the other sects. Their religious ceremony was not recognised in law, but the contracting of the two parties before witnesses was. This practice was brought to an end by Lord Hardwicke's *Marriage Act* (*see* PARISH REGISTERS). In 1768 the General Register at Dr Williams's Library began to record baptisms as well as births, but not so consistently. In the late eighteenth century, the terms Presbyterian and Unitarian were used indifferently for the same congregations, and Presbyterianism began to decline, except in Wales.

In 1837, the registers of all dissenting sects were called in to the General Register Office upon the start of civil registration. The Presbyterians obeyed, but some registers slipped through the net. Marriages were once more allowed to be performed in Presbyterian meeting-houses provided the local registrar was present.

The Public Record Office, Chancery Lane, London, has the great majority of the pre-1837 Presbyterian registers, under references RG.4, 5 and 8. Their General Register is under the heading of London. The Presbyterian Historical Society, 86 Tavistock Place, London WC1, has sixteen pre-civil-registration registers and other historical material.

Presbyterian registers are far less regularly kept than parochial ones, but they sometimes give more information (for example, wives' and mothers' maiden names, or even parents' names). As ministries had no official boundaries, and ministers often travelled far to bring services to their followers, it is worth searching the registers of all meeting-houses anywhere in the neighbourhood. Also there are many 'register entries' in Minute Books and other records.

For further reading, see *Sources for Nonconformist Genealogy and Family History*, by D.J. Steel (1973).

Presently This word used to mean 'immediately',

and still does in America. Also, 'at the present time'.

Presentment In a judicial process, the laying before the court, by a grand jury or manorial homage, of an offence, without any independent accusation having been made.

Pricket A candlestick.

Primogeniture The right or custom whereby an estate in land, or a title of dignity, descends to a person by virtue of his being the eldest male issue. In the past, when a person died intestate, his personal property, after deduction of the widow's portion, was, under Common Law, divided equally between all his children; but all his real estate (landed property) went to his eldest son.
See also BOROUGH ENGLISH; GAVELKIND.

Priory A religious house of monks or nuns, subordinate to an abbey. It was ruled by a prior. A priory would often be the feudal superior of a lord of a manor, the manor having been presented to the religious house by some magnate in FRANKALMOIGN. In the Middle Ages certain English priories were dependencies of French abbeys, and during wars with France such 'alien priories' were taken into the hands of the English Crown, their inmates being classed as 'foreign religious, subject to the King of France and his allies'. Extents of Alien Priories can be found among the Exchequer Records at the Public Record Office, Chancery Lane, London, under reference Γ.106.

A prior might, alternatively, be the dignitary of an abbey next in authority under the abbot.

Prisoners The records of prisoners in many gaols in the period 1770-1894 are at the Public Record Office, Kew, under Prisons, Records, Series I (PCOM); and those over one hundred years old are available for inspection. They consist of registers, photographs, Minute Books and Visitors' Books. Other particulars of prisoners can be found in Licences, Male & Female, Old Captions and Transfer Papers. Quarterly Prison Returns, September 1824 to March 1876 (HO.8, also at Kew) contain convicts' offences, date and place of conviction

and period of sentence. West Middlesex Family History Society has supplied the Public Record Office with a list of prisons and hulks (dismantled ships used as prisons) covered. The records of Newgate Gaol are at Kew under reference HO.10. The Corporation of London Record Office has a card index of people in London debtors' prisons from 1755. County gaol records are at the county record offices.

Prison Records *see* **Prisoners**

Privy Council In the sixteenth and seventeenth centuries, the Privy Council was, in varying degrees, the government of England under the royal prerogative. It developed out of the inner ring of the earlier Curia Regis (King's Court). Thomas Cromwell had used its members as the instruments of his policies, but after his execution it became a body of initiative with executive functions. Minutes were kept of its meetings, which were held wherever the sovereign happened to be. The privy councillors, chosen by the sovereign, were noblemen and gentry and included the chief officers of the realm (Lord Chancellor, Lord Treasurer, etc.), and of the royal household, but most of the work was carried out by a small group of executive ministers. There were a number of *ad hoc* committees, and members of the Council had other duties, such as sitting on the bench at sessions of the courts of Star Chamber, Requests and High Commission.

The Stuart kings consulted a committee of the Privy Council nominally concerned only with foreign affairs, and took decisions to which the Council was left to give merely formal approval. The names 'cabal', 'juncto' and 'cabinet council' were given to these committees of favoured ministers. Under Anne, a committee of the Privy Council met under the senior secretary of state to prepare government business, and then attended the sovereign in a meeting of her cabinet; but George I, understanding no English, never attended, so all business was done by one body, for which the name 'cabinet' survived. Its presiding officer came to be known as the Prime Minister. The records of the Privy Council Office are at the Public Record Office, Chancery Lane, London, under group PC.

Probate This term means Approval by a competent court that an instrument purporting to be the Testament of a deceased person was indeed his lawful act, together with authority to the executor(s) to carry out its terms.

From 1529 onward, no fee was charged for probate where the effects of the deceased were worth £5 or under. For larger estates, the charge was proportionate (*see* WILL).

Before 1733, the record of probate (the *Probate Act*) was written in Latin in words heavily abbreviated. The following is a typical example, unabbreviated and with punctuation inserted, and accompanied by a word-by-word translation.

Probatum fuit hujusmodi testamentum coram
Approved was this testament before

venerabile viro Ricardo Greene, artium
the worshipful [man] Richard Greene, of arts

magistro, Officiale domini Archidiaconi B——,
master, Official of the lord Archdeacon B——,

apud C—— tercio die mensis Augusti
at C—— on the 3rd day of the month of August

Anno Domini Millesimo quingentesimo
Anno Domini one thousand five hundred

duodecimo, juramento Willelmi Smith,
and twelve, by the oath of William Smith,

executoris in suprascripto testamento
the executor in the above-written testament

nominati. Et commissa fuit administratio
named. And committed was the administration

omnium et singularum bonorum et debitorum etc.
of all and singular the goods and debts etc.

defuncti prefato executori etc. de
of the deceased to the said executor etc. for

A Latin probate act (with fewer abbreviations than most) entered below the Prerogative Court of Canterbury register copy of the will of Joseph Forster (see the transcript and translation of another example under PROBATE). *Crown copyright: PROB.11*

bene et fideliter administrando ac de pleno
well and truly administering and for a full

inventario exhibendo etc, ad sancta dei
inventory delivering etc, on the holy of God

evangelia jurato in debita de juris. Potestate
gospels sworn in due form of law. Power

reservata committendo predictam
being reserved for committing the said

administrationem Agnete Smith, vidue,
administration to Agnes Smith, widow,

relicte defuncti et alii
the relict of the deceased and the other

executrici in testamento nominate.
executrix in the testament named.

From 11 January, 1858, probate of all English wills has been granted by the Probate Division (now the Family Division) of the High Court. The wills are housed at the Principal Registry of that Division at Somerset House, Strand, London, with annual indexes.

For further reading, see *A Simplified Guide to Probate Jurisdictions*, by J.S.W. Gibson (Federation of Family History Societies).

Proctor (i) Also called Procurator (the Latin term), an officer employed in admiralty, civil and ecclesiastical causes, corresponding to an attorney or solicitor at Common Law or equity.

(ii) A person licensed to collect alms for hospitals and/or lepers.

Procurator *see* **Proctor**

Professional Genealogists *see* **Association of Genealogists and Record Agents**

Proof of Age Before the institution of parish registers in 1538, there was little documentary evidence to which to refer when anyone needed to prove how old he or she might be; but this need was not infrequent, especially in the case of minors. It might be necessary to show that an heir had reached the age at which his late father's estate should be made over to him, or that a girl was of an age to be given in marriage.

Proof had to be established before the sheriff of the county with the aid of a jury. At that period the jury was not a body for deciding, impartially, facts first presented to them in court, but a group of neighbours who could swear to certain facts from personal knowledge. To prove an age in question, each member of the jury would cite some incident that he remembered as having happened at, or shortly before or after, the birth of the person concerned. If one of them mentioned that the birth had been noted by someone in writing, there is no sign that the document ever had to be produced, documentary evidence not being considered at that time as having any special value. Because of the likelihood of a proof of age being required at some time in the future, a prudent father would mark his child's birth by entertaining neighbours or giving out presents.

The records of *Proofs of Age* are at the Public Record Office, Chancery Lane, London, under references C.132-142, and calendared in print in the volumes of *Calendars of Inquisitions*. Besides the genealogical information of parentage contained in the *Proofs*, the homely incidents mentioned by the jurymen often throw interesting light on themselves and the family of the person whose age was in question.

In the period between 1538 and 1837, the evidence of baptismal registers was taken as proof of age, for instance in cases of apprenticeship and army cadetships.

When a person's age was stated in years, it was the custom, even into the early nineteenth century, to include the current year not yet completed, thus making him appear one year older than he would be considered today. However, for the Census of 1841 it was laid down that statements of age should include only completed years.
See also OCTAVE.

Prosopography History pursued through study of the social origins, family connections and economic backgrounds of relevant individuals, together with the tensions arising from the interactions of their personal careers. In this recent development, the researches of family historians can acquire an interest and value beyond the purely domestic field.

Protestation Oath Returns Following the rumours of an army plot to rescue the Earl of Stratford from the Tower, an oath 'to live and die for the true Protestant religion, the liberties and rights of subjects, and the privilege of Parliaments' was taken by members of the House of Commons on 3 May, 1641. The Protestant peers signed it the following day. A Bill imposing on all Englishmen the obligation of signing the oath was rejected by the House of Lords, but on 30 July the Commons passed a resolution that all who refused to sign were unfit to hold office in church or state.

On 4 January, 1641/2, King Charles tried to arrest five Members of Parliament; so the Protestation was printed and sent out to the sheriffs for distribution to every parish, so that every man of 18 and over should take the oath. The text was read out in the churches, and lists were made of all who signed and of all who refused to sign. Most of these lists are in the House of Lords Record Office, and some have been printed by record societies, but some survive only among parish records.

A catalogue of extant returns then known is in the *Appendix* to the *5th Report of the Historical MSS Commission* (1876), pages 120-34. The Society of Genealogists also has a list of Protestation Oath Returns, and has published a leaflet on the subject. The Returns are a valuable location record for the mid seventeenth century.

Province The area of jurisdiction of an archbishop. The province of the Archbishop of Canterbury was that part of England south of the River Trent, consisting until the nineteenth

The names of all such persons within the townshipp of Carleton in the parish of Rothwell which have taken the protestation

mr Charles Jackson
Robert Nelson
George Stones
Thomas Widowshill
William Harrison
Thomas Shawe
Thomas Townend
Thomas Clisse
Edward Scoles
Richard Scoles
William Singleton
Robert Edward
William Ellis
Thomas Wright
Robert Gamble
John Carter
William Feather
William Hader
Thomas Hey
Anthony Williman
William Mores
John Jackson
Raphe Swifte
Richard Dobson
William Illingworth
William Clisse
Robert Robinson
William Carter
John Crowmarbe
Thomas Berkett
William Steade
William Sooths
Abraham Butterfeild
John Burnell
William Corkell
John Rayner
Robert Smith
Barnabas Norton
Richard Jenkinsone
Michaell Williman
Henry Thompson
William Westerman senior
William Westerman junior
Richard Hey

Richard Lawson
William Wainewright
Robert Swineson
Thomas Brigge
Valentyne Berkett

The names of all such persons within the townshipp of Middleton in the parish of Rothwell which have taken the protestation

Sr Ferdinando Lee
Henry Gascoigne
William Gascoigne
Marell Fudworke
Thomas Lee
Robert Wilkson
William Prince
William Langfellow
Henry Lansskerie
James Saunderson
Henry Knowles
Henry Martin
William Platon
Frenett Speight
William Speight
William Skase
Thomas Skase
Thomas Dodtehson
William Beaumonte
Thomas Horne
John Horne
William Jackson
Henry Jackson
Thomas Jackson
William Meekeson
Henry Meekeson
William Wither
William Flather
William Wilkson
Thomas Walker
Xpofer Duckworth
George Duckworth
Francis Corkeran
William Casson
Thomas Walker
John Moxon
Thomas Moxon
Raphe Moxon
Gilbert Jackson
Thomas Willingsworth

John Mann
Peter Husset
John Rhoates
Joseph Lamforst
Edmund Wood
Thomas Jackson
Henry Mann
Robert Smith
Richard Currer
William Milner
William Talbert
John Parker
Gilbert Flanson
William Mann
Henry Mann
Gilbert Sabill
Thomas Sabill
George Stanforth
Richard Damell
John Damell
Francis Lupton
Edward Bowman
James Jackson
Edward Roeltingle
William Walker
Thomas Walker
John White
Gilbert Garritt
John William

The names of all such persons within the hamblett of Thorpe in the parish of Rothwell which have taken the protestation

John Gleadell
Richard Harber
Francis Holmes
George Liversedge
John Jetson
Robert Nettleton
Henry Beaumonte
William Beaumonte
Thomas Nettleton
Anthony Beaumonte
Henry Beaumonte
Nicholas Westerman
William Westerman
Thomas Westerman
Rowland Boynton
William Hurst
John Carr
Henry Casson

century of the bishoprics of Asaph, Bangor, Bath and Wells, Bristol, Canterbury, Chichester, Ely, St Davids (Exeter), Gloucester, Hereford, Lichfield and Coventry, Lincoln, Llandaff, London, Norwich, Oxford, Peterborough, Rochester, Salisbury, Winchester, and Worcester.

The province of York, to the north of the Trent, had jurisdiction over the bishoprics of Carlisle, Chester, Durham, Sodor and Man, and York.

Public Record Office (PRO).

The PRO was founded in accordance with the *English Public Record Office Act* of 1838, to have the custody of all records, etc., 'of a public nature'. All collections recognised as public were brought together and placed under the control of the Master of the Rolls. In 1854, the contents of the State Paper Office were added, and after that the records of all government departments, except the India Office, as soon as they were no longer needed for administrative purposes.

The collection now falls into two main divisions — judicial and state records — plus a large collection of records not of a public nature that have been deposited from time to time. The Office has two main repositories open to the public. The older one, built in 1856, is in Chancery Lane, London, and the newer one, opened in 1977, in Ruskin Avenue, Kew, Middlesex. There is also a separate section of the Office in Portugal Street, London, for the inspection of census returns. Some little-used records are kept at Hayes, Middlesex, and require a week's notice for production.

For regular attendance a Reader's Ticket is necessary, but Day Tickets are also issued. The Offices are open from 9.30 a.m. to 5 p.m., Mondays to Fridays.

The PRO has published a very useful volume, *Tracing your Ancestors in the Public Record Office*, by J. Cox and T. Padfield, and issues free leaflets on a number of subjects of family history interest.

LEFT Part of a Protestation Oath Roll of 1641/2, listing 'the names of such persons within the towneshipp of Carleton in the parishe of Rothwell [Yorkshire] which have taken the protestacion'. *House of Lords Record Office*

*Records kept at PRO, Kew***

Admiralty (ADM)
Advisory, Conciliation & Arbitration Service (CW)
Agriculture, Fisheries & Food, Ministry of (MAF)
Air Ministry (AIR)
Aviation, Ministry of (AVIA)
British Council (BW)
British Railways Board (AN)
British Transport Docks Board (BR)
British Transport Historical Records (RAIL)
Cabinet Office (CAB)
Captured Enemy Documents (GFM)
Certification Office for Trades Unions and Employers Associations (CL)
Channel Tunnel Advisory Groups (BS1)
Civil Service Commission (CSC)
Civil Service Department (BA)
Civil Service Pay Research Unit (CSPR)
Coal Industry Social Welfare Organisation (BX)
Colonial Office (CO)
Commonwealth Relations Office (DO)
Copyright Office (COPY)
Countryside Commission (COU)
Crown Agents for Overseas Governments and Administration (CAOG)
Customs & Excise, Board of (CUST)
Defence, Ministry of (DEFE)
Development Commission (D)
Distribution of Income & Wealth, Royal Commission on (BS.7)
Education & Science, Department of (ED)
Elizabeth Garrett Anderson Hospital (CF)
Environment, Department of the (AT)
Environmental Pollution, Royal Commission on (CY)
Exchequer and Audit Department (AO)
Export Credits Guarantee Department (ECG)
Financial Institutions, Committee to review the functioning of (BS.9)
Foreign Office (FO)
Forestry Commission (F)
Forfeited Estates, Commissioners of (FEC)
Friendly Societies, Registry of (FS)
Gambling, Royal Commission on (BS.3)
General Register Office (RG), except Census Returns (RG.9-10), Non-parochial Registers and Records (RG.4-8), and certain other registers and associated papers (RG.18, 19, 27, 30-7. 43)
Government Actuary's Department (ACT)
Health & Social Security, Department of (BN)
Health, Ministry of (MH)
Historical Manuscripts Commission (HMC)
Home Office (HO), except Census Returns (HO.107)

Housing & Local Government, Ministry of (HLG)

Hudson's Bay Company (BH), microfilm. Access by permission of the Company only.

Information, Central Office of (INF)

Inland Revenue, Board of (IR), except Estate Duty Registers (IR.26, 27)

Irish Sailors' & Soldiers' Land Trust (AP)

Iron and Steel Board (BE)

Labour, Ministry of (LAB)

Land Registry (LAR)

Lands Tribunal (LT)

Law Commission (BC)

Local Government Boundary Commission for England (AX)

Location of Offices Bureau (AH)

Lord Chancellor's Office (LCO)

Meteorological Office (BJ)

Metropolitan Police Force (MEPO)

Monuments, Ancient & Historic in Wales and Monmouthshire, Royal Commission of (MONW)

Monuments, Historic (England), Royal Commission on (AE)

Munitions, Ministry of (MUN)

National Assistance Board (AST)

National Coal Board (COAL)

National Debt Office (NDO)

National Dock Labour Board (BK)

National Health Service, Royal Commission on (BS6)

National Incomes Commission (NICO)

National Insurance Audit Department (NIA)

National Insurance Commissioners (CT)

National Savings, Department for (NSC)

National Service, Ministry of (NATS)

Operators' Licensing, Committee of enquiry into (BS4)

Ordnance Survey Department (OS)

Overseas Development, Ministry of (OD)

Parliamentary Boundary Commission (AF)

Parole Board (BV)

Paymaster General's Office (PMG)

Pensions & National Insurance, Ministry of (PIN)

Pensions Appeal Tribunal (BF)

Power, Ministry of (POWE)

Press, Royal Commission on the (BS2)

Price Commission (CX)

Prime Minister's Office (PREM)

Prison Commission (CX)

Public Building & Works, Ministry of (WORK)

Public Record Office (PRO) all classes, except transcripts (PRO.31) and certain classes of gifts and deposits (PRO.30)*

Public Trustee Office (PT)

Public Works Loan Board (PWLB)

Reconstruction, Ministry of (RECO)

Remploy Ltd (BM)

Research Institutes (AY)

Royal Fine Art Commission (BP)

Royal Mint (MINT)

Scientific & Industrial Research, Department of (DSIR)

Stationery Office (STAT)

Supply, Ministry of (SUPP)

Tithe Redemption Commission (TITH)

Trade, Board of (BT)

Transport, Ministry of (MT)

Treasury (T)

Tribunals, Council on (BL)

United Kingdom Atomic Energy Authority (AB)

University Grants Committee (UGC)

Value Added Tax Tribunals (CV)

Wallace Collection (AR)

War Office (WO)

Welsh Office (BD)

**Records are, in general, open to inspection when they are 30 years old

*PRO.30/1-3, 6-12, 16-17, 20, 22, 27, 29-33, 35-37, 39-40, 42-43, 45-46, 48, 51-52, 54-61, 63-79, 81-84, and PRO.31/20 are at Kew

Records kept at PRO, Chancery Lane (a)

Admiralty, High Court of (HCA)

Alienation Office (A)

Assize, Clerks of (ASSI)

Bankruptcy, Court of (B)

Central Criminal Court (CRIM)

Chancery (C)

Chester, Palatinate of (CHES)

Common Pleas, Court of (CP)

County Courts (AK)

Crown Estate Commissioners (CRES)

Delegates, Court of (DEL)

Durham, Palatinate of (DURH)

Exchequer (E, LR)

General Register Office (RG). Only Census Returns (RG.9-11), Non-parochial Registers and Records (RG.4-8), and certain other registers and associated papers (RG.18, 19, 27, 30-37, 43)

Home Office. Only Census Returns 1841 and 1851 (HO.107)

Inland Revenue, Board of. Only Estate Duty Registers (IR.26, 27)

Judicature, Supreme Court of (J)

Justices Itinerant (JUST)

King's Bench, Court of (KB)

King's Bench Prison (PRIS)

Lancaster, Duchy of (DL)

Lancaster, Palatinate of (PL)

Land Revenue Record Office (LRRO)
Law Officers' Department (LO)
Lord Chamberlain's Department (LC)
Lord Steward's Office (LS)
Palace Court (PALA)
Peveril, Court of the Honour of (PEV)
Prerogative Court of Canterbury (PROB)
Privy Council, Judicial Committee of the (PCAP)
Privy Council Office (PC)
Privy Purse Office (PP)
Privy Seal Office (PSO)
Public Prosecutions, Director of (DPP)
Public Record Office. Transcripts (PRO.31), and certain other classes of gifts and deposits (PRO.30) *(b)*
Queen Anne's Bounty (QAB)
Requests, Court of (REQ)
Signet Office (SO)
Special Collections (SC)
Star Chamber, Court of (STAC)
State Paper Office (SP)
Treasury Solicitor (TS)
Wales, Principality of (WALE)
Wards & Liveries, Court of (WARD)

(*a*) Some classes to be seen at Chancery Lane are housed at Hayes, Middlesex, and notice of several working days is required.

(*b*) PRO.30/5, 18-19, 21, 23-26, 28, 34, 38, 41, 44, 47, 49, 50, 53, 80, PRO.31/20 are at Kew. PRO.30/4, 13-15, 62 are no longer held in the Public Record Office

Puritanism Uncoordinated movements within the Church of England, beginning in the reign of Henry VIII and aiming to purify some of the aspects of its worship. Although all puritans were against the use of Catholic rites and of elaborate vestments and ornaments, and all believed in the Bible as their sole authority for belief and conduct, they interpreted it in many different ways.

Many groups held meetings of their own to expound the scriptures: these were known as 'prophesyings', and later as 'conventicles'. When Archbishop Whitgift attempted rigidly to enforce uniformity after 1583, the Puritans became united in opposition to an episcopalian form of church organisation. It was from the Puritan movements that the dissenting sects developed. Puritans were also called Precisians.

Purprestre An encroachment on land, especially on deer pasture under forest law or in other royal lands.

Putrid Fever The old name for a group of diseases that included typhus and smallpox.

Quakers *see* **Friends, Religious Society of**

Quarter Sessions, Court of An assembly of the Justices of the Peace of any county, riding or county town, for the joint purposes of judging suits and administering the affairs of the area. A statute of 1388 laid down that 'Justices shall keep their sessions in every quarter of the year at least', from which the name of the court is derived. They were held at Easter, Trinity (Midsummer), Michaelmas and Epiphany (January), and were presided over by the sheriff or his deputy. A leading justice was appointed the permanent official and called the Custos Rotulorum, Keeper of the Rolls.

The Tudors gave to the justices the task of enforcing a wide new range of laws. In carrying out these duties, they gradually replaced the sheriff as the main organ of local administration, and the Custos Rotulorum passed down his duties as permanent official to the Clerk of the Peace, who was often an attorney. Felonies were increasingly referred to the Assizes.

Owing to the increase in population in the eighteenth century, many Quarter Sessions could not be carried through within the usual time and had to be continued by adjournment. Several counties were therefore divided into two or more divisions for administrative purposes, each of which held its sessions 'by adjournment'. Hundred juries fell into disuse. The justices began acting in a more executive capacity and issued what were, in effect, by-laws. During the Sessions, less administrative business was done, because Standing Committees of Justices were appointed for dealing with particular problems (e.g. gaols and bridges), and new administrative offices were created: the County Treasurer, Surveyor (or Bridgemaster), Inspector of Weights and Measures, and others. In 1819 an Act of Parliament empowered justices to divide their numbers and sit in two courts simultaneously to speed up business; so the minutes may be in two series from this date.

From 1834, the scope of the justices' work was reduced by the institution of a number of *ad hoc* bodies, such as the Boards of Poor Law Guardians. The *Municipal Corporation Act*, 1835, took administrative control of the towns away from the justices, and in 1888 the *Local Government Act* transferred administrative control of the counties to county councils, in more or less the form existing today.

The Records of the Court

The *Sessions Rolls*, or *Files*, comprise all the original documents used at the Sessions (including lists of the justices in the Commission, with dots against the names of those actually present), registers of officials taking oaths of allegiance, lists of licensed religious meeting-houses, indictments, recognizances and petitions.

The *Indictment* (or *Process*) *Books* deal with judicial business. They give brief particulars of defendants, offences, pleas, verdicts and, occasionally, sentences.

The *Minute* (or *Sessions*) *Books* contain either rough notes of the proceedings, or minutes fairly written out; sometimes both are extant. In the later period there are also *Minute Books* for the Meetings of Standing Committees.

The *Order Books* are the formal records of the Court, giving the justices' decisions and edicts. The earliest extant Order Book (Devon) dates from the end of the sixteenth century, but some rolls or files are in private ownership, including, for example, those for Hertfordshire, which are at Hatfield House. Most of the extant books begin in the seventeenth century, but some are later. They were compiled both for current reference and for providing precedents. Sometimes they make reference to cases dealt with by the justices 'out of Session', i.e. in Petty Sessions. The orders are entered in chronological order, with no distinction between judicial and administrative work, since the procedure for all was judicial. However,

marginal notes of the names of persons and parishes are a help to searchers. Order Books also have contemporary indexes, which make them the most convenient of the Quarter Sessions records to search, but they often contain less detail than can be found in the rolls. Of the judicial proceedings, some were preliminary hearings of cases that would be sent on to the Assizes. The administrative business included recusancy, conventicles, taxation, rating, the Poor Law, vagrancy, highways, county bridges, ale houses, markets, outbreaks of disease and fire, sacrament certificates, registration of papists and their estates, oaths of allegiance, settlement orders, gaols, Houses of Correction and prisoners, weights and measures, and wages.

Bills of indictment were first drawn up by an official and submitted to a Grand Jury on the first day of the Session, who would examine witnesses and return the indictment marked either *billa vera* (true bill), or *ignoramus* (we do not know). In the former case the accused would stand his trial, though not always at the same session. Presentments were also made by constables, hundred juries, or the Grand Jury itself. In some counties the Sessions were always held in the county town; in others at several towns in rotation. There were separate Commissions of the Peace for each Riding of Yorkshire, and for each of the three parts of Lincolnshire.

Except during the Commonwealth, writs, indictments and recognizances were written in Latin until 1733.

A few rolls of pleas survive for the fourteenth and fifteenth centuries, and are at the Public Record Office, Chancery Lane, London, but the rest of the records are deposited at the county record offices, though a few may have got into private hands or have been lost or destroyed. Many have been calendared either in full or in extracts, and the county record offices have copies.

Judicial cases usually contain interesting biographical material about the persons concerned. Whenever a person is mentioned, his or her occupation is given. The long lists of persons registered under Acts requiring oaths of allegiance supply information about dissenters and Roman Catholics that may reveal an ancestor's religious convictions.

The Federation of Family History Societies has published a booklet, *Quarter Sessions Records for Family Historians*, by J.S.W. Gibson, which gives details of county holdings.

Quarterage County rates, payable quarterly through the parish officers.

Questman An assistant to the churchwarden. A sidesman.

Quia Emptores A law passed to prevent the loss of feudal obligations that occurred when a mesne lord granted a fee to a purchaser of the land, and required only a nominal service from him thenceforward, such as a pair of gloves annually or a rose at midsummer. The law allowed the mesne lord to dispose of land, but the feudal obligations attached to land-holding fell automatically upon the purchaser.

Quindene The day falling a fortnight after a church festival; i.e. fifteen days, including the festival itself. *See also* OCTAVE.

Quit Rent A small fixed annual rent, on payment of which a manorial or burgage tenant was quit (released) from all services to his lord. A LANDGABLE was a burgage quit rent.

Quo Warranto (i) A statute pronounced at Gloucester in 1278 by Edward I, in consequence of the abuses revealed by the RAGMAN ROLLS. By this he summoned all men who held private franchises and jurisdictions to appear before the king's judges and show by what right — *quo warranto* — they held them. Anyone failing to appear forfeited his jurisdiction to the sheriff until he proved his claim. In operating the statute, the king's lawyers refused to recognise any undocumented right, however ancient it was. This caused such injustice that in 1290 the king conceded a right to anyone who could prove by a jury of neighbours that he had held it 'since time immemorial', which meant from before the accession of Richard I in 1189.

(ii) A Writ of Quo Warranto lay against anyone who usurped a franchise or liberty against the king, or intruded himself as heir into any land.

Ragman Rolls The returns made in 1275 by commissioners appointed by Edward I to enquire throughout the country into abuses and usurpations, particularly against royal rights, committed during his absence on crusade. The king's possessions and rights, and the liberties granted by his predecessors, are listed. The Rolls are at the Public Record Office, Chancery Lane, London, under reference C.47/23.

Rape A subdivision of the county of Sussex.

Rate Books A rate is a local levy for either a specific purpose or for general purposes. The earliest extant are those of parishes and the wards of corporate boroughs for the maintenance of a local church, bridge, drainage system, or fortification. A few rate books, listing the ratepayers, survive from the Middle Ages, but the *Poor Law Acts* of 1597/8 and 1601 were the first to lay down the compulsory raising of a rate in every parish, and this was followed later in the seventeenth century by rates for the maintenance of the highways and gaols, and for dealing with vagabonds and prisoners, and, later still, for sewers and the militia. In 1738/9, many of these rates were merged with the Poor Rate.

Parochial poor rates were assessed by the Overseers of the Poor, and approved by the vestry on the basis of lands and buildings. The rate books list the ratepayers by name, showing the amounts collected and, sometimes, the assessments, often with marginal notes about either the properties or their occupiers. After 1834, both occupier and owner are named. The order in which the ratepayers were listed tended to remain the same from year to year, and in towns they are shown under street headings; so a careful comparison of the lists with other sources, such as local directories, may enable an ancestral home to be located. In towns, the parish and ward boundaries did not always coincide; so, with the additional aid of the street name, the area in which a house stood can often be closely narrowed down. Parochial rates, where they survive, have mostly been deposited by the incumbents at county record offices, but some still remain in parish churches. Borough and ward rate books are usually at the town's record office.

Recognizance (i) A legal document obliging a person to do something under a certain stated condition, in the same manner as a bond; the only difference being that the recognizance did not require the party's seal. The licensees of public houses were obliged to take recognizances before two Justices of the Peace.

(ii) A court's acknowledgement of deeds deposited, e.g. a conveyance, or a bond for good behaviour or appearance in court.

Record Cards, Genealogical Printed cards, 6 × 4 inches, with spaces allotted for card number, name of person, dates and places of birth, baptism, marriage, death, burial and probate of will; also names of father, mother, spouses and children. A useful aid for rapid reference and for identifying and linking persons for whom stray references have been found. Published by the Society of Genealogists.

Record Keeping The manner in which transcripts of family evidence should be kept is one on which there is no general agreement. The problem should be considered under three categories: (i) records of the male-line descent of the family being researched; (ii) records of collateral branches of that family; (iii) records of mentions of the same surname until they can be identified as either falling under (i) or (ii), or as referring to some other family. In each of these classifications, the purpose of the transcripts should be considered. Those in (i) are for the compilation of a family tree and eventually, perhaps, for the writing of a family history. Those in (ii) will usually be for the compilation of an extended family tree, connected with the line of descent in (i). Those in (iii) will be for storage in a condition enabling rapid reference to be made for the purposes of (i) and (ii).

(i) Records for a male-line family tree and history will include, in each generation, the ancestor and ancestress, and the ancestor's

brothers and sisters and their spouses. Transcripts should be kept in loose-leaf volumes in chronological order of the events they record. As these volumes will be for passing down to descendants they should be durable and handsome, and therefore preferably of the type that, though loose-leaf, grips the pages firmly rather than holding them loosely on rings. The chronological order is essential for the eventual writing of a narrative history. Each transcript sheet should be dated at the top right-hand corner with the date of the event it records, thus giving it a page number. The transcript must be headed with the title and reference number of the original document and its location. Any second event happening on the same day should be added on the same sheet, also any relevant background information, such as that obtained from local histories, etc., for use in writing the history. For biographical purposes, all family finds should be transcribed in generous extracts. For example, an entry from a local directory should include not only the name and address of the ancestor, but of every person in the urban street or in the village. Names of neighbours thus recorded are apt to recur in other connections, and so fill in the social background of the family.

The only exception to the rule requiring a separate sheet for each day on which an event is recorded, arises when a diary or ship's log-book is transcribed. To record each day on a separate sheet would make the total record too bulky, so each sheet should contain as many days' entries as is convenient, as long as they are all in the same month, and as long as no other event, culled from a separate source, occurs during the period recorded on the sheet.

The loose-leaf binder should contain a family tree, to act as a rough index.

(ii) Collateral lines. What method is used for this class of record depends on how much interest is taken in distant cousins of the family. If it is considerable, the same chronological method can be used in a separate loose-leaf binder for each branch, but if the collateral lines are of little concern, the information about them can be kept in the same way as in (iii), below.

(iii) This class of unconnected mentions of the surname, necessary in all genealogical research, will be of minor interest once the male-line descent has been fully established. Some genealogists recommend keeping these transcripts in files or loose-leaf binders, but files need drawers or filing-cabinets. There seems no good reason why such records should not be kept in bound MS books, provided a running index of the contents is maintained at the back for ease of reference. The index can be of names or sources, or both. A bound volume holds more than a loose-leaf binder, can be conveniently kept on a bookshelf, and is easily portable. Entries that are later found to belong properly to classes (i) or (ii) can be struck through and annotated 'Transferred to . . .'.

Record Offices As an aid to locating the offices, the Federation of Family History Societies has published a booklet with sketch town plans, entitled *Record Offices, How to Find Them*, by J.S.W. Gibson and Pamela Peskett. *See also* under county headings.

Recovery Rolls Common Recovery is a type of property conveyance first found in the fifteenth century. Like the Final Concords (*see* FINE) it took the form of a collusive legal action. The recoverer (purchaser) sued the tenant (vendor), alleging that he had no legal title because he had only come into possession after (a fictitious) Hugh Hunt had turned the recoverer out. The tenant brought a third party to court (the vouchee), who was supposed to have warranted the title to him and therefore was bound to defend the issue in his place. The recoverer then asked permission to imparl (to confer with) the vouchee. When the court reassembled, the vouchee failed to appear, so judgement was given for the recoverer. The vouchee was supposed to give land of equal value to the tenant for having misled him, but he never had any land, being often the court cryer. In later times there was usually more than one vouchee, and the procedure was recovery by double or treble voucher. The action could be heard in the Court of Common Pleas, the Court of Hustings, or a manor court. It was entered on the court rolls, and a copy of the entry, described as an exemplification, was handed to the recoverer. This procedure lasted until 1833, and the records (except those enrolled with manor court proceedings) are at the Public Record Office, Chancery Lane, London, under reference CP.43. The records of the Court of Hustings are at the Corporation of London Record Office. This procedure is sometimes found to be followed by a conveyance that restored the land to the tenant, the recovery having been merely a legal device for ending his original type of tenure.

Recto The right-hand page of an open book, the opposite of verso (the reverse, or left-hand, page).

Rector The owner of a parish benefice, who was also the recipient, until they were commuted, of the Great Tithes. He was responsible for the upkeep of the chancel of his church as his private portion of the building. *See also* INCUMBENT; VICAR.

Recusant Rolls A recusant was one who absented himself (or herself) from the services of his parish church. Under the *Act of Uniformity*, 1559, he was fined 12 pence for each absence. In 1581, the fine was raised to £20 per lunar month, and under Acts of 28 & 29 Elizabeth I, and 3 & 4 James I (their regnal years), he was liable to forfeit all his goods and two-thirds of his real property. The Recusant Rolls list the fines and forfeitures, but are by no means full lists of recusants. The properties confiscated are described in some detail. Many recusants were Roman Catholics, but in some areas the majority were Puritan dissenters; the rolls give no indication as to the religious convictions of the person penalised. Many upper-class recusants seem to have been overlooked by the authorities. The annual rolls of the county sheriffs cover the period 1592 to 1691 inclusive, but some years are missing. They are held at the Public Record Office, Chancery Lane, London, under references E.376 and E.377/1-82. The Catholic Record Society has published a number of rolls. *See also* NONCONFORMISTS; ROMAN CATHOLICS.

Reeve The foreman of the villeins — and, later, of the copyholders — of a manor. He was the official with whom the lord's bailiff dealt. He was elected by the tenants, but could pay to be excused his office. In small villages, the reeve might do double duty as constable.

Registrar General *see* General Register of Births, Deaths and Marriages

Regnal Years In the Middle Ages, documents were dated by the year of the monarch's reign: thus, a document of the third year of the reign of King Henry VI would be shown as such (and in modern calendars as 3 Henry VI). In later records, the *Anno Domini* year either replaced the regnal year or was given in addition to it. After the Restoration of the monarchy in 1660, all documents used by genealogists will bear the AD date, even though regnal years continue to appear, even (in the case of Acts of Parliament) into the present century.

The sovereigns' regnal years began on the dates shown on pp. 249-52, and continued until the same day twelve calendar months later. One exception is the reign of King John. He came to the throne on Ascension Day, which is a movable feast; so each of his regnal years starts on Ascension Day and not on the calendar anniversary of his accession.

Regrate To buy with the intention of selling retail.

Relationship, Degree of Degrees of relationship for purposes of inheritance follow a biological path, and advance by one with each person in that path, as follows:

one degree: parent and child.
two degrees: siblings (i.e via the parent); grandparent and grandchild.
three degrees: uncle or aunt, and nephew or niece; great-grandparent and great-grandchild.
four degrees: first cousins; great-great-grandparent and great-great-grandchild.

Degrees of cousinship First cousins are the children of siblings; second cousins are the children of first cousins; and so on. Cousins are once, or more, removed when they are not (in the family tree sense) both of the same generation. The removal number indicates by how many generations they differ. For example: my son's child and my daughter's grandchild are first cousins once removed. Although, logically, one might also say they were second cousins once removed, in practice the relationship is always measured from the closer cousinship.

Relief A customary manorial payment due from the heir of a deceased freeholder to the lord of the manor, for the privilege of taking up the estate of his predecessor (*see* HERIOT). Also due from the purchaser of such a freehold. Payment was usually the value of one year's rent.

Remainder (in a will) In the phrase 'with remainder to', the word indicates the right of succession to a legacy in the event of the death of the named beneficiary before the death of the testator, or before a stipulated age.

Removal Order *see* Settlement

Renders *see* Serjeanty

Replevin, Writ of A writ issued for the wrongful distraint of cattle.

Requests, Court of Petitions by poor persons, heard during the Middle Ages by justices in Eyre, and then by the Court of Chancery, were, in 1390, transferred to a committee of the King's Council functioning as a court of equity. In 1483, the Lord Privy Seal became its president. After having followed the king's movements for over a century, it was given a permanent seat in Whitehall in 1516, and for a time took its name from that palace. Eventually it became officially known as the Court of Requests. The Lord Privy Seal was assisted by four Privy Councillors, as Masters of Requests, sitting with professional judges and assessors. Although intended to be a poor man's court, it was much used by members of the royal household and came, in time, to hear complaints from all sorts of people. All evidence was taken in writing and often contains interesting biographical material. The Court was abolished in 1642.

The records are at the Public Record Office, Chancery Lane, London, under group REQ.1-3, and are calendared from Henry VII to Elizabeth I in *Lists and Indexes, Vol.21*, and indexed from

REGNAL YEARS

William I
14 Oct.

1	1066
2	7
3	8
4	9
5	1070
6	1
7	2
8	3
9	4
10	5
11	6
12	7
13	8
14	9
15	1080
16	1
17	2
18	3
19	4
20	5
21	1086

William II
26 Sept.

1	1087
2	8
3	9
4	1090
5	1
6	2
7	3
8	4
9	5
10	6
11	7
12	8
13	1099

Henry I
5 Aug.

1	1100
2	1
3	2
4	3
5	4
6	5
7	6
8	1107
9	8
10	9
11	1110
12	1
13	2
14	3
15	4
16	5
17	6
18	7
19	8
20	9
21	1120
22	1
23	2
24	3
25	4
26	5
27	6
28	7
29	8
30	9
31	1130
32	1
33	2
34	3
35	4
36	1135

Stephen
26 Dec.

1	1135
2	6
3	7
4	8
5	9
6	1140
7	1
8	2
9	3
10	4
11	5
12	6
13	7
14	8
15	9
16	1150
17	1
18	1152
19	3

Henry II
19 Dec.

1	1154
2	5
3	6
4	7
5	8
6	9
7	1160
8	1
9	2
10	3
11	4
12	5
13	6
14	7
15	8
16	9
17	1170
18	1
19	2
20	3
21	4
22	5
23	6
24	7
25	8
26	9
27	1180
28	1
29	2
30	3
31	4
32	5
33	6
34	7
35	1188

Richard I
3 Sept.

1	1189
2	1190
3	1
4	2
5	3
6	4
7	1195
8	6
9	7
10	8

John
Ascension

1	27.5.
	1199
2	18.5.
	1200
3	3.5.1
4	23.5.2
5	15.5.3
6	3.6.4
7	19.5.5
8	11.5.6
9	31.5.7
10	15.5.8
11	7.5.9
12	27.5.
	1210
13	12.5.1
14	3.5.2
15	23.5.3
16	8.5.4
17	28.5.5
18	19.5.1216

Henry III
28 Oct.

1	1216
2	7
3	8
4	9
5	1220
6	1
7	2
8	3
9	4
10	5
11	6
12	7
13	8
14	9
15	1230
16	1
17	2
18	3
19	1234
20	5
21	6
22	7
23	8
24	9
25	1240
26	1
27	2
28	3
29	4
30	5
31	6
32	7
33	8
34	9
35	1250
36	1
37	2
38	3
39	4
40	5
41	6
42	7
43	8
44	9
45	1260
46	1
47	2
48	3
49	4
50	5
51	6
52	7
53	8
54	9
55	1270
56	1
57	1272

Edward I
20 Nov.

1	1272
2	3
3	4
4	5
5	6
6	7
7	8

Edward I
20 Nov.

8	1279
9	1280
10	1
11	2
12	3
13	4
14	5
15	6
16	7
17	8
18	9
19	1290
20	1
21	2
22	3
23	4
24	5
25	6
26	7
27	8
28	9
29	1300
30	1
31	2
32	3
33	4
34	5
35	1306

Edward II
8 July

1	1307
2	8
3	9
4	1310
5	1
6	2
7	3
8	4
9	5
10	6
11	7
12	8
13	9
14	1320
15	1
16	2
17	3
18	4
19	1325
20	1326

Edward III
25 Jan

1	1326/7
2	7/8
3	8/9
4	9/0
5	1330/1
6	1/2
7	2/3
8	3/4
9	4/5
10	5/6
11	6/7
12	7/8
13	8/9
14	9/0
15	1340/1
16	1/2
17	2/3
18	3/4
19	4/5
20	5/6
21	6/7
22	7/8
23	8/9
24	9/0
25	1350/1
26	1/2
27	2/3
28	3/4
29	4/5
30	5/6
31	6/7
32	7/8
33	8/9
34	9/0
35	1360/1
36	1/2
37	2/3
38	3/4
39	4/5
40	5/6
41	6/7
42	7/8
43	8/9
44	9/0
45	1370/1
46	1/2
47	1372/3
48	3/4
49	4/5
50	5/6
51	1376/7

Richard II
22 June

1	1377
2	8
3	9
4	1380
5	1
6	2
7	3
8	4
9	5
10	6
11	7
12	8
13	9
14	1390
15	1
16	2
17	3
18	4
19	5
20	6
21	7
22	8
23	1399

Henry IV
30 Sept.

1	1399
2	1400
3	1
4	2
5	3
6	4
7	5
8	6
9	7
10	8
11	9
12	1410
13	1
14	1412

Henry V
21 Mch.

1	1412/3
2	3/4
3	4/5
4	5/6
5	6/7
6	7/8
7	8/9
8	9/0
9	1420/1
10	1421/2

Henry VI
1 Sept.

1	1422
2	3
3	4
4	5
5	6
6	7
7	8
8	9
9	1430
10	1
11	2
12	3
13	4
14	5
15	6
16	7
17	8
18	9
19	1440
20	1
21	2
22	3
23	4
24	5
25	6
26	7
27	8
28	9
29	1450
30	1
31	2
32	3
33	4
34	5
35	6
36	7
37	1458
38	9
39	1460

Restored
9 Oct.

49	1470

Edward IV
4 Mch.

1	1460/1
2	1/2
3	2/3
4	3/4
5	4/5
6	5/6
7	6/7
8	7/8
9	8/9
10	1469/0
11	1471/2
12	2/3
13	3/4
14	4/5
15	5/6
16	6/7
17	7/8
18	8/9
19	9/0
20	1480/1
21	1/2
22	1482/3

Edward V
9 Apr

1	1483

Richard III
26 June

1	1483
2	4
3	1485

Henry VII
22 Aug.

1	1485
2	6
3	7
4	8
5	9
6	1490
7	1

Henry VII
22 Aug.

8	1492
9	3
10	4
11	5
12	6
13	7
14	8
15	9
16	1500
17	1
18	2
19	3
20	4
21	5
22	6
23	7
24	1508

Henry VIII
22 Apr.

1	1509
2	1510
3	1
4	2
5	3
6	4
7	5
8	6
9	7
10	8
11	9
12	1520
13	1
14	2
15	3
16	4
17	5
18	6
19	7
20	8
21	9
22	1530
23	1
24	2
25	3
26	4
27	5
28	6
29	7
30	1538
31	1539
32	1540
33	1
34	2
35	3
36	4
37	5
38	1546

Edward VI
28 Jan.

1	1546/7
2	7/8
3	8/9
4	9/0
5	1550/1
6	1/2
7	2/3

Jane
6 July

1	1553

Mary I
6 July

1	1553
2	4

Philip & Mary
25 July

1/2	1554
2/3	5
3/4	6
4/5	7
5/6	1558

Elizabeth I
17 Nov.

1	1558
2	9
3	1560
4	1
5	2
6	3
7	4
8	5
9	6
10	7
11	8
12	9
13	1570
14	1
15	1572
16	3
17	4
18	5
19	6
20	7
21	8
22	9
23	1580
24	1
25	2
26	3
27	4
28	5
29	6
30	7
31	8
32	9
33	1590
34	1
35	2
36	3
37	4
38	5
39	6
40	7
41	8
42	9
43	1600
44	1
45	1602

James I
24 Mch.

1	1602/3
2	3/4
3	4/5
4	5/6
5	6/7
6	7/8
7	8/9
8	9/0
9	1610/1
10	1/2
11	2/3
12	3/4
13	4/5
14	5/6
15	6/7
16	7/8
17	8/9
18	1619/20
19	1620/1
20	1/2
21	2/3
22	3/4
23	4/5

Charles I
27 Mch.

1	1625
2	6
3	7
4	8
5	9
6	1630
7	1
8	2
9	3
10	4
11	5
12	6
13	7
14	8
15	9
16	1640
17	1
18	2
19	3
20	4
21	5
22	6
23	7
24	1648

Charles II
30 Jan.

1	1648/9
12	1659/60
13	1660/1
14	1/2
15	2/3
16	3/4
17	4/5
18	5/6
19	6/7
20	7/8
21	8/9
22	9/0
23	1670/1
24	1/2
25	2/3
26	3/4
27	4/5
28	1675/6
29	6/7
30	7/8
31	8/9
32	9/0
33	1680/1
34	1/2
35	2/3
36	3/4
37	1684/5

James II
6 Feb

1	1684/5
2	5/6
3	6/7
4	7/8
till	12.12.88

Wm. & Mary
13 Feb.

1	1688/9
2	9/0
3	1690/1
4	1/2
5	2/3
6	1693/4

William III
28 Dec.

6	1694
7	5
8	6
9	7
10	8
11	9
12	1700
13	1
14	1702

Anne
8 Mch.

1	1701/2
2	2/3
3	3/4
4	4/5
5	5/6
6	6/7
7	7/8
8	8/9
9	9/0
10	1710/1

Anne	
8 Mch.	
11	1711/2
12	2/3
13	3/4

George I	
1 Aug.	
1	1714
2	5
3	6
4	7
5	8
6	9
7	1720
8	1
9	2
10	3
11	4
12	5
13	1726

George II	
11 June	
1	1727
2	8
3	9
4	1730
5	1
6	2
7	3
8	4
9	5
10	6
11	7
12	8
13	9
14	1740
15	1
16	2
17	3
18	4
19	5
20	6
21	7
22	8
23	9
24	1750
25	1
26	2
27	3
28	4
29	1755
30	6
31	7
32	8
33	9
34	1760

George III	
25 Oct.	
1	1760
2	1
3	2
4	3
5	4
6	5
7	6
8	7
9	8
10	9
11	1770
12	1
13	2
14	3
15	4
16	5
17	6
18	7
19	8
20	9
21	1780
22	1
23	2
24	3
25	4
26	5
27	6
28	7
29	8
30	9
31	1790
32	1
33	2
34	3
35	4
36	5
37	6
38	7
39	8
40	9
41	1800
42	1
43	2
44	1803
45	4
46	5
47	6
48	7
49	8
50	9
51	1810
52	1
53	2
54	3
55	4
56	5
57	6
58	7
59	8
60	1819

George IV	
29 Jan.	
1	1820
2	1
3	2
4	3
5	4
6	5
7	6
8	7
9	8
10	9
11	1830

William IV	
26 June	
1	1830
2	1
3	2
4	3
5	4
6	5
7	1836

Victoria	
20 June	
1	1837
2	8
3	9
4	1840
5	1
6	2
7	3
8	4
9	1845
10	6
11	7
12	8
13	9
14	1850
15	1
16	2
17	3
18	4
19	5
20	6
21	7
22	8
23	9
24	1860
25	1
26	2
27	3
28	4
29	5
30	6
31	7
32	8
33	9
34	1870
35	1
36	2
37	3
38	4
39	5
40	6
41	7
42	8
43	9
44	1880
45	1
46	2
47	3
48	4
49	5
50	6
51	7
52	8
53	9
54	1890
55	1
56	2
57	3
58	4
59	5
60	6
61	1897
62	8
63	9
64	1900

Edward VII	
22 Jan.	
1	1901
2	2
3	3
4	4
5	5
6	6
7	7
8	8
9	9
10	1910

George V	
6 May	
1	1910
2	1
3	2
4	3
5	4
6	5
7	6
8	7
9	8
10	9
11	1920
12	1
13	2
14	3
15	4
16	5
17	6
18	7
19	8
20	9
21	1930
22	1
23	2
24	3
25	4
26	1935

Edward VIII	
20 Jan.	
1	1936

Henry VIII to James I in *Supplementary Lists and Indexes 7* (4 volumes), under the names of the parties, places and subjects.

Residence, Certificate of In the sixteenth and seventeenth centuries, certificates were issued to people who had moved their abode, to show that they had made their Lay Subsidy payment in a certain place and were therefore to be excused elsewhere. A duplicate of the certificate was attached to the subsidy return. This practice began in the reign of Edward VI and continued until that of Charles II.

The certificates, now detached from the returns, are in 462 bundles among the Exchequer records at the Public Record Office, Chancery Lane, London. They are calendared, by surname only, under reference E.115. The calendars are on the shelves of the Round Room. Against each surname is shown the county of residence, but it must be remembered that this may not be the county of residence already known for that person. The certificates are a valuable aid for tracing a family move.

Roe, Richard A fictitious personage introduced into many legal documents; as also John Doe and Hugh Hunt. These imaginary persons were introduced to enable the Common Law to cope with new situations and needs, while still, to outward appearance, preserving its ancient forms.

Rogationtide The Monday, Tuesday and Wednesday before Ascension Day, originally kept as a period of fast and supplication, especially for the coming harvest. In Roman Catholic England, litanies were chanted in procession, but after the Reformation the processions lost their religious significance and became simply the perambulation of the parish boundaries.

Rogue Money A payment due annually from each parish to the High Constable of the hundred, for the maintenance of prisoners in the county gaol.

Roman Catholics From 1559, the history of English Catholics became a subject separate from that of their compatriots, as a result of the

Acts of *Supremacy* and *Uniformity*. The latter made non-attendance at services of the Church of England an offence, called recusancy. A fine of one shilling for each absence was collected by the churchwardens and used for the relief of the parish poor.

In 1569, many Catholic nobles took part in the 'Rising of the North' in favour of Mary Queen of Scots, which led to the active persecution of their co-religionists. However, English Catholics trained for the priesthood at the theological college at Douai in France, and, from 1574 onward, entered the country secretly to keep the faith alive against the time when Mary, the heir presumptive, should succeed her cousin, Elizabeth.

From 1581, fines were raised to £20 per month for absenteeism, 100 marks plus one year's imprisonment for attending a Catholic Mass, and 200 marks plus the same imprisonment for celebrating the Mass. Three years later it became high treason for laymen to receive the ministrations of Catholic priests.

In 1586, non-payment of fines became punishable by seizure of all one's movable goods and two-thirds of one's lands. The missionary priests were concealed by wealthy co-religionists in hiding holes in their country houses. Such priests had no geographical boundaries for their missions, and they naturally tended not to keep registers because these would have constituted documentary evidence against their flock. Catholics, however, were baptized and even married by their missionary priests, but they usually went through a Church of England marriage too, to avoid a fine, to obtain legal registration and to avoid any doubt about the legitimacy of their children. Burials were usually only possible in parish churches. Catholicism survived mainly in the north. In 1678, the Popish Plot invented by Titus Oates temporarily revived the persecution of Catholics, whose legal disabilities had for some years not been too strictly enforced. (For Roman Catholics of the mid seventeenth century, *see* ROYALIST COMPOSITION PAPERS).

At the end of the seventeenth century, so many Catholics were not having their children baptized by the parish priest that they were obliged by law to inform him of the births of their children, and were fined for noncompliance. Therefore many Catholic births (not baptisms) can be found recorded in parish registers of that period.

At the turn of the century, anti-Catholic feeling grew sharper as the danger of a Catholic heir to the throne became imminent. Papists were forbidden to buy or inherit land. In 1701, the *Act of Settlement* barred Catholics from the throne of England.

With the accession of George I, an Act was passed compelling all persons over the age of 18 to take an Oath of Allegiance, in the wording of which they renounced the Catholic Church. Lists exist of people of property who refused to take this oath. Papists were compelled to register the value of their lands, whether freehold, copyhold or leasehold, with the Clerk of the Peace. On the death of a registered landowner, his heir had to register. Sometimes a copy of the will would be attached. Some papists forfeited their lands; all were liable to special taxes. From 1754, only marriages in Church of England churches were legal. In 1778, an Act was passed 'to relieve, upon conditions and under restrictions, persons professing the Popish religion'. This is popularly known as 'the repeal of the penal laws' (the years from the Reformation until 1778 are called by Catholics 'the penal times'). Catholics were now allowed to take an Oath of Allegiance and attend the law courts, and it is from this year that a number of Catholic registers begin. However, the Act provoked the Gordon Riots in London and disturbances elsewhere, and remained largely a dead letter.

The *Catholic Relief Act* of 1791 enabled Catholics to worship at their own registered churches under registered priests, and many churches were built. Several thousand priests fled from the French Revolution to England, and gathered congregations here.

In 1829, the *Emancipation Act* enabled Catholics to vote, sit in Parliament and hold property unconditionally. This resulted in a great increase in church building.

In 1837, the Catholic Church, like the nonconformist churches, was asked to deposit its existing registers of baptisms and burials with the newly appointed Registrar General. Only 79 Catholic chapels agreed, mostly in Yorkshire. Their registers are now at the Public Record Office, Chancery Lane, London, under reference RG.4; the rest are held at the Catholic churches. Reference should be made to the published yearbook, *The Catholic Directory*.

In 1850, the law permitted the creation of a Roman Catholic hierarchy in Britain. Immigration from Ireland, as a result of the famine there, increased the number of Catholics in Britain. The House of Lords Record Office has lists of eighteenth- and late seventeenth-century papists.

In 1904, the Catholic Record Society was founded. In addition to many registers, it has published recusant lists and other sources, and a series of monographs. It issues a journal, *Recusant History*, twice yearly. The Secretary of the Society is Miss R. Rendel, Flat 5, Lennox Gardens, London SW1X 0BQ.

An index of Catholic marriages in London postal districts north of the River Thames, 1837-70, has been compiled. Enquiries should be addressed to Catholic Marriages, 1 Cliffsea Grove, Leigh-on-Sea, Essex.

The most useful original sources are:

Pipe Rolls 1581-91

Recusant Rolls 1592-1691 (with some gaps), containing details of lands forfeited to the Crown, and fines for non-attendance at church. However, not all the recusants listed can be assumed to be Catholics; some are Protestant nonconformists. The Rolls are among the Exchequer Records at the Public Record Office, Chancery Lane, London, under reference E.377.

Assize Court Records, Quarter Sessions Records and *Bishops' Visitation Books* have details of the presentment of recusants, and sometimes reveal the religious beliefs of the accused.

Marriages 1754-1837. Church of England registers should be searched.

Catholic Burial Grounds Enquire of local parish priests, whose names are obtainable from the yearbook, *The Catholic Directory*.

Oath of Allegiance Records and the *Register of Roman Catholic Estates* are at the county record offices.

The English Catholic Ancestor, a society for Catholic family history, has recently been formed. Its address is, c/o Mr M.L. Brooks, Hill House West, Crookham Village, near Aldershot, Hampshire.

For further reading, see *The National Index of Parish Registers, Vol.3* (Phillimore, 1974), *Roman Catholicism in England from the Reformation to 1950* by E.I. Watkins (Oxford University Press), and *Sources for Recusant History* (Catholic Record Society, 1983).

Rotulet A small roll of parchment, or a small membrane bound up in a roll.

Rovers The expression 'at rovers' meant 'at random'.

Royal Air Force This arm of the fighting services was formed in April, 1918, and so falls outside the scope of a manual of ancestral research for which that year has been taken as the appropriate terminal date. During the First World War there were two separate services, the Royal Flying Corps and the Royal Naval Air Service, under the authority of the War Office and Admiralty respectively. Their records are at the Public Record Office, Kew, among those of the Army and the Royal Navy.

Royal Artillery The Royal Regiment of Artillery came into existence in 1716 under the direction of the Board of Ordnance. During the eighteenth century its guns were distributed among the infantry, and it was not until 1802 that brigades of artillery were formed and the organisation of an independant corps took shape. In 1855, the Board of Ordnance was abolished and the Royal Artillery was placed under the authority of the War Office.

Research into 'gunners' depends upon whether the man being sought was an officer or ranker.

For *Officers*, the first source to consult is the printed *List of Officers of the Royal Regiment of Artillery, 1716-1899*, by J. Kane, available at the Public Record Office, Kew. It supplies the date on which each officer started as a Gentleman Cadet, and his age in years and months at that time. The date of each promotion follows, and, under 'Remarks', details of how and when his active career ended. A 'Supplementary Remarks' column gives such details of his career as medals, decorations and overseas postings. Medical officers are listed separately. In the Royal Artillery, promotion was always by seniority, not purchase, and was slow. The second step is to consult the printed *Battery Records of the Royal Artillery*, by Lt.-Col. M.E.S. Laws, also starting from 1716. The two volumes show, for each year, where each company of each battalion was stationed; so, by comparing it with the 'Supplementary Remarks' mentioned above, it is possible to identify the officer's company, or at least narrow it down to two or three. Against each battalion is shown a list of the WO.10 records at the Public Record Office, Kew, containing the monthly musters of the companies. Officers were liable to be moved from one company or assignment to another. Once the officer's unit is identified, histories of the Royal Artillery in the library of the National Army Museum will provide descriptions of campaigns and actions in which his company took part. The annual *Army Lists* will supply further details, such as the times when an officer was on furlough.

The Royal Military Academy, Woolwich, was founded in 1741 to train cadets and untrained officers for the artillery and engineers. In 1774, an entrance examination was introduced. In 1806, entrance was confined to cadets, and a few years later the entrance ages were fixed at 14 to 16. The Academy was also opened to men for the Royal Corps of Signals. Applications were usually accompanied by certified copies of baptismal entries.

For *Other Ranks*, there are the following original records at the Public Record Office, Kew.

Pay Lists and *Muster Rolls*, 1760 onward, give date of enlistment, movements and date of discharge or death. They are arranged by regiments in twelve-monthly volumes, again under reference WO.10. 'Men becoming Non-effective' are listed on a form at the end of each quarter, with their birthplaces and dates of enlistment. In the Muster Roll the record of a man's enlistment will show his age at that time.

Description Books (WO.54/260-316 and WO.69/74-80) supply information on a man's height and colour of hair, eyes and complexion. The books for the Royal Irish Artillery, 1756-74, are under WO.69/620.

Depot Description Books are under WO.67/1-34.

Casualty Returns are under WO.54/317-337.

Records of Service (WO.69/1-16, 7-177, 626-641) end in 1877.

Regular Soldiers' Documents exist for the period 1760-1900. Those before 1760 refer to pensioners only.

For marriages and children from *c.*1868, see the end of the Musters and Pay Lists, except for regiments in India, where they generally appear at the beginning. *Regimental Registers of Soldiers' Marriages* and the births and baptisms of their children, are at the General Register Office.

If a man's station is known but not his unit, the battalions stationed at that place can be found from the *Monthly Returns* (WO.17, and, from 1859, WO.73). *Depot Musters* exist until 1872. A regiment's depot can be found in *Hart's Army Lists*. The musters may be bound up with the other musters of the regiment; if not, they may be at the end of the WO.12 List (WO.12/12122-13184). *Medal Rolls* 1793-1904 (WO.100/1-371) contain a few details about the men who won decorations.

Royal Engineers

Royal Engineers The first engineers used in war were not regarded as military men at all, but as gentlemen engaged as consultants on the construction and destruction of fortifications, minor defence-works and roads. The manual work, too, was done by civilians (i.e. by smiths, carpenters, wood cutters, sappers and miners) under the generic term 'artificers', who were engaged for the occasion or for the campaign. This state of affairs continued, with modifications, for centuries. Throughout this time, the engineers were closely linked with the artillery.

Seventeenth century. The term 'engineers' came into use for the artificers, and the title of 'King's Engineer' was bestowed upon officials responsible for fortifications.

1716 The engineers and artillery were separated, both still remaining under the Board of Ordnance, but engineers were still considered the experts to decide on the number, siting and mounting of the artillery's guns.

1741 The Royal Military Academy, Woolwich, was founded to train men for the engineers and artillery.

1757 Engineers were, for the first time, given regular military rank, all as officers.

1772 The first Corps of Military Artificers was formed for service at Gibraltar.

*c.*1787 The title Royal Engineers was conferred on the officer engineers.

1780s Companies of military engineers were formed for service along the south coast of England.

1791 The Ordnance Survey was instituted for the mapping of Great Britain by military engineers.

1812 The School of Military Engineering, Chatham, was founded to give technical instruction to both officers and men.

1813 Four companies of Royal Sappers and Miners were formed by the Duke of Wellington in Spain, under Royal Engineer officers. The name replaced 'military artificers' for the other ranks. At Waterloo (1815) Wellington had a brigade of engineers with each division.

1853 In the Crimea, Royal Engineers were in service as telegraphists.

1855 The Board of Ordnance was abolished, and the Royal Engineers and Royal Artillery were placed under the War Office. The engineer officers and the sappers and miners were at last amalgamated, as the Corps of Royal Engineers.

1862 Following the transfer of the administration of India to the Crown, the Indian corps of engineers were incorporated into the Royal Engineers.

1875 The Institution of Royal Engineers was founded for the study of the military science and history of engineering.

Unlike the army, commissions in the Engineers could not be bought. Promotion was by seniority and tended to be slow.

Published works: *List of Officers of the Corps of Royal Engineers, 1660-1898*, by T.W.J. Connolly.

Manuscript sources at the Public Record Office, Kew: *Pay Lists and Muster Rolls* (WO.11); *Description Books* (WO.54/260-316, WO.69/74-80); *Casualty Returns* (WO.54/317-337): and for officers, *Returns of Officers' Services, 1796-1935, Commission Books of the Board of Ordnance, 1740-1852*, and *Returns of Engineer Officers, 1786-1850*.

Royal Historical Society The object of the Society is to promote the study of history by issuing publications. Founded in 1868 as the Historical Society, it attained its present title in 1887 by royal permission. In 1897 the Camden Society was amalgamated with it, and that society's *Camden Series* of texts with introductions was continued. Other publications are the Society's *Transactions*, containing the papers read before its members, and *Miscellanies*, containing several short texts. Publications of particular value to genealogists have been the *Handbook of British Chronology*, edited by Sir Maurice Powicke and Dr E.B. Fryde, the *Handbook of Dates*, by Professor C.R. Cheney, and *Texts and Calendars*, by E.L.C. Mullins.

Royal Marines The corps was founded in 1664 as the Duke of York and Albany's Maritime Regiment of Foot. They were disbanded by William III, but not long afterwards he raised two regiments, called the 1st and 2nd Marines, for the duration of the war with France.

On the outbreak of the War of the Spanish Succession in 1702, six Marine Regiments were formed, again for the duration. For the War of the Austrian Succession in 1755, ten regiments were raised, but this time they became a permanent body and were transferred from the Army to the Navy as the Marine Corps. In 1802, they became the Royal Marines. Two years later, companies of Royal Marine Artillery were formed, known, from their uniform, as the Blue Marines, to distinguish them from the Royal Marines, who wore red. The artillery companies were amalgamated with the Royal Marines in 1923.

The records are all at the Public Record Office, Kew. The Description Books (ADM.158) cover 1750-1888, and summarise in convenient alphabetical order the information given on the Attestation Forms, 1790-1883 (ADM.157) — i.e. the birthplace, pre-service trade, height, eyes, complexion and hair, and enlistment details of each recruit, with some details of his service and discharge. A number of Description Books are missing. From 1842 to 1905, similar details can be obtained from the *Registers of Service* (ADM.159). No records of officers' services, similar to other services, have been published.

For further reading, see *Tracing Your Ancestors*

in the PRO, by J. Cox and T. Padfield (HMSO, 1983). A free leaflet, *Royal Marines Records in the Public Record Office*, is available at the Public Record Office.

Royal Navy Under William the Conqueror, the Cinque Ports (Dover, Sandwich, Hastings, Romney and Hythe) were responsible for providing ships and men for the defence of the realm. By the time of Henry I, the Court of Admiralty was in existence. In Henry VIII's reign, the Navy Board was formed to take over from the Cinque Ports. The Lord High Admiral's Council was formed to assist the Lord High Admiral in carrying out the executive functions of the Navy. This later became the Admiralty Board.

Naval Accounts and Inventories were kept, and these have been published by the Navy Records Society. They include the names of some officers and officials. From the reign of Henry VIII onward, references to the Navy and some naval men can be found in the published *Calendar of State Papers*. At the Restoration (1660) the occupation of naval officer became a regular career, providing half-pay for some men on reserve, but ratings continued to be taken on only as required and mainly by pressing those men who 'used the sea', such as merchant seamen, ferrymen, etc. At this time, the personnel of the Navy was divided into Commissioned Officers, Warrant Officers and Ratings. The records of these classes differ, as follows.

For *Officers*, there are printed or typescript sources for the outlines of their careers. *Navy Lists* have ben printed since 1749; they became annual in 1782 and official from 1814. There is also the *List of Sea Officers* from 1800. The *Seniority Lists* (ADM.118) are annotated lists of officers from 1717. There is also a printed list, *Commissioned Sea Officers of the Royal Navy, 1660-1815*. A number of collections of naval biographies have also been printed, including *Lives of the British Admirals* (to 1816), by J. Campbell and W. Stevenson, *Royal Naval Biography*, by J. Marshall, *Biographia Navalis, 1794-8*, by J. Charnock, and *Naval Biographical Dictionary* (1849), by W.R. O'Byrne.

Original official sources are in the Public

Record Office, Kew, and include the following. *Records of Officers' Services* (ADM.196), from the last quarter of the eighteenth century; *Lieutenants' Passing Certificates* of both the Navy Board (ADM.107) and Admiralty (ADM.6), covering the period 1691 to 1902 with some gaps. There is a complete cumulative typescript index for 1789-1818 of the Navy Board series. From 1789, the certificates have baptismal certificates attached. *Returns of Officers' Services* (ADM.9) consist of two censuses, one of officers alive in 1817-22, annotated to 1828, and the other of officers living in 1846, in which their ages are mentioned. ADM.11/10 shows the ages of officers serving in 1847. ADM.6/30 covers lieutenants, mates, midshipmen and others, from 1799 to 1854, showing dates of birth and baptism, place of birth, and parents' names.

Other returns available are: *Appointments and Commissions*, 1695 onward (ADM.6 and 11); *Officers Appointed 1660-88* (ADM.10/10); *Lieutenants unfit for service, 1804-10* (ADM.6/123); *Officers who passed HMS Excellent gunnery school* (ADM.6/60).

Warrant Officers were heads of departments, e.g. boatswain, carpenter, cooper, engineer, gunner, master, sailmaker, surgeon. They are included in *Records of Officers' Services* (ADM.196), already mentioned. Other records are, *Warrant Officers' and Seamen's Services* (ADM.29), which give brief service records of men superannuated after 1802; the *Seniority Lists* (ADM.118); the *Commission and Warrant Books* (ADM.6 and 11). There are also censuses of boatswains, carpenters, gunners and pursers among miscellaneous registers in ADM.6 and 11.

For *Engineers* see ADM.196 13/200-6 and ADM.11/48-9. *Surgeons* 1774-1886 are recorded in ADM.104/12-29, and see also ADM.11/40 and ADM.106/2952-3. Selected *Surgeons' Journals* are in ADM.101. *Masters' Qualifications* 1660-1830 (ADM.106/2908-50) include certificates of baptism, as do some *Passing Certificates* 1851-63 (ADM.13/72-4). For *Clerks' Passing Certificates* see ADM.13/75-8 and 196-9.

For *Midshipmen* see also ADM.196, and *Passing Certificates* 1857-99 in ADM.13/102 and 240-5. Those serving in 1814 are shown with their ages and birthplaces in ADM.6/182, and an index is available.

Chaplains are listed in *Chaplains of the Royal Navy, 1626-1903*, by A.G. Kealy. See also ADM.82, 24 and 30/7.

For *Ratings* it is necessary to know the name of the ship in which a man served. *Ships' Musters* from 1667 onward are under ADM.36-9. The men's ages and birthplaces are often shown, and *Description Books* may be among them, giving ages, height, complexion, scars, tattoos, etc. Ships' *Pay Books* (ADM.31-5) survive from 1669. In 1853, Continuous Service Engagement for ratings was first introduced; *CS Engagement Books* cover the period 1853-72. If a man is known to have been serving in a given area at a certain time, but not in which ship, the *List Books* 1673-1893 (ADM.8) show the whereabouts of vessels.

During the Napoleonic Wars, a kind of naval militia was raised called the Sea Fencibles, and the paylists of this body for 1798-1810 are under ADM.28. For officers and men killed in action or dying from wounds there are records of petitions from widows, orphans or mothers, in the *Bounty Papers* (ADM.106/3023-4) for the period 1675-1822. These include evidence of kinship and often give details of the death. Records of the estates of the deceased, including some wills, are under ADM.44, 48, 141 and 142.

For biographical details, see the *Log-books of Captains* 1669-1852 (ADM.51/1-4563), and the *Log-books of Masters* 1672-1840 (ADM.52/1-4660).

For further reading, see *Tracing Your Ancestors in the PRO*, by J. Cox and T. Padfield (HMSO, 1983). *Naval Records for Genealogists*, by N.A.M. Rodger, is available at the Public Record Office. The Navy Records Society has been publishing volumes of records since 1894.

The Naval Historical Library, Ministry of Defence, Empress State Building, London SW6 1PR is open to the public by previous appointment (tel: 01.385.1244. Ext.3246).

Royalist Composition Papers

In 1643, a Parliamentary Committee was set up called the Committee for the Sequestration of Delinquents' Estates, to confiscate the lands of those who were taking the Royalist side in the Civil War. Papists and other recusants were also included, even though not taking an active military part.

When a person was accused, his estate was seized pending investigation of his case. If found guilty, his whole estate was confiscated, but one-fifth was allowed him for the maintenance of his family and another fifth of the proceeds of the estate went to the informer. In cases of mere recusancy, one-third of the estate was allowed to the guilty party. In 1653, the war being over, the work of the Committee was taken over by the Committee for Compounding the Estates of Royalists and Delinquents. The accused were urged to confess, and if they pledged their loyalty to the Commonwealth government they were allowed to compound in proportion to their guilt. One-sixth was taken from anyone who had taken part in either the first or second civil war (i.e. before or after 1647), one-third from those who had been active in both. Delinquent Members of Parliament lost half their estates. The records of both Committees are at the Public Record Office, Chancery Lane, London, the first under reference SP.20 and the second under SP.23 in volumes G1-269. The PRO has issued a free leaflet, *Confiscations, Sales and Restoration of Crown and Royalist Lands, 1642-60*.

Rutland The country was merged with LEICESTERSHIRE in 1974. The Leicestershire Family History Society holds regular meetings and issues a journal. Enquiries should be sent c/o the Federation of Family History Societies, 31 Seven Star Road, Solihull, West Midlands B91 2BZ, marked 'Please forward' and enclosing a stamped self-addressed envelope.

Record Repository Oakham Library, Oakham.

Parish Registers and Indexes (*see* comment under COUNTY) Most of the registers that have been deposited are at Leicestershire County Record Office (CRO). The Society of Genealogists has copies of a few. Pallot's Marriage Index covers 19, mostly from 1780. The INTERNATIONAL GENEALOGICAL INDEX (IGI) also has some. The Bishops' Transcripts are at the Northamptonshire CRO.

Marriage Licence Records These are at the Northamptonshire CRO.

Wills before 1858 are at the Northamptonshire CRO, some on microfilm. Exceptions are those proved in the Peculiar Courts of Caldecott and Ketton & Liddington, which are at the Leicestershire CRO.

As the county lay in the Diocese of Lincoln until 1541, and then in that of Peterborough, and always in the Province of Canterbury, wills could also be proved in the Consistory Courts of those dioceses, and in the Prerogative Court of Canterbury.

Non-parochial Registers Six registers are at the Public Record Office (PRO), Chancery Lane, London, and are also covered by the IGI.

Census Returns These are at the PRO, Portugal Street, London, and at Leicestershire CRO, Oakham Library, and Loughborough University.

Heralds' Visitation Pedigrees have been printed for 1681-2.

S

Sac and Soc The privilege of holding courts, trying causes and imposing fines, as in a MANOR.

Sacrament Certificate In 1673 the (*First*) *Test Act*, directed against Popish recusants, compelled every person holding civil or military office to take the oaths of supremacy and allegiance, accepting the king as 'the only supreme governor of this realm', and acknowledging that his authority existed 'as well in all spiritual and ecclesiastical things or causes as temporal'. It also compelled every such person to receive the sacrament of the Lord's Supper according to the usage of the Church of England, and to deliver into Quarter Sessions a certificate to that effect, signed by the minister, churchwarden and two witnesses. He also had to make a declaration against transubstantiation. These certificates frequently give the occupation of the man and of his witnesses. A register had to be kept of all persons who took the oaths. The law was not repealed until 1828, but from 1750 fewer certificates were made out.

In 1688 a new form of oath was required of all office-holders, namely:

I, [A.B.], do swear that I do from my heart abhor, detest and abjure, as impious and heretical, that damnable doctrine and position 'That Princes excommunicated or deprived by the Pope or any Authority of the See of Rome may be deposed or murdered by their Subjects or any other whatever.' And 'I do declare that no foreign prince, person, prelate, state or potentate hath, or ought to have, any jurisdiction, power, superiority, pre-eminence, or authority, ecclesiastical or spiritual within this Realm. So help me God.'

Some Protestants were allowed to practise 'occasional conformity', i.e. taking the sacrament a certain minimum number of times.

The certificates are among the Quarter Sessions records at county record offices.

Sad An adjective that meant 'discreet' or 'serious'.

Saints' Days *see* **Calendar**

Salt Library, William *see* **Staffordshire**

Sampler From the seventeenth to the early twentieth century it was the custom for a young girl to embroider a piece of material as an example of her skill in needlework. The embroidery of the sampler normally included a pattern, the alphabet in capitals and lower case, the numerals, a pious verse, quotation or motto, the maker's name and age, and the date on which she completed her work. These examples of the childish skill of little girls tend to be treasured and passed down the generations, long after all other material evidence of the family past has disappeared. A register of all surviving samplers is being compiled by Mrs Charlotte Soares, 61 Sunnyside Road, Chesham, Buckinghamshire.

Sanctuary The privilege of safe refuge in a consecrated place. Sometimes the right of sanctuary for a fleeing criminal or refugee applied to the whole church, but more often to the chancel only. To remove a person from there within forty days of his reaching it was sacrilege.

There were two kinds of sanctuary: general and peculiar. General sanctuary applied to every church, and only to felonies; peculiar sanctuary was a right granted by charter to certain churches, and covered even treason, and for life.

The procedure laid down obliged the fugitive to confess his crime in detail to one of the clergy, surrender his weapons, and pay an admission fee. Within the forty days, and in the church, he could confess his crime to the coroner and take an oath of Abjuration of the realm. He would then be convicted, suffer attainder, and forfeit his goods. To leave the realm, he would have to travel on foot, dressed in a long white robe, bare-headed and carrying a wooden cross. He had to keep to the highway, stay no more than two nights at any one place, and make straight for the coast. Sometimes his port of embarkation was laid down by the coroner.

Sanctuary for crime was abolished in 1623, but for civil processes it hung on in certain places, the best known of which was Whitefriars, between Fleet Street and the River Thames in London. These relics of sanctuary were abolished by Acts of 1697 and 1723.

Scavenger An urban official responsible for keeping the streets clean. Under him he had 'rakers', who went around three times per week doing the actual work of clearing the night-soil and rubbish put out by householders. The scavenger sometimes combined other respon-sibilities with that of the cleanliness of his area.

Schools The most accessible and informative of school records are the registers that have been published by public schools, anciently endowed grammar schools, and charity schools. They usually provide the pupil's date of birth, father's name, period at the school and a few details of his later career. The Society of Genealogists has a collection of these. For some ancient schools the minutes of Governors' Meetings survive. Another numerous class of record consists of the Log Books kept by the masters or mistresses of the thousands of schools begun in the early and middle nineteenth century, and administered under the auspices of either the National Society for Promoting the Education of the Poor (Church of England) or the British and Foreign

Schools Society (Nonconformist); both societies receiving government aid from 1839. An Act of 1879 set up local school boards all over England and Wales, which founded Board Schools wherever there was need. The Log Books of pupil attendance, and other records, may still be in the custody of the school, parish or local education authority, but many of those that survive have found their way to the county record offices. Though they contain little genealogical information, the noted causes of absences throw light on the ways of life of the children and their families. A prospectus of the archives of the British and Foreign Schools Society may be obtained from their Archives Centre, West London Institute of Higher Education, Borough Road, Isleworth, Middlesex TW7 5DU.

Scot The parochial poor rate, as distinct from Lot, which was for church maintenance.

Scottish Genealogy Despite the fact that the Crowns of both England and Scotland became vested in King James VI of Scotland and I of England in 1603, and notwithstanding the subsequent *Act of Union* of 1707, Scotland has had, and continues to have, a completely separate identity from England.

There are still many differences between the two countries (for example, Scotland continues to have quite a different legal system, her national religion is Presbyterianism and she operates the feudal system of land tenure), and they all serve to emphasise that we are dealing with a separate nation, the origin of whose people is Celtic in contrast to the rather mixed origins of their English neighbours.

Scotland's history, riddled as it is with hardship and strife, has helped to mould the Scottish character, in which devotion to the family and to the larger concept of the clan is paramount. Moreover, the comparatively small number of surnames, its relatively small population, the massive emigration, coupled with the precision of the Scottish temperament, has made Scotland notorious for its genealogical and heraldic awareness.

Insofar as research into Scottish records is concerned, we should continue to follow the same procedures and guidelines as described in the Guide to Genealogical Research, at the beginning of this book. Nevertheless, as one might expect with a separate country, there are many different records to search; but, fortunately, most of these are centralised and housed in Edinburgh, either at New Register House or at the Scottish Records Office.

Public Registers

(a) The General Register of Births, Deaths and Marriages for Scotland is housed at New Register House, Edinburgh, and dates from 1 January, 1855. It is more comprehensive than the English system, and Scottish certificates give the following additional information:

Births — date of marriage of parents (except 1856-61), thus eliminating the need for much searching; qualification of informant and his residence, if out of the house at which the birth occurred.

Marriages — how married (e.g. after proclamation); exact ages of parties; the maiden surname of the mother to each party of the marriage.

Deaths — name, surname, rank or occupation of deceased's father; maiden name of deceased's mother (with a notation if they are deceased); qualification of informant and residence, if out of house in which the death occurred.

(b) Although there has been an official Census Return every ten years since 1801, as in England, those of genealogical value started in 1841 (with the same limitations as its English equivalent), being followed in 1851 by the more comprehensive Return.

Census Returns can be consulted at New Register House in Edinburgh.

Parochial Records

(a) All the Presbyterian Parish Registers of Scotland are in the custody of the Registrar General for Scotland, where they can be inspected, and in much the same way as in England they give details of baptisms, marriage proclamations and burials.

The records of some 900 parishes were kept by their Presbyterian ministers, and most date from about 1740 (except the Western Isles). However, no uniform method for recording baptisms, proclamations or burials was in force and therefore the details vary considerably from one parish to another.

(b) Scotland, too, was racked by religious dissention, and for non-Presbyterian or nonconformist records, the Scottish Record Office has various valuable and useful collections of records, and the Registrar General has custody of a small collection of nonconformist records, a handlist of which is available from New Register House.

Naming Customs

Although there are some variations on the theme, many families in Scotland followed a highly developed system for naming their children, whereby the eldest son is named after his paternal grandfather; the second son after his maternal grandfather; the third son after his father; the eldest daughter is named after her maternal grandmother; the second daughter after her paternal grandmother; the third daughter after her mother.

Thus, it is important to note the names and details of any sponsors or witnesses where they occur in records, which, when examined in the light of the naming customs, can provide useful leads.

Wills

There are many printed indexes to wills (testaments) and Letters of Administration (Testament Dative), which have been published by the Scottish Record Society, giving details of testaments recorded in the Commissary courts, the earliest of which was in Edinburgh and dates from 1514.

There are also indexes for all Commissariots until 1800, and typescript indexes are available for the twenty years or so thereafter, until the Commissariot jurisdiction was transferred to the Sheriff courts.

Thereafter, records of testaments and their indexes formed part of the Sheriff Court Records, which are kept in the Scottish Record Office.

Unfortunately there is no national index as such, and it is necessary, therefore, to search in the regional indexes. However, a *Register of Confirmations*, giving the value of the estate, the executors and the sheriffdom in which the testament was confirmed, is available from 1876 onward, as also is a printed *Register of Defuncts* (testators) largely culled from Sheriff Court Records for part of the nineteenth century. Present-day confirmations are dealt with at Register House, whereas the older records prior to 1823 are held in the Scottish Record Office.

Monumental Inscriptions

Certain additional information as to trades or professions is sometimes incorporated on Scottish tombstones. In the eighteenth century it was common practice to put only the initials of the head of the family and his wife, and the year in which the stone was erected (often that of the first death in the family, or the date of acquisition of the lair, or grave-plot), together with certain symbols denoting trades (as listed below), as well as those denoting mortality.

Baker — baker's peel or shovel with loaves on it
Barber — scissors and comb or razor, and occasionally a bleeding bowl
Butcher — a cleaver
Cooper — a head knife
Farmer — plough-share or coulter, or oxen yoke
Gardener — spade and rake
Hammerman — crown and hammer
Maltman — spade and broom
Mariner — ship/compass/coil of rope, nautical quadrant (like a sextant) or mariner's cross/star
Mason — mell and chisel
Merchant — a pair of scales, or the figure 4
Miller — the mill-rind (the heraldic molin)
Shoemaker or Cordiner — a crown and a circular knife
Smith — crown and hammer, with pincers and horseshoe
Tailor — scissors and tailor's 'goose' (iron)
Weaver — shuttle or stretcher

A comprehensive collection of lists giving details of monumental inscriptions is available at the Scottish Record Office, or local lists are available at local libraries.

Services of Heirs

This register is useful in that it identifies many people who died intestate, together with the jury's decree as to whom the deceased's heirs should be. The registers, which are partly indexed, span some 500 years until 1847 (when the system was superceded by decrees of sheriffs) and are housed at the Scottish Record Office.

Register of Sasines

The General Register of Sasines, which is housed in the Scottish Record Office, dates from 1617, when the Scottish Parliament decreed that General and Particular Registers should be kept. It is still in use and exceeds 50,000 volumes. The register provides fairly comprehensive registration of the ownership of all land in Scotland from then until now, except for land within the royal burghs which was recorded from 1681. Through it, it should be possible for the researcher to trace the ownership of even a small piece of land over many generations. As land usually descends within a family, details of relationships can often be gleaned. There is also an abridged printed register dating from 1781, referring to the main registers, which can reduce the amount of searching required.

Registers of Deeds

The Registers of Deeds housed in the Scottish Record Office, and exceeding 12,000 volumes, have been described as 'an inexhaustible store of information about the private life of our forefathers'. It dates from 1554 and includes bonds, indentures, marriage contracts, protests and writs, together with a vast array of other material with which the researcher can clothe the skeleton. Other records include the *Calendar of Deeds* from 1554 to 1595, and the *Register of Acts and Decrees*, together with indexes from 1750 onward (except 1755 to 1770).

The Registers of Deeds are a vast repository of information. Greater detail can be obtained from *The Public Records of Scotland*, by J. Maitland Thomson (1922).

Hearth and Poll Tax Records

The Hearth Money accounts of 1690-3, giving the names of the heads of households which had hearths, and the Poll Tax records of 1694 and 1695 are kept at the Scottish Record Office.

In addition, various other tax rolls, including valuation rolls and window tax rolls, are available for the sixteenth, seventeenth and eighteenth centuries; and from 1855 the

Valuation Rolls, giving details of proprietors and tenants of all properties, are also available.

Service Records

Service Records peculiar to Scotland are housed at the Scottish Record Office, and are included in the Register of the Privy Council for Scotland, 1545-1691.

The Treasury records include many muster rolls.

Prior to the Union, records become rather more specialised, and reference should be made to the bibliography of the publications mentioned in the General section below, which relate to service records.

Heraldry

The Court of the Lord Lyon at New Register House is the Scottish equivalent of the College of Arms. However, in Scotland heraldry is governed by statute law, and the Lord Lyon King of Arms as a judge of the Lyon Court sits in judgement. Unlike England, he is armed with sufficient powers to command rather greater respect and obedience, and besides his role as a judge he is also a Minister of the Crown, and responsible direct to the Sovereign for all Scottish heraldic and genealogical matters, as well as for all matters relating to clans, their chiefs, tartan, badges and designations, etc. The records of his court, and particularly those dating from 1672 (which contain the *Public Register of All Arms and Bearings in Scotland* in 64 volumes, and the *Public Register of All Genealogies and Birthbrieves* in 4 volumes) form part of the public records of Scotland and can be inspected by the public on payment of a nominal fee. There are many practical differences between English and Scottish heraldry, but in simple terms only the eldest son of someone rightly entitled to arms inherits his father's arms undifferenced. All younger sons have only the right to matriculate a differenced version of their paternal arms, and this then forms the basis of the arms of that line. The system encourages cadets to update their pedigrees, and this is invaluable for the researcher and makes the Lyon Office records an exceedingly valuable source of information, especially bearing in mind that in 1707 a third of the population were deemed to have been noble. Details of all

Scottish Coats of Arms from 1672 to 1973 are given in *An Ordinary of Scottish Arms, 1672 to 1902*, by Sir James Balfour Paul, with Volume 2 by David Read (of Robertland) and Vivien Wilson covering 1902 to 1973.

For further information about Scottish heraldry, see *Scots Heraldry*, by Sir Thomas Innes of Learney, revised by Malcolm Innes of Edingight.

General

In so short an article, one cannot possibly do justice to the many record repositories and sources covering many hundreds of years. There are equivalent Scottish records for newspapers (from 1700) and estate and family papers in abundance, many of which are catalogued in the National Register of Archives at the Scottish Record Office. For those wishing to pursue the subject in greater detail, the following general books are particularly recommended.

Hamilton-Edwards, Gerald *In Search of Scottish Ancestry* (Phillimore)

Steel, D.J., *The National Index of Parish Registers*, Vol.XII (Phillimore)

Whyte, Donald, FHG, *Scottish Genealogical Research*

Each of these publications contains a valuable bibliography for those wishing to study a particular subject in depth. It is probable that the researcher will need to employ expert help in consulting many of these rather specialised records. Not only are the language and the handwriting very different, but many of the registers are exceedingly voluminous, which makes the services of an experienced record searcher all the more valuable. The Association of Scottish Genealogists and Record Agents has a number of members who have specialised in Scottish research.

by P. de V.B. Dewar, FSA (Scot.)

Scutage An annual money payment to a feudal lord. The practice (which developed within a century after the Conquest) of holding land of more than one lord made Knight Service difficult to operate. Also, knights grew old and might be succeeded by daughters only; so tenants in respect of whom such conditions arose were allowed to pay in lieu of service a sum of money which the lord would use towards paying a man-at-arms. This payment was called scutage, or 'shield-money', from the Latin *scutum* (a shield). In the twelfth century it was assessed at 20 shillings per whole knight's fee, payable annually in two instalments, at Easter and Michaelmas.

Sea, Births and Deaths at Since 1 July, 1837, ships' captains have returned a certificate of each event to the Registrar General of Shipping and Seamen, giving the name(s) of the person(s) concerned, the date and place (latitude and longitude), the sex, occupation, rank or rating, and nationality; and, in cases of death, the age, birthplace, last place of abode, and cause of death. The *Marine Register Books* recording these events are at the General Register Office.

See also MERCHANT SEAMEN.

Secretary Hand The great majority of sixteenth- and seventeenth-century records are written in this script. By the year 1700 it had given place to the italic hand which is very like our own. Two alphabets of Secretary Hand are shown here: the first consists of extracts from a sixteenth-century copybook and shows how the letters were meant to be formed; the second shows examples of how the letters are usually found in seventeenth-century texts written by clerks who were no calligraphers.

The first sight of a document in Secretary Hand can be daunting, but fluent reading is simply a matter of getting used to it and being aware of certain difficulties presented by it — difficulties that were almost certainly responsible for its eventual supercession. These are:

Lower case letters

a The only difficulty with this letter occurs when it is written with a diagonal ascender, which gives it a very unexpected look.

b and *l* These can look very alike if the circle of the b is small.

c and *t* These are often difficult to distinguish, and c is sometimes used where today we use a t; for example, in words ending in -ation.

d, e and *o* The e is most frequently found written without the pen having been taken off

A Secretary Hand alphabet extracted from a sixteenth-century copybook, showing how the letters were meant to be written. They should be compared with the examples shown on pages 266-7. (C.H.= draws attention to Court Hand letters radically different from their Secretary Hand counterparts.)

the paper, which makes it look very like an o with a small, accidental-looking circle at the top. Sometimes, too, this continuous action with the pen disconnects the smaller circle altogether from the larger one, and makes the letter look very like a d. For an example of this, compare the examples of e shown in the seventeenth-century alphabet with the second and third d.

f and *s* The f should have a short stroke across it, which is absent from the s, but sometimes it is missing. Both letters are often written with loops, both in the ascender and the descender. The s at the end of a word is written as the last two examples shown in the copybook alphabet and the second, fourth and sixth in the seventeenth-century alphabet. At that period, many words were spelt with a final e that is not used now; the plural 'es' was represented by what looks like a curly figure 9.

g, y and *th* The descender of the g tails away to the left, and that of the y to the right. The sound 'th' at the beginning of a word is often represented by the Anglo-Saxon letter called 'thorn'. It can be confused with the y, but, unlike that Secretary Hand letter, it is open at the top and its descender tails away to the left. This makes it identical with a modern y, but it should always be transcribed as it sounded, i.e. as 'th'.

h This letter is nearly always scrawled as in the last three examples shown in the seventeenth-century alphabet, but it is easily recognised from having both an ascender and a descender, and the latter, unlike those of f and s, tails away to the right.

i, m and *n*, also *u* and *j* The first three are made up of minims. A minim is a single short downward stroke, which by itself represents the letter i. Two of them form an n, and three make up either m, 'in' or 'ni' (the dot is often missing). To make matters worse, the letter u, as generally written, is indistinguishable from n. Also, the letters i and j were largely interchangeable, so that three minims can also represent 'ju'.

j See above.

k and *t* The lower, smaller loop of the k is often difficult to make out, and the larger loop, in the ascender, fails to ascend much, so that the latter looks at first glance like a t. But any sign of a loop indicates a k. (For t, see also c and t above.)

l, m, n and *o* See above.

Secretary Hand alphabets showing the letters as they are often found. They should be compared with the copybook alphabet on page 265, on which they are based. *Drawn by Alf Ison*

p The letter itself is fairly simple, though it can sometimes look like a carelessly written y; but with variations it can represent any one of several syllables. The sounds 'par' (as in parish) and 'per' are indicated by the letter p with its descender curving up to the left and turning back across itself to the right. Sometimes this appears as no more than a stroke across the descender. The syllables 'pre' and 'pri' are indicated by keeping the pen on the paper after

Sample letters from the 17th century

contractions

	mañõr	manner
	tõmõy	common
	ŧᵗ	that
	Mᴿ	Mr (Mister)
	Maᵗⁱᵉ	Majestie

and horizontal line developed to:

Joħ	John
Wᵗᵗ	William
Wiłts	Wiltshire

Signs

ℛ	= er	vᵉʳy	every
ℯ	= es	dayℯ	day
		dayℯ	days

propertie

Runes

Þ (thorn)	yᵉ	the
	yᵐ	them
	yᵗ	that
Ȝ (yog)	Monȝier	

Numbers etc.

11 2 2 33 ጻ 4 4 5 ς 5 б б 1 7 8 8 3 9 9 0 ø

= per, par

= pre, pri

= pro

- - - ~
.... indicate omission

the the the the = the

the = she her = her his = his

parish parish parish = parish

---

finishing the p, and making an upward flourish to the right of the letter and curving back to the left above it. The sound 'pro' is formed by continuing the curve of the p across the descender and then down and across again to the right.

q presents no difficulty.

r A letter often difficult to recognise, because it tends to be written in different ways, even in the same document.

s and *t* See above.

u and *v* These are largely interchangeable. At the beginning of a word, u is usually written as a v. (For *u*, see also above.)

w This is formed as a double v.

x This letter is also used for the ampersand, '&'. With a c following it, it stands for 'et cetera'.

y See above.

z This letter is very like the modern version.

A neatly written sixteenth-century example of Secretary Hand. It reads: 'In the name of God Amen. the Fyvetene daye of March In the Yere of our Lord God A thousand Fyve hundreth three score & Seventene, I, / Symond Josslyn of Felsted in the Countie of Essex, yoman, beyng of holle Mynde & in good & parfight Remenbrance, I prayse & thanke / Almightie God for yt, do make & ordayne thys my present Testament & last Wyll in Maner & forme followyng, that ys to saye / Fyrst & pryncypallye I comend my Sowle to Almightie God my Maker, savior & onlye Redemer, And my bodye to be buryed / in the Church or Churchyerd of Felsted Aforsayd. Item, I gyve & bequeth to Margarett, my Wyffe, & Raffe Josslyn, my sonne, / all & every those my landes, tenementes, leazes, medowes, pastures & growndes Whych I holde by copye of Courtt Roule of the maner of / Felsted To have, hold to occupye togither from the daye of my death forthwardes duryng all the tyme & As long as she, the sayd /'. Apart from the handwriting, these lines from a will supply instructive examples of the kind of spelling and capitalisation to be expected, and the use of 'y' where we write 'i'; also the ampersand and the commonly found abbreviated syllable 'pre-' in 'present'. *Courtesy Essex Record Office*

Capitals

These are more difficult than the lower case letters, partly because there is usually more than one way in which they could be written, and partly because they so often (but by no means always) begin proper names, which themselves tend to be difficult because they cannot be deduced from the sense of the text, as other words so often can. Compare the letters closely with all the examples given in these two alphabets. The capital letter F was formed by combining two lower case ones, and should be transcribed as a capital, not as two small ffs.

Abbreviations and contractions

Medieval Latin texts were written in an exact system of these, and English texts came to be treated in the same way, but to a lesser extent. For the Latin there were various signs above the line to indicate exactly the nature of the shortening in each case, but by the sixteenth century these had degenerated into mere dashes or flourishes above the word, which did little more than indicate the use of some unspecified abbreviation or contraction. Often the writer merely kept his pen on the paper at the end of the word, and his superscribed sign became just a flourish curling up from the last letter. When a flourish of this sort (except after p) occurs in the middle of a word, it indicates the missing letters 'er'.

The contractions of syllables starting with a p have been described above. Sometimes an abbreviation is indicated by writing only one or two letters above the line. Our cardinal numbers (e.g. 1st, 2nd) are a survival of this practice.

Spelling

When trying to make out a word, remember that it may not be spelt as it is today, or even as elsewhere in the same text.

Two pieces of general advice can be given. When you first need to read a Secretary Hand text, set out to transcribe it in full. Leave a gap for any word or part of a word that you cannot read, and press on to the end. By the time you get there you will be more used to the handwriting and will be able to fill in some of the gaps. Then, read your transcript through, and the sense of the document will enable you to fill in still more. If any unsolved difficulties remain, study them carefully and search the record for other occurrences of them. These, in their context, may have caused you no trouble and will now enable you to complete your transcript.

The second piece of advice is to transcribe in full the first example of each particular type of document you consult. You can then use your transcript as a guide on future occasions, because the same words and phrases will crop up in all documents of the same type, and knowing what to expect is half the battle.

At first sight, Secretary Hand may look formidable, but one does not have to be clever to read it. Every seventeenth-century schoolboy did so. It is simply a matter of practice.

For further reading, see *Secretary Hand: a beginner's introduction*, by Lionel Munby (1984), in typescript from the Society of Genealogists. *See also* HANDWRITING.

Secular Clergy Priests not in any monastic order.

Seisin Legal possession with occupation. To disseise is to dispossess.
See also LIVERY; TERRE TENANT.

Seize Quartiers It is said that to gain admission to the court of Louis XIV, French nobles had to be able to show that all their (sixteen) great-great-grandparents were of armigerous families. In England the term has been adopted to refer to any person's complete set of great-great-grandparents, without any armorial connotation. For young people of the late twentieth century, the identifying of all members of their great-great-grandparents' generation is often not difficult, thanks to the General Register of Births, Deaths and Marriages.

Selion A strip of arable land in the common fields of a manor, normally about 22 yards (20 metres) in length. The team ploughing it kept going in the same direction, round and round the strip in narrowing turns, so that each furrow turned the soil inwards, eventually making a ridge along the centre of the selion. The lowest furrow round the outside acted as a drain. This practice is known as 'ridge and furrow ploughing'. Several adjacent selions made up a furlong. A selion was also called a 'land' or 'strip'.

Seneschal Another word for steward, from the Latin *seneschallus*.

Sentence A judgement of an ecclesiastical court regarding a disputed will. Alternatively referred to as 'decree'.

Serf An inhabitant of a manor whose status was even lower than that of a villein, in that even his body belonged to his lord. In England, serfdom, common at the time of Domesday, soon thereafter became extinct.

Sergeant-at-Law In the Middle Ages, a highly qualified lawyer. He was said to be 'of the degree of the coif', from the white silk coif that he was entitled to wear. The equivalent of the modern Queen's Counsel.

Serjeanty A type of tenure intermediate between knight service and socage. Land was held on condition of the performance of a certain individual service, other than those classed under knight service. This might be anything from service in the army of a special kind, escort service, keeping a gaol, or providing an armed man, down to rendering up some small article such as a sword or dagger each year, or even a specified flower at midsummer. These small payments were called 'renders', and tenure by virtue of them was known as petty-serjeanty. The more onerous services constituted grand-serjeanty, and the holder of such a tenure was liable to wardship if he inherited while he was under age.
See also WARDS AND LIVERIES, COURT OF.

Sessions, Special Monthly meetings of Justices of the Peace on an informal basis. Few records survive, but some may be found at the county record office.

Settlement A legal right to poor relief, arising out of a settled place of abode. By the *Poor Law Act* of 1601, a person was recognised as being legally a settled inhabitant of a parish after a month's abode. Parish vestries soon began to use this principle to operate an unofficial system of refusing relief to paupers who had settlement elsewhere.

The *Settlement Act* of 1662 laid the basis of the law of settlement for the next two centuries. Anyone entering a township and occupying a tenement worth less than £10 per annum might, within the next forty days, be removed by the parochial Overseers of the Poor, acting on an order from two Justices of the Peace who had examined him on oath. He would then be escorted, by the constable or by a series of constables along the route, back to the place where he was considered to be legally settled, unless he could give security for indemnity against becoming chargeable to the parish. However, if he managed to stay for forty days, he obtained settlement at his new abode.

In a family, a child's place of settlement was

RIGHT A handsome example of Secretary Hand in a parish apprenticeship from 1673. *Courtesy Berkshire Record Office*

Voluntary

Guildford Town, IN THE COUNTY OF **Surrey.** §§.

The Examination of *Dorothy Brinkwell* now residing in the Parish of *The Blessed Virgin Mary* in the said Town *Now Widow* taken on Oath the *seventh* day of *July* 18*20* before *John Nealds Esquire Mayor and Samuel Russell Esquire Two* of his Majesty's Justices of the Peace for the said Town,

Who on *her* Oath saith That upwards of forty years ago she hired herself as a yearly Servant to The Earl of Winterton of Shillingley in the parish of Kirdford in the County of Sussex and lived with him as a yearly Servant upwards of five years and she believes that the last forty days of her Service were performed in the said parish of Kirdford That on quitting the Service of the Earl of Winterton she intermarried with John Brinkwell of the parish of the Blessed Virgin Mary in Guildford aforesaid Plumber and Glazier And that the said John Brinkwell at the time of his death which happened about twenty eight years ago he was a settled parishioner in the said parish of the Blessed Virgin Mary And this Examinant further Saith that she hath done no Act whatever since the decease of her said Husband whereby to gain a legal Settlement either by renting a Tenement or by Service or otherwise

Sworn before Me,

John Nealds
Mayor

S. Russell

Dorothy Brinkwell
her mark

the same as his father's until he or she was apprenticed, which could happen at the age of seven. Then his place of apprenticeship would become his parish of settlement. Unmarried persons not apprenticed could obtain a new settlement after service in a parish for one year. At marriage, a woman took on the same settlement as her husband.

Illegitimate children were granted settlement where they were born. This led Overseers to try to get rid of women pregnant with bastards. If the child was born while the mother was actually under an order of removal, it was given the same settlement as hers.

From 1685, the forty days' removal period began from the date of delivery in writing to the Overseers of a notice of residence. This led to private compassionate arrangements between paupers and Overseers; so, in 1691, the forty days were made to begin from the publication of the notice in church. It is from this year that records of removal begin.

In 1697, an Act circumvented paupers who hired themselves to serve a master or mistress for a year but actually quitted their service after a few weeks. It also took the important step of authorising the Overseers to issue Settlement Certificates to paupers of their parish, but this issue was of grace, not of right. The document eased the pauper's temporary acceptance into another parish (e.g. for helping with the harvest), since it enabled the parish authorities there to send him back where he had come from if he even looked like becoming chargeable to them. In fact, the parish into which he moved was given the right of demanding such a certificate.

In 1795, removal by the Overseers was forbidden unless the pauper became actually chargeable to the parish, which did away with much of the injustice of the law. Though the *Settlement Act* was repealed in 1834, the principle of settlement remained substantially in force until 1876.

A Settlement Examination revealing valuable biographical information. Note that the word 'Earl' has been accidentally omitted from the second line.
Courtesy Guildford Muniment Room

The main documents relating to settlement are:

(i) The *Indemnity Certificate of Settlement*, given to the pauper by his own churchwardens.
(ii) The *Examination* of the pauper by churchwardens or a magistrate, prior to the issue of a *Removal Order*. This mentions his family, recent moves, and other valuable information.
(iii) The *Removal Order*, made out in duplicate, after application by the Overseer to two Justices of the Peace; one copy was for each parish concerned.
(iv) Quarter Sessions records of appeals against removal orders, sometimes with counsel's opinion on the case.
(v) Vestry minutes and the accounts of overseers and constables.

Most of the above are to be found at county record offices, but some of the parochial records may still be kept at parish churches. In these records, 'pass' was a term meaning 'send to his/her parish of settlement'.

Severalty Land 'in severalty' was held outside the conditions of common tenure customary in a manor. 'Several' meant 'separate', and so 'private'.

Shack The right of grazing upon the common arable and meadow lands of a manor after the crop has been taken.
See also LAMMAS.

Sheffield and District Family History Society *see* Yorkshire

Sheriff The chief official of a county. At the Conquest, the administration of the shires was placed in the hands of the earls, but as that rank became hereditary, and the work increased, the authority and duties passed to the sheriff. The office was for a time elective, but later by royal appointment through the Exchequer. Sometimes one man held the post for two adjacent counties. The sheriffs' functions were progressively reduced as many of them were passed to Commissioners of Array, coroners, Justices of the Peace, tax-collectors and, in the sixteenth century, to Lieutenants.

Shop A workshop. Not until the nineteenth century was the term used to mean a retail outlet, although in earlier times goods were quite often sold direct from the workshop in which they were made.

Shot (i) Another name for furlong, or, in some places, for a selion.

(ii) A body of soldiers or militiamen armed with firearms.

Shropshire The Shropshire Family History Society holds regular meetings and issues a journal. Enquiries should be sent c/o The Federation of Family History Societies, 31 Seven Star Road, Solihull, West Midlands B91 2BZ, marked 'Please forward' and enclosing a stamped self-addressed envelope.

Record Repositories Shropshire Record Office, The Shirehall, Abbey Foregate, Shrewsbury (tel: 0743.222406); Shropshire County Library, Local Studies Department, St Mary's Hall, St Mary's Place, Shrewsbury; Shrewsbury Borough Archives, Guildhall, Shrewsbury.

Parish Registers and Indexes (*see* comment under COUNTY) A large proportion of the registers of the 229 ancient parishes are now at the county record office (CRO), and copies of many of them are in the library of the Society of Genealogists. Boyd's Marriage Index covers 125. Pallot's Marriage Index covers 119, mostly from 1790, and an index for 1813-37 is in the care of R.E. Gwynne, 38 Meadow Road, Newport, Shropshire. The INTERNATIONAL GENEALOGICAL INDEX (IGI) treats over 200 registers, and a copy is at Lichfield Record Office (*see* STAFFORDSHIRE). The Bishops' Transcripts for the Diocese of Lichfield (northern part of the county) are at the Lichfield Record Office, for the Diocese of Hereford (southern part of the county) at Hereford Record Office (*see* HEREFORDSHIRE), and a few for the Diocese of St Asaph at the National Library of Wales, Aberystwyth.

Marriage Licence Records These are at the same repositories as the Bishops' Transcripts.

Wills before 1858, proved in the following courts, are at Lichfield Record Office:

Royal Peculiar (Pec.) Court of Bridgnorth
Pec. Court of Buildwas Abbey

Pec. Court of Wombridge Abbey
Manorial Court of Ellesmere
Manor Court of Longton-on-Tern
Prebendal Court of Prees or Pipe Minor

Those for the Pec. Court of Ashford Carbonal are at Hereford Record Office.

As the county lay in the three dioceses of Lichfield, Hereford and St Asaph, as well as in the Province of Canterbury, wills could also be proved in the appropriate Consistory Court and in the Prerogative Court of Canterbury.

Non-parochial Registers Fifty-five of these are at the Public Record Office (PRO), Chancery Lane, London. The IGI covers a similar number.

Census Returns These are at the PRO, Portugal Street, London, and at the Shropshire County Library.

Heralds' Visitation Pedigrees have been printed for 1623 and 1663.

The *Shropshire Archaeological Society* has published a number of county records.

Siblings Brothers and/or sisters with at least one parent in common.

Sigla A word abbreviated to a single letter, sometimes preceded and followed by a full stop; for example, .s. (*scilicet*), .f. (*folio*) and .n. (*enim*). Commonly encountered in documents written in medieval Latin.

Silly Innocent, simple.

Single A 'single person' was a divorced person; a 'single woman' was one who had borne a child, though unmarried.

Sir (i) The title, placed before both Christian name and surname, of baronets and knights, and before the Christian name alone in the oral form of address.

(ii) Until the sixteenth century, a courtesy title for a priest who was not a university graduate; translated into Latin as *dominus*.

Sister A term often used to designate a sister-in-law. Sometimes, to make clear which is meant, a real sister is referred to as 'my own sister'.

Size A kind of candle.

Slavery After a court decision of 1772, all slaves in this country became free, but this ruling did not affect those in the colonies. In 1807, an Act of Parliament abolished the slave-trade in the British dominions and this provision was strengthened by an Act of 1811, but the ownership of existing slaves remained. To check that the trade from Africa to the colonies was not continuing, slaves on the plantations had to be registered, and the lists were checked from time to time against the facts. These records, arranged under islands, parishes and plantations, are at the Public Record Office, Kew, under reference T.71. They give the slaves' names, ages and occupations, 'colour' (negro, mulatto or mestee), and 'country' (African or Creole). In 1833, an Act converted all British-owned domestic slaves into apprenticed labourers as from 1 August, 1834, and they were to be made completely free in 1840. This latter date was later brought forward to August, 1838, but by then many plantations had already freed their slaves. The T.71 class of record also lists the numbers of slaves as at 1 August, 1834, giving their value and the proportional compensation to be paid for them by the British Government.

Smoke-penny One of the dues once payable at Eastertime to the incumbent of a parish by his parishioners; in this case, from the occupier of a house with a fireplace.

Socage A form of feudal tenure in which the land was held in return for a money rent. Although no knight service was required, the tenant still had to do fealty to the king.

Society of Genealogists *see* **Genealogists, Society of**

Socman An early term for a tenant who held his land in socage.

Soiled Land Land originally held freehold, but converted to villein or copyhold tenure.

Sojourner A temporary resident in a parish.

Soke Another name for a LIBERTY.

Solemn League and Convenant On 25 September, 1643, the Members of the House of Commons took a covenant to which, in the following year, all males above the age of 18 in areas controlled by Parliament were expected to subscribe. It committed them to the reformation of religion (Protestantism), the extirpation of popery and prelacy, the preservation of the rights of Parliament and the person and authority of the king, and the exposure of all malignants (Royalists). The returns were kept locally among the parish records and only the names of refusers were sent in to Westminster. Surviving lists will now be either in church vestries or at county record offices.

Solar (i) An upper room or loft.

(ii) A room for the owner of the house, separate from the hall, which was commonly used by all the household.

Somerset The northern part of the ancient county is now in the new county of Avon. The Somerset and Dorset Family History Society holds regular meetings and issues a journal, *The Greenwood Tree*. Enquiries should be sent c/o The Federation of Family History Societies, 31 Seven Star Road, Solihull, West Midlands B91 2BZ, marked 'Please forward' and enclosing a stamped self-addressed envelope.

Record Repositories Somerset Record Office, Obridge Road, Taunton (tel: 0823.87600); Somerset County Reference Library, Binford Place, Bridgwater; Bath City Record Office, Guildhall, Bath.

Parish Registers and Indexes (*see* comment under COUNTY) Registers of most of the ancient parishes have been deposited at the county record office (CRO), and the Society of Genealogists has copies of nearly 400. Boyd's Marriage Index covers 120 parishes. Pallot's Marriage Index covers 160, mostly for 1790-1812. The family history society has a marriage index in progress in the care of G. Smith, Middle Whites Farm, Burtle, Bridgwater. The INTERNATIONAL GENEALOGICAL INDEX (IGI) treats about 100 registers. The Bishops' Transcripts are at the CRO.

Marriage Licence Records These are at the CRO.

Wills before 1858. Until 1942, the probate records of the Diocese of Bath and Wells were housed at the Probate Registry, Exeter, but they were then destroyed by bombing. However, indexes, calendars and extracts have been collected at the CRO, and also Estate Duty Office copies from 1812. As the county lay in the Province of Canterbury, wills could be proved in the Prerogative Court of Canterbury.

Non-parochial Registers Ninety-six registers are at the Public Record Office (PRO), Chancery Lane, London, and the IGI covers some of them. Copies of almost all of them, on microfilm, are at the CRO.

Census Returns These are at the PRO, Portugal Street, London, and at the CRO.

Memorial Inscriptions The Society of Genealogists has transcripts from about 150 churchyards, and the family history society has more in progress.

Heralds' Visitation Pedigrees have been printed for 1623.

The *Somerset Record Society* has published a number of county records.

Son-in-law

Son-in-law A term often used to mean 'stepson'. The existence of a son-in-law is often concealed, when his surname is not mentioned, under the term 'son'.

Soul-Scot A customary payment to the parish incumbent for a burial, paid at the open grave.

Specialty A 'debt with specialties' was one documented under seal, for instance in a bond.

Spelling Until the mid eighteenth century, spelling was not considered a matter of great importance. In manuscripts, surnames are often spelt in various ways, even in the same document. However, the appearance of the dictionaries of Nathan Bailey (1730) and Samuel Johnson (1755) were a strong influence, both directly and through the standardisation of pronunciation, toward standardising spelling on an etymological basis. It must be remembered that in most records a surname was written not by the bearer, but by a clerk who often had only the sound of the word to guide him. Thus names starting with an H may often be found written

and indexed under the second letter, and vice versa for names starting with a vowel. The addition of a final s was, and still is, a common error. Many names have a number of customary spellings, for example Shephard, Shepherd, Shepard, Sheperd, Sheppard and Shepperd.

It has been well said that most of us have inherited the sounds of our names, rather than the spelling, and in the Gothic Revival of the 1820s and 1830s a number of people changed the spelling of their surnames to what they fancied was the original form. Smith became Smythe, and Fitzhugh became FitzHugh; and one or two families of names starting with F changed to a double small f, from a misunderstanding of the capital F of SECRETARY HAND. *See also* HANDWRITING.

Spiritualities The property of a monastery or church, such as its charters, communion vessels, etc.; and income from 'spiritual' sources, e.g. tithes, offerings, glebe and land held in FRANKALMOIGN. Secular assets were called Temporalities.

Sports September 1983 saw the inaugural conference of the British Society of Sports History. Details can be obtained from Derek Benning, Madeley School of Physical Education, North Staffordshire Polytechnic, Madeley, Crewe, Cheshire CW3 9HY.

Staffordshire The southern end of the ancient county is now in the new county of West Midlands. The Birmingham and Midland Society for Genealogy and Heraldry has a Staffordshire branch (*see* WARWICKSHIRE). Enquiries should be sent c/o The Federation of Family History Societies, 31 Seven Star Road, Solihull, West Midlands B91 2BZ, marked 'Please forward' and enclosing a stamped self-addressed envelope.

Record Repositories Staffordshire County Record Office, County Buildings, Eastgate Street, Stafford (tel: 0785.3121); Lichfield Joint Record Office, Bird Street, Lichfield (tel: 05432.56787); Sandwell District Library, High Street, Smethwick (tel: 021.5580497); Dudley Public Library, Archives and Local Studies Department, St James's Road, Dudley (tel: 0384.55433);

Staffordshire County Library, First Terrace, Stafford; William Salt Library, 19 Eastgate Street, Stafford.

Parish Registers and Indexes (*see* comment under COUNTY) About half the registers of the ancient parishes have been deposited, nearly all at the county record office (CRO). The Society of Genealogists has copies of many of them. Pallot's Marriage Index covers 27 registers, mostly for 1790-1812. The INTERNATIONAL GENEALOGICAL INDEX (IGI) treats about 200 registers, and a copy is at Lichfield Joint Record Office. The family history society has a marriage index in progress in the care of Mrs Jean Dunn, 11 Common Walk, Huntington, Cannock. The Bishops' Transcripts are at the Lichfield Joint Record Office.

Marriage Licence Records These are also at the Lichfield Joint Record Office.

Wills before 1858. The records are all at the Lichfield Joint Record Office. As the county lay in the Province of Canterbury, wills could also be proved in the Prerogative Court of Canterbury.

Non-parochial Registers There are 72 registers at the Public Record Office (PRO), Chancery Lane, London. A few of them are covered by the IGI.

Census Returns These are at the PRO, Portugal Street, London, and at the CRO.

Heralds' Visitation Pedigrees have been printed for 1583, 1614 and 1663-4.

The *William Salt Archaeology Society* has published a number of county records.

Stallage A tax levied by city and borough corporations for the privilege of setting up a stall for a market or fair.

Star Chamber, Court of The Court of the Lords of the Council at Westminster, popularly known as the Court of Star Chamber from its place of session, was one of the courts that grew out of the King's Council to afford justice that complainants found difficult to obtain in the ossified procedure of the courts of Common Law. It sat without a jury and its hearings were public. It was liked and respected until the reign of Charles I, when its decisions were used to favour the causes of the king and the Anglican Church, an abuse which led to its being abolished by the Long Parliament in 1641.

Records of the proceedings are at the Public Record Office, Chancery Lane, London, under group STAC, and those of Elizabeth I's reign have been indexed in *Lists and Indexes, Supplementary 4*, Vols 1-5. The Order Books showing how suits ended were destroyed during the Civil War. All evidence was taken in the form of written depositions, and these often reveal intimate information about a person's or family's circumstances and way of life.

State Papers A collection of correspondence by royal officials, starting from early in the reign of Henry VIII. The State Paper Office was established in 1578 with two Secretaries of State, for the Northern and Southern Departments respectively. The records subsequently became separated into Domestic, Foreign and Colonial. The first and last have been calendared to the early eighteenth century, and the Foreign Papers for the reign of Elizabeth I.

In 1782, the Foreign Office was created, with the Secretary of State for the Northern Department as its head. The *State Papers* series are now at the Public Record Office, Chancery Lane, London. The calendared volumes can also be found on the open shelves at the British Library, British Museum Reading Room, and contain, among much political material, items of biographical data, mainly of the gentry. The references to original documents in this series are: Edward VI's reign, SP.10; Mary, SP.11; Elizabeth, SP.12; Domestic Addenda, SP.13. The piece numbers are those of the volumes shown in the calendar, not those of the calendar volumes.

Steward The senior administrative official of a manor, or of a monastery (for its temporal affairs); he was often a lawyer. The steward of a manor represented the lord, appointed the bailiff for the day-to-day management of the manor, and presided at manor courts unless the lord himself was present. Also termed the Seneschal. Monasteries commonly had a steward and a sub-steward. The latter did all the work, but the former had influence which he used in the monastery's favour.

Stewhouse Originally a public bath-house, but the term came to apply to a brothel. A street of stewhouses was called 'the stews'.

Stint *see* **Gate** *and* **Waste**

Stocks A wooden structure for the punishment of petty offences. The delinquent sat on a bench in a public place, such as a village green, with his ankles through apertures in boards that were then locked in position. He was thus exposed to public ignominy and possible reprisals for a specified number of hours. This form of punishment dated from Anglo-Saxon times and was last used in 1865 at Rugby.

Stray A term, recently introduced into family history circles, to mean a recorded reference to a person in connection with a parish, county or country, other than that in which he or she was normally resident. Family history societies maintain lists of such references found in their respective areas.

Strip *see* **Selion**

Subinfeudation The process by which a tenant-in-chief or his sub-tenant (a mesne lord) granted one or more of his fees to a further sub-tenant. The feudal service required of the sub-tenant might be knight service, or a portion of it, or something purely nominal such as the provision of a falcon or a rose at midsummer. In the last-mentioned case, the superior lord was giving away all his rights except those of wardship and escheat. A stop was put to this practice by the *Statute of Quia Emptores* in 1291. A mesne lord's own feudal obligations arising from the land always passed to his sub-tenant. *See also* MESNE LORD.

Subsidy *see* **Clerical Subsidy** *and* **Lay Subsidy**

Succession, Law of In the Middle Ages the land of a deceased person could not pass by testament (*see* WILL). Under the Common Law it passed to the eldest male heir (*see* BOROUGH ENGLISH; BURGESS TENURE; GAVELKIND; PRIMO-GENITURE). A man's movable goods were divisible at death into three parts: one for his widow, one for his children, and one that he could leave by testament as he wished. This practice gradually became obsolete. In cases of intestacy (which were the majority) the custom grew that one-third went to the widow and two-thirds to the children. If the wife had predeceased her husband, everything went to the children. If there was a widow but no children, half of the movable goods went to her and half to the deceased's next-of-kin (*see* CHATTELS). This practice was confirmed by the *Statute of Distributions* in 22 & 23 Charles II (his twenty-second and twenty-third regnal years). When a will appears at first sight to give a widow less than her due, this Law of Succession should be borne in mind.

Suit of Court The duty of attendance at the manor or hundred court. Absentees were obliged to provide excuses (essoins). Those who did not were listed as defaulters, and fined.

Suffolk The Suffolk Genealogy Society holds regular meetings and issues a journal, *Suffolk Roots*. Enquiries should be sent c/o The Federation of Family History Societies, 31 Seven Star Road, Solihull, West Midlands B91 2BZ, marked 'Please forward' and enclosing a stamped self-addressed envelope.

Record Repositories Bury St Edmunds and West Suffolk Record Office, Schoolhall, Bury St Edmunds (tel: 0284.63141); Ipswich and East Suffolk Record Office, County Hall, Ipswich (tel: 0473.55801).

Parish Registers and Indexes (*see* comment under COUNTY) Nearly all the registers of the 504 ancient parishes have been deposited at their appropriate record office, and the Society of Genealogists has copies of many of them. Boyd's Marriage Index covers 489 registers. Pallot's Marriage Index covers 57, mostly from 1790 to 1812 or 1837. The INTERNATIONAL GENEALOGICAL INDEX (IGI) includes about 150.

Marriage Licence Records Those for the Archdeaconry of Sudbury are at the West Suffolk Record Office, and those for the Archdeaconry of Suffolk at the East Suffolk Record Office.

Wills before 1858, proved in the following courts, are at the following record offices.

At the West Suffolk Record Office:

Archdeaconry of Sudbury

Peculiar Courts of Isleham (*see* CAMBRIDGE-SHIRE) and Freckenham

At the East Suffolk Record Office:

Archdeaconry of Suffolk

At the Essex Record Office:

Deanery of Bocking

As the county lay in the Diocese of Norwich and the Province of Canterbury, wills could also be proved in the Consistory Court of Norwich (*see* NORFOLK), and in the Prerogative Court of Canterbury.

Non-parochial Registers There are 66 registers at the Public Record Office (PRO), Chancery Lane, London, and the IGI covers about the same number.

Census Returns These are at the PRO, Portugal Street, London, and at both county record offices.

Memorial Inscriptions The Society of Genealogists has transcripts from a few churches, and the family history society has transcription in progress.

Heralds' Visitation Pedigrees have been printed for 1561, 1612 and 1664-8.

The *Suffolk Records Society* has published a number of historical records.

Suling A measure of land about twice the size of a HIDE, used in southeastern England.

Summoner The official who summoned people to appear before an ecclesiastical court. Also called an Apparitor.

Supporters Representations of creatures, real or imaginary, placed at the sides of an armorial shield in an achievement, and appearing to support it. The right to supporters is limited to peers, Knights of the Garter, Thistle and St Patrick, and Knights Grand Cross and Grand Commanders of other Orders, though exceptions to this rule have been made. The hereditary right of peers to supporters is limited to the actual holders of the title. Some local authorities have been granted supporters.

See also ARMS, COAT OF; HERALDRY.

Surety (i) A godparent.

(ii) A person pledged to give security for the performance of a bond, or for the proper carrying out of duties.

Surgeons The early history of London surgeons is bound up with that of the Barber Surgeons' Company (*see* BARBERS). Elsewhere, surgeons were licensed by the church authorities (*see* ECCLESIASTICAL COURTS; ECCLESIASTICAL VISITATIONS).

In 1745, the surgeon members broke away from the barbers and formed a separate Company, which, in 1800, obtained a charter founding the College of Surgeons, now the Royal College. Even after this date, the profession of surgeon did not carry the same prestige as that of physician. The early records of the Barber Surgeons are at the Guildhall Library, London, and of the later period, at the College. New entrants to the profession were apprenticed to a surgeon, and details of their apprenticeship can be found among the records of the hospital in which they served.

Details of the College's fellows have been published in Plarr's *Lives of the Fellows of the Royal College of Surgeons*. Surgeons of the Royal Navy kept *Medical Journals*, which are at the Public Record Office, Kew, under reference ADM.101. The annual *Medical Directory* has given details of surgeons since 1845.

See also APPRENTICES; DOCTORS, MEDICAL; PHYSICIANS.

Surnames A surname is a name borne hereditarily by all members of a family in male-line descent. In Anglo-Saxon times people had personal names only, even when they were known by an additional 'to-name' (e.g. Edmund Ironsides).

Hereditary surnames were first introduced into England by some of the leading followers of the Conqueror, and most were derived from the place-names of their estates, either in France or in England. They were usually inherited only by the eldest son. The custom of applying a man's to-name to all his children began in the late twelfth century and spread slowly, with the manorial classes and the south of England leading the way. In 1267 is found the first legal recognition of an hereditary surname (de

Cantebrigg). By 1400, three-quarters of the population are reckoned to have borne hereditary family names and the process was complete by about 1450. It is these names that make genealogy possible.

Surnames had five main origins: place-names, location of abode, occupations, nicknames and patronymics.

Place-name surnames, derived from towns and villages, indicated either where a person had come from (the majority), or of what place he was lord of the manor or most important resident. In early documents the names were prefaced by 'de' ('from' or 'of'). The large number of 'from' names is evidence of early family mobility.

Location-of-abode surnames were originally often prefaced by 'At' or 'Att' ('at the') — for example, Attwell — and include such names as Wood, Ford, Lane and Hill. It is not always possible to be sure to which of these two geographical groups (place-names and locations) a name belongs. A fourteenth-century person called Mayfield may have been so named because he came from the Sussex village of that name, or he may have himself lived beside a field of mayweed in any county. These two geographical groups together account for nearly half our surnames.

Occupation surnames are the second most common, and it is reckoned that most of them originated in medieval towns. Examples are: Carter, Mercer, Hayward, Thatcher and Smith. Some were adopted from their form as written in Latin documents; for example, Faber (Smith). The reason for the prevalence of Smith today is that there were so many kinds of craftsmen in the Smith category — blacksmith, shoesmith, arrowsmith, swordsmith, goldsmith, silversmith, tinsmith, etc. A less immediately obvious type of occupation name is that formed from the personal name or even surname of an employer; e.g. Roberts (meaning Robert's man), or Abbot (abbot's man), or simply the employer's personal name of Luke, Thomas, etc., as mentioned under Patronymics, below.

Nicknames, the third most numerous class, arose from a custom especially prevalent among peasants, and so are thought to point to a village

origin. They may be obviously descriptive (such as Short, Brown, Smart), or from a likeness to something else, often an animal (Bull, Byrd, Peacock).

Patronymics are derived from the personal name or occupation of a person's father or, more rarely, mother or other relative (e.g. Johnson, Fitzwalter, Smithson). Such personal names mentioned above as showing occupational origin may, alternatively, have originated as patronymics (e.g. the first Richards may have been either Richard's man or Richard's son).

It is never safe to draw a quick conclusion about the origin of a surname from its modern form. Corruption of sound and spelling has gone on for centuries, and is still continuing. Jerningham, which looks very like a place-name, is in fact a corruption of Jernegan, a personal name. To be reasonably sure of an origin, the line of descent of the family concerned must be traced back as far as possible, and its earliest-found spelling considered. Unrelated families of the same surnames may well trace back to different name-origin groups.

It should be remembered that all people of the same surname do not necessarily descend from a common ancestor, even when at an early date they are found inhabiting the same district.

The English Surname Survey has as its objects not merely the etymology of surnames, but their whole history from the period when hereditary names first appeared until about 1700. It publishes volumes dealing with the subject county by county, showing the differences which existed between various regions, social classes and types of surname, why some names became common while others remained rare, and how married women came to take the surname of their husbands. Volumes so far published cover West Yorkshire, Norfolk and Suffolk, Oxfordshire, Lancashire and Sussex. The Survey is under the direction of Mr R.A. McKinley, the Marc Fitch Research Fellow in English Surnames, in the Department of Local History at the University of Leicester.

It has always been legally possible to change one's surname. A sixteenth- or seventeenth-century change is sometimes discernible when a person is found mentioned in a record as 'Smith alias Brown' (*see* ALIAS). By the seventeenth century, the convenience of having a record of the change was recognised, and wealthier people would resort to a private Act of Parliament. The last time this was done was in 1907. Another method, in use since the seventeenth century, was by Royal Licence. After 1783, applications for this were referred to the College of Arms, but nowadays this is necessary only when arms also have to be changed. The issue of a Royal Licence was normally advertised in the *London Gazette*. A third, and now the most common, method is by Deed Poll, accompanied by enrolment in the Close Rolls of Chancery (until 1903) and later in the Enrolment Books of the Supreme Court. The earliest enrolment was in 1851. The indexes of the Close Rolls at the Public Record Office, Chancery Lane, London, show the name used by the person concerned in making his declaration, usually his old name. From 1905 until 1941, both names are indexed. A fourth method of making a change is simply by advertisement in the press. A fifth, by making a Statutory Declaration before a Justice of the Peace, or Commissioner for Oaths.

By an Act of 1916, enemy aliens — and by another of 1919, all aliens — are allowed to change their names only by Royal Licence or special permission from the Home Secretary. Such changes are advertised in the *London Gazette*.

To find a recorded change, the first step is to consult *An Index to Change of Name, 1760-1901*, edited by W.P.W. Phillimore and E.A. Fry (London, 1905), available at the Society of Genealogists. Further information can be traced as indicated there. Omitted from it are only those changes by Royal Licence not advertised in the *London Gazette*, and those by Deed Poll not advertised in *The Times*. From the late nineteenth century, deeds poll enrolled can be found at the Public Record Office (PRO), Chancery Lane, London, in classes C.54 and J.18; and from 1914 they were published in the *London Gazette*. A free leaflet, *Change of Name*, is available at the PRO.

For further reading, see *The Origin of English Surnames* and *A Dictionary of British Surnames*, both by P.H. Reaney; and *Change of Name*, by J.F. Josling (1974).

Surrender A document extinguishing an

owner's right in property. Conditional surrender was a mortgage of a manorial copyhold. If the copyholder failed to repay his loan, he would surrender his rights to the mortgagee, but the latter would need to apply to the lord of the manor for acceptance as his tenant.

Surrey Many of the county's northern parishes are now in the Greater London area. The West and the East Surrey Family History Societies both hold meetings in their areas and issue journals. Enquiries should be sent c/o The Federation of Family History Societies, 31 Seven Star Road, Solihull, West Midlands B91 2BZ, marked 'Please forward' and enclosing a stamped self-addressed envelope.

Record Repositories Surrey Record Office (CRO), County Hall, Kingston-upon-Thames (tel: 01.546.1050); Guildford Muniment Room (branch of the CRO), Castle Arch, Guildford (tel: 0483.66551); County Reference Library, Fairfield Road, Kingston-upon-Thames; Surrey Archaeological Society's Library, Castle Arch, Guildford; Minet Library, 52 Knatchbull Road, London SE5 (tel: 01.733.3279).

Parish Registers and Indexes (*see* comment under COUNTY) Most of the registers of the 146 ancient parishes have been deposited either at the CRO, its Guildford branch, the Greater London Record Office (*see* LONDON AND MIDDLESEX), the Guildhall Library, or the Minet Library. The Society of Genealogists has copies of more than 100. The West Surrey Family History Society (FHS) has a marriage index of the county complete except for the South London parishes. Pallot's Marriage Index covers 39, mostly from 1790 to 1812. The INTERNATIONAL GENEALOGICAL INDEX (IGI) includes nearly 200. The Bishops' Transcripts are at the Greater London Record Office.

Marriage Licence Records Those for the Archdeaconry of Surrey are at the Greater London Record Office, and the CRO and the Society of Genealogists have copies of an indexed calendar. The few for the Peculiar Court of Croydon are at Lambeth Palace Library, Lambeth Palace Road, London SE1. The Minet Library has a large collection of original licences.

Wills before 1858, proved in the Archdeaconry

and Commissary Courts of Surrey, are at the Greater London Record Office. Those for the Peculiar Court of the Archbishop of Canterbury in the Deanery of Croydon are at Lambeth Palace Library, and the Society of Genealogists has an index of them.

As the county lay in the Diocese of Winchester until 1847, and in the Province of Canterbury, wills could also be proved in the Consistory Court of Winchester (*see* HAMPSHIRE), and in the Prerogative Court of Canterbury. The West Surrey Family History Society has published an index to the Archdeaconry Court wills, 1752-1858.

Non-parochial Registers Forty-seven are at the Public Record Office (PRO), Chancery Lane, London, and have been indexed by the West Surrey Family History Society.

Census Returns These are at the PRO, Portugal Street, London, and at the CRO.

Memorial Inscriptions The West Surrey FHS has nearly completed transcribing for West Surrey. The Society of Genealogists also has a number of transcripts.

Heralds' Visitation Pedigrees have been printed for 1572, 1623 and 1662-8.

The *Surrey Archaeology Society* and the *Surrey Record Society* have published a number of historical records.

Surrogate A deputy presiding over a court; for example, on behalf of an archdeacon.

Sussex The Sussex Family History Group holds regular meetings and issues a journal, the *Sussex Family Historian*. Enquiries should be sent c/o The Federation of Family History Societies, 31 Seven Star Road, Solihull, West Midlands B91 2BZ, marked 'Please forward' and enclosing a stamped self-addressed envelope.

Record Repositories East Sussex County Record Office, Pelham House, St Andrew's Lane, Lewes (tel: 07916.5400); West Sussex County Record Office, John Edes' House, West Street, Chichester (tel: 0243.85100); Brighton Area Library, Church Street, Brighton; Hastings Area Library, Brassey Institute, 13 Claremont, Hastings; Hove Area Library, 182-6 Church Street, Hove.

Parish Registers and Indexes (*see* comment under COUNTY) Most of the registers of the 305 ancient parishes have been deposited at the appropriate county record offices (CROs). The Guildhall Library, London, has copies of all Sussex Registers, and the Society of Genealogists has copies of nearly 200. Pallot's Marriage Index covers 24, mostly from 1790 to 1812, and the family history society has a marriage index in progress. The INTERNATIONAL GENEALOGICAL INDEX (IGI) includes about 100. The Bishops' Transcripts are at the West Sussex record office.

Marriage Licence Records These are at the West Sussex record office.

Wills proved in the following courts are at the West Sussex record office:

> Episcopal Consistory Court for the Archdeaconry of Chichester
> Peculiar (Pec.) Court of the Dean of Chichester
> Pec. Court for the Deaneries of Pagham and Tarring

Those proved in the following courts are at the East Sussex record office:

> Episcopal Consistory Court for the Archdeaconry of Lewes
> Pec. Court for the Exempt Deanery of South Malling
> Exempt Jurisdiction of the Deanery of Battle

As the Diocese lay in the Province of Canterbury, wills could also be proved in the Prerogative Court of Canterbury.

Non-parochial Registers Fifty-six registers are at the Public Record Office (PRO), Chancery Lane, London, and the IGI covers a similar number.

Census Returns These are at the PRO, Portugal Street, London, and at Brighton Area Library.

Memorial Inscriptions The Society of Genealogists has transcripts from about eighty churches.

Heralds' Visitation Pedigrees have been printed for 1570 and 1634.

The *Sussex Record Society* has published many historical records of the county.

Sweating Sickness Once a common epidemic disease, swift in fatal effects. Its symptoms began with cold shivers, giddiness, headache and pains in the neck and shoulders, but the cold soon turned to heat and sweating, followed by intense thirst, palpitations and delirium. Some sufferers died within three hours of its onset, but any who survived for twenty-four hours were considered safe. It was also known as the English disease.

Swedenborgians *see* **New Jerusalemites**

T

Table This article of furniture, when mentioned in inventories, is often simply a board laid on trestles, though the two constituents are sometimes listed separately as such. A 'joined table' was a carpentered one.

The word 'tables' was also used for the game of backgammon.

Tabular Pedigree *see* **Family Tree**

Tallage A medieval tax that could be levied by a feudal lord upon his villeins, by a borough upon its burgesses, and by the king upon towns and his demesne manors. As it became the practice to summon representatives of boroughs to Parliaments, which were called for the purpose of obtaining approval for subsidies to the king, the royal tallaging of towns fell out of use. Also, restrictions were laid on the freedom of lords and boroughs to levy tallage, by making it compulsory to obtain royal licences for the same.

Tallet A hay-loft over a stable.

Tally A stick notched to act as a record of an amount of money received. The stick was then split into two, from top to bottom; the payer received one half and the payee the other. In case of any dispute, the two halves had to 'tally'.

Tavern Originally a house in which wines could be consumed on the premises. The owner or occupant was known as a vintner, and, in London, would be a member of the Vintners' Company. However, by the seventeenth century taverns also served beer. In the same century, there was a shortage of minted coins for small change, so tavern keepers used to issue tokens to make up the deficiency, and these were accepted in payment later by the same tavern. The servers of drinks were called 'tipplers'.

Telephone Directories A collection (not complete) of telephone directories from 1880 onward is housed at the British Telecom Museum, Baynard House, 135 Queen Victoria Street, London EC4V 4AT (open Monday to Friday, 9.30 a.m. - 12.30, and 2.00 - 4.00 p.m.). Other collections are at the Guildhall Library, London, the Department of Printed Books, Bodleian Library, Oxford, and the Historical Telephone Directory Library, 7th Floor, 211 Old Street, London EC1V 9PS.

Temporalities The income of monasteries and churches arising from purely secular sources, such as rents.
See also SPIRITUALITIES.

Tenant-in-Chief In the Middle Ages, this term denoted a person holding feudal land directly from the king. Often shown as a 'tenant in capite'. In most cases such a tenant would hold a number of manors, which he would subinfeud to sub-tenants (*see* SUBINFEUDATION). *See also* MESNE LORD.

Tenement Originally a holding of land and buildings in manorial terms, or a fee farm held from a superior lord. Later, any holding of land and buildings. A roweless (roofless) tenement was one without any building on it.

Tenths and Fifteenths Lay Subsidies were originally levied as a certain fraction of a householder's movable goods, after allowing for a certain minimum and specified exempt goods. The fraction differed from subsidy to subsidy, but after 1294 two fractions were commonly indicated in the heading to the Subsidy Rolls from the practice of levying separate rates on urban and rural areas, with the larger fraction bearing upon townspeople.

Tenure In feudal times, all land was held of a superior lord, in a series culminating in the king as sole absolute owner.

There were several forms of tenure: (i) Knight Service, i.e. a freeholding by military service when required, sometimes commuted to SCUTAGE; (ii) Socage, a freeholding by payment of rent; (iii) Frankalmoign, i.e. by prayers only, a tenure for ecclesiastical bodies; (iv) Villeinage, by agricultural services rendered by unfree tenants of a manor; (v) Serjeanty, by various unclassifiable services.

Knight Service was formally abolished in 1662, but already tenure by secular bodies had become either freehold, copyhold or leasehold. The first was a development from knight service and socage, the second from villeinage, and the third was by rent for a term of either years or lives. A freehold tenure passed at death either by fee tail (*see* ENTAIL) or by fee simple (*see* FEE). *See also* MESNE LORD; TENANT-IN-CHIEF; TERRE TENANT.

Terre Tenant The lord of a manor or freeholder in actual occupation of the land, as distinct from his superior lord.
See also KNIGHT SERVICE.

Terrier A written description of a landed property by acreages and boundaries. Manorial estate records usually include a terrier of the estate. Glebe Terriers are those dealing with the land belonging to a parish incumbent's benefice. The boundaries are described by reference to the holders of adjacent lands.

Tertian Ague Malaria; strictly speaking, of the type in which the symptoms recurred at forty-eight hour intervals. It was formerly not uncommon in England, and before the discovery of quinine treatment in the seventeenth century it was often fatal.

Testament *see* **Will**

Time Immemorial A legal term meaning all time prior to the accession of Richard I in 1189. In 1291, it was laid down that a person who held a franchise without any charter of authority, but who could prove that he had possessed it from 'time whereof the memory of man runneth not to the contrary' (or, more briefly, since 'time immemorial' or 'time out of mind'), could be granted a charter for that franchise.
See also QUO WARRANTO.

Tining An enclosure formed by a fencing of dead wood. A tine was a stake.

Tinker A mender of brass kettles, pans and other metalware. In country districts he was usually an itinerant worker.

Tippler A retailer or server of ale in a tavern or ale-house.

Tithe A tenth part of anything, but especially that of the profits and stock of parishioners, due, under Canon Law, to their incumbent for his support. It is in AD 747 that the tithe system in England is first mentioned, and throughout the Middle Ages every parishioner of a tithable parish was expected to contribute one-tenth of his crop, animal produce and other trade products, directly or indirectly, to the rector of the parish. Normally, the rector was the parish priest. He received the tithes directly, and stored them in his tithe barn; but sometimes the rectorship had been bestowed upon a local monastery, which received the tithe and accepted the responsibility of paying the stipend of a parish priest, who was called the vicar (i.e *vicarius*, substitute).

An Act of 1391 obliged monastic rectors to devote part of their tithes to the poor of the parish. Tithes were of two kinds, Great and Small. The Great Tithes were those of corn, hay and wool; all others were Small. The usual custom was for a monastic rector to pass the Small Tithes to the vicar. Tithes of produce from the ground were predial tithes; those from the profits of labour were personal tithes; those that were partly one and partly another (e.g. calves, lambs, chickens, dairy produce) were called mixed tithes.

At the Dissolution of the Monasteries in 1538, the rectorship of many parishes passed to the new lay owners of the former monastery lands.

In 1571, the bishops caused Glebe Terriers to be drawn up. These listed church lands and endowments in each parish, including tithes.

New, up-to-date terriers were made from time to time, until about 1836.

In the seventeenth century, the numerous nonconformists resented having to pay tithes to Church of England clergy, and Quakers were forbidden by George Fox to pay them at all. At this time began the gradual commutation of tithes from payments in kind to cash payments, and this continued until 1836, effected by private Acts of Parliament. Also, tithes were often commuted when the lands of the parish were enclosed under *Inclosure Acts*.

The *Tithe Commutation Act*, 1836, enabled commutation to be made more easily by commissioners, in negotiation with the inhabitants of each parish, on the basis of a professional land valuation. The commissioners' decisions were called Tithe Awards. They are incorporated in schedules, arranged alphabetically under parish landowners, and show the occupiers, the acreage of each parcel of land, the annual money tithe payable, and a numerical reference to an accompanying large-scale map of the parish. The map shows houses, boundaries, acreages, land-use and field names, and has cross-reference back to the schedule. These awards continued through half a century. Tithe Awards were drawn up in three copies. The one retained by the commissioners is now at the Public Record Office, Kew, under reference IR.18; the one for the bishop is either at the diocesan registry or the county record office; and the incumbent's copy may be still in the parish chest or deposited at the county record office. The *Return of all Tithes Commuted and Apportioned under the Acts for Commutation of Tithes* (British Sessional Papers, House of Commons, Vol. LXIV) lists all districts for which awards exist, and is on the shelves at the Public Record Office. Tithe Awards may be used to confirm residence or ownership of land in a parish, and to throw light on an ancestor's way of life.

For records of commutations down to 1836, *see* ACTS OF PARLIAMENT (Private). Tithe Books of the seventeenth and eighteenth centuries have been preserved in a few parishes, as also have miscellaneous papers referring to tithe. These may be in church vestries or at the county record office. The records of ecclesiastical courts have mentions of enforcements of tithe payments.

The Exchequer Court of Pleas, and other lay courts, also have cases of disputes between clergy and laity about tithes.

Tithing (i) A group of men and boys, originally ten in number, who were held responsible to the manor court for its members' good conduct. Every male of the age of 12 and over was obliged to be in a tithing. The tithing list of the manor was checked at each View of Frankpledge, and all boys who had reached the eligible age were enrolled. The elected representative of the tithing was the Tithingman. He was responsible for presenting to the manor court all misdemeanours committed by members of families within his tithing.

(ii) Later the term came to mean a subdivision of a parish.

Title Deed A legal document drawn up to transfer property and/or rights from one person to another. The vendor is always required to produce the deed by which he acquired the property, and also, until recently, the series of deeds by which the property passed through earlier hands, perhaps through hundreds of years. In 1925, the *Law of Property Act* made it unnecessary to pursue the title back further than thirty years, provided the previous transfer had taken place within that period. This Act rendered a huge number of ancient documents unnecessary for further legal use, so they flooded in to county and other record offices from owners, solicitors, bankers and mortgagees. As many properties had titles going back to the seventeenth century or earlier, the result has been that there are now several millions of these documents in local repositories. They describe the properties in varying detail, and, since 1840, include a plan. They mention vendors and purchasers, and sometimes give details of transactions carried out many years earlier, and of documents then in possession of other people. The records of the nineteenth and twentieth centuries are of three kinds: the 'abstract' of the title, which is a lawyer's summary looking back over the title position; the title deeds; and extraneous papers such as contracts for sale, auctioneers' catalogues, and so on.

The procedure by which property has changed hands has varied a number of times since the Middle Ages, so that title deeds have taken several different forms. Our present conveyance document dates from 1840.

A free leaflet, *Private Conveyances in the Public Record Office*, is available at the Public Record Office.

See also BARGAIN AND SALE; FEET OF FINES; LEASE AND RELEASE; RECOVERY ROLLS.

Toft A plot of land on which a building stood, or, as the word is more often used, had formerly stood. In a manor, it had manorial Rights of Common attached to it.

Toleration Act This Act of 1688 allowed Protestant dissenters, other than Unitarians, to engage in organised public worship as long as their meeting-places were registered and were all organisationally independent of one another. This resulted in the setting up of a large number of nonconformist congregations all over the country. Registration was carried out at the office of the diocesan or archidiaconal authority, or with Quarter Sessions. The information recorded included the name of the minister, the denomination of the group, the name of the person in whose house the meetings were held, and generally the names of several leading members as supporters or witnesses. From 1812, registration had to be effected at all three authorities. The records are at the county record offices or diocesan registries (*see* DIOCESE).

Tontine A form of annuity in which the total amount of money to be shared each year in interest by the investors remained the same, so that as investors died each survivor received an increased amount, and the last survivor received the income from all the investments.

The first scheme was launched by the government as a means of raising money in 1693, and was repeated in 1773, 1775, 1777 and 1789. The second, third and fourth were nominally Irish schemes, but many English people invested in them. Other tontines were organised by corporate boroughs, e.g. Newcastle-upon-Tyne in 1797. It was the practice for the 'Subscriber' to invest on behalf of a small child, usually a relative (the nominee) since long-lasting membership was necessary to obtain the maximum benefit, though nominees were divided into classes according to their ages. The registers show the names and parishes of abode of the subscribers and nominees, and the ages, dates of death, and executors of the latter.

The records of the eighteenth-century government tontines are at the Public Record Office, Kew, under reference NDO.3 (for 1773, 1775 and 1777), and NDO.2 (for 1789). A printed list of the nominees of the 1693 scheme is in the British Library. Mr F.L. Leeson has issued *A Guide to the Records of British State Tontines and Life Annuities of the 17th and 18th Centuries*, which is available in the library of the Society of Genealogists.

See also ANNUITIES.

Tory A political epithet of abuse directed at the court party in the country and Parliament; first used in the reign of Charles II. It was derived from the Irish *toiridhe* (pronounced similarly), meaning a pursued person, a Catholic guerilla fighter against the English colonists, because the court party was then considered to be pro-Catholic. This was not true of all Tories, but all English Catholics supported the court party.

Tory is now the colloquial name for the Conservative and Unionist Party.

See also WHIG.

Total Descent A term denoting a chart that shows all ancestral lines of ascent, male and female. Also called a Blood Descent, or Birth Brief. The chart is similar to that used for pure-bred dogs and racehorses, in which cases it is called a pedigree; but for human beings a pedigree means something different (*see* FAMILY TREE).

In a Total Descent chart, the arrangement of the ancestral generations may be either vertical or horizontal, only ancestors and ancestresses are shown, with their dates of birth/baptism, marriage and death/burial. In theory, the number of ancestors doubles at each generation, so it is usual for a Total Descent sheet to have room to show no more than five generations, leaving continuation sheets to show the ancestors of each of the sixteen great-great-grandparents at the head of the first sheet, and so on. In practice, the number of ancestors does not

A Total Descent chart prepared
for the Prince of Wales.

keep doubling, because two separate lines of descent will sooner or later converge to people who are cousins, then to siblings, and then to a parental couple common to both lines.

For many families, the number of generations from 1975 to the Conquest is twenty-seven, so the number of theoretical ancestors in the generation of 1066 would be 41,508,864; but the whole population of England at that time is reckoned to have been about 1,250,000, made up of three generations — grandparents, parents and children. The middle, parental,

generation will then have been about 600,000 persons, or 300,000 couples. It is reasonable to assume that the descent of at least half of those will have died out at various times during the last 900 years, so surviving lines will lead back to about 150,000 couples. If these pairs have to embrace all the 41,508,864 theoretical ancestors of each of us who is of English descent, it seems statistically inevitable that all the 150,000 couples are our ancestors, and that includes William the Conqueror himself and his queen. Admittedly Scottish ancestors and foreigners

287

PEDIGREE CHART

1. Mary SMITH
BORN 17 May 1914
WHERE Richmond, Surrey
WHEN MARRIED 7 Sep 1937
DIED
WHERE

NAME OF HUSBAND OR WIFE: Victor HUGHES

2. Philip SMITH
BORN 21 Oct 1884
WHERE Richmond, Surrey
WHEN MARRIED 27 July 1918
DIED 31 Jan 1923
WHERE Worthing, Sussex

3. Dorothy BROWN
BORN 20 Dec 1886
WHERE Hounslow, Mddx
DIED 23 Jan 1952
WHERE Walton-on-Thames, Sy.

4. Joshua SMITH
BORN 26 July 1845
WHERE London
WHEN MARRIED 16 May 1876
DIED 9 Sep 1928
WHERE Richmond, Surrey

5. Helen ROBINSON
BORN 2 May 1848
WHERE Benson, Oxfordshire
DIED 31 Oct 1945
WHERE Richmond, Surrey

6. William BROWN
BORN 12 July 1846
WHERE London
WHEN MARRIED
DIED 3 April 1929
WHERE

7. Katherine CLARKE
BORN 5 Feb 1849
WHERE
DIED 1905
WHERE

8. Robert SMITH
BORN 18 June 1817
WHERE Bristol
WHEN MARRIED 8 June 1843
DIED 8 March 1898
WHERE London

9. Emma BOX
BORN
WHERE
DIED 11 Dec 1904
WHERE Teddington, Mddx

10. Walter ROBINSON
BORN 12 June 1809
WHERE Benson, Oxm.
WHEN MARRIED 6 Dec 1832
DIED 24 July 1906
WHERE

11. Sophia BAKER
BORN 6 Oct 1808
WHERE Wantage, Oxm
DIED
WHERE

12. William BROWN
BORN 17 June 1817
WHERE
WHEN MARRIED
DIED
WHERE

13. Charlotte HILL
BORN 24 July 1817
WHERE
DIED 2 Jan 1899
WHERE

14. Francis CLARKE
BORN 1812-3
WHERE
WHEN MARRIED 1 June 1843
DIED
WHERE

15. Marianne BOX
BORN 25 Apr 1819
WHERE
DIED
WHERE.

16. James SMITH
17. Sarah CRABBE
18. Joshua BOX
19. Anne MILLER
20. James ROBINSON
21. Sarah WOOD
22. Abraham BAKER
23. Harriet HAYES
24. Henry BROWN
25. Elizabeth LANG
26. Thomas HILL
27. Charlotte JUDD
28. Hugh CLARKE
29. Elizabeth PARK
30. Joseph BOX
31. Sarah

A Total Descent chart, showing all ancestors back to great-great-grandparents.

will affect the figures to some extent, but the extent of compression of a constantly doubling number of theoretical ancestors into the constantly 'contracting' population, seems more than great enough to outweigh the effect of 'alien' lines. The above conclusion has been objected to on the grounds of exclusive class divisions and the static position of families in remote valleys, but this alleged difficulty seems to overlook the facts that class divisions have never been absolute in England, and that family immobility is largely irrelevant when all female descents are included, since only a minority of brides and bridegrooms have been 'both of this parish', and only one bride from outside the valley is needed to break any segregation of descent.

Total Descents can be conveniently charted in book form. On the page devoted to the male-line descent, the spaces for the ancestresses' names can be cut out, so that their names show through from where they are written on other pages, on which their own male-line descents are charted.

Tourn A medieval court, often called the Sheriff's Tourn, held in each hundred twice a year before the sheriff or his deputy. Every freeholder in the hundred was required to be present, but certain important magnates, both lay and clerical, had exemption.

Tournament A jousting contest between mounted men in armour. Such sporting functions were given encouragement by Edward III, and became popular social gatherings for the upper classes. Royal tournaments were arranged by the king's constable and marshal, and the proceedings included elaborate banquets. The colourful devices on the competitors' shields, surcoats and banners, and the caparisons of their horses, helped to develop the rules and art of heraldry, to disseminate knowledge of it and to popularise the bearing of arms among the gentry. The ladies present, although only spectators, played a part in the formalities as supporters of individual competitors. Provincial nobles, smaller gentry and chartered boroughs followed the king's lead in organising jousting contests. Their meetings attracted all the side-shows customary at fairs.

Tournaments were the most striking manifestations of the Edwardian cult of chivalry.

Town Down to the seventeenth century, this term was applied not only to towns but also to villages and hamlets.

Township A civil division of a parish for the levying of a separate Poor Rate. Each township had its own constable. An earlier term was 'Vill'.

Trade Tokens From time to time, and especially in the mid seventeenth century, a shortage of small change caused traders all over England to issue their own brass or copper tokens for small amounts, mostly farthings and halfpennies, but also some pennies. Depending upon the worth of the issuer's reputation, these would be acceptable at a number of establishments within his neighbourhood. A token usually showed, in addition to its value, the issuer's name or initials (and sometimes his wife's, too), his trade, and the street where his shop or tavern lay. A considerable list of such tokens is to be found in *Trade Tokens Issued in the 17th Century in England, Wales and Ireland*, by W. Boyne, revised by G.C. Williamson (in two volumes, 1889-92), but many other tokens have come to light since then.

Tranqueter A maker of hoops.

Transcript An exact copy of the wording of an original document, not involving the imitating of its handwriting. Spelling, abbreviation, capitalisation and punctuation should be reproduced as closely as possible. During the process of transcribing, no mark should be made on the original document, no page-corner turned down, no finger run down a column of names, and no use made of the document as a pad on which to rest the paper for transcribing. The use of pencil, on which record repositories insist, requires the subsequent making of a fair copy in ink or typescript for family record purposes (*see* RECORD KEEPING), but the pencilled transcript should be kept for possible later checking. All transcripts should be headed with the name, reference number and location of the original. Any omissions should be indicated by dashes. Dots should be used only for transcribing omissions already made in published records and indicated there by dots.

Faded handwriting can often be made more legible by viewing it under ultra-violet light. Provision for this is available at many record offices.

When the transcriber is faced with a very long document of which he requires a copy in full, he can usually by-pass the pencil-copy stage by ordering a photocopy.

See also ABSTRACT.

Transported Convicts In 1597, the *Vagrancy Act* empowered justices in Quarter Sessions to banish offenders to such parts beyond the seas as should be assigned by the Privy Council; and in 1619, 'a hundred dissolute persons' were transported to Virginia. A later Act of 1666 empowered justices to transport notorious thieves from Cumberland and Northumberland to America. From 1718 onward, many were sent to Maryland and Virginia, and some stayed as settlers when their sentences expired. For the period 1719-44 a list has been printed from the Public Record Office Treasury records.

Transportation to America was ended by the War of Independence in 1776, so an alternative place of exile had to be found. In March, 1787, nine transport ships took the 'First Fleet' from England to New South Wales. Their original destination was Botany Bay, but on arrival there the ships immediately left for Port Jackson, where Sydney now stands. Until 1813, some prisoners were also sent to Norfolk Island.

In 1822, a prison on Sarah (or Settlement) Island, Macquarie Harbour, Tasmania, was founded as a place of 'secondary' punishment for serious and regular offenders; and in 1825, the prison on Norfolk Island was re-opened for long-term convicts and 'secondary' punishment. In 1830, Port Arthur, on the Tasman Peninsula, was opened as Tasmania's main penal station, and shortly after, in 1834, Sarah Island prison was closed.

Norfolk Island prison closed in 1835, and in 1871 transportation was finally abandoned. Port Arthur prison remained open for prisoners already there, but closed in 1877.

For information about the offences for which prisoners were convicted, reference should be made to the records of the Assizes and Quarter Sessions. Old Bailey Sessions papers are in the Guildhall Library, and those of the Middlesex Sessions are at the Greater London Council Record Office. Sometimes information concerning a person convicted in the provinces will be found in the local newspaper's report of the session.

At the Public Record Office, Kew, *Convict Transportation Registers* (HO.11) cover the whole period of transportation to Australia from 1787 to 1871 in 21 volumes, which contain lists under the transport ships' names. The order is roughly that of departure. Each volume has an index of the ships included in it. Registers show full name of convict, term of transportation, and date of conviction.

Convicts, New South Wales and Tasmania (HO.10) is a class of 64 volumes, which could be described as a series of censuses for those colonies for various years between 1788 and 1859. They also contain names of numerous members of the convicts' families who were not transported, and are described as 'Came Free' or 'Born in the Colony'. The census of 1828 (HO.10/21-27) is the most complete. It shows the names of 35,000 persons with their ages, religions, families, abodes, occupations, and stock and land held, along with the name of the ship and the year of arrival. Some of the earlier volumes in this class give date and place of trial in England.

New South Wales Original Correspondence (CO.201) commences in 1784 and shows numerous lists of both emigrant settlers and convicts, 1801-21. There is an index on the shelves of the Search Room in the Public Record Office, Kew, for the period 1823-33.

Entry Books Relating to Convicts (CO.207) have lists of names for New South Wales, 1788-1825.

Some lists have been published in *The Convict Settlers of Australia* by L.L. Robson (Melbourne, 1965).

Prisoners were sometimes pardoned and did not sail. Details of Pardons can be found at the Public Record Office, Kew, under reference HO.10. Applications by convicts' families for passages to Australia are registered under reference CO.386 at Kew.

The names of Prison Hulks and of the convicts kept in them prior to transportation are to be found in the Quarterly Prison Returns, 1824-76 (HO.8) at Kew.

For further reading, see *English Convicts in Colonial America*, by P.W. Coldham (1974-6), and *The Crimes of the First Fleet Convicts*, by J. Cobley (1970).

Trespass, Writ of A writ against a person who 'with force of arms and against the king's peace' carried off the plaintiff's goods, or did him some other injury.

Trinodas Necessitas The three feudal obligations attached to landholding; namely, military service, the maintenance of roads and bridges, and the upkeep of castles.

Turbary The right of a manorial villein or copyholder to cut turf or other fuel.

Tyburn Ticket A certificate issuable to a person who had captured a felon later found guilty. It gave him exemption from serving parochial office. It was transferable and often fetched a high price.

Tyne and Wear A county formed in 1974 out of parts of NORTHUMBERLAND and DURHAM.

U

Unitarians At the beginning of the eighteenth century, the Socinian belief in the divinity of God the Father, and in the humanity of Jesus Christ, began to permeate Presbyterian and Congregationalist assemblies. An attempt, in 1719, to make a belief in the Trinity the official Presbyterian doctrine failed to secure a majority vote, and, as a result, congregations all over the country became divided on the issue. In some, traditional Presbyterian doctrines prevailed and members holding Unitarian views had to set up new chapels; in other places it was a Unitarian majority who retained the chapel, but many such majorities still considered themselves

Presbyterians. Much the same divisions occurred in Congregationalist chapels.

When nonconformist registers were deposited with the Registrar General in 1837-40 (now held at the Public Record Office, Chancery Lane, London, under references RG.4, 5 and 8), most of the Unitarian records dating from 1762 were classed as Presbyterian. Nevertheless, in 1851 there were 229 Unitarian places of worship in England. Other records of the movement are at Unitarian Headquarters, 1 Essex Street, London WC2. The Unitarian Historical Society publishes records, and the Secretary's address is 6 Ventnor Terrace, Edinburgh EH9 2BL.

For further reading, see *Sources for Nonconformist Genealogy and Family History*, by D.J. Steel (1973).

Universities Details of graduates of the two ancient English universities of Oxford and Cambridge, including their parentage, have been published as *Alumni Oxonienses* and *Alumni Cantabrigienses*. These, and also the annual calendars of Durham (1832), London (1836) and other universities and colleges, are available in the library of the Society of Genealogists. For the period of the Middle Ages, Dr A.B. Emden has produced biographical registers of both Oxford and Cambridge from a variety of sources, but they contain virtually no genealogical information.

Upholder (i) An undertaker.
(ii) An upholsterer.

Use In the late fifteenth century, the conveyance of land to trustees for the use of a third person, who was in fact often the transferer himself, created a 'use'. The transferer retained the right to change the user by a later deed expressing his wish, or will, in the matter; so, when he was dying he would issue his Last Will, naming the person to whom the land was to pass on his death, usually one of his younger sons, who would otherwise be excluded from it under the Common Law provision that land passed on death to the heir (i.e. the eldest son). An attempt was made to prevent the creation of uses, by the *Statute of Uses* of 1535-6, because it deprived the king and other lords of their fines and escheats, avoided forfeiture in cases of felony, and defeated the provisions of the statutes of MORTMAIN. By the *Statute of Uses*, possession of the land passed direct to any person named as user, instead of to the trustees. However, because of the pressure of public opinion, the *Statute of Wills* of 1540 allowed land to be legally devised on the death of its holder. The joint deed known as the *Last Will and Testament* came into existence as a consequence of this statute.

Utas *see* **Octave**

Uterine A uterine brother or sister is one born of the same mother but by a different father.

V

Valet In the late Middle Ages, the term for boys of the upper and middle classes who were put out to other families to learn manners and obedience. They carried out many household duties and were a kind of social apprentice. The modern use of the word for a man's personal servant derives from this custom.

Valor Ecclesiasticus In 1535, Parliament decreed an annual tax of one-tenth of the net income of all spiritual benefices. This necessitated a survey of church wealth. The resulting report has been published by the Record Commissioners in six volumes, but not all of the original report has survived. Details of Berkshire, Cambridgeshire, Essex, Hertfordshire, Northumberland, Rutland and parts of Middlesex and Yorkshire are missing, but the summaries of benefice incomes are complete. Some county record societies have published extracts translated from the original Latin.
See also SPIRITUALITIES; TEMPORALITIES.

Variant Among other uses, a term denoting an alternative spelling of a name.

Vassal A person who held land of a superior lord, and had sworn homage to him.

VCH *see* **Victoria History of the Counties of England**

Vellum The finer types of parchment, made from the younger and therefore more delicate skins of calves (the name means veal), and kids, or even of still-born or newly born calves and lambs. *See also* MEMBRANE.

Verso *see* **Recto**

Vert and Venison The forest laws (*see* FOREST) were professed to be for the protection of Vert and Venison. By 'Vert' was meant anything that bore green leaves and so afforded food and shelter for the game; 'Venison' meant all living beasts of the chase that provided food for man, and not, as today, solely the flesh of deer.

Vestry The governing body of a parish. The name was derived from the room in the church building in which its meetings were held. The assembly consisted of the incumbent (as chairman), the churchwardens and other respected householders of the parish, who were either co-opted by existing members ('close' or 'select' vestries) or elected by the parishioners ('open' vestries), according to the custom of the parish. Of these, there might be any number from a dozen in a country parish, to forty or more in a city.

During the sixteenth and seventeenth centuries, the meeting gradually took over the functions of the manor court as the basic unit of local government. In each parish the change proceeded at its own pace. The office of churchwarden was often filled by house-row, i.e. the occupiers of certain properties in turn. The vestry appointed the Constable and the Overseers of the Poor, and the Surveyor of the Highways, subject to the approval of the Justices of the Peace. Minutes were kept of all meetings, and the books containing these (where they survive) may be either still with the incumbent or deposited at the county record office or borough record office. They tell the history of the parish, the background of our ancestors' lives, and mention the names of many of the parishioners. They are supplemented by the account books of the Wardens, Overseers,

Surveyor and Constable. The *Local Government Act* of 1894 transferred the civil functions of the parish to parish councils and parish meetings.

Vicar A parish incumbent. In the past he differed from the rector in that he did not receive the Great Tithes (*see* TITHE). These went to the rector, who may have been a monastery or an ecclesiastic, or even a layman, who then paid the vicar a salary. Since the commutation of tithes, the difference between a vicar and a rector has been purely historical.

Vicar General The deputy of an archbishop or bishop. He dealt mainly with administrative matters of the province or diocese, while the Official (or Official Principal) was responsible for judicial cases. The two posts could, however, be held by the same person.

Victoria History of the Counties of England Usually known as the Victoria County History, and abbreviated to VCH. This series of volumes was launched in 1899 by Mr (later Sir) Laurence Gomme and Mr Arthur Doubleday, a member of the publishing firm of Constable and Company, with a subsidy of £20,000 and a list of subscribers. Queen Victoria consented to be the first subscriber to the project.

In the first nine years, fifty volumes appeared, but the First World War put a stop to progress and in 1920 the publishing syndicate was put into liquidation. However, the second Lord Hambledon took over the burden of its finances and enabled work to continue until his death. The assets were then acquired by the editor, Dr W. Page, who in 1933 transferred them to the University of London. Since then the work has been in the charge of the Institute of Historical Research of that university. Page was succeeded as editor by Mr L.F. Salzman, and volumes continued to appear slowly. However, after the Second World War the university was able to increase the *History*'s grant and enable a regular staff to continue the work. Mr P.B. Pugh became General Editor of the series. Local authorities now raise money to pay county editors to work on their individual volumes. The work, which has always been carried out through local committees, is divided into forty-five county

sets, not exactly corresponding with the original county areas. Monmouthshire and Northumberland are excluded. A separate history of the latter has been published with the aid of material transferred by the VCH to the County History Committee. The current General Editor (1985) of the VCH is Mr C.R. Elrington.

Each county set starts with one or more volumes devoted to general subjects, such as political, social and economic history, religious houses, archaeology and, originally, natural history. A portion is also devoted to a translation and commentary on the county's section of the *Domesday Book*. The remaining volumes are filled with the individual histories of the towns, parishes and hamlets of the county. The earliest published volumes naturally reflect the thoughts of their own period, in that they deal largely with the descent of manors and advowsons, and the edifices of the Established Church. Later volumes include accounts of nonconformity, education, the enclosure of the fields, parish government and the physical development of the towns and villages.

Though more than 150 volumes have appeared, and a number of county sets have been completed, many more volumes have yet to come. A great deal of information can be found in them on families of manorial status, often covering several generations. Unfortunately, many of the volumes are still unindexed. They are often to be found in the larger public reference libraries.

Victuallers Persons supplying food and drink to the public had to be licensed annually by the Quarter Sessions. The licence records are to be found at the county record office.

Vi et Armis Latin for 'By force of Arms'; an expression sometimes found in legal pleading. It would be inserted in order to enable the case to be heard in a certain court; for example, the Court of Star Chamber, the original jurisdiction of which was over cases of violence. It was usually a complete fiction.

Vill A district or group of houses that bore a name. A parish might contain several vills. It is an early term, more or less synonymous with the later 'township'.

Villein The term was introduced in Norman times to denote a tenant of manorial land who held by agricultural service. He was free in regard to everyone except his feudal lord, which meant that he was bound to his holding (*see* NATIVO HABENDO). Even there, he held his land hereditarily only by right of the custom of the manor. His work service was of two kinds: week work, i.e regular agricultural work done each week; and boon work, which was extra work done at important stages in the agricultural year (e.g. harvest).

A villein could not bring a suit in the king's court, and could not marry without his lord's permission; but he had rights, even against his lord, which were protected by the manor court. His holding — a house and, usually, a garden plot — carried with it the right to a certain number of arable strips of land, the right to graze a certain number of beasts in the pasture, and the right to a certain crop of hay from the meadow. In addition to his work service, he paid rent of assize (commutation of earlier rent in kind), which remained fixed for centuries in spite of the continuous fall in the value of money. At death, his chattels were forfeit to the lord but might be bought by his heir.

Villein status virtually died away by 1500, after which time the villeins' descendants became entirely free and held their land of the lord of the manor by copyhold.

Vintner The term was used for either a wine merchant, or the keeper of an inn or tavern who sold wine. There is a London livery company of Vintners.

Virgate Usually thirty acres of arable land scattered among the common fields of a manor, but it varied from as little as ten acres to as many as eighty in some parts of the country. It was a quarter of a HIDE, and was also known as a 'yardland'.

Viscount The title of the fourth rank in the peerage, between earl and baron. In Norman times the terms 'Viscounte', and the Latin *Vicecomes*, were applied to the sheriffs of the counties in their capacity of deputies to the earls (*comes*), but that usage died out. The first creation of a Viscounty in the English peerage was in 1440, when John, Lord Beaumont, was made Viscount Beaumont with precedence over all barons. A viscount is spoken of as 'Lord So-and-So'.

Visitations *see* **Arms, Coat of** *and* **Ecclesiastical Visitations** *and* under each county heading.

W

Wales *see* **Welsh Genealogy**

Wales, National Library of In addition to its printed books, this library, at Aberystwyth in the county of Dyfed, houses records essential to genealogists of Welsh families; e.g. wills and administrations before 1858, Bishops' Transcripts, manorial and legal documents, and some parish registers. It also contains records of the county of Herefordshire. Welsh records formerly at the Public Record Office have been transferred to Aberystwyth.

Walford's County Families *see* **County Families, Walford's**

Waltham Forest Family History Society *see* **London and Middlesex**

Wapentake A subdivision of a county in the area of the former Danelaw; a term originally used in the shires of Derby, Leicester, Lincoln, Nottingham and York, but now usually replaced by 'hundred'. The word derives from the Scandinavian for the clash of arms by which those assembled in the court of the district used to express their assent to its decisions.

Ward Money A payment made by a medieval tenant as commutation of his service of castle-guard. The money was used to pay a professional garrison.
See also SCUTAGE.

Wardmote The assembly of citizens that administered the affairs of a city ward. Many early Wardmote Books of the City of London are kept at the Guildhall Library.
See also MOTE.

Wards and Liveries, Court of The Court for administering funds received by the king for his rights of wardship, marriage and livery. Land held of the king in chief, either by Knight Service or Grand Serjeanty, was subject to royal guardianship if it fell by inheritance to a son under 21 or a daughter under 14. The king had the right to the management and profits of it until either the minority ended or the ward was given in marriage during minority. He had also the right of choosing the spouse. In practice, the king sold his rights, usually to a near relative of the minor, and also the use of the land, not necessarily to the same person. A further payment, for livery, was due from the estate when the heir came of age. The business of wardship and marriage was transferred from Chancery to the newly instituted Court of Wards in 1540, to which liveries were added two years later.

The occurrence of a minority in a tenancy-in-chief would be revealed by the Inquisition Post Mortem, but often the family avoided the holding of any inquisition, so the Crown relied also on informers who were rewarded by being allowed a low price for the wardship, and the land to their own use. As wardship was avoided or terminated by marriage, the child of a sickly or elderly father tended to be married off as soon as possible, which could be at 12 for a girl and 14 for a boy. A ward who refused the bride or bridegroom found for him or her by the guardian, or who married someone without the guardian's consent, caused a fine to the estate. However, guardians were obliged to undertake not to 'disparage' their wards by marriage (i.e. not to marry them below their social status) and they were allowed an 'exhibition' by the Court for their maintenance and education. In the seventeenth century, Roman Catholics were excluded as guardians. Wardships often meant the ruin of a gentleman's estate, since the guardian had only a short-term interest in its exploitation. The system and the Court were abolished in 1646, and the abolition was confirmed at the Restoration in 1660. The records of the Court are at the Public Record Office, Chancery Lane, London, under reference WARDS.1-15.
See also PROOF OF AGE.

Warranty The grantor of land to a sub-tenant by FEOFFMENT had the obligation to guarantee (warrant) his tenant's title against any possible counter-claims. So any relative with even a remote potential claim was called upon to associate himself with the grant by 'warranting' to the grantor. The same principle applied when land was transferred from one person to another by Final Concord (*see* RECOVERY ROLLS).
See also FEET OF FINES.

Warren, Right of Free The right to preserve and hunt in a stated area anything furred or feathered, except deer and boar.

Warwickshire The northwest area of the ancient county, including Birmingham and Coventry, is now in the new county of West Midlands. The Birmingham and Midland Society for Genealogy and Heraldry holds regular meetings at several places and issues a journal, *The Midland Ancestor*. Enquiries should be sent c/o The Federation of Family History Societies, 31 Seven Star Road, Solihull, West Midlands B91 2BZ, marked 'Please forward' and enclosing a stamped self-addressed envelope.

Record Repositories Warwickshire County Record Office, Priory Park, Cape Road, Warwick (tel: 0926.43431); Birmingham Reference Library, Birmingham B3 3HQ (tel: 021.235.4217); Shakespeare Birthplace Trust Record Office, Guild Street, Stratford-upon-Avon (tel: 0789.4016); Coventry Local Studies Centre, Broadgate House, Broadgate, Coventry.

Parish Registers and Indexes (*see* comment under COUNTY) The registers of virtually all of the 208 ancient parishes have been deposited, mostly at the county record office (CRO). The Society of Genealogists has a number of copies. Pallot's Marriage Index covers 31, mostly from 1790 to 1812. The INTERNATIONAL GENEALOGICAL INDEX (IGI) includes over 200, and both the CRO and the family history society (FHS) have copies. The FHS has a marriage index in hand; one for

Birmingham and Environs, 1801-37, has been compiled by Mr F.W. Winchurch, 3 Dunns Copse, Ledbury, Herefordshire; and one for the rest of the county is in the care of Mrs M. Newman, 132 Melton Avenue, Solihull, West Midlands. The Bishops' Transcripts for Lichfield Diocese are at the Lichfield Joint Record Office, Staffordshire; those for the Worcester Diocese are at the Hereford and Worcester Record Office, Herefordshire.

Marriage Licence Records These are at the same repositories as the Bishops' Transcripts (see above).

Wills before 1858, proved in the following courts, are located as shown.
At the county record office:

> Manorial Courts of Barston, Knowle, Packwood, Temple Balsall, Baddesley Clinton

At the Shakespeare Birthplace Trust Record Office:

> Peculiar (Pec.) Court of Stratford-upon-Avon
> Pec. Court of Hampton Lucy

At Lichfield Joint Record Office:

> Dean and Chapter's Court of Lichfield
> Pec. Court of Bishop's Itchington
> Pec. Court of Merevale
> Pec. Court of Bishop's Tachbrook

At the National Library of Wales, Aberystwyth:

> Pec. Court of the Royal Free Chapel of Shrewsbury St Mary

As the county lay partly in the Diocese of Lichfield, partly in that of Worcester, and wholly in the Province of Canterbury, wills could also be proved in the Consistory Courts of those two dioceses and in the Prerogative Court of Canterbury. The Society of Genealogists has a number of will indexes.

Non-parochial Registers Fifty-five registers are at the Public Record Office (PRO), Chancery Lane, London, and a similar number are included in the IGI.

Census Returns These are at the PRO, Portugal Street, London, and at the CRO.

Memorial Inscriptions The Society of Genealogists has transcripts from a few churches, and the FHS has transcription in progress.

Heralds' Visitation Pedigrees have been printed for 1619 and 1682-3.

The Dugdale Society has published a number of historical records of the county. The FHS has published *Tracing Your Ancestors in Warwickshire*, by F.C. Markwell.

Waste The land of a manor, not devoted to arable, meadow or wood. It usually lay on the manorial boundaries and was used for pasture, and was gradually assarted (brought under cultivation) over the centuries. As the population increased during the twelfth and thirteenth centuries, some of the waste was used for new villages. In 1236, the *Statute of Merton* allowed the lord of a manor to enclose part of the waste, provided he left sufficient for the needs of his free tenants. As the waste decreased, many manors had to limit the number of beasts each tenant was allowed to graze on it. These limits were called 'stints' or 'gates'.
See also COMMON, RIGHTS OF.

Watch and Ward The patrolling of an area both by night (watch) and by day (ward), a duty to which citizens of towns were liable in their town.

Waynage A villein's implements of work.

Waywarden Another name for the Surveyor of the Highways.

Week Work The amount of time each week that a villein had to work on the demesne land of the lord of his manor. The obligation to do week work was the hall-mark of villeinage.

Welsh Genealogy Wales has been administered with England since Tudor times, so that the standard genealogical sources are the same. However, research in Wales can be affected by some basic differences.

First, many classes of records have not survived on the same scale as in England, and rarely have early starting dates. Secondly, settled surnames were not adopted in many parts of Wales until quite modern times, in some areas as late as the nineteenth century. As a result, one has to be aware of the possible survival of the patronymic naming system, whereby a man took his father's forename (for example, Dafydd ap Morgan, meaning David, son of Morgan). The main problem which has arisen from this is that a few popular forenames have provided the majority of modern Welsh surnames, making identification difficult. Thirdly, Welsh, though not used as an official language until recently, has to be taken into account in many areas where it will certainly appear (particularly in personal documents). Finally, the greater incidence of nonconformity in Wales increases the probability that records will not be found in the Anglican registers, particularly of the nineteenth century.

All these factors must be borne in mind, but their significance varies greatly from area to area within Wales, so that it is important that the family historian takes background reading and local history seriously, and that Welsh ancestors are placed in their social, geographical and occupational context, not least to help distinguish them from others of the same name. Much greater emphasis has to be placed on oral and family evidence, and on sources which elsewhere may be considered minor, such as educational records, newspapers, chapel histories, etc.

Some time has to be spent in locating possible sources which will, again, vary according to area. The National Library of Wales has long been a repository for the major classes of document, but the county record offices have considerable collections in their own right, including, in many cases, original parish registers. The 1985 joint publication, *The Parish Registers of Wales* (see below) will assist searchers greatly. It is advisable to make enquiries, in advance, of both record office and National Library to establish whether their holdings meet a researcher's needs, and detailed guides and lists are available on request. It is difficult to generalise about the wide range of material in the còunty record offices, but among the vast collection at the National Library the following have particular interest for the family historian: Bishops' Transcripts, probate records, parish and nonconformist records, tithe documents, estate papers and printed and manuscript pedigrees.

The manuscript holdings of other reference and university libraries in Wales should not be forgotten, nor should the collections of Welsh material in the British Library and the College of Arms. Local libraries have, in some cases, genealogical collections as well as valuable Local Studies Departments. Census microfilms and the microfiche of the INTERNATIONAL GENEALOGICAL INDEX are frequently to be found in these locations.

Little has been published on research into Welsh ancestry in genealogical handbooks, but the six family history societies which cover Wales print articles in their journals on sources typical of, or unique to, their area, as well as useful aids, such as to monumental Welsh — the language used on gravestones. All are transcribing and publishing records. Collectively, as the Association of Family History Societies in Wales (for their address, see below), they plan to produce a booklet, the first of a series, on Welsh sources. Articles on Welsh families and records appear frequently in the publications of local historical societies.

The addresses given here are grouped according to the Welsh counties as they were reorganised in 1974, with an indication of which historic counties they contain; Glamorgan is an exception to this, as reorganisation there led to subdivisions which are not particularly relevant to the family historian. All societies listed are voluntary bodies, and enquiries should be addressed to the Honorary Secretary, enclosing a stamped self-addressed envelope.

The National Library of Wales, Aberystwyth, Dyfed SY23 3BU (tel: 0970.3816/7).

Cardiff Central Library, The Hayes, Cardiff CF1 2QU (tel: 0222.382116).

University College of Swansea Library, Singleton Park, Swansea SA2 8PP (tel: 0792.25678).

University College of North Wales Library, Bangor, Gwynedd LL57 2DG (tel: 0248.51151).

Association of Family History Societies of Wales, 2 Pen Lôn, Menai Bridge, Gwynedd LL59 5LW.

Clwyd (Denbighshire, Flintshire)

Clwyd Record Office, The Old Rectory, Hawarden CH5 3NR (tel: 0244.532364) and 46 Clwyd Street, Ruthin LL15 1HP (tel: 08242.3077).

Clwyd Family History Society, 27 Mile Barn Road, Wrexham LL13 9LX.

Denbighshire Historical Society, Gorffwysfa, Llansannan, Denbigh LL16 5HN.

Flintshire Historical Society, 50 Hafod Park, Mold CH7 1QW.

Dyfed (Cardiganshire, Carmarthenshire, Pembrokeshire)

Carmarthenshire Record Office, County Hall, Carmarthen SA31 1JP (tel: 0267.233333).

Cardiganshire Record Office, Swyddfa'r Sir, Marine Terrace, Aberystwyth SY23 2DE (tel: 0970.617581).

Pembrokeshire Record Office, The Castle, Haverfordwest SA61 2EF (tel: 0437.4591).

Dyfed Family History Society, 175 Penybank Road, Penybank, Ammanford SA18 3QP.

Cardiganshire Antiquarian Society, Tal-y-Werydd, Aberarth, Aberaeron SA46 0LX.

Carmarthenshire Antiquarian Society, Rock Villa, Trelech, Dyfed.

Pembrokeshire Local History and Record Society, The Castle, Haverfordwest SA61 2EF.

Glamorgan

Glamorgan Archive Service, County Hall, Cathays Park, Cardiff CF1 3NE (tel: 0222.28033).

West Glamorgan Area Record Office, County Hall, Oystermouth Road, Swansea SA1 3SN (tel: 0792.471589).

Glamorgan Family History Society, Llanishen Fach Farmhouse, Heol Erwin, Rhiwbina, Cardiff.

Glamorgan History Society, 24 Canon Street, Barry, South Glamorgan.

Gwent (Monmouthshire)

Gwent County Record Office, County Hall, Cwmbran NP4 2XH (tel: 06333.67711).

Gwent Family History Society, 18 Greenway Drive, Griffithstown, Pontypool, Gwent.

Gwent Local History Council, 8 Pentonville, Newport.

Gwynedd (Anglesey, Caernarfonshire, Merionethshire)

Caernarfon Area Record Office, County Offices, Shirehall Street, Caernarfon LL55 1SH (tel: 0286.4121).

Anglesey Area Record Office, Shire Hall, Llangefni LL77 7TW (tel: 0248.723262).

Dolgellau Area Record Office, Cae Penarlâg, Dolgellau LL40 2YB (tel: 0341.422341).

Gwynedd Family History Society, Cwm Arian, Pensarn Fawr, Penysarn, Anglesey LL69 9BX.

Anglesey Antiquarian Society and Field Club, Llangefni Library, Anglesey.

Caernarvonshire Historical Society, County Offices, Caernarfon.

Merionethshire Historical and Record Society, Area Record Office, Dolgellau.

Powys

Archivist, County Library Headquarters, Llandrindod Wells LD1 5LD (tel: 0597.2212).

Powys Family History Society, 61 Rockes Meadow, Knighton, Powys LD7 1LE.

Brecknock Society, Tynant, Groesffordd, Brecon, Powys.

Powysland Club, Branch Library, Red Bank, Welshpool.

Radnorshire Society, College of Further Education, Llandrindod Wells, Powys.

Reference and Further Reading

Benwell, R.M. and G.A., 'Interpreting the parish registers and Bishops' Transcripts for Anglesey and Llŷn', and 'Interpreting the census returns for rural Anglesey and Llŷn', from *Anglesey Antiquarian Society Transactions* (1975, 1973).

The Dictionary of Welsh Biography Down to 1940 (4th edn, ed. R.T. Jenkins, 1959).

McDonald, R.W., 'The Parish Registers of Wales', from *National Library of Wales Journal* (1976).

Morgan, P.J. and T.J., *Welsh Surnames* (University of Wales Press, 1985).

Morgan, P.J. and D. Thomas, *Wales: the Shaping of a Nation* (David & Charles, 1984).

Pitt-Lewis, C.J., 'Using the IGI for Wales and Monmouthshire', from *Where to Find the IGI* (Federation of Family History Societies, 1984).

Williams, C.J. and J. Watts-Williams, *Cofrestri Plwyf Cymru/The Parish Registers of Wales* (National Library of Wales and Welsh County Archivists' Group, in association with the Society of Genealogists, 1985).

Pre-parish register and gentry families

Bartrum, P.C., *Welsh Genealogies,* AD *300-1400*

(1974), and *Welsh Genealogies, AD 1400-1500* (1983).

Clark, G.T., *Limbus Patriae Morganiae et Glamorganiae* (1886).

Dwnn, Lewys, *Heraldic Visitations of Wales* (ed. Meyrick, 1846).

Griffith, J.E., *Pedigrees of Anglesey and Carnarvonshire Families* (1914).

Jones, Major Francis, 'An Approach to Welsh Genealogy', from *Transactions of the Honourable Society of Cymmrodorion* (1948).

Lloyd, J.Y.W., *History of Powys Fadog* (1881-7).

Nicholas, T., *The Annals and Antiquities of the Counties and County Families of Wales* (1872).

West Wales Historical Records, ed. Francis Green (14 Vols. 1912-29).

by Mrs Sheila Rowlands.

West Midlands A county formed in 1974 out of parts of STAFFORDSHIRE, WARWICKSHIRE and WORCESTERSHIRE.

Westmorland Now a part of the new county of Cumbria. The Cumbria Family History Society holds regular meetings and issues a newsletter. Enquiries should be sent c/o The Federation of Family History Societies, 31 Seven Star Road, Solihull, West Midlands B91 2BZ, marked 'Please forward' and enclosing a stamped self-addressed envelope.

Record Repositories Cumbria Record Office (Carlisle), The Castle, Carlisle (tel: 0228.23456); Cumbria Record Office (Kendal), County Offices, Kendal (tel: 0539.21000); Cumbria Record Office, 140 Duke Street, Barrow-in-Furness; Kendal Public Library, Kendal.

Parish Registers and Indexes (*see* comment under COUNTY) Most of the registers of the 68 ancient parishes have been deposited at the county record office (CRO), Kendal. The Society of Genealogists has copies of 29. Pallot's Marriage Index covers 14, mostly from 1790 to 1812. Most of the registers appear in the INTERNATIONAL GENEALOGICAL INDEX (IGI). The Bishops' Transcripts are at the CRO, Kendal.

Marriage Licence Records These are at the CRO, Carlisle.

Wills before 1858, of testators in the northeast part of the county, were proved in the Consistory Court of Carlisle and are at the CRO, Carlisle. Those of testators in the southwest part of the county were proved in the Consistory Court of the Archdeaconry of Richmond (Western Deaneries), and are at the Lancashire CRO (*see* LANCASHIRE), as also are the records of three Peculiar Courts.

As the southwest part of the county lay in the Diocese of Chester, and the whole county lay in the Province of York, wills could also be proved in the Consistory Court of Chester and the Prerogative Courts of York and Canterbury.

Non-parochial Registers Nine registers are at the Public Record Office (PRO), Chancery Lane, London, and are included in the IGI.

Census Returns These are at the PRO, Portugal Street, London, and at the CRO, Kendal.

Memorial Inscriptions The family history society has transcription in progress.

Heralds' Visitation Pedigrees have been printed for 1664-5.

The *Westmorland Antiquarian and Archaeological Society* has printed a number of historical records of the county.

Whig One of the great English political parties from the late seventeenth to early nineteenth century. It was the party that looked to the great landed nobles for leadership, in opposition to the Tories who looked to the king and the court. There are several theories about the origin of the name. One is that it came from the Scottish word for whey, the favourite drink of the Scottish Covenanters, a party opposed to Charles I. Another is that it derived from the shortened form of 'Whiggamore' (a Scottish driver of horses), because in 1648 a group of drivers marched to Edinburgh to demonstrate against Charles I and the Duke of Hamilton. A third theory is that the term was one for a Scottish rustler of horses and cattle, a nickname of abuse already used for Presbyterians. Yet another version is that it was made up of the initials of 'We hope in God', the motto of the political club from which the party took its rise. As the name of the political party, the word came into use in 1679 in the heated opposition to the party's bill to exclude the Catholic Duke of York from the succession to the throne.

By the end of the Napoleonic Wars the growth of towns and industries gave rise to new radical ideas, to which those who opposed them gave the name 'Liberal', taken from revolutionary parties in France and Spain. The word, however, grew in respectability through the 1820s and was accepted to cover those views that both the more progressive Whigs and the Radicals could share, and in 1839 it became the official name of the erstwhile Whig Party.

Whip Land Manorial land not marked out by permanent meres, but measured out before each year's ploughing by a whip's length.

Whitmore, J.B. The compiler of *A Genea-logical Guide*. That volume, published in 1953, continues the list of printed pedigrees contained in the earlier *Genealogist's Guide* by G.W. Marshall.
See also NATIONAL PEDIGREE INDEX.

Wife Selling Until the end of the nineteenth century, it was a common misapprehension that a wife was her husband's chattel and so could be sold by him if he wished. The customary practice was to take her to a market-place, hang a halter round her neck — ones of ribbon and straw are mentioned — and put her up for auction. Recorded cases of wife sale occur from the late seventeenth century, though the custom is said to be much older. As the most usual source of evidence is the press, mentions become more numerous with the increase in the number of newspapers, but at least one parish register entry, a baptism in 1782 at Purleigh, Essex, is known to mention that the mother was a bought wife. The practice was not confined to country districts where ignorance of the law might be excused. In 1823, the French Chargé d'Affaires in London reported to his chief that the current price at Smithfield Market was 22 shillings, having recently doubled. Prices recorded from all over the country vary between 4 pence and £50. In 1891, the Lord Chancellor of the day ruled that no law gave a husband complete dominion over the person of his wife, but further instances of wife-selling in the later 1890s are known. Reference to press reports can

be found under 'Marriage' in the documentary collections of the Society of Genealogists.

Will The document now properly known as a Last Will and Testament was originally two separate ones, each directing the disposal of a deceased person's property according to his wishes while living. The earliest that survive are from the Anglo-Saxon period.

The feudal system, which attained its full form after the Conquest, was based on obligations and rights arising out of the holding of land, so freehold lands and buildings, except those held in GAVELKIND and BURGESS TENURE, could not be allowed to be divided between a man's sons. They were not bequeathable, but descended by Common Law intact to a man's heir — his eldest son, if he had one. Copyhold land descended according to the custom of the manor. Only leaseholds could be bequeathed. However, the church, influenced by Roman law, made all other types of property (known as 'personalty') bequeathable, subject to one-third going to the widow and one-third to the children (*see* SUCCESSION, LAW OF).

The document describing the owner's wishes was called a Testament, and required to be granted probate by an ecclesiastical court. It was, therefore, the custom for the testator to start by bequeathing his soul to God and to give instructions as to where his body was to be buried. He then left legacies to his local church, and sometimes to the mother church (the cathedral of the diocese), and then to the poor. After this, he itemised legacies of his personal property to his family and friends. Besides appointing the executor or executors of the testament, an overseer would usually be nominated to whom the executor could refer in case of any difficulty or dispute.

In the fifteenth century, the law forbidding the devising of land was circumvented by conveying real estate, during life, to trustees known as the 'feofees to uses' ('to hold to the use of the owner's will'), and the document instructing the trustees was known as his Will. This device was made illegal by the *Statute of Uses* in 1535-6; but such dissatisfaction was caused to small landowners who were thereby deprived of the means of providing adequately for their younger sons, that in 1540, by the *Statute of Wills*,

> *In the Name of God Amen*
>
> *I Richard Godfrey of the Inner Temple London Esquire do make this my last Will and Testament as followeth First I bequeath my Soul to my own Great Creator that gave it hopeing through the merritts of his blessed son my only Saviour to obtain Everlasting life my body I desire may be buryed in the same Grave with my Dear wife and Daughter in St Brides Church London frugally decently and at the discretion of my Executrix And whereas I am intitled by law to dispose of the Guardianship of my Daughter ffranklyn Godfrey dureing her Infancy I doe hereby give and dispose thereof to my worthy good friend Thomas Bennett Esq: one of the Masters in Chancery untill she arrives at the age of one and Twenty years intreating him to accept thereof*

A typical religious preamble to a will of 1732. *Crown copyright: PROB.11*

owners in fee simple (*see* FEE) holding under tenure of SOCAGE were permitted to devise all, and those holding by Knight Service to devise two-thirds of their lands. This enabled the two documents to be combined under the title of the Last Will and Testament, now popularly known as the Will. When a will does not mention, or seem to do justice to, the relict or eldest son, or devise any land, it must be remembered that they benefitted under the provisions of the Common Law. Until 1837, a will could be made by any male over the age of 14, and female over the age of 12. After that date, a testator had to be 21 or over. Until 1882, a married woman could make a will only with her husband's consent.

During the Civil Wars, the 300 or so probate courts became disrupted by the hostilities, except that of the Prerogative Court of the Archbishop of Canterbury (PCC); and under the Commonwealth, an Act of 8 April, 1653, abolished all ecclesiastical jurisdictions in probate matters. All wills and administrations had to be brought before 'Judges for the Proving of Wills and Craving of Letters of Administration' in London, and their records were incorporated into the PCC series. However, the old courts were restored on the Restoration of the monarchy in 1660. By an Act of the following year abolishing military tenures, all restrictions on the devising of freehold land were removed.

Before 1750, people in modest circumstances might let wills go unproved — and so

unrecorded — if there was no dispute about how the estate was to be dealt with, thus saving the expense of probate. Between 1717 and 1791, the wills of all Catholics had to be enrolled either in one of the central courts or in Quarter Sessions. Before 1882, a married woman could not normally make a will without her husband's consent, because her property was considered to be her husband's; but there were occasional special circumstances, for example when she held specifically devised property from a previous husband.

As from 11 January, 1858, all ecclesiastical and peculiar jurisdictions were abolished by the *Probate Act*, and their powers were passed to the Probate Division (now the Family Division) of the High Court. England and Wales were divided into civil probate districts, each with a District Probate Registry, and a Principal Probate Registry in London. All wills since that date can now be consulted at the Principal Registry of the Family Division, Somerset House, London. Indexes are also available at district probate registries and at certain record offices and libraries in the provinces. For further reading on these, see 'Printed Indexes to Probate Records after 1850' by J.S.W. Gibson, in *The Local Historian* Vol.15, No.4.

Probate Jurisdictions Before 1858, a testator having all his property within the area of one archdeaconry would normally have his will proved in the Archdeacon's Court, presided over by the Archdeacon's Official, though not all archdeaconries had testamentary jurisdiction. If some of the property lay outside the archdeaconry but in the same diocese, the will could be proved in one of the Bishop's Courts, i.e. either in the Consistory Court or the Commissary Court (*see* CHURCH OF ENGLAND HIERARCHY). Some bishoprics claimed probate rights over all noblemen, gentlemen-at-arms, rectors, vicars, and other clergy whose lands lay wholly within the diocese, even if they lay wholly within one archdeaconry. The indexes kept by some courts suffer from a number of omissions of wills actually proved.

Every three years or so, the bishop 'visited' his diocese, i.e. he summoned the clergy and lay officials of the diocese to him, and during this ecclesiastical visitation all lower courts were inhibited for a period of from three to six months. During a vacancy in a bishopric, the Court of the Dean and Chapter or of the Archbishop normally took over jurisdiction.

If a testator had property in more than one diocese, his will had to be proved in the Prerogative Court of the archbishop of the province, either Canterbury or York. If property was held in both provinces, then the will had to be proved in the court of Canterbury, which also had jurisdiction over people owning property in England or Wales who died in Scotland or Ireland, at sea, or in 'foreign parts'. All these regulations did not preclude persons of substance, willing to pay the higher fees, from proving a will at a Prerogative Court to gain the advantages of the highest authority, the best record keeping, and privacy from local enquiries, even though their estate lay entirely in one archdeaconry. Prerogative Court wills date from 1383.

In the larger courts there were often several 'seats' dealing with different districts and keeping separate records, so their record volumes are liable to overlap one another chronologically.

In addition to the main courts described, a number of smaller courts existed. They belonged either to ecclesiastical dignitaries outside the archdeaconry, or to city corporations, colleges or lords of manors, and were known as Peculiar Courts. They could grant probate on wills of property lying wholly within their borders. Otherwise the will had to be proved in either the Bishop's Court or the archbishop's Prerogative Court. Peculiars were of many

kinds. Their jurisdiction could cover a parish or parishes (not necessarily contiguous), a city, borough, township, liberty, manor, cathedral or church precinct, deanery or college precinct. Sometimes a place might lie in more than one Peculiar; indeed, one whole Peculiar is occasionally included within another. They were variously presided over by an archbishop, bishop, dean, dean and chapter, sub-dean, chancellor, precentor, succentor, vice-chancellor, prebendary, rector, vicar, lord of manor, or mayor, each, of course, able to appoint a commissary to do the actual work. Some were inhibited during visitations.

Appeals from the Bishops' Courts of the southern province lay to the Court of Arches of the Archbishop of Canterbury, so-called because it was once held at the Church of St Mary-le-Bow (*de arcubus*) in London. Appeals from that court and from both Prerogative Courts lay, after the Reformation, to the Court of Delegates of England.

Procedure and Documents The executor(s) took the will to the appropriate probate court. There it went through several procedures, each of which gave rise to a document. Many of these are still available for perusal, and are of the highest genealogical value. They are as follows:

Probate Act The Court, being satisfied that the testament was in order, passed a probate act, approving it and authorising the executors to carry out their functions, and then recorded the fact in its Probate Act Book (*see* PROBATE). The original will was annotated with a copy of the Probate Act and filed in a 'bundle' in the court's records. These originals bear the signature of the testator and often a seal, which may show his arms or crest (*see* ARMS, COAT OF).

A Probate Copy of the will and act was then made and given to the executors as their guide and authority. Until about 1600, it was usual to give the original will back to the executors, and file the Probate Copy. Any document given to the executors is now usually lost or hard to trace.

Testamentary Bond Some courts obliged the executors to enter into a bond to execute the will faithfully.

Registered Copy of the Will A further copy of the will and probate act was usually written into a book of registered wills, for office use and public reference. This is the copy of easiest access to the genealogist.

Unproved Wills Some courts have collections of these.

Inventory Before 1700, it was usual for the executors to be obliged to supply an inventory of the goods of the deceased, attested by the overseer or supervisor of the will named by the testator. There is often a separate file for these inventories. They are rare after 1750. A reference in the calendar of wills, marked 'rpt' ('respited'), means that no inventory was demanded. These records often reveal a man's occupation, either explicitly or from his stock-in-trade or tools.

Nuncupative Wills Until 1838, these were testamentary intentions expressed by the deceased's word of mouth before 'credible witnesses', who later made sworn statements before the probate court. By the *Statute of Frauds*, 1678, there had to be at least three witnesses who had heard the deceased's wishes spoken in his own house and during his last illness. They needed to have them written down within six days, and not proved until fourteen days after the death. Since 1838, nuncupative wills can be made only by soldiers on active military service, and by seamen at sea. Freehold land could not be devised by a nuncupative will, nor could a written will be revoked by one.

Bond of Tuition, Curation or Guardianship When a minor was left fatherless, the court could appoint a guardian for him. This guardian had to give a bond, and such documents are filed either with the will or administration, or separately. Normally, tuition was for boys under 14 and girls under 12. Curation was for children older than that, but under 21.

The wills' calendar may contain some cases noted as 'Administration with Will Annexed', which usually means that the executors named in the will were not available, possibly dead; so administration was granted to the next-of-kin to act as executor. Sometimes, during a long testamentary trust, the trustees and/or beneficiaries died, which made further court action necessary. The particulars were generally entered on the margin of the register copy of the will, and are often of genealogical value.

Unsigned, Amended and Unwitnessed Wills In such cases, witnesses had to be sworn as to the handwriting or intentions of the testator. Their sworn statements are usually filed with the original will, and copied into the register book.

Caveats When someone with an interest in the estate wished to prevent probate being granted without his objection being considered, he could enter a Caveat. This was written into either a Caveat Book or the Act Book, and would give rise to a Sentence, which would be registered. Caveats sometimes reveal interesting family antagonisms.

Assignations When an executor or administrator was thought to have infringed the conditions of his bond, a person interested in the estate could summon the sureties of the bond to show why probate should not be assigned to someone else. An Assignation was an interlocutory order issued in consequence of such an application, and was copied into the Probate or Admon. Act Book.

Original wills see ARMS, COAT OF.

Apart from the wills in the archives of the probate courts (for which *see* under the relevant county heading), there are at the Public Record Office (PRO), Chancery Lane, London, a number of wills contained in other classes of record, for example among the manor court rolls. The PRO has an index of these. Also at the PRO are indexes (IR.26 and 27) from the Estate Duty Office, of wills proved and admons granted in all the probate courts of England and Wales during the period 1796-1857. They fall into two groups: those for 1796-1811, and those for 1812-1857. The first group is divided into three sections, the *PCC Will Index* (IR.27/1-16), *PCC Admon. Index* (IR.27/17-20), and the *County Court Indexes* (IR.27/67-93). From 1812 onward, the sections are: *Will Indexes* (IR.27/140-323), and *Admon. Indexes*, subdivided into PCC (IR.27/21-66) and *County Courts* (IR.27/94-139). These indexes, which are not available to the public until they are seventy-five years old, not only lead to finding the estate duty arising in connection with a will, but can also speed the finding of the will itself in the probate court records. The Society of Genealogists has copies of indexes of earlier wills and admons. at various courts.

When a will cannot be found in the period shortly after a man's death, it is worth searching the period after the death of his widow, because if the husband left his wife a life interest in his estate, the will was sometimes not proved until after she had died. However, the neglect of an executor to prove a will — as well as other reasons — has sometimes resulted in many years elapsing between death and probate. So far the longest period known is seventy-six years.

Because wills usually mention several members of a family of two or three generations, they are one of the most valuable sources available to the genealogist. They are often the only means of establishing the truth, or otherwise, of a family tree hypothetically compiled from parish registers alone.

Brief details of archdeaconry and diocesan probate records are shown under county headings, but searchers will do well to consult also one or more of the following guides: *A Simplified Guide to Probate Jurisdictions: Where to Look for Wills* (Federation of Family History Societies, 1982). More detailed works are, *Wills and Their Whereabouts*, by Anthony J. Camp (1974) and *Wills and Where to Find Them*, by J.S.W. Gibson (1974), both out of print but available in libraries. Free leaflets, *Probate Records* and *Death Duty Registers*, are available at the PRO.

Maps showing the boundaries of probate jurisdictions have been published by the Institute of Heraldic and Genealogical Studies, and are also shown in *Wills and Where to Find Them* and the above-mentioned *Simplified Guide*.

Williams's Library, Dr Dr Daniel Williams (c.1643-1716) was a Presbyterian minister of the type whose faith developed later into Unitarianism. He bequeathed his collection of books and manuscripts for public use, and in 1729 it was opened as a library in London, where it was known as 'The Dissenters' Library in Red Cross Street'. After several moves, it settled permanently in 1890 at 14 Gordon Square. It is administered by a Board of twenty-three trustees, most of whom are usually Unitarians. However, the books and records cover the history of English nonconformity generally.

All the books and pamphlets in the library, published between 1653 and 1800, have been catalogued under the title *Bibliography of Early Nonconformity*. The contents are listed under subject and author, and chronologically. There are histories of individual nonconformist churches and congregations, arranged under counties, *Transactions* of denominational historical societies, and the publications of national and other historical societies.

Collections made by other people have been donated to the library. One of the most useful genealogically is that of Roger Morrice (d. 1701/2), compiled as material for a general history of Puritans which he never managed to write. It was taken over by John Evans (c.1680-1730), who added a list of dissenting congregations and ministers of the period 1715-29. It finally formed the basis of Daniel Neal's *History of the Puritans*. There is another list of congregations, with some histories, dated 1722, by Joseph Thompson, and also the Conventicle Returns of 1669, included in G. Lyon Turner's *Records of Nonconformity*.

As nonconformist ministers continued to neglect register-keeping, the Protestant Dissenting Deputies of the Three Denominations (Baptist, Presbyterian and Congregationalist) formed the General Register of Births and arranged with the trustees of Dr Williams's Library to house it, and for the librarian to act as Clerk. The Register began on 1 January, 1742/3. It was open not only to Londoners and nonconformists, but to any parents ready to sign a certificate of their child's birth and to spend 6 pence on registering a copy. Even some births abroad are included. The certificates, in addition to the usual details of parentage, gave the exact place of birth and the name of the mother's father.

Attempts were made to persuade ministers to register their baptisms, but with little success; the first volume contains only 36 entries. Another attempt to encourage use of the register was an offer to post-register without fee any birth before 1742. This brought in some from as early as 1713. However, by 1769 there were only 303 entries, so the Registry was made a repository for ministers to deposit their register books. In 1831, the original certificates were bound into books, and in 1837 the records were transferred to the Registrar General, along with most other nonconformist registers. They contain 48,975 entries of birth. Those for the final six months overlap those in the civil General Register. They have now passed from the Registrar General to the Public Record Office, Chancery Lane, London, where they are in group RG.

Dr Williams's Library has a handlist of manuscripts with an index of names; also a card index of Congregationalist ministers from *c.*1640 until the present century. The library is open from 10 a.m. to 5 p.m. on Mondays, Wednesdays and Fridays, and from 10 a.m. to 6.30 p.m. on Tuesdays and Thursdays. Subscribers to the library can borrow books. Application to become a subscriber must be accompanied by the names of two guarantors.

Wiltshire The Wiltshire Family History Society holds regular meetings and issues a journal. Enquiries should be sent c/o The Federation of Family History Societies, 31 Seven Star Road, Solihull, West Midlands B91 2BZ, marked 'Please forward' and enclosing a stamped self-addressed envelope.

Record Repositories Wiltshire Record Office, County Hall, Trowbridge (tel: 02214.3641); City of New Sarum Record Office, The Council House, Bourne Hill, Salisbury.

Parish Registers and Indexes (*see* comment under COUNTY) Most of the registers of the 318 ancient parishes have been deposited, nearly all at the county record office (CRO). The Society of Genealogists has copies of more than 150. Pallot's Marriage Index covers 83, mostly from 1790 to 1812. The Nimrod Index of Marriages, c/o Mrs B. Carter, 28 Okus Road, Swindon, is in progress. A number of registers are included in the INTERNATIONAL GENEALOGICAL INDEX (IGI). The Bishops' Transcripts are at the CRO.

Marriage Licence Records These are at the CRO.

Wills before 1858, proved in the Archdeaconry Courts of Salisbury and Wiltshire, and a number of Peculiar Courts, are nearly all at the CRO.

As the county lay in the Diocese of Salisbury and the Province of Canterbury, wills could also be proved in the Consistory Court of Salisbury (these wills are now at the CRO), and in the Prerogative Court of Canterbury.

Non-parochial Registers The registers of 71 chapels are at the Public Record Office (PRO), Chancery Lane, London, and the IGI includes a small number.

Census Returns These are at the PRO, Portugal Street, London, and the Wiltshire Library and Museum Service, Bythesea Road, Trowbridge, has copies.

Memorial Inscriptions The family history society has transcription in progress, and there are a few transcripts in the library of the Society of Genealogists.

Heralds' Visitation Pedigrees have been printed for 1565, 1623 and 1677.

Window Tax In 1696, a new tax on houses replaced the Hearth Tax which had been ended a few years earlier. One of the chief objections to the latter had been that it could involve the intrusion of inspectors into private dwellings; in contrast, the window tax was assessed from outside. Nevertheless, it was objected to on the grounds that it was a tax on light and air.

The tax was imposed upon the occupiers, not the owners, and small dwellings whose occupants did not pay poor or church rate were exempt; others were charged on an increasing scale. All paid a basic 2 shillings; houses with between ten and twenty windows paid 8 shillings, and the rates for large houses were increased in 1709. Householders would reduce their totals by blocking-up non-essential windows, and for this reason (but mainly because the tax was badly administered) the total yield over the years fell instead of rising. In order to check this, the Act was repealed in 1747 and a new one passed. By this new Act, in addition to the basic tax, houses with ten to fourteen windows paid 6 pence per window; those with fifteen to nineteen paid 9 pence; and those with over twenty windows paid one shilling per window. At first the yield rose, but the blocking-up of windows was resumed, and during the 1750s and 1760s the tax was again increased. It was not until 1851 that it was abolished, although it was not strictly enforced at the end.

The records are among those of the Exchequer (E.181 for *Drafts of Receivers'*

Accounts) at the Public Record Office, Chancery Lane, London. They provide the name and address of the tax payer, the number of windows in his house, and the amount paid in tax.

Windsor, Slough and District Family History Society *see* Berkshire

Witch In the Middle Ages, witchcraft was evil-doing by supernatural means, and it was only the evil act that attracted judicial punishment. If the deed or intent was not serious (such as causing the victim to break out into boils) the punishment was light, sometimes the stocks or pillory, or a penance in church. It was in the reign of Henry VIII that witchcraft — a compact with the devil to commit an evil act — first became a crime under the law; but the statute against it was repealed under Edward VI in 1547. However, an Act of 1563 made it a felony to invoke an evil spirit for any purpose, good or bad, and a spate of trials before the Assizes resulted in a number of hangings.

When James VI came to the throne, he wrote a book on Demonology, and his Act of 1604 made the penalties more severe and widened the scope of the law to include a mere covenant with an evil or wicked spirit, regardless of any deed or purpose. For evidence, the devil's mark (which might be a wart) was searched for, or the accused might be thrown, bound, into a stream to see whether she floated or sank. The 1604 Act caused a rise in the number of people put to death, after a decline since the early years of the previous statute; but thereafter numbers declined again to nothing at all, until the year 1645/6, when a failed lawyer, Matthew Hopkins, became active as a professional witch-finder and caused an epidemic of witch hysteria in the southeastern counties. After his death in 1646, the number of hangings again fell away sharply. The last person to be executed for the offence was hanged at Exeter in 1682, and in 1735 all Acts against witchcraft and sorcery were repealed. It has been estimated that about 500 people (nearly all of them women) suffered death for witchcraft in England, and by hanging, not burning. The evidence is to be found in the records of the Assizes.

Without that An obsolete expression, meaning either 'except' or 'denying', according to the context. It was followed by a second 'that'; for example, 'without that that he had ever seen . . .'. Often found in law suit depositions.

Wood An obsolete word, meaning 'mad'.

Woolwich and District Family History Society *see* Kent

Worcestershire The northern parishes of the ancient county are now in the new county of West Midlands. The remainder is now part of the new county of Hereford & Worcester. The Birmingham and Midland Society for Genealogy and Heraldry holds meetings at Stourbridge, and issues a journal. Enquiries should be sent c/o The Federation of Family History Societies, 31 Seven Star Road, Solihull, West Midlands B91 2BZ, marked 'Please forward' and enclosing a stamped self-addressed envelope.

Record Repositories County of Hereford & Worcester Record Office (H.O.), County Hall, Spetchley Road, Worcester WR5 2NP, and the Worcester Branch at St Helen's, Fish Street, Worcester (tel: 0905.23400); City of Worcester Records, The Registrar, Guildhall, Worcester.

Parish Registers and Indexes (*see* comment under COUNTY) Some of the registers of the 209 ancient parishes have been deposited at the county record office (CRO). The Society of Genealogists has a number of register copies. Pallot's Marriage Index covers 50, mostly from 1790 to 1812. The INTERNATIONAL GENEALOGICAL INDEX (IGI) includes about 100, and both the CRO and the family history society (FHS) have copies. The Bishops' Transcripts are at the CRO.

Marriage Licence Records These are at the CRO.

Wills before 1858, proved in the Consistory Court of Worcester, and a number of Peculiar Courts, are at the CRO. A number of parishes in the west of the county lay in the Diocese of Hereford, so wills were proved in the Episcopal Consistory Court of Hereford and are at Hereford Record Office.

As the county lay in the Province of Canterbury, wills could also be proved in the Prerogative Court of Canterbury. The Society of Genealogists has an index of the Consistory Court of Worcester wills.

Non-parochial Registers The registers of 39 chapels are at the Public Record Office (PRO), Chancery Lane, London, and a few are included in the IGI.

Census Returns These are at the PRO, Portugal Street, London, and at the CRO.

Memorial Inscriptions The Society of Genealogists has transcripts of a few churchyards.

Heralds' Visitation Pedigrees have been printed for 1533, 1569, 1634 and 1682-3.

Workhouses Some parochial 'convenient houses of dwelling' for the impotent poor were set up as a result of the *Poor Law Act* of 1601, but workhouses became numerous only in the eighteenth century. An Act of 1723 enabled parishes to set them up either singly or in combination with neighbouring parishes. Generally, they were so ill-administered that they were said to be either 'houses of terror' or 'houses of debauchery'. *Gilbert's Act*, 1782, forbade the admission of able-bodied paupers. In 1834, under the *Poor Law Amendment Act*, newly constituted Poor Law Unions took over responsibility for the poor from the parishes, and each union was obliged to set up a workhouse. Except in serious cases, relief to the poor was confined to those who would enter the workhouse.

The records of these institutions, and the Minute Books, are at the county and borough record offices.
See also GUARDIANS OF THE POOR.

Writ In law, an instrument in writing (under seal) issued by a court, commanding or forbidding the performance of some act by the person to whom it was addressed; e.g. a Writ of Mandamus, Writ of Summons. In civil cases, an 'original' writ was issued by the Court of Chancery, under the great seal, summoning the defendant to appear. This initiated the case. The term itself is thought to derive from the fact that even in early times, when proceedings at law were conducted orally, these instructions had always been in writing.

Writer Until the nineteenth century this was the term for a commercial clerk, much of whose time, before the age of the typewriter and carbon

paper, was taken up in writing out and copying. The term is still used in the Royal Navy.

Writ of Capias *see* **Outlawry**

Writ of de Libertate Probanda *see* **Libertate Probanda, Writ of**

Writ of Exigend *see* **Outlawry**

Yardland An area of about thirty acres.

Yeoman In the Plantagenet period, the word meant a knight's servant or retainer. There were also Yeomen of the King's Chamber, who were minor court officials under the Chamberlain. At that period, there was a class of freemen called Franklins, and under the Tudors the name of yeoman gradually became attached to them. Broadly speaking, they constituted a stratum of cultivators of the soil, either freeholders or tenants, who differed from the minor gentry more by their way of life than by any economic category. The yeoman would put his own hand to work that the gentleman would employ servants to do, and his wife likewise; but many a young man of gentle and even armigerous family was styled yeoman, as long as he lived like one (i.e. until he inherited his father's estate).

Below the yeoman class came the equally ill-defined stratum of Husbandman, whose land-holding was normally smaller. The standing of the yeomanry is reflected in the later use of the word for the local volunteer force, mounted on their own horses, as distinct from the (infantry) militia.
See also CLASS, SOCIAL.

Yorkshire The ancient county is now divided into the new counties of North, West and South Yorkshire, Cleveland, and Humberland. The Family History and Population Studies Section of the Yorkshire Archaeological Society, the East Yorkshire Family History Society, the Cleveland Family History Society, the York Family History Society, the Sheffield and District Family History Society, and the Doncaster Society for Family History, all hold meetings and issue journals. Enquiries should be sent c/o The Federation of Family History Societies, 31 Seven Star Road, Solihull, West Midlands B91 2BZ, marked 'Please forward' and enclosing a stamped, self-addressed envelope.

Record Repositories Borthwick Institute of Historical Research, St Anthony's Hall, York (tel: 0904.59861); North Yorkshire County Record Office, County Hall, Northallerton (tel: 0609.3123); North Yorkshire Record Office, The York Archives, Exhibition Square, York; West Yorkshire and Diocese of Wakefield Record Office, Newstead Road, Wakefield (tel: 0924.67111); South Yorkshire Record Office, Cultural Activities Centre, Ellin Street, Sheffield (tel: 0742.29191).

Cleveland County Libraries Archives Department, 81 Borough Road, Middlesborough (tel: 0642.210944); Humberside County Record Office, County Hall, Beverley (tel: 0482.887131); South Humberside Area Record Office, Central Library, Town Hall Square, Grimsby (tel: 0472.53481).

Kingston-upon-Hull City Record Office, 79 Lowgate, Kingston-upon-Hull (tel: 0482.222015); Doncaster Archives Department, King Edward Road, Balby, Doncaster; Wakefield Metropolitan District Archives Department, Balne Lane, Wakefield (tel: 0924.71231); Calderdale Metropolitan Borough Archives Department, Central Library, Lister Lane, Halifax (tel: 0422.60425); Sheffield City Archives Department, Central Library, Surrey Street, Sheffield (tel: 0742.734756); Leeds Archives Department, Sheepscar, Chapeltown Road, Leeds (tel: 0532.628339); Bradford Central Library Archives Department, Princes Way, Bradford (tel: 0274.33081).

Parish Registers and Indexes (*see* comment under COUNTY) Most of the registers of the ancient county have been deposited, mainly at the record offices of the new counties. The Society of Genealogists has copies of nearly 300. Boyd's Marriage Index covers 174. Pallot's Marriage Index covers 93, mostly from 1790 to 1812. The INTERNATIONAL GENEALOGICAL INDEX (IGI) includes nearly 400. The East Yorkshire family history society (FHS) has a marriage index in progress. The Bishops' Transcripts of the county are at the Borthwick Institute, except for those parishes in the northwest of the county which were in the Archdeaconry of Richmond; these are at Leeds Archives Department.

Marriage Licence Records These are at the Borthwick Institute.

Wills before 1858. There were many Yorkshire probate courts. At the Borthwick Institute there is a Deanery Book listing every parish, and showing in which of the twenty-five deaneries and numerous Peculiars each one lay. The search can then be directed to the relevant repository; i.e. either the Borthwick Institute, Leeds Archives Department, the Dean and Chapter of York Library, Hull Record Office, or Bradford Record Office. As the county lay in the Province of York, wills could be proved in the Prerogative Courts of both York and Canterbury. The Society of Genealogists has indexes to a number of Yorkshire courts.

Non-parochial Registers There are 423 registers at the Public Record Office (PRO), Chancery Lane, London, and the IGI includes over one hundred.

Census Returns These are at the PRO, Portugal Street, London, and at the central libraries at Northallerton, Leeds, Wakefield and Middlesborough, as well as (for local areas) at libraries in several other towns.

Memorial Inscriptions The Society of Genealogists has transcripts from about 100 churches, and the family history societies have transcription in progress.

Heralds' Visitation Pedigrees have been printed for 1530, 1584-5, 1612 and 1665-6.

The *Yorkshire Archaeological Society* has published many historical records.

A

B

C

D

E

F

G

H

I J

K

L

M

N

P

QR

S | *T*

Useful Addresses

Association of Family History Societies of Wales 2 Pen Lôn, Menai Bridge, Gwynedd LL59 5LW

Association of Genealogists and Record Agents 1 Woodside Close, Caterham, Surrey CR3 6AU

Association of Scottish Genealogists and Record Agents 106 Brucefield Avenue, Dunfermline, Fyfe KY11 4SP

Bodleian Library University of Oxford, Oxford

Borthwick Institute of Historical Research St Anthony's Hall, University of York, York

British Library British Museum, Great Russell Street, London WC1

British Newspaper Library Colindale Avenue, London NW9

Corporation of London Record Office Guildhall, Gresham Street, London EC2

Federation of Family History Societies 31 Seven Star Road, Solihull, West Midlands B91 2BZ

General Register Office St Catherine's House, 10 Kingsway, London WC2

Greater London Council Record Office 40 Northampton Road, London EC1

Guildhall Library Aldermanbury, London EC2

House of Lords Record Office Houses of Parliament, London SW1

Institute of Heraldic & Genealogical Studies Northgate, Canterbury, Kent

International Genealogical Institute Church of Jesus Christ of Latter-Day Saints, 50 East Smith Temple Street, Salt Lake City, Utah, U.S.A.

Lambeth Palace Library Lambeth Palace Road, London SE1

National Library of Wales Aberystwyth, Dyfed SY23 3BU

New Register House 3 West Register Street, Edinburgh EH1 3YY

Principal Registry of the Family Division Somerset House, Strand, London WC2

Public Record Office Chancery Lane, London WC2

Public Record Office Portugal Street, London WC2

Public Record Office Ruskin Avenue, Kew, Surrey

Scottish Record Office West Register Street, Edinburgh EH1 3YY

Society of Genealogists 14 Charterhouse Buildings, London EC1M 7BA